The Pilgrim's Guide to Rome's Principal Churches

Joseph N. Tylenda, S.J.

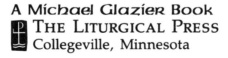
A Michael Glazier Book
THE LITURGICAL PRESS
Collegeville, Minnesota

A Michael Glazier Book published by The Liturgical Press.

Cover design by Ann Blattner.
Cover photo by Beth Hay.

1   2   3   4   5   6   7   8   9

Library of Congress Cataloging-in-Publication Data

Tylenda, Joseph N.
    The pilgrim's guide to Rome's principal churches / Joseph
N. Tylenda.
        p.   cm.
    "A Michael Glazier book."
    Includes bibliographical references.
    ISBN 0-8146-5016-3
    1. Churches, Catholic—Italy—Rome—Guidebooks. 2. Rome (Italy)-
-Buildings, structures, etc.—Guidebooks. I. Title.
NA5620.A1T96   1993
726'.5'0945632—dc20   92-42870
                                                                          CIP

RSG
a faithful friend is a sure shelter
he who finds one finds a treasure

Sirach 6:14

Contents

Introduction

Christian pilgrims have always made their way to Rome to pray at the tombs of Sts. Peter and Paul, and to visit the city's great basilicas. In the early years of the Christian era—beginning with the persecution of Nero (emperor 54–68)—the faithful showed special reverence for the martyrs, who had courageously faced death rather than deny their faith in the one true God. After the peace brought by Constantine (emperor 306–337), religious edifices were erected over these martyrs' tombs, and these churches, in turn, became the cherished goals of Christian pilgrims.

Sometime before the first millenium, the pious custom had grown among the faithful of visiting Rome's five major basilicas, namely, S. Pietro in Vaticano, S. Giovanni in Laterano, S. Maria Maggiore, S. Paolo fuori le Mura, and S. Lorenzo fuori le Mura. The visits were to be done within the same liturgical day, that is, between the vespers of one evening and the vespers of the following. With the passage of time, two other churches were added, namely, S. Croce in Gerusalemme and S. Sebastiano. Since the pilgrims, on their way from S. Lorenzo to S. Giovanni in Laterano, had to pass S. Croce, they also began to visit this church to reverence the major relics of Our Lord's Passion housed there. Then on their way from S. Giovanni to S. Paolo, the pilgrims had to pass the church and catacombs of S. Sebastiano, with its relics of that beloved martyr. The number of churches to be visited in a single day was thus fixed at seven, and these churches became known as the "Seven Churches." The road which today leads from S. Sebastiano to S. Paolo still bears its medieval name, "Sette Chiese."

The present volume offers descriptions of fifty churches. The first group, which stands apart from the others, forms the famous "Seven Churches," of which St. Pius V (1566–1572), referring to the ancient pious practice of visiting them, wrote in his Bull, *Egregia populi Romani*: "These basilicas are celebrated for their antiquity, their religious services, the relics of the martyrs venerated within, the indulgences gained and, finally, for the mystical significance of the number seven." Of the remaining forty-three churches, some are included because of their antiquity (such as S. Sabina and S. Clemente), or because of their architectural magnificence (for example, S. Andrea al Quirinale and S. Andrea della Valle), or for their artistic treasures (S. Luigi dei Francesi and S. Maria del Popolo), or because of the saints whose bodies are there venerated (S. Maria sopra Minerva and Il Gesù). This present collection of fifty churches is merely a selection; all of Rome's churches are worthy of a prayerful visit. The asterisks after a church's name indicate its relative importance.

For each church here described there is a simplified floor plan with superimposed numbers to indicate the places where items mentioned in the text are located. In no way do these plans pretend to be architecturally exact drawings of the edifice; they are merely indicatory.

The descriptive text dealing with each church is divided into three sections. First, the history of the church's origin is briefly given, then a general description of the church's exterior. Since this guide was written for the pilgrim, architectural terms are kept to a minimum. A glossary of terms, however, has been added at the end of the volume. The third section describes the church's interior. This is the book's meaty portion. The reader is first invited to step into the sacred edifice and enjoy the fullness of its beauty, and then see it in its individual parts. In general, the description of each church follows the same counter-clockwise pattern: beginning with the chapels on the right of entrance, progressing toward the front and main altar, and then back along the church's left side.

Most of these fifty churches have been the objects of detailed studies (see Bibliography), and the information found in the following pages has been culled from those volumes, and in large part personally verified. The subject matter or theme of the majority of the paintings and statues in these churches has been identified and, whenever possible, their artists as well. I have, in general, withheld personal comment with regard to artists and their works, hoping to lead viewers to arrive at their own opinion. Now and then a personal preference or prejudice has slipped through.

The book is meant to be used as you make your way through the church, visiting chapel after chapel. Once you have completed your visit of the entire edifice with book in hand, you may want to give the chapels, paintings, and statues that have especially appealed to you another quick glance. I suggest a leisurely walk down the main aisle or nave, allowing yourself the minute or two needed to imprint this particular painting or that striking statue in your memory. Finally, before leaving, give the church another overall glance, to bring everything together into a unified experience.

The text also includes reproductions of church facades by two of Rome's greatest engravers, Giovanni Battista Falda (1648–1678) and Giuseppe Vasi (1710–1782). Those taken from the former first appeared in his *Il nuovo teatro delle fabriche, et edificii in prospettiva di Roma moderna*, 3 vols. (Rome: 1665–1669); those from the latter are from his *Magnificenze di Roma antica e moderna*, 10 vols. (Rome: 1747–1761).

The author is grateful to Pietro Vanetti, S.J., for the use of the photographs of the engravings published in this book.

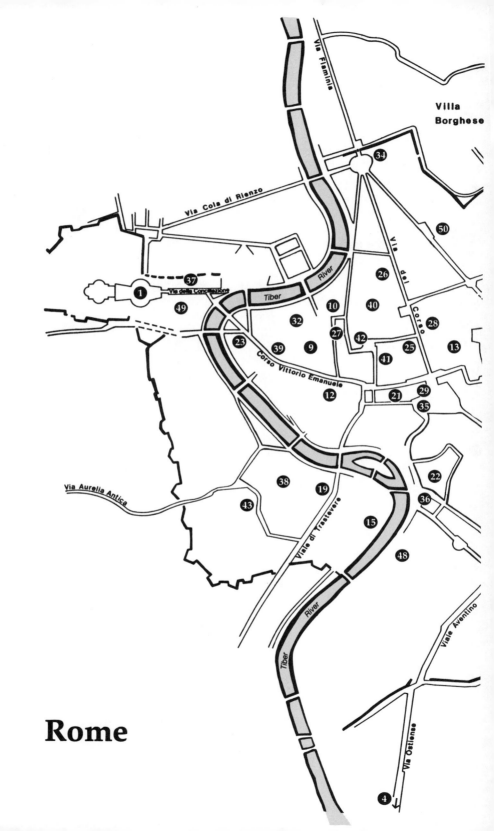

Rome

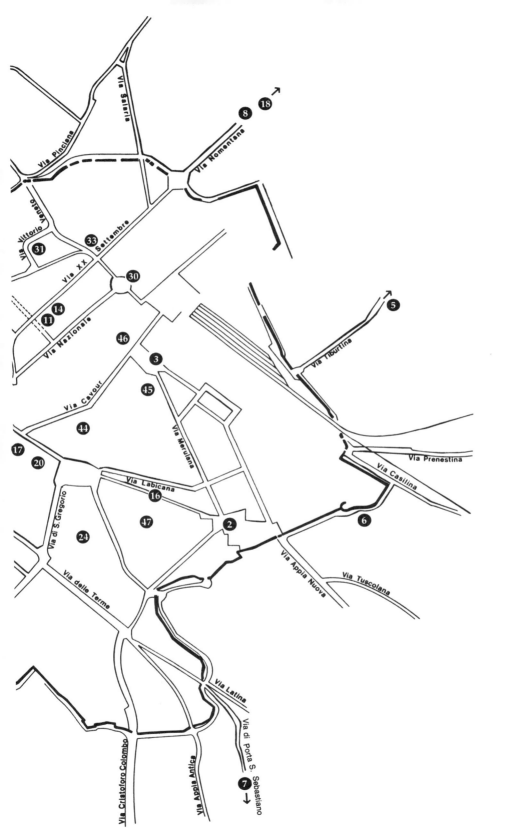

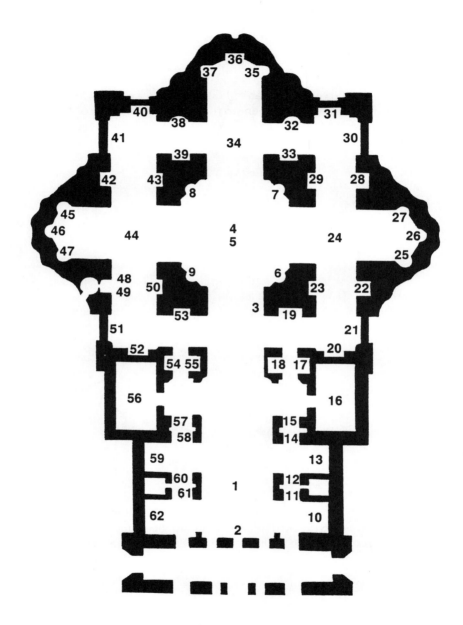

S. Pietro in Vaticano

1 S. Pietro in Vaticano***
Vatican City

History. The Apostle Peter came to Rome some time after the year 50 and was martyred on Vatican Hill about 64-67. Over his tomb Pope Anacletus (ca. 79--ca. 91) built an oratory, which was replaced by Constantine (emperor 306-337). The Constantinian basilica was begun about 320 and consecrated by Sylvester I (314-335) on 18 November 326; it was not completed, however, until the reign of Constans (emperor 337-350). The basilica was large, with a *quadriporticus*, and over the years, enriched with mosaics and frescoes; it also housed many monuments of popes, emperors, and famous personages.

When the building threatened to collapse in the fifteenth century, Nicholas V (1447-1455) began (1452) its restoration. With his death work came to a halt and remained so for half a century, except for a brief period under Paul II (1464-1471). It was Julius II (1503-1513) who decided that restoration would not suffice, but that a new building was needed. *Donato Bramante* was placed in charge and Julius II laid the first stone (in what is now the St. Veronica pier) on 18 April 1506. After Bramante's death (1514), Leo X (1513-1521) put the construction in the hands of *Raphael*, who changed Bramante's Greek cross plan to a Latin cross. After Raphael's death (1520) the newly appointed *Baldassarre Peruzzi* returned to Bramante's plan. Work was necessarily suspended during and immediately after the Sack of Rome (1527), and when *Antonio da Sangallo the Younger* took over he reinstated the form of a Latin cross. After his death in 1546 Paul III (1534-1549) appointed *Michelangelo* architect of St. Peter's.

Michelangelo reverted to Bramante's plan, but added the dome. Work progressed and succeeding architects faithfully followed Michelangelo's plans. In 1607 Paul V (1605-1621) appointed *Carlo Maderno* architect and instructed him to complete the basilica in the form of a Latin cross. The pope's decision was based on two factors: he wanted the new basilica to occupy the same area as the old basilica, and a building in the form of a Latin cross was better suited for important liturgical functions. By adding three chapels on each side to the eastern portion of Michelangelo's building, Maderno created the nave we now see. He is sometimes taken to task because his extension necessarily conceals the lower part of Michelangelo's dome. The basilica was completed in 1614; the facade, however, was completed in 1612. Urban VIII (1623-1644) consecrated the basilica on 18 November 1626, the thirteen-hundredth anniversary of its first consecration. New St. Peter's was thus 120 years (1506-1626) in the making.

Piazza. St. Peter's Piazza is one of the most successful architectural constructions (1656–1667) that man has conceived. It is the undoubted masterpiece of *Gian Lorenzo Bernini,* done at the request of Alexander VII (1655–1667). The lower part of the piazza is an ellipse (some 790 feet wide), formed by two semi-circular colonnades, while the upper part is an irregular rectangle with three flights of gently graded steps (total of 22) leading to the basilica. Each colonnade has four rows of Doric columns, forming three interior corridors, the middle one wide enough for a cardinal's carriage to have traversed its way to the Apostolic Palace. There are a total of 284 columns and 88 pilasters in the colonnades; the trabeation above has a total of 88 statues of saints, and at the ends of the colonnades the name and coat of arms of Alexander VII. (In the entire piazza 153 statues are visible.) At the upper end of the right colonnade is the Bronze Door, entrance to the Apostolic Palace.

In the center of the piazza is an Egyptian obelisk of red granite, without hieroglyphics, resting on four bronze lions lying on a tall plinth. The obelisk was brought from Hierapolis to Rome by Caligula (emperor 37–41) in the year 37 and erected in his circus which, in time, became known as that of Nero (emperor 54–68). The circus was located on the left side of the basilica, and the obelisk stood near to where the sacristy stands today. Sixtus V (1585–1590) had the obelisk moved to its present site. It took four months (30 April to 10 September 1586) to move it some 825 feet, and on the day of its erection in the piazza, 40 winches were used, with more than 800 workers and 140 horses. The spectacular feat was accomplished by *Domenico Fontana,* and to show his gratitude and joy, the pontiff raised him to the nobility. The story that the pontiff had ordered perfect silence under penalty of death, and that a sailor in the crowd, when he noticed that the ropes were giving way, cried out, "Water on the ropes," thus turning certain tragedy into an overwhelming victory, seems to be a later concoction merely to enhance the story. Alexander VII had the obelisk topped with his insignia, in which a relic of the true cross was enclosed. The distance from the ground to the tip of the cross is about 135 feet.

In the pavement surrounding the obelisk are sixteen stone markers indicating the names of the winds and the direction whence they come. The bronze lampstands date from 1852.

The fountains in the piazza are 46 feet high. The one on the right (as you face the basilica) dates from the time of Innocent VIII (1484–1492), and was moved here from another location by Maderno at the request of Paul V. It was later rebuilt by Bernini and then duplicated on the other side by *Carlo Fontana.*

Midway between the obelisk and the fountains, on both sides, is a

Basilica di S. Pietro in Vaticano (G. Vasi, 1753)

stone disk in the pavement with the words "centro del colonnato." Standing on the disk and looking directly at the colonnade, one only sees the first row of columns, as if the colonnade had but a single row.

The oversized statues of Sts. Peter (by *Giuseppe Fabris*) and Paul (by *Adamo Tadolini*), done in 1838 for St. Paul Outside-the-Walls, were placed here in 1847 by Pius IX (1846–1878), as replacements for two from the fifteenth century that were taken into the Apostolic Palace.

Facade. The facade, in travertine, was begun by Maderno in the spring of 1608 and completed in July 1612, two years before the nave was finished. The inscription translates: "In honor of the Prince of the Apostles, Pope Paul V Borghese, a Roman, in the Year 1612, the seventh of his pontificate." The facade is of one order, with eight massive semicolumns and four pilasters supporting the entablature, which is then topped by a triangular pediment with the Borghese coat of arms. Five entrances, alternating in size, lead into the portico; the free standing africano marble columns in the first, third, and fifth entrances are from the old basilica. Above the middle entrance is a bas-relief (1612–1614) of "Christ Gives the Keys to Peter," by *Ambrogio Buonvicino*. Above the entrances is the Benediction Loggia; it is from the balcony of the center window that the news of the election of a pope is announced to the world. It is likewise from that window that the pope gives his *urbi et orbi* ("to the city and to the world") blessing on Christmas and Easter. An attic with a balustrade carrying thirteen statues (Christ, eleven apostles, and John the Baptist), done in 1614, crowns the facade.

The facade is 376 feet long and 149 feet high. Maderno has been criticized for a facade whose length was not in proportion to its height, but the facade we see is not the one that Maderno envisaged. Immediately after the facade was completed (1612), Paul V insisted that bell towers be added and that the basilica be linked to the Apostolic Palace. Thus, the two end sections with arched openings were added and by 1613 the bell tower on the side near the Apostolic Palace was under way. Construction halted with the pope's death in 1621, and then Maderno died eight years later. Construction was resumed by Bernini under Urban VIII; the projected towers now took on a more elaborate design. Bernini began (1637) with the southern tower, on the facade's left, but since he did not allow for the weakness in the lower portion, due to the large arch, serious cracks appeared in the substructure and construction was necessarily halted. The tower was eventually demolished in 1646. Pius VI (1775–1799) then had clocks, designed by *Giuseppe Valadier*, installed in the end sections. The basilica's six bells, electronically operated since 1931, are under the clock on the left. The oldest bell is from 1288.

The exterior length of the basilica, including the portico is 694 feet; the tip of the cross that surmounts the dome is 435 feet from the ground.

Portico. The portico was completed in 1612, but its decoration took several years. On the pilasters inside the three middle entrances, there are large tablets listing the cardinals and prelates present (1 November 1950) for the solemn definition of the Virgin Mary's assumption into heaven. The vault (completed 1619), with scenes from the Acts of the Apostles in the medallions, and the coat of arms of Paul V, is the stucco work of *Giovanni Caslani* and *Simone D'Aria*. Statues of thirty-six popes, venerated as martyrs, are in nineteen lunettes; their names are at their feet and they were done by Buonvicino. The lunette above the middle portal has a relief of "Christ Entrusts His Flock to Peter," by one of Bernini's assistants. Opposite this is the famous "Navicella," a mosaic by *Giotto*, done ca. 1298, and originally in the *quadriporticus* of old St. Peter's. The donor of the mosaic was Cardinal Jacopo Stefaneschi (1270–1341); he appears in the mosaic on the extreme right bottom, at the Savior's left foot. The mosaic was reconstructed here in 1619 and has been restored several times.

Five doorways lead into the basilica, the same number as in the former one. The first, third, and fifth have fluted columns from the earlier basilica. The pediments alternate between triangular and segmental; a cherub's head is in each tympanum. The inscriptions on the architraves inform us that the portals date from the fourteenth year of Paul V's pontificate, that is, 1619.

The **central bronze doors** (1433–1445) are from the former basilica and were done by *Filarete* (Antonio Arevulino) in Florence for Eugenius IV (1431–1447). For them to fit into the larger doorways of the new building, panels were added (1620) at the top and, thus, Paul V's name is found there. There are six principal panels. The uppermost depict the Savior and Virgin Mary. The central panels have Paul (left) and Peter giving the keys to Eugenius IV (right); "Eugenius IV, Venetian" is found directly beneath the pope's figure. The lower panels have scenes from Paul's life and martyrdom (left) and from Peter's life and martyrdom (right). Filarete's signature ("The work of Antonio of Florence") is visible at the top center of the bottom left panel, and the place of casting is found on top of the bottom right panel together with Ethiopic characters. Between the upper and the middle, and between the middle and lower principal panels there are others, depicting various events of Eugenius' pontificate: for example, lower left, Eugenius crowns Sigismund of Hungary in St. Peter's, and lower right, the Armenians and Nestorians come to Rome to meet Eugenius. The text above translates: "These are the famous events of Eugenius IV; these document his noble soul." The doors are bordered with a magnificent frieze of tendrils, fruit, animals, and mythological figures, as well as portraits of emperors and other personages.

The other four bronze doors are of recent date. At the far left is that by *Giacomo Manzù*, and is known as "Door of Death" (1964). The large panels at the top illustrate the death of the Virgin (left) and Christ taken down from the cross (right). The second panel in the bottom row is the death of Pope John XXIII (3 June 1963).

The next bronze door (1970–1977), known as "Door of Evil and Good," is the creative work of *Luciano Minguzzi*. The left door treats evil: the first panel is the martyrdom of Vitalis and Agricola—in death servant and master are equal; "Enslavement of Humanity" is the second panel in the second row, and the long panel below has religious and political martyrs. The door treating good has "St. Augustine's Preaching Overcomes Heresy" at the top; the second panel in the second row shows an African cardinal giving Communion to a soldier, and the long panel below depicts Vatican Council II, with John XXIII on the left and Paul VI (1963–1978) on the right.

The bronze door (1965) on the right of the central door is by *Venanzo Crocetti* and is named "Door of the Sacraments." The panels on the left and right side are: an angel announces the grace of the sacraments that unites all mankind; baptism; confirmation; penance; Eucharist; marriage; orders; anointing. These three sets of doors were financed through a legacy of Prince George Wittelsbach of Bavaria, a canon of the basilica.

The last door on the right is the Holy Year Door. It is opened and closed by the pope himself. The first Holy Year was proclaimed by Boniface VIII (1294–1303) in 1300, but the Holy Door came into existence for the Holy Year of 1500, during the time of Alexander VI (1492–1503). The last Holy Year was 1983–1984, proclaimed by John Paul II (1978–). These bronze doors date from 1949; they are the work of *Ludovico Consorti* and are the gift of the Swiss Catholics. The sixteen panels treat the themes of forgiveness, pardon, and redemption. The two panels on the top left show Adam and Eve expelled from paradise, while the top two on the right represent the annunciation. The second row: Jesus' baptism; finding the lost sheep; the prodigal son; Christ cures the paralytic. The third row: Christ forgives a sinner; Peter asks Christ how many times we ought to forgive; Christ forgives Peter after his denial, and Christ forgives the good thief. Last row: Thomas' unbelief; institution of the sacrament of penance; Paul's conversion; Pius XII (1939–1958) opens the Holy Door in 1950.

Inscriptions are on the walls next to the portals. The one between the first and second doorways on the left speaks of the donation made by Gregory II (715–731) of fifty-six olive trees, so that there would always be a supply of oil for the lamps on St. Peter's tomb. That on the left of the Holy Door is Boniface VIII's promulgation of the first Holy Year. On the right of the same door is a tablet commemorating the meeting (26 October 1967) between Paul VI and Patriarch Athenagoras I (1886–1972), and the meeting (6 December 1987) between John Paul II and Patriarch Dimitrios I (d. 1991). The text is in Latin and Greek.

An equestrian statue is at each end of the portico; to the right is Bernini's Constantine, depicted at the moment when he sees the sign of the cross in the sky, and hears the words "In this sign you will conquer." The statue (1654–1670) is at the foot of the *Scala Regia*, which leads into the Apostolic Palace. The four statues in the niches here are allegorical representations of the three theological virtues (faith, hope, and charity) and of the Church. At the other end of the portico is *Agostino Cornacchini's* Charlemagne (1725), the first emperor to be crowned in old St. Peter's. The four statues in the niches are the four cardinal virtues (fortitude, justice, prudence, and temperance).

The pavement was designed by Bernini, then restored (1888) by Leo XIII (1878–1903); it was again refurbished by John XXIII prior to the opening (11 October 1962) of Vatican Council II. John XXIII's coat of arms is in front of the central door, while that of Clement X (1670–1676) is to the left and Leo XIII's to the right.

Interior. (1) The first impression is of grandeur and greatness; each architectural detail has been planned to produce a proportioned unity. The visitor's focus is immediately directed to the Confession of St. Peter with its majestic baldachin, framing Bernini's luminous "Glory" in the apse.

The nave is separated from the two aisles by piers, whose paired fluted pilasters with Corinthian capitals rise to the trabeation, on which the barrel vault rests. The first three arches, near the entrance, form the extension that Maderno made to the building; these piers are narrower than those of Michelangelo and emphasize the building's height. Though the basilica was structurally complete in 1614, it was for the 1650 Holy Year that Innocent X (1644–1655) made the final push to complete its interior decoration. The pilasters in the two aisles have a total of 108 medallions, of which 56 are of the early popes, venerated as saints. These relief-portraits, supported by putti, were designed by Bernini and done (1647–1648) in Carrara marble by assistants. Above and below the medallions is Innocent's heraldic charge of dove with laurel branch; he was a Pamphili by birth. The allegorical figures (1647–1650) in the spandrels above the arches are also by Bernini's assistants.

The nave's coffered ceiling was decorated (1780) during the time of Pius VI, as the papal coat of arms in the vault indicates. The niches have statues of the founders and foundresses of religious orders and congregations. The fifteen in the nave area are: left side, bottom, rear to front, Sts. Peter of Alcantara (1499–1562), Camillus de Lellis (1550–1614), Ignatius of Loyola (1491–1556), and Francis of Paola (1416–1507); top, Sts. Lucy Filippini (1672–1732), Louis Grignion de Montfort (1673–1716), Anthony Mary Zaccaria (1502–1539), and Peter Fourier (1565–1640); right side, bottom rear to front, Sts. Teresa of Jesus (1515–1582), Vincent de Paul (1581–1660), and Philip Neri (1515–1595); top, Sts. Madeleine-Sophie Barat (1779–1865), John Eudes (1601–1680), John Baptist de La Salle (1651–1719), and John Bosco (1815–1888). It was in this nave that Vatican Council II (1962–1965) was held.

The inscriptions running above the pilasters of the basilica deal with St. Peter. That on the left wall of the nave translates: "I have prayed for you, O Peter, that your faith may never fail. You in turn must strengthen your brothers" (Luke 22:32). The one on the right wall reads: "Whatever you declare bound on earth shall be bound in heaven; whatever you declare loosed on earth shall be loosed in heaven" (Matt 16:19).

Though the putti supporting the holy water stoups (1722–1725) on the first two piers appear to be of normal size, they are, in reality, over 6 feet high. The interior length of the basilica is 611 feet, and the height of the nave is 145 feet.

(2) The rear wall has three inscriptions over the doors: the one on the left commemorates Paul V's completion of the basilica and his build-

ing of the confession; the middle one recalls Innocent X, who decorated the pilasters and had the pavement laid; the third honors Urban VIII, who consecrated the basilica, had the baldachin made and decorated the four piers surrounding the confession. Still higher are two clocks.

On the very bottom right of the central bronze doors, if there is enough light, one can see an interesting panel on which Filarete has left his pictorial signature. An Antonio, so identified beneath the figure, leads his students in a dance. They carry the instruments of their trade. On the panel's left, on the doorway from which the workers emerged is written, "Antonio di Pietro of Florence made this on the last day of July 1445." Now that the doors have been completed, master and students take time off and rejoice on a commission superbly fulfilled. They had every right to be proud of these doors.

In front of the main door is a large porphyry disk that was once in front of the main altar of the old basilica. On this disk Charlemagne knelt, on Christmas 800, to be anointed and crowned Holy Roman Emperor by Leo III (795–816). Some twenty other emperors likewise knelt on this disk and received the imperial crown from the hands of the pope.

As we walk the length of the nave, with eyes cast downward we see bronze markings in the floor indicating the length of other world-famous basilicas or cathedrals. A total of twenty-seven are given. The shortest is that of St. Patrick's in New York City (340 feet). The pavement, with pieces from the pavement of the old basilica, was designed by *Giacomo Della Porta* but completed by Bernini at the request of Innocent X. Thus, we have Innocent's seal in the floor, recalling that the pavement was finished for the 1650 Holy Year. Further down we meet another seal, that of Pius XI, commemorating the 1933 Holy Year.

(3) Next to the last pilaster on the right is a bronze statue of a seated St. Peter. As a result of the countless pilgrims who touch or kiss the statue's right foot, which extends over the pedestal, it is well worn. The statue is most probably from the thirteenth century and attributable to *Arnolfo di Cambio*. The above mosaic medallion of Pius IX was placed here in 1871 by the clergy of the basilica to commemorate the fact that in that year Pius was the first pope to equal the legendary twenty-five years of St. Peter's pontificate. Pius died several years later (1878). Leo XIII (1878–1903) likewise exceeded Peter's twenty-five years, but only by five months.

(4) **Dome.** The lantern was added to the dome in 1593, but it was only in 1603 that Clement VIII (1592–1605) commissioned *Cavalier d'Arpino* to prepare the cartoons for its decoration. It took several years, how-

ever, before the cartoons were turned into mosaics. The sixteen windows in the drum supply abundant illumination for this area. The vertical lines of the double pilasters in the drum drive upward until they converge at the lantern. The sixteen compartments in the dome are decorated with figures in six concentric circles. The lunettes near the drum have half busts of sixteen popes, whose relics are venerated in the basilica; then come the large figures of Christ, Mary, St. John the Baptist, the twelve apostles, and St. Paul. The third row has angels with symbols, the next has tondi with seraphim, and the fifth and sixth likewise have angels and seraphim. In the lantern God the Father is giving his blessing.

The words at the base of the drum translate: "You are Peter and on this rock I will build my church. I will entrust to you the keys of the kingdom of heaven" (Matt 16:18). The interior measurement of the dome's diameter is approximately 139 feet.

The medallions in the pendentives have the four evangelists. John and Luke were designed by *Giovanni De Vecchi,* who also did the mosaic work; Mark and Matthew were designed by *Cesare Nebbia,* but others transformed his cartoons into mosaics. The angels in the remaining spaces are by *Cristoforo Roncalli.* The diameter of each medallion is 29 feet; the pen in Mark's hand is 5 feet, and that in Matthew's 8 feet.

(5) Confession of St. Peter—baldachin. The papal altar does not stand directly beneath the dome's center but directly above the tomb of St. Peter, as did the altar in the original basilica. The altar overlooks the confession, and faces east. The present altar dates from 1594, when Clement VIII had the earlier altars of St. Gregory the Great (590–604) and Callistus II (1119–1124) enclosed within it. Only the pope, or the cardinal whom he deputes, may celebrate at this altar.

In 1613 Paul V asked Carlo Maderno and *Martino Ferrabosco* to make an open sunken confession under the dome, in front of the tomb of the apostle. Maderno then had the pavement and walls lined with precious marbles and placed a balustrade around it. Two flights of stairs lead down and at the bottom there are two alabaster columns with small statues of Sts. Peter and Paul. In the wall is the Niche of the Pallia, with a silver casket (1700) in which the pallia are kept until 29 June, the feast of Sts. Peter and Paul, when the pope confers them on the newly appointed metropolitan archbishops. Behind the urn is a ninth-century mosaic of Christ "Pantocrator." This is the only item from the old St. Peter's that is still in its original location. Directly beneath this niche is St. Peter's tomb. Immediately above the niche is a gilded bronze triptych with busts of Christ (center), Sts. Peter (left) and St. Paul (right). The niche is flanked by four cotognino alabaster columns and bronze statues (1616–1618) of both apostles by Buonvicino. Seven lamps hang before the niche. At the bottom of the stairs, and on both sides of the confession, is Paul V's coat of arms.

On the balustrade, staircase, and in front of the altar overlooking the confession are 89 cornucopia-shaped bronze oil lamps, always burning.

Since a temporary baldachin had been placed over Clement VIII's altar, Urban VIII asked Bernini to prepare something more permanent. He began work on it in the summer of 1624, and it was not until 28 June 1633 that the finished product was unveiled. Four spiral columns, decorated with olive branches, genii, and bees, support a simulated cloth baldachin, whose sides are concave to imitate drapery, and whose flaps (with seraphim heads and bees, Urban's heraldic device) and tassels appear to be wafted by a breeze. Four graceful angels stand on the columns and four volutes curve inward and upward until they join at a point upon which a globe surmounted by a cross is fixed. On the front, two putti playfully handle the papal tiara. The underside portion of the baldachin has the Holy Spirit with a sunburst background. Bernini's choice of spiral columns came from his desire to copy the columns that surrounded the apostle's tomb in the old basilica. These ancient Constantinian columns have been incorporated elsewhere in this basilica, as we shall see.

The four bronze columns rest on marble bases approximately 8 feet high, with the sculpted coat of arms of Urban VIII. There is a bit of concealed humor in these sculptures, and the story is told that at the time when these were being prepared, Urban VIII's niece was about to give birth. Face the confession and look at the coat of arms on the front column on the left; at the top, somewhat hidden by the folds of the marble, the sculptor has placed a feminine head. By going around the baldachin in clockwise fashion, you will notice that each coat of arms has a similar head, but the expressions change as to indicate the pain of labor. The surprise is on the front side of the fourth and final column. Worthy of note on these same sculptures are the grotesque masks that appear at the base of the coats of arms.

To produce his baldachin Bernini used the bronze ribs that had recently been added to the dome of St. Peter's, but when this was not enough, Urban had the bronze trusses and beams (replacing them with wood) taken from the porch of the Pantheon. Though the pope was convinced that he was giving this bronze a more noble character by transforming it into decoration for Peter's tomb, nevertheless, the pasquinade current at the time was "Quod non fecerunt barbari, fecerunt Barberini" ("What the barbarians did not do, the Barberini did"). Urban VIII was a Barberini. The baldachin is 96 feet high, and weighs approximately 93 tons or 208,320 pounds.

(6–9) Piers. While working on the baldachin, Bernini was asked (ca. 1627) to decorate the four massive piers supporting the dome and to create a setting worthy of the holiest relics possessed by the basilica. The relics were: Longinus' lance, which was given to Innocent VIII by Sultan Bajazet II in 1489; a piece of the true cross, given the basilica by Urban VIII; Veronica's veil, which is known to have been in the basilica as early as 1000; and the head of the Apostle Andrew, which was brought to Venice by Thomas Paleologos and given to Pius II (1458–1464) in 1462. (The relic of Andrew's head was returned to the Greek Church by Paul VI in 1964.) Thus, the four statues (each 16 feet 6 inches high) in the niches would be of Longinus, St. Helena, St. Veronica, and St. Andrew. Of these four Bernini did Longinus (1635–1638), *Andrea Bolgi* did St. Helena (1630–1639), *Francesco Mochi* St. Veronica (1629–1632), and *François Duquesnoy* sculpted St. Andrew (1633–1639). Bernini however designed the decorations for the piers. Above each saint's statue is a balcony with Urban VIII's coat of arms, and above this an aedicule whose spiral columns come from the decoration that surrounded the altar over St. Peter's tomb in the old basilica. Within the aedicule is a relief of angels holding the relic that had been deposited in the small niche beneath them.

Longinus **(6)** is depicted as gazing upward toward the cross, convinced that Christ is, indeed, the Son of God. St. Helena **(7)** holds aloft the true cross that she discovered. St. Veronica **(8)** speeds on her way to tell her companions of the image she found on her veil. St. Andrew **(9)** joyfully embraces his cross of martyrdom.

The inscription running above the piers refers to Peter as the source of unity in the Church: "Thus, one faith shines in the world, thus, one priesthood arises."

(10) Chapel of the Pietà. This is Michelangelo's celebrated marble group, sculpted (1498–1499) when he was about twenty-five, for the French cardinal Jean de Bilhères de Lagraulas (or Jean Villiers de la Groslaye), ambassador of Charles VIII to Pope Alexander VI. The cardinal commissioned it for his tomb in St. Peter's, but never lived to see it. He died on 6 August 1499, and the statue was placed on the tomb in 1500. During the building of the new St. Peter's and afterwards, the statue was moved several times; it was finally placed here in 1749. This is the only extant work that Michelangelo has signed; his name is on the diagonal band crossing the Virgin's breast. The statue was restored after a crazed man's attack on 21 May 1972. The chapel previously had a crucifix (#11) and, thus, the vault has *Giovanni Lanfranco's* fresco of the "Triumph of the Cross," the only fresco remaining in the basilica. This, as well as several other chapels in the basilica, is flanked by handsome columns of red and white cottanello marble. The mosaic in the cupola outside the chapel represents

"Salvation through the Cross" and the pendentives have Old Testament figures (Noah, Abraham, Moses, and Jeremiah). These mosaics are based on cartoons by *Pietro da Cortona* and *Ciro Ferri*. To the right of the chapel is the Holy Door and over it a mosaic of St. Peter, after a design by Ferri and placed here by Clement X (1670–1676) for the 1675 Holy Year.

(11) The statue (1836) of Leo XII (1823–1829) is by *Giuseppe Fabris;* the pontiff, however, is buried beneath the pavement in front of the altar of St. Leo the Great (#41). The door beneath leads to an elliptical chapel, which has a thirteenth-fourteenth-century wooden crucifix attributed to *Pietro Cavallini.* It was carved for a chapel in old St. Peter's, and was then placed in the chapel to the right until 1749, when Michelangelo's *Pietà* was moved there. In that year the crucifix was transferred here. Within is also an elevator.

(12) Monument to Queen Christina of Sweden (1626–1689). Queen Christina was the daughter of King Gustavus Adolphus and reigned from 1644 to 1654, when she abdicated. She became a Catholic the following year, came to Rome and died here. The monument, with her portrait in a large medallion, is by *Carlo Fontana.* The relief (ca. 1702) is by *Jean-Baptiste Théodon* and represents the queen abjuring heresy and entering the Catholic Church. The ceremony took place (3 November 1655) in Innsbruck, Austria. Her tomb is in the grottoes below.

(13) Chapel of St. Sebastian. The altar has "Martyrdom of St. Sebastian," a mosaic copy of *Domenichino's* fresco now in S. Maria degli Angeli. Beneath the altar is the body of Blessed Innocent XI (1676–1689), placed here after his beatification in 1956; his tomb is in the left aisle (#55). On the right is the monument (1940) to Pius XI (1922–1939) by *Francesco Nagni;* Pius' tomb is in the grottoes. On the left is the monument (1964) to Pius XII (1939–1958) by *Francesco Messina;* Pius' tomb is likewise in the grottoes. The darkish columns here and at several other altars are of africano marble and come from the earlier building. The cupola has mosaics of the "Lamb Adored by Martyrs," and the pendentives portray Abel, Ezekiel, Isaiah, and Zechariah; all are after models provided by Pietro da Cortona and *Guidobaldo Abbattini.*

(14) The tomb of Innocent XII (1691–1700) was designed by *Ferdinando Fuga;* the statue (1746) of the pontiff and those of Charity (left) and Justice (right) are by *Filippo Valle.*

(15) This monument to Matilda (1046–1115), countess of Tuscany, was designed by Bernini at the request of Urban VIII and executed by *Andrea Bolgi.* The relief (1635) on the urn is by *Stefano Speranza* and depicts the incident at Canossa when Gregory VII (1073–1085) reconciled (25 January 1077) the penitent Emperor Henry IV of Germany. Countess Matilda stands on the pope's left. Since she was a staunch protector of the papacy, her statue holds a papal tiara. Urban VIII had her ashes brought (1635) here from the Benedictine monastery at Polirone, near Mantua. Matilda was the first woman to be buried in St. Peter's.

(16) Blessed Sacrament Chapel. The gilded bronze tabernacle (1673–1674) on the altar is by Bernini and is modelled after Bramante's *tempietto* at S. Pietro in Montorio. The two adoring angels are likewise by Bernini. Over the altar is "The Trinity," a painting (1628–1631) by Pietro da Cortona. This is the only painting presently in St. Peter's; in all other cases mosaic copies have replaced the originals. The altar on the right has a mosaic copy of "St. Francis in Ecstasy" by Domenichino; the original is in S. Maria della Concezione. The two spiral columns on the altar are from the altar over St. Peter's tomb in the old basilica. The vault has gilded stuccoes with scenes from the Old and New Testaments done by *Giovanni Caslani* and *Simone D'Aria*. The cupola outside the chapel depicts the "Mystery of the Eucharist" and the pendentives have Aaron, Elijah, Melchizedek, and a high priest dispensing the bread of proposition; all based on designs by Pietro da Cortona and *Raffaele Vanni*.

(17) Monument to Gregory XIII (1572–1585). The statue (1720–1723) of the pontiff and those of Religion (left) and Fortitude (right) are by *Camillo Rusconi*. The Gregorian Calendar derives its name from this pope and the relief on the sarcophagus shows papal mathematicians and astronomers presenting (24 February 1582) their revision of the Julian calendar to the pontiff. The new calendar went into effect 4-15 October 1582. The relief is by *Bernardino Cametti* and *Carlo Francesco Melloni*. The winged dragon beneath the urn is the heraldic charge of the Buoncompagni family, of which the pope was a member.

(18) Tomb of Gregory XIV (1590–1591). Gregory reigned a mere ten months. Originally Gregory XIII's tomb was located here and had decorations by *Prospero Bresciano*. When Rusconi's new tomb for the pope was ready (1723) across the aisle, Gregory XIII's remains were transferred there. The remains of Gregory XIV were placed in this niche in 1842. The figures on the side are Religion (left) and Justice (right).

(19) The altar, flanked by two columns of cottanello marble, has a mosaic copy of the "Last Communion of St. Jerome" by Domenichino; the original is in the Vatican Pinacoteca. St. Jerome (340?–420), supported by disciples in his Bethlehem monastery, receives Communion from St. Ephraem.

(20) The tomb of Gregory XVI (1831–1846) is the work (1854) of *Luigi Amici*. The statue on the left is Wisdom, the other is Prudence, holding its symbols of a mirror and a serpent in its left hand. The relief on the urn recalls Gregory's promotion of Catholic missions; the kneeling figures represent other nations coming to the faith.

(21) This chapel, known as the Gregorian Chapel, is named after Gregory XIII (1572–1585), during whose pontificate it was completed. The altar, faced with marble and having verde antico columns, has an eleventh-century image of the Virgin known as "Our Lady of Succor." Gregory had the image placed here in 1580. Beneath the altar are the relics of St. Gregory Nazianzen (ca. 329–389), Patriarch of Constantinople and Doctor of the Greek Church, brought here by Gregory XIII from the church of the Benedictine nuns at S. Maria in Campo Marzio. The mosaics in the cupola refer to the Virgin (after models by *Girolamo Muziano* and *Nicola La Piccola*) and the pendentives have, besides St. Gregory Nazianzen, other Doctors of the Church (Sts. Jerome, Gregory the Great, and Basil the Great).

(22) Tomb of Benedict XIV (1740–1758). *Pietro Bracci* designed the monument (1769) and did the statue of the standing pontiff imparting his blessing during the 1750 Holy Year. He also did Wisdom (left); Disinterestedness (right) is by *Gaspare Sibilla*. Sibilla's signature will be found on the coins near the putto's left foot.

(23) The altar dedicated to St. Basil (ca. 329–379) has a mosaic of the "Mass of St. Basil"; the original painting by *Pierre Subleyras* is in S. Maria degli Angeli. In the year 372, on the feast of the Epiphany, St. Basil celebrated Mass in the basilica of Caesarea in Cappadoccia, with the Arian Valens (emperor 364–378) present. The emperor was so taken by the devotion with which St. Basil celebrated Mass, that he fell into a swoon. Beneath the altar is the body of St. Josaphat Kuncewycz (ca. 1580–1623), archbishop of Polotsk (Belorussia) and martyr for the cause of Christian unity.

(24) It was in this right transept that Vatican Council I (1869–1870) was held. The eight statues here are: bottom west wall Sts. Bruno (d. 1101), Joseph Calasanz (1556–1648); top Sts. Paul of the Cross (1694–1775), Bonfiglius Monaldo (d. 1261); bottom east wall Sts. Cajetan of Theine (1480–1547), Jerome Emiliani (1486–1537); top Sts. Frances Cabrini (1850–1917), Joan Antida Thouret (1765–1826). The inscription over the pilasters translates: "O Peter, you said, 'You are the Christ, the Son of the living God.' Jesus answered, 'Blessed are you Simon, son of Jonah, for flesh and blood has not revealed this to you'" (see Matt 16:16-17).

(25) The altar is dedicated to and has a mosaic of St. Wenceslaus (ca. 907–929), King of Bohemia. The mosaic is based on *Angelo Caroselli*'s original. Ovals are on either side of the altar: St. Cyril (ca. 826–869) on the left, with St. Methodius (ca. 815–885) on the right. Both saints are "Apostles to the Slavs" and copatrons of Europe. The columns here are of granite.

(26) "The Martyrdom of Sts. Processus and Martinian" is a mosaic

copy of *Jean de Boulogne*'s painting in the Vatican Pinacoteca. Sts. Processus and Martinian were jailers at the Mamertine prison at the time of St. Peter's incarceration. They were converted and baptized by the apostle and then suffered martyrdom. Their relics are under the altar. The altar has two porphyry columns, which came from the medieval baldachin over the high altar in the old basilica. The columns framing the chapel are giallo antico. The oval on the left has a portrait of St. Anthony Claret (1807–1870), founder of the Missionary Sons of the Immaculate Heart of Mary (Claretians), and that of St. Joaquina de Vedruña (1783–1854), foundress of the Carmelite Sisters of Charity, is in the oval on the right.

(27) The altar has "Martyrdom of St. Erasmus," a mosaic copy of *Nicolas Poussin*'s painting, now in the Vatican. St. Erasmus was bishop of Formia and was martyred under Diocletian (emperor 284–305). On the occasion of the celebration of the millenium (1988) of the evangelization of the Ukraine, mosaics of Sts. Vladimir (956–1015) and Olga (ca. 890–969) were placed in the ovals. Vladimir became Grand Duke of Kiev in 980 and was baptized in 988; he then introduced Christianity to Kievan Russia. Olga was Vladimir's grandmother and had become a Christian ca. 955.

(28) This neoclassical monument (1782–1792) to Clement XIII (1758–1769) is by *Antonio Canova*. The pontiff kneels in prayer; Religion is on the left and has the Hebrew words "Holy God" on her forehead and "Doctrine and Truth" on her belt. The disconsolate winged Death sits next to the urn; at the base are two lions, one of which is sleeping.

(29) "Christ Walks on the Water and Saves St. Peter" is a mosaic (1727) copy of G. Lanfranco's original. The episode is from Matthew 14:24-31. The columns are of yellow Sienese marble.

(30) The altarpiece of St. Michael is a mosaic copy of *Guido Reni*'s painting in S. Maria della Concezione. The mosaics in the cupola treat the "Heavenly Militia," while the pendentives have Fathers of the Church (Dionysius the Areopagite, Flavian of Constantinople, St. Leo the Great, and St. Bernard), who have written on the angels.

(31) The altar has "Burial of St. Petronilla"; *Guercino*'s original is in Rome's Capitoline Museum. Paul I (757–767) had the saint's relics brought to St. Peter's from the cemetery of Domitilla; in 1606 they were placed under this altar.

(32) Monument to Clement X (1670–1676). This monument of different marbles was designed (1684) by *Mattia De Rossi*, but executed by various artists. The pope's statue is by *Ercole Ferrata*, that of Beneficence (left) by *Lazzaro Morelli*, and Clemency (right) by *Giuseppe Mazzuoli*. The bas-relief on the urn depicts the opening of the Holy Door for the 1675 Holy Year and is by *Leonardo Reti*.

In the pavement, in front of the monument, a bit to the right and facing the altar of St. Michael, is a simple stone marking the burial place of Sixtus IV (1471–1484) and Julius II (1503–1513). When the tomb of Sixtus IV, in which Julius II's body had likewise been placed, was removed from the Blessed Sacrament Chapel (#16) in 1922, their remains were placed here (1926). Sixtus' magnificent tomb may now be seen in the Treasury (#49), but Julius, to whom this basilica owes its beginning, never had a tomb of his own. He had commissioned Michelangelo to prepare one; it was to have 40 statues, and the "Moses," now in S. Pietro in Vincoli, was to be part of it, but the tomb never came to be.

(33) "St. Peter Raises Tabitha," a mosaic (1760) after the original of *Placido Costanzi* in S. Maria degli Angeli. The miracle is recorded in Acts 9:36-43.

(34) The eight statues of founders and foundresses in the niches in this area of the basilica are: south wall, bottom, Sts. Benedict (480–546) and Francis of Assisi (1182–1226); top, Sts. Frances of Rome (1384–1440) and Alphonsus Liguori (1696–1787); north wall, bottom, Elijah (ninth century B.C.) and St. Dominic (1170–1221); top, Sts. Francis de Sales (1567–1622) and Francis Caracciolo (1563–1608).

Beneath the statues on the lower level are marble tablets; the one in the presbytery on the left says that the tablets commemorate the solemn definition of the dogma of Mary's Immaculate Conception by Pius IX on 8 December 1854; the other three record the names of the cardinals and prelates present.

The inscription in the apse reads: "O Shepherd of the Church, you feed all of Christ's lambs and sheep." This is in Latin on the left side and in Greek on the right.

(35) The tomb of Urban VIII (1623–1644) is by Bernini. Urban was Bernini's patron, and in 1628/1629 the pope commissioned him to begin work on his tomb, which was only completed in 1647, three years after the pope's death. The majestic statue of the pontiff is in bronze, with white marble statues of Charity (left) and Justice (right). Also in bronze is the symbol of death, which rests on the urn and records the pope's name. The three Barberini bees are likewise on the tomb; two are on the upper portion of the plinth and one on the urn.

(36) The **Chair of Peter** is the symbol of the pope's teaching office. In 1656 Alexander VII asked Bernini to prepare a fitting ambience for what was then thought to be St. Peter's episcopal throne. Up to that time it was kept in a reliquary in the baptistery. The throne is wooden with ivory inlays, and we know today that it was given to John VIII (872–882) by Charles the Bald, most probably on the occasion of the latter's coronation as emperor in 875. Bernini's creation, eight years in the making, was

unveiled on 17 January 1666, the feast of the Chair of Peter. The gilded bronze throne, in which the remains of the ninth-century throne are enclosed, hovers in the air. At its sides are four Doctors of the Church. In the rear are Sts. Athanasius and John Chrysostom representing the Eastern Church; in front are Sts. Ambrose (left) and Augustine (right) for the Western Church. These four do not carry or support the chair, they rather point toward it. The base on which they stand is red Sicilian jasper on black-and-white French marble. The papal coat of arms at the base is that of Alexander VII. The statues are approximately 16 feet 6 inches high.

Bernini himself carved the "Feed my lambs" relief on the back of the chair; two small figures are at its sides, and the two putti above the throne hold aloft a tiara and each brandishes a key. Gilded clouds so fill the area behind the chair, that only the capitals of the two columns are visible. The window is surrounded with a "Glory" in which angels and putti fly in what appears to be reckless abandon. An alabaster window with the Holy Spirit is in the center; sunburst rays pass through the "Glory" and extend to the top and to the bottom's right and left sides.

The vault above has three round gilded stucco scenes by *Luigi Vanvitelli;* "Crucifixion of St. Peter" (left), "Christ Gives the Keys to St. Peter" (center), and "Beheading of St. Paul" (right). The bronze free-standing altar toward the front of the platform dates from 1980 and is the creation of *Albert Friscia.*

(37) The tomb (1551–1575) of Paul III (1534–1549) is by *Guglielmo Della Porta.* The pope's statue is bronze, while the reclining figures of Justice (left) and Prudence (right) are of marble. The tomb was first located in another part of the basilica and moved here in 1629.

(38) Tomb of Alexander VIII (1689–1691). The bronze statue (1706–1715) of the pope is by *Angelo De Rossi,* also the marble statues of Religion (left) and Prudence (right). The relief on the base is likewise his and represents the rite of offering gifts to the pope during the canonization ceremony of 16 October 1690.

(39) The mosaic (1760) on the altar is "St. Peter Cures a Paralytic," after an original by *Francesco Mancini* in the Quirinal Palace. The miracle is recorded in Acts 3:7.

(40) Altar of St. Leo the Great (440–461). The magnificent relief (1646–1653) in Parian marble, by *Alessandro Algardi,* is "Pope Leo I Meets Attila." Of all such massive reliefs, this is the richest and most perfect. The scene is said to have taken place outside Rome in 452, when Leo successfully persuaded Attila (ca. 406–453), king of the Huns, to spare Rome. Sts. Peter and Paul also appeared expressing their willingness to protect their city. Leo was the first pope buried in old St. Peter's; prior to this

the popes were buried in the cemeteries outside the city. Leo's remains are beneath the altar, placed here in 1606.

(41) Chapel of Our Lady of the Column. The chapel receives its name from the image of the Virgin which had been painted on a column in the nave of old St. Peter's and placed here in 1607. Since Vatican Council II the chapel has been known as *Mater Ecclesiae* (Mother of the Church). The altar is especially rich in the variety of marbles used. Beneath the altar are the remains of Sts. Leo II (682–683), III (795–816), and IV (847–855); the remains of the three popes were united in one urn during the reign of Paschal II (1099–1118). In the pavement in front of the chapel and facing the altar of St. Leo the Great is the burial place of Leo XII (1823–1829), with an inscription which the pope himself dictated prior to his death. In it, the pope refers to himself as "least among the heirs of so great a name." Leo XII's monument is in the right aisle (#11). The cupola above has symbols based on invocations in the Litany of Loreto; the original designs were by *Giuseppe Zoboli*. The pendentives have Doctors of the Church (Germanus of Constantinople, John Damascene, Bonaventure, and Thomas Aquinas).

(42) Tomb of Alexander VII (1655–1667). This was designed by Bernini and dates from his final years (1672–1678); most of the work is by his disciples but done under his supervision. Bernini himself may have done the pontiff's head. The pope kneels in prayer, with Justice and Prudence rising behind him; in the foreground are Charity (left) and Truth (right). Death rises from beneath a shroud of Sicilian jasper and holds aloft an hour glass to inform the pope that his time has run out.

(43) The mosaic (1921), "Sacred Heart of Jesus Appears to St. Margaret Mary," depicts an event that took place on 27 December 1673. She was canonized in 1920.

(44) The statues in the niches of the left transept are: east wall, bottom, Sts. John of God (1495–1550) and Peter Nolasco (ca. 1182–1249/56); top, Sts. Mary Euphrasia Pelletier (1796–1868) and Louise de Marillac (1591–1660); west wall, bottom, Sts. Giuliana Falconieri (1270–1341) and Norbert (1080–1134); top, Sts. Angela Merici (1474–1540) and William of Vercelli (1085–1142). The inscription along the building reads: "Three times Jesus says to you, Peter, 'Do you love me?' You answer, O chosen Peter, saying, 'Lord, you know everything. You well know that I love you'" (see John 21:15-17).

(45) The altarpiece represents "St. Thomas' Unbelief," a mosaic after *Passignano's* original. Beneath the altar are the relics of St. Boniface IV (608–615), placed here in 1606. The left oval has a mosaic of St. Maria Domenica Mazzarello (1837–1881), foundress of the Daughters of Our Lady Help of Christians, canonized in 1951. The oval on the right has a portrait of St. Maddalena Canossa (1774–1835), foundress of the Daughters of Charity of Canossa, canonized in 1988.

(46) The middle altar has a mosaic of "St. Joseph, Patron of the Universal Church," after a painting by *Achille Funi*. The mosaic was placed here in 1963. The two porphyry columns on the altar come from the main altar of the old basilica. The mosaic medallions (1858) on the sides portray the apostles Sts. Simon and Jude; their relics were placed beneath the altar in 1605.

(47) The "Crucifixion of Peter" is a mosaic (1822) after G. Reni's painting in the Vatican Pinacoteca. In 1606 the remains of St. Leo IX (1049–1054) were placed here. The oval on the left has St. Lawrence Ruiz (d. 1637), the first canonized (1987) Filipino saint; on the right St. Antonio Maria Gianelli (1789–1845), bishop of Bobbio, canonized in 1951.

(48) Tomb of Pius VIII (1829–1830). The neoclassical figures (1853–1866) are by *Pietro Tenerani*; Christ sits with arms outstretched, ready to embrace the kneeling pontiff. St. Peter is on the left and St. Paul on the right. The two reliefs on the lower level are of Justice (left) and Prudence (right).

(49) The door below the tomb leads to the Sacristy and Treasury. The sacristy is a separate building, joined to the basilica by two passageways; it was built in 1776–1784 by order of Pius VI (1775–1799). A sixteenth-century statue of St. Andrew dominates the vestibule; on the wall, to the statue's right, a large marble tablet listing the popes buried in the basilica, from St. Peter to John Paul I, a total of 147 popes.

Halfway down the corridor leading to the treasury is the way to the sacristy proper, which is not open to the public. The **treasury** is housed in the rooms on the western side of the building; the items are conveniently arranged, well displayed, clearly identified, and fully illuminated. Among the treasures are vestments, reliquaries, crosses, chalices, monstrances, candlesticks, etc. Each item, with its matchless beauty and exquisite workmanship, is a witness to the artistic heritage of past Christian centuries. Of special interest: the bronze monument-tomb of Sixtus IV (1471–1484), the masterpiece of *Antonio del Pollaiolo*, executed (ca. 1490–1495) not long after his arrival in Rome, and the extraordinary sarcophagus of Junius Bassus (d. 359), prefect of Rome.

(50) The altarpiece is the "Punishment of Ananias and Sapphira," a mosaic (1768) after an original by *Cristoforo Roncalli*. The scene is from Acts 5:1-10; because both Ananias and Sapphira had lied to the Holy Spirit, they were immediately punished. Sapphira is stricken in the foreground, while Ananias is being carried out in the background.

(51) The Clementine Chapel is named after Clement VIII (1592–1605), during whose pontificate it was completed. The mosaic (1772) is the "Miracle of St. Gregory the Great," after *Andrea Sacchi*'s original in the Vatican Pinacoteca. Gregory I (590–604) cuts into a cloth from which, because it had touched the relics of martyrs, blood miraculously flows. In 1606 St. Gregory's remains were placed beneath the altar. The mosaics in the cupola have Clement VIII's coat of arms, and the pendentives have Doctors of the Church (Ambrose, Augustine, Athanasius, and John Chrysostom); all have been reproduced from Roncalli's designs.

(52) Tomb of Pius VII (1800–1823). This monument, by the Danish sculptor *Bertel Thorvaldsen*, is frigid when compared to Bernini's baroque creations. The pontiff sits rigidly and gazes sternly upon the viewer; Fortitude is on the left, Wisdom on the right. Thorvaldsen is the only non-Catholic artist represented in St. Peter's.

(53) The altarpiece is an enlarged mosaic version of *Raphael*'s "Transfiguration." Raphael's painting was first in S. Pietro in Montorio and was later taken to France; on its return to Italy it was placed in the Vatican Pinacoteca.

(54) Monument to Leo XI (1605). The statue (1642–1644) of the seated pontiff is by *Alessandro Algardi*. The two standing figures represent Majesty (left) and Liberality (right); the former is by *Ercole Ferrata* and the latter by *Giuseppe Peroni*. The relief on the urn depicts Leo, while still a cardinal, acting as Clement VIII's legate in absolving (17 September 1595) Henry IV of France from the ecclesiastical censures he had incurred. Leo was pope for twenty-seven days, and beneath the statues are roses with the words *sic florui*, "thus I flourished," recalling the brevity of his pontificate.

(55) Monument to Blessed Innocent XI (1676–1689). The monument was designed by *Carlo Maratta* and executed (1697–1704) by the French sculptor, *Étienne Monnot*. The relief below represents the Christian victory over the Turks at Vienna on 13 September 1683 under John III Sobieski, king of Poland, the most important event during Innocent's pontificate. The statues are of Faith (left) and Fortitude (right). Monnot's signature will be found on the front of the shield. The pope's body is under St. Sebastian's altar (#13).

(56) The canons' chapel was designed by *Carlo Maderno*. The mosaic altarpiece is the "Immaculate Conception with Saints" (John Chrysostom, Francis of Assisi, and Anthony of Padua) after an original by *Pietro Bianchi*. The relics of St. John Chrysostom (347–407), patriarch of Constantinople and Doctor of the Church, were placed beneath the altar ca. 1626. In the pavement in front of the altar is a stone tablet indicating the place of burial of Clement XI (1700–1721), founder of the Vatican Museum. The gilded stucco work in the ceiling is by G. Caslani and S. D'Aria. The

choir stalls (1622–1644) were designed by Bernini. The mosaics in the cupola outside the chapel represent "Eternal Father Surrounded by the Four Animals of the Apocalypse" and is based on cartoons by Maratta and Ferri. They also supplied the designs for the David, Daniel, Jonah, and Habakkuk in the pendentives.

(57) Monument to St. Pius X (1903–1914). The monument (1923) was designed by *Florestano Di Fausto*, with the statue of the pope by *Pier Enrico Astorri*. The pope is represented in the act of invoking peace; World War I had begun weeks before the pope's death, which occurred 20 August 1914. The relief on the left of the doorway recalls the pope's lowering the age for receiving Holy Communion, and on the right the learned accepting the Church's teaching. The panels in the door likewise recall his deeds, for example, the middle panel on the left refers to his rearranging the Vatican Pinacoteca, and that on the right to his reform of Church music. The pope's relics are beneath the altar in the next chapel.

(58) Tomb of Innocent VIII (1484–1492). This bronze tomb (1498), by Antonio del Pollaiolo, is the only tomb transferred (1619) from the old basilica to the new. The pope holds in his left hand the holy lance of Longinus, which Sultan Bajazet II had given (1489) the pontiff. Innocent is also depicted recumbent in eternal sleep. The reliefs on either side of the enthroned pope are the four cardinal virtues. There is a slight error in the inscription at the base of the monument. It states that the New World was discovered while Innocent was reigning; the pope died on 25 July, one week before Columbus set sail.

(59) Chapel of the Presentation. The altar has a mosaic version of *Giovanni Francesco Romanelli*'s "Presentation of Mary in the Temple." Beneath the altar are the relics of St. Pius X, canonized in 1954. On the right wall is the bronze monument to John XXIII (1958–1963) by *Emilio Greco*; it represents the pope and bishops (the Church of Vatican Council II) engaged in corporal works of mercy. The pope is buried in the grottoes below. On the left wall, the monument to Benedict XV (1914–1922) by *Pietro Canonica*. Since Benedict was pope during World War I, he is represented as praying for peace in the world. The bronze relief behind has the Virgin and Child, and a world devastated by war. The cupola, which depicts "Glory of Mary and the Fall of Lucifer," and the pendentives (Miriam, Moses, Noah, and Aaron) are after designs supplied by Maratta and *Giuseppe Chiari*.

(60) Monument (1745) to Maria Clementina Sobieski (1702–1735), wife of the Old Pretender, James Edward Stuart [James III], after a design by *Filippo Barigioni*. The figure represents Charity; in one hand she holds a heart and with the other she supports a mosaic portrait of the deceased, after an original by *Ignaz Stern*. The tomb identifies her as "Queen of Britain, France, and Ireland." Under the monument is one of the entrances to the cupola.

(61) Monument to the last of the Stuarts. A. Canova designed the monument (1817–1819) in the form of a stele, with the portraits and half busts of James Edward [James III] (1688–1766), Old Pretender to the English throne, and his sons Charles Edward [Bonnie Prince Charlie] (1720–1788), also pretender to the throne, and Henry Benedict (1725–1807), cardinal of York. Their tomb is in the grottoes below. Two mournful genii, holding fasces, stand near a doorway.

(62) Baptistery. The porphyry baptismal font (1694) was formerly used as the cover for the tomb of the Holy Roman Emperor Otto II (955–983), who is buried in the grottoes. The bronze cover of the font is after the design (1725) of *Carlo Fontana*. The mosaic behind the font is of the "Baptism of Christ," a copy of Maratta's original in S. Maria degli Angeli. On the left side is a mosaic copy of *Giuseppe Passeri*'s "St. Peter Baptizes Sts. Processus and Martinian," and on the right a copy of *Andrea Procaccini*'s "St. Peter Baptizes the Centurion Cornelius." The baptismal theme is continued outside the chapel; the mosaics in the cupola represent baptisms of water, desire, and blood, while the pendentives have allegorical figures of the four then known continents: Africa, Asia, America, and Europe. These are all based on cartoons by *Francesco Trevisani*.

Grottoes

Entrance to the grottoes may be had at four different points, each near one of the statues in the four piers supporting the dome. The following order presumes that the entrance is the one near the statue of St. Longinus.

(1) Chapel of St. Longinus. The altar has a mosaic, "Beheading of St. Longinus," after a painting by *Andrea Sacchi*. Since the chapel had been formerly dedicated to St. Helen, the walls have frescoes of the "Crucifixion," "Finding of the True Cross," etc.

(2) Chapel of the Patrons of Europe. In 1964 Paul VI (1963–1978) proclaimed St. Benedict patron of Europe, and in 1980 John Paul II (1978–) proclaimed Sts. Cyril and Methodius copatrons as well. The chapel dates from 1981.

(3) Chapel of Our Lady of Czestochowa. The chapel is dedicated to the "Black Madonna" of Poland and was built in 1958. It was extended and rededicated in 1982. The reliefs of the evangelists that flank the painting of our Lady come from the tabernacle of Innocent VIII (1482–1492). The walls have seven Polish saints.

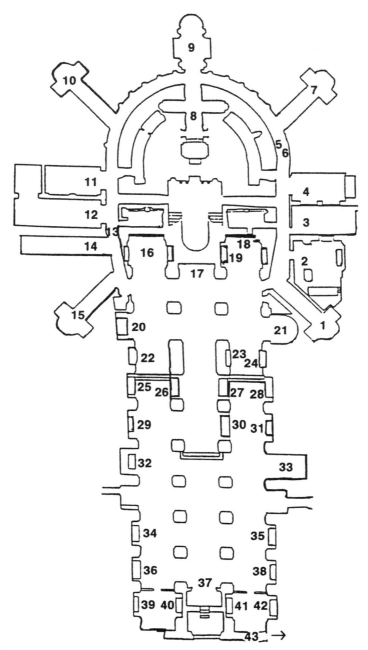

Grottoes

(4) Chapel of St. Columban. The chapel was constructed in 1954; the mosaic represents St. Columban (543–615) and monks leaving their monastery in Ireland to evangelize Europe.

(5) Relief of the head of St. Andrew. This was most probably part of a tabernacle holding the relic of the head, which had been brought to Rome in 1462. Paul VI returned the relic to the Greek Church in 1964.

(6) Marble statues of the apostles. The statue in this and succeeding niches were part of a tabernacle that Sixtus IV (1471–1484) had ordered for the main altar, over the tomb of St. Peter, in the old basilica.

(7) Chapel of St. Helen. At the end of the passage is an altar dedicated to her. The chapel was originally in honor of St. Andrew and, thus, the wall decorations represent Pius II (1458–1464) receiving the relic of St. Andrew's head.

(8) Chapel of St. Peter. The altar was erected by Clement VIII (1592–1605), and the base of the red wall (so called because it was lined with red plaster), directly behind the altar, touches St. Peter's tomb below. Excavations done beneath the basilica (1940–1950) have unearthed the ancient cemetery where St. Peter was buried.

(9) Tomb of Pius XII (1939–1958). It was during Pius' pontificate that the excavations under St. Peter's took place.

(10) Chapel of St. Veronica. The altarpiece is "St. Veronica Wipes the Face of Jesus" and the walls represent scenes of popes displaying Veronica's veil for veneration.

(11) Chapel with the tomb of Cardinal Joseph Beran (1889–1969) of Prague. Above the tomb is a seventeenth-century fresco by *Giovanni Battista Ricci* depicting the Oratory of John VII (705–707), which was dedicated to our Lady and joined to old St. Peter's. The fresco was placed here in 1988 by order of Pope John Paul II. The fourteenth-century image of the Virgin over the altar, "Madonna della Bocciata," is from the old basilica. On the wall outside the chapel, but facing it, is a large stone cross; the inscription next to it, dated 1606, states: "This cross was once at the top of the facade of the old basilica."

(12) Chapel of Our Lady of Childbirth. This fifteenth-century fresco, called "Madonna delle Partorienti," perhaps by *Melozzo da Forlì*, was originally in old St. Peter's and was brought to these grottoes in 1605. The walls have fragments from the earlier basilica; on the right a bust of Boniface VIII (1294–1303).

(13) The mosaic of Virgin and Child is thought to have been part of the tabernacle of the Holy Face, in the chapel dedicated to the Virgin by John VII (705–707). The figures on the sides may be of Constantine and St. Helen. The statues next to the mosaic probably come from the monument to Callistus III (1455–1458); St. John (left) holds a book to indicate that he is an evangelist, and St. Bartholomew (right) holds a knife to recall that he met death by being flayed.

(14) In the Lithuanian chapel the walls have reliefs recalling saints and events in Lithuania's history. The image of the Virgin over the altar is Our Lady of Ostrabrama. The chapel dates from 1970.

(15) Chapel of St. Andrew. The altarpiece is "St. Andrew Contemplates His Cross of Martyrdom." The chapel was originally dedicated to St. Longinus and, thus, one wall has a "Crucifixion" and the other "Innocent VIII Carries the Relic of the Holy Lance in Procession."

(16) This chapel to Our Lady of Guadalupe was dedicated by John Paul II in May 1992. A mosaic of the Virgin, in a Mexican silver frame, is on the front wall. The silver-covered bronze reliefs in the two alcoves also come from Mexico: the one on the left depicts Bl. Juan Diego kneeling before the bishop and holding his cloak with the Virgin's image; that on the right portrays John Paul II giving his blessing from the loggia of the Guadalupe basilica. This recalls the pope's two visits (1979 and 1990) to the shrine.

(17) Direct view into the confession in front of the papal altar. The urn in the niche is where the pallia are placed after being blessed by the pope. They remain there until the pope gives them to newly appointed metropolitan archbishops.

(18) The "Madonna of the Orsini," by *Isaia da Pisa*, is over the altar; it came from one of the dozen or so chapels built by the Orsini family in old St. Peter's. At the Virgin's feet are two members of that family, Nicholas III (1277–1280) and Cardinal Giovanni Gaetano (d. 1335). Sts. Peter and Paul are with the Virgin.

(19) Tomb of Pius VI (1775–1799). Pius had been Napoleon's prisoner in France, where he died. He was first buried in a cemetery in Valence; in 1802 his remains were brought to Rome and placed in this ancient, simple sarcophagus. The relief (fourth century) on top of the tomb was placed there by Pius XII and depicts "Joseph Sold by His Brothers" (left) and "Adoration of the Magi" (right).

(20) Tomb of Pius XI (1922–1939). The tomb (1941) and the figure of the pope are by *G. Castiglione.*

(21) Tomb of John XXIII (1958–1963). It was Pope John XXIII who convoked Vatican Council II. On the wall is a Renaissance relief of the Virgin and Child, flanked by two angels, attributed to *Luigi Capponi.*

(22) Tomb of Cardinal Rafael Merry del Val (1865–1930). Born in London of Spanish parents, he was secretary of state (1903–1914) to Pius X. The tomb is in onyx from Majorca, the gift of the Spanish people.

(23) Tomb of Carlotta di Lusignano (1442–1487), queen of Cyprus. Carlotta became queen in 1458, but had to abandon the island the following year, leaving the crown to her half-brother. Sixtus IV (1471–1484) offered her asylum in Rome in 1461. The tomb was transferred from the old basilica to the grottoes in 1610.

(24) Tomb of Queen Christina of Sweden (1626–1689). The tomb's simplicity contrasts with her monument in the basilica above.

(25) Tomb of the last of the Stuarts, that is, of James Edward [James III] (1688–1766), and his sons Charles Edward [Bonnie Prince Charlie] (1720–1788), and Cardinal Henry Benedict (1725–1807), duke of York. Their remains were united (1939) in this single tomb, which bears royal insignia.

(26) Tomb of Cardinal Federico Tedeschini (1873–1959), archpriest of the basilica.

(27) Tomb of Benedict XV (1914–1922) by *Giulio Barberi.*

(28) Tomb of Innocent IX (1591). He was pope for only two months; his tomb was moved (1606) here from the old basilica.

(29) Tomb of Innocent XIII (1721–1724). His tomb was at first upstairs; in 1836 his remains were brought to the grottoes and placed in this ancient sarcophagus.

(30) Tomb of John Paul I (1978). He succeeded Paul VI (1963–1978) and was pope from 26 August to 28 September, a bit more than a month. He was known as the "smiling pope."

(31) Tomb of Marcellus II (1555). Marcellus was pope for twenty-two days; on his election he retained his baptismal name. Brought here in 1607; his coat of arms is above.

(32) Tomb of Urban VI (1378–1389). It was during Urban's reign that the Great Western Schism (1378–1417) began.

(33) Tomb of Paul VI (1963–1978). Paul succeeded John XXIII (1958–1963); he successfully completed Vatican Council II and saw to its implementation. The fifteenth-century relief of Virgin and Child is from the school of *Donatello.*

(34) Sarcophagus of Pius III (1503). His pontificate was less than a month. His remains were taken from his tomb and temporarily placed (1608) in this early Christian sarcophagus; after the tomb had been moved to S. Andrea della Valle, his remains were also transferred there (1614).

(35) Tombstone of Innocent VII (1404–1406). The stone was brought to the grottoes in 1606.

(36) Tomb of Hadrian IV (1154–1159). Hadrian was born Nicholas Breakspeare and, so far, the only Englishman to be elected pope. The tomb is of red Egyptian granite and dates from the third century; the pope's remains were placed in it in 1606.

(37) Statue (1822) of Pius VI (1775–1799) by *Antonio Canova* and assistants. This was Canova's last work.

(38) Tomb of Nicholas V (1447–1455). It was Nicholas who decided to restore old St. Peter's, and brought Italy's greatest painters to Rome to decorate the rooms in the Vatican.

(39) Tomb of Gregory V (996–999). Gregory was named pope when he was twenty-four years old and died as a result of malaria when he was twenty-seven. His body was exhumed in 1609 and placed in this early Christian sarcophagus.

(40) Tomb of Emperor Otto II (955–983). Otto was Holy Roman Emperor from 973 to 983. The tomb was originally located in the *quadriporticus* of old St. Peter's.

(41) Tomb of Nicholas III (1277–1280). Nicholas was buried in the Chapel of St. Nicholas, which the pope had ordered built in old St. Peter's. During the rebuilding of the new basilica, his tomb was destroyed and his remains were then placed in this fourth-century sarcophagus.

(42) Tomb of Boniface VIII (1294–1303). Boniface instituted the first Holy Year in 1300. The tomb is the work of *Arnolfo di Cambio.*

(43) This early fourteenth-century fresco of the Virgin, in a sculptured Renaissance aedicule, is attributed to *Lippo Memmi.* On the sides are Doctors of the Church; these were once a part of the tomb of Callistus III (1455–1458).

On leaving the grottoes we see bases of columns from the fourth-century basilica as well as portions of the wall. On the right is the cover for the tomb of Callistus III; at the time of the rebuilding of St. Peter's his remains were taken to the Spanish church of S. Maria de Monserrato. The above relief of Christ is from Callistus' original monument in St. Peter's, as are the reliefs of Sts. Vincent Ferrer and Osmond, both of whom were canonized by Callistus.

Near the exit, on the left, a statue of a seated St. Peter, which was originally located, until about 1575, near the entrance of the old basilica. The statue is from the third century, perhaps of a philosopher; the head and hands are later additions, perhaps from the thirteenth century.

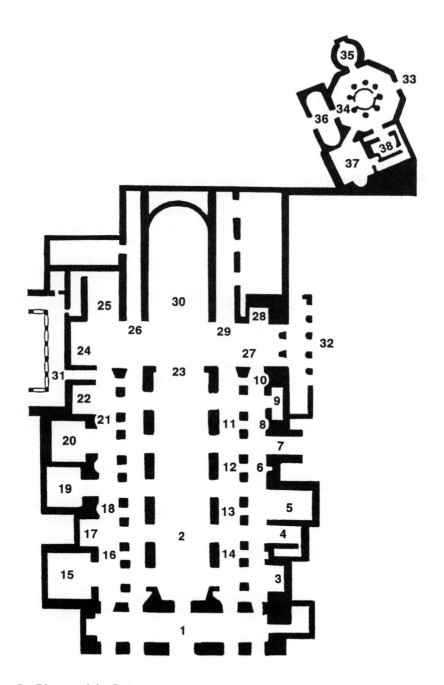

S. Giovanni in Laterano

2 S. Giovanni in Laterano***
Piazza di Porta San Giovanni

History. This is Rome's cathedral. In the early part of the fourth century, Constantine (emperor 306–337) gave Pope Melchiades (311–314) a parcel of imperial property, together with its buildings, for a church and papal residence. The property was known as "Lateran"; years previously it had belonged to Plautius Lateranus. Melchiades may have begun, but Sylvester I (314–335) completed converting the buildings into a basilica, which he then consecrated in 324 and dedicated to the Savior. The basilica was sacked by Alaric in 408 and by Genseric in 455; it was restored by Leo the Great (440–461), and again, centuries later, by Hadrian I (772–795). The basilica suffered from an earthquake in 896 and was rebuilt by Sergius III (904–911), who also dedicated it to St. John the Baptist. In the twelfth century Lucius II (1144–1145) added St. John the Evangelist to the dedication. After the fires of 1308 and 1360 the church was again rebuilt. Later Clement VIII (1592–1605) had the transept redone, and Innocent X (1644–1655) asked *Francesco Borromini* to modernize (1646–1649) the nave. This is the interior the visitor sees today.

Five ecumenical councils (1123, 1139, 1179, 1215, 1512) were held in the basilica and adjoining palace. The popes resided here from the time of Constantine until 1304, when they moved to Avignon; but on their return (1377), they made the Vatican their usual residence. Excavations (1934–1938) beneath the basilica have uncovered remains of Christian and pagan buildings, portions of paved streets, and the foundations of the fourth-century Constantinian basilica.

Exterior. The travertine facade, commissioned by Clement XII (1730–1740) and designed by *Alessandro Galilei*, was completed in 1735. It is of a single order with tall pilasters; the center portion is flanked by paired semicolumns with composite capitals. This single order, in turn, is divided into a portico and a balustraded loggia with arches. Between the portico and loggia is a running medieval inscription from the earlier facade declaring that the pope and emperor want this temple to be considered the first and mother of all churches. This phrase "omnium urbis et orbis ecclesiarum mater et caput" is repeated on the bases of the center columns. A triangular pediment surmounts the central arch and in its tympanum two angels hold an ancient mosaic of the Savior from the original facade. A balustrade runs along the top; a statue of the Savior with those of Sts. John the Baptist and John the Evangelist are in the center. The other twelve statues are of Doctors of the Eastern and Western Churches. The dedication is: "Clement XII, in His Fifth Year as Pope, to the Savior in Honor of Saints John the Baptist and Evangelist." Clement XII's coat of arms is on the bases of the middle pilasters.

(1) Five entrances lead to the portico and the church likewise has five doorways. The central bronze doors come from the Curia (Roman Senate) in the Forum; they were brought here (1660) by Alexander VII (1655–1667) and enlarged by having bronze strips added, on which Alexander's star, his heraldic device, was attached. The Holy Door is on the far right, last opened in 1983–1984. Above three doorways and the niche on the left are four eighteenth-century reliefs with scenes from the Baptist's life. In the niche a fourth-century statue of Constantine, originally in the Baths of Constantine on the Quirinal; it was placed here (1737) by Clement XII, whose coat of arms is on the coffered ceiling and in the pavement.

Interior. (2) By enclosing the earlier basilica's columns in massive piers, Borromini transformed (1646–1649) a basilican-styled building into a baroque edifice, having a nave and four aisles. Statues of the apostles in grey marble aedicules, with flanking verde antico columns and a pediment, in which the Pamphili (Innocent X was a Pamphili) dove is displayed, line the nave. The statues (1700–1719) are by various sculptors, all followers of *Gian Lorenzo Bernini*. The most interesting are, perhaps, the four by *Camillo Rusconi:* St. Matthew and St. James the Greater (right side), and St. Andrew and St. John (left side). The names of the apostles are beneath. Above the aedicules are reliefs, designed (1650) by *Alessandro Algardi*, of scenes from the Old (left) and New (right) Testaments. Between the windows further up, medallions with prophets, whose names are above.

The Renaissance coffered ceiling, attributed to *Pirro Ligorio*, was begun in 1562 during the pontificate of Pius IV (1559–1565). It was finished under Pius V (1566–1572), and restored by Pius VI (1775–1799). The names and coats of arms of these popes are in the ceiling. The triumphal arch, at the end of the nave, is supported by two granite columns; the spandrels have the basilica's patrons, John the Baptist (left) and John the Evangelist (right). The old cosmatesque pavement was restored (1425) by Martin V (1417–1431).

(3) "Mary Immaculate and Saints," a fresco by *Placido Costanzi*.

(4) The Torlonia Chapel, enclosed by an ornate bronze gate, was designed (1830–1850) by *Quintiliano Raimondi*. The marble group (1844) on the altar is *Pietro Tenerani*'s "Christ Taken from the Cross." The altar's frontal is of malachite, lapis lazuli, and alabaster. The tomb on the right

Basilica di S. Giovanni in Laterano (G. Vasi, 1753)

is that of Prince Giovanni Torlonia (1775–1829), and on the left, of his wife Anna. Both tombs are by *Giuseppe Barba*. The statues in the niches represent the four cardinal virtues (fortitude, justice, prudence, and temperance), and the reliefs in the pendentives are of the evangelists. All these are by *Pietro Galli*.

(5) *Giacomo Della Porta* designed the chapel; *Sermoneta*'s "Crucifixion" (ca. 1575) is over the altar. On the right wall, *Cavalier d'Arpino*'s "St. John Evangelist and Disciples."

(6) Tomb of Cardinal Cesare Rasponi (d. 1675). The monument is by *Filippo Romano*; Fame (winged female) entrusts a relief-portrait of the deceased to Time (winged male).

(7) The door leads to the passage, built by Innocent X, connecting the basilica with the Lateran palace. That pope's image is above the door. In the niche to the left, the monument to Cardinal Pietro Gasparri (1852–1934), who had been secretary of state (1922–1930) to Pius XI (1922–1939). Gasparri negotiated the Lateran Treaty between the Vatican and Italy; it was signed (11 February 1929) by him and by Benito Mussolini (1883–1945) in the adjoining Lateran palace. The monument (1932) is by *Enrico Tadolini*.

(8) Cosmatesque tomb of Cardinal Giussiano de Casate (d. 1287) of Milan. In the relief above, Cardinal Giacomo Colonna (ca. 1250–1318), who commissioned the tomb, is presented to the Savior by St. John the

Evangelist. Many of the basilica's monuments were reconstructed by Borromini and, thus, have both ancient and modern elements.

(9) "St. John's Vision on the Isle of Patmos," fresco by *Lazzaro Baldi.*

(10) The tomb (1460) of the Portuguese Cardinal Antoā Martins Chavez (d. 1447) by *Isaia da Pisa.* The three central figures represent the theological virtues (faith, hope, and charity). The other two are Justice and Fortitude.

(11) An eighteenth-century monument to Sergius IV (1009–1012), with fragments from the original tomb.

(12) Monument to Alexander III (1159–1181), erected (1660) by Alexander VII (1655–1667).

(13) Monument to Sylvester II (999–1003), the first Frenchman to be pope. The Catholics of Hungary added (1909) the upper commemorative relief to recall that it was Sylvester who sent (1000) the crown, by which St. Stephen was crowned the first king of Hungary. The inscription was part of the original tomb.

(14) This fresco fragment attributed to *Giotto* depicts Boniface VIII (1294–1303) proclaiming the first Holy Year in 1300. The fresco had been on the loggia outside the Lateran Palace; when the loggia was pulled down (1586), the fresco was moved to the cloister, and then placed here (ca. 1786).

(15) The Corsini Chapel, with its handsome chancel, was built (1732–1735) by Galilei at the request of Clement XII, a Corsini. The altar has a mosaic reproduction of *Guido Reni's* "St. Andrew Corsini"; the original is in Florence. The relief above the altar depicts the battle of Anghiari (1440), during which St. Andrew Corsini miraculously aided the Florentines. On the left is the monument to Clement XII; the pope's statue in bronze is by *Giovanni Battista Maini.* The porphyry urn at the base had been in the Pantheon and once contained the ashes of the consul Marcus Agrippa (63–12 B.C.), son-in-law of Augustus (emperor 27 B.C.–A.D. 14). The monument on the right, also by Maini, is to Cardinal Nereo Corsini (1624–1678), Clement XII's uncle. The four cardinal virtues are in the niches and in the pendentives. The crypt below has a marble "Pietà" by *Antonio Montauti.*

(16) Over the confessional, the tomb of Cardinal Gerardo Bianchi (d. 1302) of Parma. He was the basilica's first archpriest; his figure is incised on the tombstone.

(17) Directly over the altar, a fourteenth-century fresco, in the style of Giotto, of the "Dormition of Our Lady." This was originally in the Lateran palace; Benedict XIII (1724–1730) had it brought into the basilica. Above is the "Assumption with Sts. Dominic and Philip Neri," begun by *Giovanni Odazzi* but completed by *Ignaz Stern.*

(18) Over the confessional, the tomb of Cardinal Bernardo Caracciolo (d. 1255) of Naples.

(19) The altar has a marble figure of the Crucified Lord, by *Aurelio Cioli*, on a gilded bronze cross. Below is an image of "Our Lady of Grace," a fifteenth-century painting by a follower of *Perugino*. Beneath the altar, a third-century Roman sarcophagus. On the left wall, tomb of Cardinal Giulio Antonio Santori (d. 1602) with bust by *Giuliano Finelli*. On the opposite wall, Tenerani's monument in memory of the Pontifical Zouaves killed (1860) in battle; flanking the Savior are Faith (left) and Justice (right).

(20) The Lancelotti chapel was designed (1585-1590) by *Francesco da Volterra* and later (1675) rebuilt by *Giovanni Antonio De Rossi*. "St. Francis of Assisi Receives the Stigmata," by *Giovanni Battista Puccetti*, is the altarpiece. The stucco work (1675) in the vault is by *Filippo Carcani* and depicts scenes in the life of St. Francis that are connected with the basilica.

(21) Above the confessional, the tomb of Cardinal Girolamo Casanate (1620-1700), founder of the famous Roman library that bears his name. The reclining figure (1707) of the deceased is by *Pierre Le Gros*.

(22) The chapel's fresco (1660) is of St. Hilary of Poitiers by *Guillaume Courtois*. In the left alcove, monument to Ilario Mauri of Parma, the chapel's founder. To the right the tomb of Cardinal Pietro Duraguerra (d. 1302).

(23) The Gothic papal altar (reconstructed in 1851 during the time of Pius IX [1846-1878]) dates from 1367; it was commissioned by Urban V (1362-1370) and executed by *Giovanni di Stefano*. The tall, stately baldachin is supported by four columns (three granite and one marble), and is decorated with saints' statues on the corners; the frescoes (1369), three on each side, are by *Barna da Siena*. Behind the grille are two gilded silver busts, which contained what were once thought to be relics of the heads of Sts. Peter and Paul. The altar beneath the baldachin is of white marble, ornamented with small mosaic columns; it was restored in 1851 and, thus, has Pius IX's coat of arms in the center. Its upper portion contains a wooden altar, which legend says was used by the earliest popes, from St. Peter to Sylvester I. The confession in front has the tomb of Martin V (1417-1431); the bronze slab, bearing the pope's image, is by *Simone Ghini*. There is also a statue of St. John the Baptist.

(24) The transept was renovated (1597-1601) by Clement VIII, whose coat of arms is on the ceiling. The ceiling also has a bust of the Savior in the center with those of Sts. Peter and Paul and full-length images of John the Baptist and John the Evangelist. Each end of the transept has four late sixteenth-century tapestry-like frescoes, done in mannerist style,

narrating the history of Constantine and the basilica. The story begins left of the altar in the left transept, goes the length of the transept, then returns to end on the altar's right: "Constantine's Victory" (*Bernardino Cesari*), "Constantine Dreams of Sts. Peter and Paul" (*Cesare Nebbia*), "Constantine's Legionnaires Search for Pope Sylvester" (*Paris Nogari*), "Constantine's Baptism" (*Cristoforo Roncalli*), "Laying the Basilica's First Stone" (Nogari), "Dedication of the Basilica" (*Giovanni Battista Ricci*), "Image of the Savior Appears in the Basilica" (Nogari), and "Constantine Presents Gifts to the Basilica" (*Giovanni Baglione*). Above these, next to the windows, are apostles and saints. The evangelists in the spandrels of both triumphal arches (facing each other) are by *Agostino Ciampelli*.

The altar, designed by *Pier Paolo Olivieri* (ca. 1599), has four large ancient fluted bronze columns, which are said to have been in Rome's Temple of Jupiter Capitolinus. The tabernacle on the altar is ornamented with jasper and lapis lazuli, and stands between four columns of verde antico. Above the altar is a bronze relief of the Last Supper, behind which is a fragment of wood thought to be from the table our Lord used at the Last Supper. The statues in the side niches are (left to right): Aaron (*Silla da Viggiù*), Melchizedek (*Nicolas d'Arras*), Moses (*Flaminio Vacca*), and Elijah (*Camillo Mariani*). These same sculptors did the reliefs above their statues. Roncalli's "Eternal Father" is in the tympanum, and on the wall above, Cavalier d'Arpino's splendid "Ascension." It was because of this fresco and his supervision of the artistic decoration of the transept that Clement VIII made him "Cavalier."

(25) The Colonna Chapel was constructed (1625) after designs by *Girolamo Rainaldi*. The altar has four columns of rare pink alabaster and a painting by Cavalier d'Arpino of "Savior between Sts. John the Baptist and John the Evangelist." The ceiling has *Baldassarre Croce*'s fresco "Coronation of the Virgin." Left of the altar is the marble and bronze tomb of Lucrezia Tomacelli (d. 1625), wife of Prince Filippo Colonna (ca. 1578–1639), the chapel's founder. Walnut choir stalls, decorated with saints' statues, line the walls. The Colonna coat of arms is in the pavement.

(26) The tomb (1907) of Leo XIII (1878–1903), by *Giulio Tadolini*, is over the door leading to the sacristy. A majestic Leo stands erect with outstretched arm; the laborer on the left recalls Leo's encyclical *Rerum Novarum*, which dealt with labor and its problems, and on the right Religion. Visits to the sacristy are not permitted, but among the tombs on the way, there are those of two famous painters, *Giuseppe Cesari* (1568–1640), better known as *Cavalier d'Arpino*, and *Andrea Sacchi* (1599–1661).

(27) The story of Constantine and the basilica continues on the walls of the right transept, as explained earlier. Above the side exit is a baroque organ (1598) by Luca Blasi of Perugia, with carved wooden angels on top.

The marble busts of David (left) and Ezekiel (right), directly over the door-ways, are by *Ambrogio Buonvicino*. The two giallo antico columns, supporting the organ, come from Trajan's Forum.

(28) This small chapel has an eighteenth-century crucifix on the altar. To the altar's right is a marble relief of a kneeling Boniface IX (1389–1404) with cosmatesque decorations. On the right wall, *Antonio D'Este*'s tomb (1803) for Cardinal Carlo Rezzonico (d. 1799). Above is *Francesco Grandi*'s fresco "Presentation of Christ in the Temple." The left wall has his "Adoration of the Shepherds," and, below, the sixteenth-century tomb of an unknown senator.

(29) The monument-tomb of Innocent III (1198–1216) by *Giuseppe Lucchetti*. Innocent died in Perugia and was buried there. When Leo XIII, who had been bishop of Perugia, became pope, he had Innocent's remains brought here and had the monument erected (1891). The figures in the side niches are Wisdom (left) and Fortitude (right). The door beneath leads to the museum and souvenir shop.

(30) **Apse mosaic.** The Constantinian basilica had an apsidal mosaic, and it is believed that when Nicholas IV (1288–1292) commissioned the friars *Iacopo Torriti* and *Iacopo da Camerino* to restore (1292) it, the artists preserved as much of the original as possible. When the apse was again in need of repair in the nineteenth century, Leo XIII had the presbytery extended (1876–1886) by *Virginio Vespignani* and his son *Francesco,* and had Vatican mosaicists remove the thirteenth-century mosaic from the old tribune and reconstruct it in the new apse. Leo's coat of arms is on the ceiling.

The mosaic's topmost portion has a bust of Christ with angels in adoration. This depicts the miraculous appearance of Christ in the basilica's apse at the time of its consecration by Sylvester and may be a remnant of the fourth-century mosaic. Below, placed in the center on a solid gold background, is a jewelled cross over which the Holy Spirit hovers. Beneath the cross flow the four rivers of Paradise, from whose waters deer and sheep slake their thirst. The rivers then flow into the Jordan, which runs along the bottom of the mosaic and in which children and sea creatures play. This lower portion with its animals and river may also be from the fourth century.

The saints that occupy the middle area are of different sizes, an indication of their relative importance. In resetting these figures the two friars may have salvaged as much as possible from the earlier mosaic, but they likewise added figures of their own. The Virgin Mary and St. John the Baptist are on either side of the cross. Then come Sts. Paul and Peter on the left, with Sts. John the Evangelist and Andrew on the right. Inserted between St. Peter and the Virgin is St. Francis of Assisi (1182–1226), and between Sts. John the Baptist and John the Evangelist is St. Anthony of Padua (1195–1231). These two Franciscan saints were added because the two mosaicists were Franciscan friars, and Nicholas IV, who commissioned the mosaic, was likewise a Franciscan. Nicholas also appears in the mosaic, kneeling at the Virgin's right; she gently places her hand on his head. The pope's name appears beneath him: "Nicholas IV, servant of the Mother of God." On the far left bottom is the autograph: "This is the work of Iacopo Torriti," and there used to be on the far right, "and of his assistant Iacopo da Camerino."

Next to the windows below are the other nine apostles; between the second and third apostle on the left, and the same on the right, is the figure of a friar craftsman; perhaps the two mosaicists meant these as self-portraits. The papal throne and wall beneath the mosaic are decorated with panels and disks of porphyry. The upper side walls have two large frescoes by Grandi: on the left, 'Leo XIII Approves the Plans for the Apse," and on the right, "Innocent III Approves the Franciscan and Dominican Orders." Both organs (1886) are by Morettini of Perugia. The walls are lined with forty-two modern walnut choir stalls. The spandrels of the triumphal arches have Doctors of the Church.

(31) The **cloister** dates from 1215–1223 and is by *Pietro Vassalletto* and his son. The arches facing the garden are richly decorated with mosaics. The upper gallery was constructed later. The well in the center is from the ninth century The cloister's walls have fragments of monuments from the old basilica, among them a papal throne. A room entered from the cloisters has an exhibition of vestments.

(32) This is the basilica's north entrance, built (1586) by *Domenico Fontana* at the time of Sixtus V (1585–1590), and divided into a portico and loggia, each having five arches. It is decorated with sixteenth-century frescoes by various artists. A bronze statue (1608) of Henry IV of France, a benefactor to the Lateran chapter, stands in the alcove at one end; it was designed by *Nicolas Cordier.* The two bell towers are from the twelfth century and were restored in the fifteenth.

The Egyptian obelisk in the square is of red granite, the tallest and oldest in Rome. It dates from 1500 B.C.; originally erected by Thutmose IV (king ca. 1420–1411 B.C.) in Thebes, it was brought to Rome (357) by Constantius II (emperor 337–361) and placed in the Circus Maximus. It was then erected here in 1588 by Fontana, by order of Sixtus V.

(33) **Baptistery.** The baptistery was also built by Constantine, about the same time as the basilica. It was restored and transformed into an octagonal-shaped brick building by Sixtus III (432–440). The entrance in use today was opened by Gregory XIII (1572–1585) for the 1575 Holy Year.

A frieze with Alexander VII's heraldic charges runs along the top of the building.

(34) A colonnade of eight porphyry columns (four with Ionic and four with Corinthian capitals), taken from the imperial palace, together with a circular balustrade, marks off the baptismal area. The Latin couplets in praise of baptism on the octagonal architrave are by Sixtus III. A row of smaller columns of white marble rests on the architrave and supports the cupola. The eight oil paintings in the cupola, depicting scenes from the Baptist's life, are modern copies of *Andrea Sacchi*'s originals. The step-down circular area was used for baptism by immersion; in the center is an urn of green basalt, on which baptisms are now performed. A seventeenth-century gilded bronze tabernacle-like cover, with reliefs, once stood on the urn; it is now placed to the side.

The walls have five frescoes (1580–1650) done during the pontificate of Urban VIII (1623–1644). These represent scenes connected with Constantine and run from right to left (beginning on the right after the entrance): "Constantine's Vision of the Cross" (*Giacinto Gemignani*), "Constantine's Victory at the Milvian Bridge" (*Andrea Camassei*), "Constantine's Triumphal Entry into Rome" (Camassei), "Adoration of the Cross and the Destruction of Idols" (*Carlo Maratta*), and finally "Burning of Heretical books on the Lateran Steps" (*Carlo Magnoni*). Above are medallions with portraits of Constantine and popes, together with sketches of Roman churches. Next to the entrance are frescoes of Constantine (left) and Sylvester I (right), and next to the opposite doorway John the Baptist (left) and John the Evangelist (right). Urban's coat of arms is in the ceiling as well as in the pavement.

(35) Four chapels surround the baptismal area. This chapel, dedicated to the Baptist, was built by Pope Hilary (461–468). The altar has a statue of the Baptist by *Luigi Valadier.* The bronze doors (fifth century) may be from the Baths of Caracalla and, because silver was included in the alloy, they sing as they move on their hinges (see custodian).

(36) This was the original narthex and entrance to the baptistery and was converted into a chapel by Anastasius IV (1153–1154). The chapel on the left is dedicated to Sts. Cyprian and Giustina, whose relics are beneath the altar. The apse mosaic of twisting vine tendrils is said to be from the fifth century To the left is the monument of Alessandro Borgia (d. 1764), archbishop of Fermo.

The chapel opposite is dedicated to Sts. Rufina and Secunda, whose relics are here. The altar has a painting of the Savior placing crowns on their heads. To the left is an image of the Virgin and Child by *Sassoferrato* and to the right one of St. Philip Neri, attributed to Reni. The monument to the left is to Cardinal Nicola Maria Lercari (1675–1757), who had been secretary of state to Benedict XIII, and on the right the one to Nicola Lercari (1705–1757), archbishop of Rhodes.

Since this had been the original entrance to the baptistery, a few steps through the doorway will give a glimpse of what the Christians of centuries past saw when they approached the baptistery. The doorway is flanked by two porphyry columns with decorated bases and composite capitals, supporting a highly decorated entablature.

(37) This chapel, dedicated to St. Venantius, missionary bishop in Dalmatia (martyred 257), was built by Pope John IV (640–642) and completed by Pope Theodore (642–649). John was a Dalmatian by birth, and had the relics of St. Venantius and of eight martyrs brought to Rome from Salona and placed beneath the altar. The Byzantine-style mosaic dates from this period. At the top are the four symbols of the evangelists, together with the cities of Jerusalem and Bethlehem; lower down the martyrs of Salona, four on each side. In the apse, Christ has the central position with two angels, and below, the Virgin in the center with hands raised in prayer, with six saints (Venantius, Peter, Paul, John the Baptist, John the Evangelist, and Domnus) together with John IV and Theodore. Unfortunately, the baroque altar obscures most of the mosaic. To the left is the tomb of Cardinal Francesco Adriano Ceva (1585–1655) and to the right that of the Marquis of Ceva; both are by *Francesco Fancelli*. The carved cedar ceiling is from the early sixteenth century.

(38) This chapel, built by Pope Hilary in fulfillment of a vow, is dedicated to St. John the Evangelist. When Hilary was papal legate in Ephesus, a grave disturbance broke out (449) in the city and he succeeded in finding refuge at the tomb of St. John the Evangelist. In gratitude he promised a chapel in the saint's honor. The vault is richly decorated with a fifth-century mosaic representing the Lamb of God framed by flower and fruit garlands. A bronze statue of the evangelist, modelled by *Taddeo Landini*, is on the altar and is flanked by two columns of Oriental alabaster. The bronze doors are from 1196 and come from the ancient papal residence; they replace an earlier set of doors.

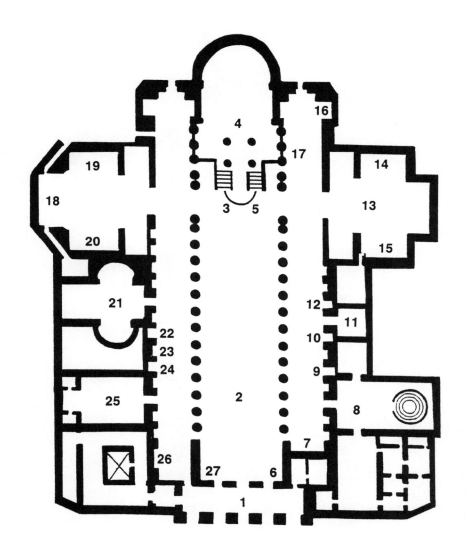

S. Maria Maggiore

3 S. Maria Maggiore***

Piazza di S. Maria Maggiore

History. This is one of the five patriarchal basilicas and is sometimes called "Basilica Liberiana" in a desire to identify it with a church built by Pope Liberius (352–366). According to the medieval legend, the Virgin appeared in a dream (4 August 352) to a wealthy Roman patrician named Giovanni, and told him to build a church on the site where he would find snow the following morning. Befuddled, he went to tell Pope Liberius of his dream, but that night the Virgin had also appeared to the pope and told him that he would find snow on the Esquiline Hill, and there he was to outline the size of a new church. A document from the time of Damasus I (366–384) mentions a "Basilica Liberiana," but it is not certain that it was on the site of the present basilica.

The first church known to have been on this site was that built by Sixtus III (432–440) immediately after the Council of Ephesus (431), at which it was defined, against the erroneous teaching of Nestorius (d. ca. 451), that the Virgin Mary is "Theotokos," that is, Mother of God. Thus, Sixtus' church was the first church dedicated to the Virgin, and since it was, with the passage of time, the largest and most important church dedicated to her, it became known as St. Mary Major. Subsequent centuries brought minor changes to the basilica, but the first important transformation was done by Nicholas IV (1288–1292), when he had the apse redone. Clement X (1670–1676) later had *Carlo Rainaldi* redo the rear facade, and Benedict XIV (1740–58), in preparation for the 1750 Holy Year, had *Ferdinando Fuga* reconstruct the main facade and totally resystematize the interior. For the most part, the basilica, as we see it today, is that of Fuga.

Exterior. The travertine facade, cleaned in 1991, is Fuga's work (1741–1742), and is flanked by twin buildings; the one on the right is from 1605, that on the left from 1721. The facade has two orders; the lower is a portico, which replaces that of Eugenius III (1145–1153), and has five entrances. The entrances on the ends have triangular pediments with putti holding papal insignia, while the one in the center has a segmental pediment with the figures of Humility and Virginity. Benedict XIV's coat of arms is over the central entrance. The second order is a large loggia with three arches, the middle one being the tallest with a triangular pediment.

A balustrade runs the length of the facade and divides the two orders; the statues at the ends are of St. Charles Borromeo (1538–1584) on the left and Blessed Nicholas Albergati (1375–1443) on the right. Both were archpriests of the basilica. Another balustrade is above the loggia and continues the length of the adjoining buildings. Five statues are on the upper balustrade, the Virgin and Child in the center, the other four being popes. The Romanesque campanile is from 1377, has a pyramidal top (fifteenth century) and is the highest in Rome (248 feet); it replaces the one from 1100 and was restored by Paul V (1605–1621), whose coat of arms is above the clock. The oldest bell is from 1289.

(1) Portico. Five doors give entrance into the basilica. The one on the far left is the Holy Door, open only when a Holy Year is announced. The one in the center has bronze doors (1949) by *Ludovico Pogliaghi;* they were the gift (1949) of Pius XII (1939–1958), as the inscription above indicates. The doors' panels illustrate scenes from the Virgin's life; Pius' coat of arms is in the pavement in front. Four reliefs depicting episodes connected with the basilica are over three of the doorways and the statue on the right. From left to right: "Martin I Receives the Exarch Olympius," "Gelasius Burns Heretical Books," "Hilary Holds a Council in the Basilica," "Patrician Giovanni and His Wife Offer Their Goods to Pope Liberius." The reliefs are all from 1742–1743. The eight granite columns in the portico are from the previous portico. To the right is a bronze statue (1692) of Philip IV (1605–1665) of Spain by *Girolamo Lucenti;* Philip was a benefactor of the basilica's chapter.

Loggia. The doors to the left of the Holy Door lead to the loggia with the mosaic decorations of the old facade. The mosaics were commissioned by the Colonna cardinals, Giacomo (ca. 1250–1318) and Pietro (1260–1326), and executed by *Filippo Rusuti,* toward the end of the thirteenth or the beginning of the fourteenth century, after those of the apse had been completed. The mosaics are in two orders. Between the arches of the loggia, in the upper order, an enthroned Christ with four angels is in the center; on the left are the Virgin and Sts. Paul and James, with St. Jerome covered by the masonry. On the right, Sts. John the Baptist, Peter and Andrew, with St. Matthew covered. Symbols of the evangelists are above. The artist included his signature beneath the Savior's feet. The lower order has four scenes, dealing with the basilica's foundation: "Virgin Mary Appears to Pope Liberius," "Virgin Mary Appears to Giovanni the Patrician," "Giovanni Meets Pope Liberius," "Pope Liberius Outlines the Church in the Snow." Much of this was done by assistants; the mosaics were restored in 1825. The four gilded bronze angels, at the sides of the doorways, once crowned the baldachin over the main altar, but were removed (1932) by Pius XI (1922–1939) to allow a better view of the apse mosaic.

Basilica di S. Maria Maggiore (G. Vasi, 1753)

Interior. (2) The church is basilican in style with a wide central nave and two lateral aisles, separated by forty columns of which thirty-six are bianco greco marble and four granite. This is one of the best examples of the basilican style in Rome. The columns uniformly have Ionic capitals and they directly support the trabeation with its handsome fifth-century mosaic frieze of green acanthus leaves on a gold background.

Immediately above the trabeation is a series of square-shaped panels, eighteen on each side of the nave, mostly with mosaics from 431–440, the time of Sixtus III. The series starts on the left, near the main altar and depicts Old Testament scenes, from the lives of Abraham, Isaac, and Jacob (on left) and of Moses and Joshua (on right). They are heavily restored, portions are painted in, and a few are missing with paintings as replacements (e.g., those at the end on both sides near the entrance). The mosaics are high and, unfortunately, natural light is sometimes insufficient to appreciate them properly.

Above the mosaics and between the windows is a series of twenty-two frescoes, begun in 1593, representing scenes from the New Testament, principally the life of the Virgin. They were done by seven artists, among whom were *Giovanni Battista Ricci* and *Baldassarre Croce.* Over the arches leading to the Sistine (#13) and Pauline (#18) chapels are two other frescoes: Croce's "Death of the Virgin" (1593) over the left arch, and *Aureliano*

Milani's "Birth of the Virgin" (1742) over the right arch. Milani's replaces an earlier version of the same subject.

The gold coffered ceiling was begun by *Giuliano da Sangallo* under Callistus III (1455–1458) and completed by *Antonio da Sangallo the Elder* under Alexander VI (1492–1503). Both popes were Borgias and their heraldic charge was a bull. Callistus' coat of arms appears in the ceiling twice, but that of Alexander appears three times. Tradition claims that Alexander used the first gold brought from the New World, a gift of Ferdinand and Isabella, to gild the ceiling. The ceiling was last restored (1975) by Paul VI (1963–1978). The frieze immediately below the ceiling is also from the time of Alexander and displays the Borgia bull.

The cosmatesque pavement is from the time of Eugenius III (1145–1153) and has been several times restored. On the rear wall, over the inscriptions placed above the doors are three coats of arms: on the left that of Cardinal Domenico Pinelli (d. 1611), who is remembered for his decorations (1593) in the nave; in the center is that of Benedict XIV, remembered for his restorations (1740–1750) and his consecration (30 September 1750) of the new altar; on the right, Cardinal Girolamo Colonna (1708–1763), archpriest of the basilica during Benedict XIV's restorations. Above these three is the coat of arms of Clement VIII (1592–1605), pontiff during the 1593 renovations in the nave.

(3) The **mosaic on the triumphal arch** is from the time of Sixtus III (432–440); his name appears at the top of the arch, "Sixtus, Bishop, to the People of God." In the center is a jewel-studded throne with an upright cross, the symbol of the Savior. There are also symbols of the evangelists, each holding a crown, as well as Sts. Peter (left) and Paul (right). The remainder of the mosaic is divided into four rows with scenes from Christ's nativity and infancy. The scenes are based upon the apocryphal gospels and are not in chronological order. First row, left: "Annunciation" (in which the Virgin is dressed as a Byzantine princess) and "Angel Appears to Joseph"; on the right "Presentation" and "Angel Instructs Joseph to Take the Child to Egypt." Second row: "Adoration of the Magi" and "In Egypt Christ Meets Aphrodisius." Third row: "Slaughter of the Innocents" and "Magi with Herod." Bottom: the cities of Jerusalem and Bethlehem with lambs, symbols of the apostles and faithful.

(4) The superb **apse mosaic** is some eight hundred years later than that of the triumphal arch. When Nicholas IV (1288–1292) tore down Sixtus' apse, he replaced it with a larger one and commissioned a new mosaic. Nicholas was a Franciscan, and he asked the Franciscan friar *Iacopo Torriti*, who had just completed the mosaic in St. John Lateran, to do this one too. The mosaic, "Coronation of the Virgin," was completed in 1295, three years after Nicholas' death.

Dominating the mosaic are the figures of the Savior and Virgin. Both are seated on the same cushioned and jewelled throne; the Savior places a crown on the Virgin's head. Their feet are on footrests, and the Savior, whose figure is larger than that of the Virgin, holds a book in his left hand on which is written "Come, my chosen one, and I will place you on my throne." Both figures are encircled by stars, with the sun and moon toward the circle's bottom. On each side nine angels look upward toward the scene.

On the mosaic's left are four figures. The first is Pope Nicholas IV, diminutive in size to indicate his unworthiness to be among personages as great as these. Then Sts. Peter, Paul, and Francis of Assisi (1182–1226). On the mosaic's right the figures are Cardinal Giacomo Colonna (ca. 1250–1318), who, with Nicholas, defrayed the expenses of the mosaic, then Sts. John the Baptist, John the Evangelist, and Anthony of Padua (1195–1231). Sts. Francis and Anthony were added because they were not only recently canonized and popular with the faithful, but also because Nicholas and Torriti were Franciscans. At both ends of the mosaic is the stem of a hearty acanthus plant, whose branches rise upward and fill the mosaic with admirably symmetrical designs on which exotic birds (e.g., peacocks and phoenixes) perch. Running at the base is a river, with river gods at the ends holding jars from which water flows; children and aquatic birds play, men fish, and animals slake their thirst. At the extreme left of the mosaic is Torriti's signature.

Torriti likewise did the five scenes from the Virgin's life immediately below the apse mosaic; left to right: "Annunciation," "Nativity," "Dormition of the Virgin," "Adoration of the Magi," and "Presentation." The Virgin's dormition was placed in the center to serve as a prelude to the mosaic above; that is, it was after the Virgin's death (the Savior holds her soul in his hand) that she was assumed into heaven and crowned.

The outside arch has an enthroned lamb at the top center, with seven candlesticks and the evangelists holding gospels. Below are the twenty-four elders from the Apocalypse raising their hands to the Savior. Beneath these on the left is "St. Jerome Explains the Scriptures to Paola and Eustochia," and on the right "St. Matthew Preaches to the Hebrews." Both these scenes may appear out of place, but Jerome's and Matthew's bodies were brought from the East and placed in the basilica. This mosaic on the outside arch was covered in 1593, when a vault was built over the main altar. The vault was removed in 1931 by Pius XI and the mosaic, thus, was redone (1933), but based on earlier sketches.

In the center of the apse's lower portion is *Francesco Mancini*'s pleasing "Nativity" (1750) in a giallo antico frame. The reliefs imbedded in the wall, two on either side of the painting, were originally part of the ciborium that was once over the main altar. They are the work (ca. 1474) of *Mino del Reame*; left to right: "Nativity," "Liberius Outlines the Basilica in the Snow," "Assumption," "Adoration of the Magi."

(5) The present main altar (1747) is by Fuga; he used the four porphyry columns that formed part of the fifteenth-century ciborium. The gilded bronze palm branches, encircling the columns and twining upward, were added by *Giuseppe Valadier* in 1823. The columns have bronze Corinthian capitals, and Benedict XIV's coat of arms is on the base of the columns. A series of gilded seraph heads serve as the flaps of the canopy. The baldachin is now surmounted merely by the papal insignia, but it once also had angels (now in the loggia) on the corners. The urn beneath the main altar is of porphyry with gilded bronze decorations; enclosed are the relics of the Apostle Matthew and other martyrs. Four bronze putti support the altar table.

In front of the main altar is the confession, which Pius IX (1846–1878) had *Virginio Vespignani* enlarge (1862–1864). The walls are covered with polychrome marble. The relic of Christ's manger is placed in a gold and silver reliquary, designed by Valadier in 1802. The relic is supposed to have come to Rome at the time that St. Jerome's body was brought from Bethlehem. The reliquary is placed between two porphyry columns; the side walls have frescoes by *Francesco Podesti.* The statue of Pius IX, kneeling in prayer, is by *Ignazio Iacometti.*

(6) The monument (1671) of Clement IX (1667–1669) is by C. Rainaldi and was designed to match that of Nicholas IV (1288–1292), which was, originally, opposite it in the presbytery. It was moved here by Fuga, at the time of his renovations. The baroque statue of the pontiff is by *Domenico Guidi;* Charity (left) is by *Ercole Ferrata* and Faith (right) by *Cosimo Fancelli.* Clement's coat of arms is at the top. The pope is buried, however, in front of the confession.

(7) In front of the altar (1610–1612) is a marble slab indicating the place where members of the Patrizi family of Rome are buried. The family claims descent from Giovanni, the patrician, who is said to have built the "Basilica Liberiana." The altar painting (1635) is "Virgin Appears in a Dream to Giovanni and His Wife." In the painting, by *Giuseppe Puglia,* the Virgin points to the miraculous snowfall. The handsomely framed bust of Costanzo Patrizi (d. 1623) on the altar's right is by *Alessandro Algardi.* The tomb on the altar's left is that of Maximilian Pernstein, a Bohemian youth, who died (1593) in Rome at age eighteen. Up to the time of Fuga's eighteenth-century renovations, the tomb of the artist *Girolamo Muziano* (1528–1592) was also in this area.

(8) The former choir of the canons was transformed into a Baptistery by *Flaminio Ponzio* (1605), and later (1825) redone by Valadier. The room

is divided by two red granite columns; the baptismal font, a porphyry basin, gift of Leo XII (1823–1829), was placed here in 1825. The statues of the Baptist and putti on the cover, as well as the cherub heads and garlands that decorate the base, are the work of the goldsmith *Giuseppe Spagna*. The large relief on the back wall is the "Assumption" (1608–1610) by *Pietro Bernini*. Near the bottom on the right wall, the bust of Benedict XIII (1724–1730) by *Pietro Bracci*, commissioned (1725) by the canons of the basilica in memory of the pontiff's repairing the basilica's roof. The vault over the baptistery area was painted (1608–1610) by *Passignano*, with the "Assumption" in the center, and prophets and Doctors of the Church in the other panels. The lunettes have putti and scenes from the Virgin's life.

The door to the right leads to the sacristy, decorated by Passignano. The vault has "Coronation of the Virgin," with scenes from the Virgin's life in the lunettes. The door on the left leads to the fifteenth-century chapel of St. Michael; the vault frescoes depict the evangelists and are, perhaps, by *Piero della Francesca*, but they are in a ruinous state.

(9) Altar with "Holy Family and St. Ann" (1723) by *Agostino Masucci*.

(10) Altar with *Stefano Pozzi*'s painting of Blessed Nicholas Albergati (1375–1443), who had been archpriest of the basilica.

(11) The Chapel of the Relics was designed (ca. 1748) by Fuga. Porphyry columns (ten) and pilasters flank the fifteenth-century wooden crucifix in the center and the aedicules containing reliquaries on the side walls.

(12) Altar with "Annunciation" (ca. 1740) by *Pompeo Batoni*.

(13) This is the Sistine Chapel, named after Sixtus V (1585–1590), and begun (1585) by him when he was still a cardinal. The chapel, in the form of a Greek cross with cupola, is the work of *Domenico Fontana*. The polychrome marbles used here were salvaged from older Roman buildings in ruin. The frescoes (1587–1589) are by a group of Roman painters (*Lattanzio Mainardi, Paris Nogari, Giovanni Battista Pozzi*, and *Giacomo Stella*) under the direction of *Cesare Nebbia* and *Giovanni Guerra*, and depict the ancestors of the Lord (in pendentives, lunettes, and underarches) as well as scenes related to his birth and infancy (on the walls). The cupola has the angelic hierarchies. The subject matter of these frescoes derives from the presence of the Oratory of the Manger in this chapel, which we shall soon discuss. These frescoes were restored in 1871, with much repainting.

The chapel's back wall has frescoes of "Sts. Paul and John the Evangelist" (left) and "St. Peter Enters Rome" (right). The statues in the niches, St. Paul (left) and St. Peter (right), are by *Leonardo Sormani*.

The altar in the chapel's center has an especially beautiful ciborium (1590) composed of four gilded bronze angels, holding a *tempietto*, similar to the chapel itself. In front of the altar is a confession into which Fontana had (1587) the Oratory of the Manger transported (walls, niches, and statues) from its original location, which may have been at the end of the right aisle. That oratory had been built ca. 1289 by *Arnolfo di Cambio*, and housed the relic of Christ's manger, now located in the confession in front of the main altar. Of Arnolfo's work there remain but a few traces: the David and Isaiah in the spandrels outside the entrance arch, and in an alcove (around and behind the altar) the few pieces from a Nativity group, namely, St. Joseph, the ox and ass, and three Magi. The Virgin and Child are from the sixteenth century.

(14) This is the tomb (1586–1589) of St. Pius V (1566–1572). It is divided into two orders; the pontiff's statue (1587), by Sormani, is in the center of the lower order, with two reliefs, separated by verde antico columns. The reliefs illustrate events during the pope's reign; that on the left is "Pius V Gives the Banner from Lepanto to Marcantonio Colonna" and on the right "Pius V Gives the Military Baton to Count Sforza di Santa Fiora" to fight the Huguenots. Both are by *Nicolas d'Arras*. Those above, separated by caryatids, depict, left to right: "Battle of Lepanto," "Coronation of Pius V," and "Victory over the Huguenots." The middle relief is by Nicolas d'Arras, while the other two are by *Giles de Rivière*. Pius' coat of arms surmounts the tomb. The urn that once contained the pope's body was added after his beatification (1672); the silver panel (1697–1698) with the image of the pope in death is by *Pierre Le Gros*. Since Pius was a Dominican, statues of St. Peter Martyr (left) by *Valsoldo* and St. Dominic (right) by *Giacomo Della Porta* are in the side niches. Pius V's tomb was included in Sixtus V's chapel because it was Pius who had made Sixtus a cardinal.

(15) Sixtus V's tomb (1588–1589), in the chapel's right arm, is similar to that of Pius V. The pope's statue (1589), unveiled in the pontiff's presence, is by Valsoldo, who also did the relief on the lower left, "Sixtus V's Works of Faith and Charity." The relief on the right, "Sixtus V's Works of Justice and City Improvement," is by Nicolas d'Arras, while the three above, left to right, "Canonization of St. Diego of Alcalà," "Coronation of Sixtus V," and "Peace between Sigismund of Poland and the Emperor of Austria" are by Giles de Rivière. Sixtus was a Franciscan and, thus, statues of St. Francis of Assisi (left) by *Flaminio Vacca*, and St. Anthony of Padua (right) by *Pier Paolo Olivieri* are in the side niches. Sixtus' coat of arms is at the top. The sacristy (1590), whose door is to the right of Sixtus' tomb, is frescoed by the same artists who worked on the chapel's vault. The altar has "Adoration of the Shepherds," attributed to G. B. Pozzi, and the lunettes have landscapes attributed to *Paul Bril*.

There are two tiny chapels on the sides as one enters this larger chapel.

The one on the left is dedicated to St. Jerome; the altarpiece (1817) portraying the saint is by *Giovanni Micocca.* The right wall has "St. Jerome Washes the Feet of His Disciples," by *Andrea Lilio.* St. Jerome's remains were brought from Bethlehem and placed in the basilica; the exact place is no longer known. The chapel on the right is that of St. Lucy; the altar has Nogari's "Communion of St. Lucy"; G. B. Pozzi's "Massacre of the Innocents" is on the left wall.

The vault in the right aisle, at the entrance to this chapel, has the four evangelists by Lilio and *Ferdinando Sermei.*

(16) This is the medieval Gothic tomb of Cardinal Consalvo Rodriguez (d. 1299), bishop of Albano. Under an elegant baldachin, with a mosaic "Virgin and Child with Sts. Matthew and Jerome," rests the recumbent figure of the cardinal, slightly tilted forward. The cardinal also appears in the mosaic at the feet of the Virgin.

(17) The inscription on the step reads: "Gian Lorenzo Bernini, who brought honor to art and to the city, here humbly lies." The marker in the floor has: "The noble Bernini family here awaits the resurrection." *Gian Lorenzo Bernini's* father *Pietro* is also buried here. Special permission was granted for burial so close to the papal altar because Gian Lorenzo's son, Pierfilippo, happened to be a canon of the basilica.

(18) This is the Borghese Chapel, also known as the Pauline Chapel, named after the Borghese pope Paul V (1605–1621). In his desire to erect a chapel for the icon of the Virgin, still venerated in this chapel, Paul V gave the task to *Flaminio Ponzio.* Work began on the chapel in 1605 and Ponzio repeated the architectural patterns that Fontana used in the Sistine Chapel, on the other side of the nave. The chapel's main feature is the altar (1609–1612) with the ninth/twelfth-century image of the Virgin known as "Salus Populi Romani." The icon is handsomely framed and surrounded by five gilded bronze angels, designed by *Camillo Mariani.* The altar was designed by *Pompeo Targoni* and *Girolamo Rainaldi;* the columns flanking the icon are of Oriental jasper and support a pediment on which two angels by *Guillaume Bertholet* rest. The icon was placed in the chapel on 27 January 1613. The relief (1612) above the altar is by *Stefano Maderno* and depicts Pope Liberius marking off the dimensions of his basilica in the new-fallen snow. The altar table was the gift (1749) of Princess Agnese Colonna Borghese and her coat of arms is found on either side of the altar. The statue of St. John the Evangelist (1611) on the left is by Mariani, and that of St. Joseph (1612) on the right is by *Ambrogio Buonvicino.*

The ornate frieze with exuberant putti and garlands of fruit, between the Corinthian capitals, is by *Pompeo Ferrucci* and *Valsoldino.*

The vault was done (1610–1612) by Rome's best artists of the period.

Cavalier d'Arpino was in charge, and he clearly chose for himself the areas most visible to the public. The lunette over the altar has his "Virgin Appears to Sts. John the Evangelist and Gregory Thaumaturgus"; he likewise did the prophets (Isaiah, Jeremiah, Ezekiel, Daniel) in the pendentives, and the tondo (St. Luke) in the underarch over the altar. The other two panels (1775) in that same underarch depicting Sts. Ignatius of Antioch and Theophilus (left) and Sts. Irenaeus and Cyprian (right) are by *Domenico Corvi*. *Ludovico Cardi* did the cupola (1612), perhaps his last work; it represents Paradise, with the Virgin and apostles in the lower portion. Since Galileo (1564–1642) had recently discovered (1610) craters on the moon, the artist painted his version of the moon with craters beneath the Virgin's feet.

Guido Reni did the frescoes near the windows and in the underarches above the tombs. Near the windows over Paul V's tomb: "Narses Victorious over Totila" (left) and "Heraclius Victorious over Chosroes" (right). St. Francis and St. Dominic are in the underarch. Near the window over Clement VIII's tomb: "Vision of St. John Damascene" (left) and "Vision of St. Ildephonse" (right). In the underarch on the left are three bishops (Cyril, Ildephonse, and John da Marsciano), and on the right three queens (Pulcheria, Gertrude, and Kunigunda). The underarch near the entrance is by *Giovanni Baglione*. The tondo in the center has "Death of Julian the Apostate" and the panels have "Punishment of Constantine V Compronimus" (left) and "Leo V the Armenian" (right).

(19) The tomb (1610–1614) of Clement VIII (1592–1605) matches that of Paul V on the opposite wall. The statue of the pontiff is by *Silla da Viggiù;* the relief on the lower left is "Papal Victory over the Ferrara Insurgents" by Buonvicino, with Mariani's "Conquest of Strigonia" on the lower right. In the upper level, left to right: "Peace between Philip II of Spain and Henry IV of France," by *Ippolito Buzzi;* "Coronation of Clement VIII," by P. Bernini; "Canonization of Sts. Hyacinth and Raymond," by Valsoldino. The four charming caryatids of the upper level are also by P. Bernini. Clement's coat of arms crowns the tomb. In the niches on the altar's sides are statues of Aaron (left) and St. Bernard of Clairvaux (right), both by *Nicolas Cordier*. Paul V had Clement's tomb placed here because it was Clement who made Paul a cardinal.

(20) The tomb (1610–1615) of Paul V is in the chapel's left arm. The pope's statue is also by Silla da Viggiù, but the head is by Cordier. Not caring for the head that Silla gave the statue, Paul V had it replaced by one to his liking. As customary, the reliefs depict major events during the pope's reign. That on the lower left is "Emperor Rudolph of Hungary Goes into Battle," by *Stefano Maderno*, and that on the lower right is Buonvicino's "Paul V Orders the Fortification of Ferrara." The reliefs in

the upper level, left to right: "Canonization of Sts. Charles Borromeo and Frances of Rome," by Valsoldino; "Coronation of Paul V," by Buzzi; "Paul V Gives Audience to Persian Ambassadors," by *Cristoforo Stati*. The caryatids here are by Ferrucci and Buzzi. The statues of St. Denis (left) and David (right) in the niches are by Cordier.

The door on the altar's right leads to the sacristy, which has decorations by Passignano. The altarpiece is of the Virgin, and the vault has saints of the Carmelite, Carthusian, and Cistercian orders.

Of the two small chapels on the sides as you enter this chapel, that on the left is dedicated to St. Frances of Rome (1384–1440) and is decorated by Baglione; that on the right, dedicated to St. Charles Borromeo (1538–1584), has a mediocre modern painting of the saint on the altar. Baglione also did the frescoes (Doctors of the Church) in the vault in the aisle outside the chapel.

(21) The Sforza Chapel was commissioned by Cardinal Guido Ascanio Sforza di Santa Fiora (1518–1564); begun (1556) by *Tiberio Calcagno*, it was completed (1573) by Giacomo Della Porta. The altar has *Sermoneta*'s "Assumption" (1573) and above is Nebbia's fresco "Coronation of the Virgin." The prophets next to the window are also by Nebbia. The tombs of the two Sforza cardinals are in the lateral apses; the left has the tomb (ca. 1573) of Cardinal Guido Ascanio and the right that (1582) of his brother Cardinal Alessandro (1534–1581). The oil portraits of the cardinals over the tombs may be by Sermoneta. Two tablets over the confessionals outside the chapel's entrance recall the benefactions of both cardinals to this chapel and the fact that both had been archpriests of this basilica.

(22) The altar has *Placido Costanzi*'s painting "St. Francis in Ecstasy."

(23) "Regina Pacis" by *Guido Galli*, placed here (1918) by Benedict XV (1914–1922) in thanksgiving for the end of World War I.

(24) Altar has "Vision of St. Leo the Great" (1750), by *Sebastiano Ceccarini*.

(25) The Cesi Chapel, dedicated to St. Catherine of Alexandria, was founded (ca. 1560) by Cardinal Federico Cesi, and done by Giacomo Della Porta. The altar has "Beheading of St. Catherine" (ca. 1567), by Sermoneta. Also his are the frescoes by the window and in the spandrels. The large figures, on the altar's sides, of Sts. Peter (left) and Paul (right), are by G. B. Ricci, but the two above of Sts. John (left) and Matthew (right) are by Sermoneta. The four large paintings on the walls depict scenes from the life of St. Catherine of Alexandria: left front "St. Catherine's Mystical Espousal" (1660), by *Carlo Cesi*; left rear "St. Catherine Taken to Heaven by Angels," by an anonymous artist; right front "St. Catherine Victorious over the Wheel," by *Luigi Gentile*; right rear "St. Catherine

Disputes with Philosophers" (1659), by *Giovanni Angelo Canini.* On the left wall is the tomb of Cardinal Paolo Emilio Cesi (1481–1537) and on the right, the chapel's founder, Cardinal Federico Cesi (1500–1565). The bronze recumbent figures of the cardinals are prior to 1568.

(26) At end of the nave is the baroque monument to Bishop Agostino Favoriti (d. 1638), done in 1685 by *Filippo Carcani,* after a design by *Ludovico Gemignani.* The statue of Faith on the left is especially striking; Fortitude is on the right.

(27) The remains of Nicholas IV (1288–1292), who commissioned the apse mosaic, was discovered near the presbytery in 1572, and a tomb designed by D. Fontana was erected (1574) for him in the presbytery. The statues of the pontiff, Religion (left), and Justice (right) are by Sormani. The tomb was moved here in 1746, during the Fuga renovations.

It is worth a walk around the basilica to see the rear facade with its wide stairs leading up to the basilica. At the request of Clement X (1670–1676), whose coat of arms is in the center of the apse, C. Rainaldi transformed (1673) the octagonal apse into a semicircular one. A balustrade with four statues, done (1672–1673) by *Francesco Fancelli,* runs along its edge.

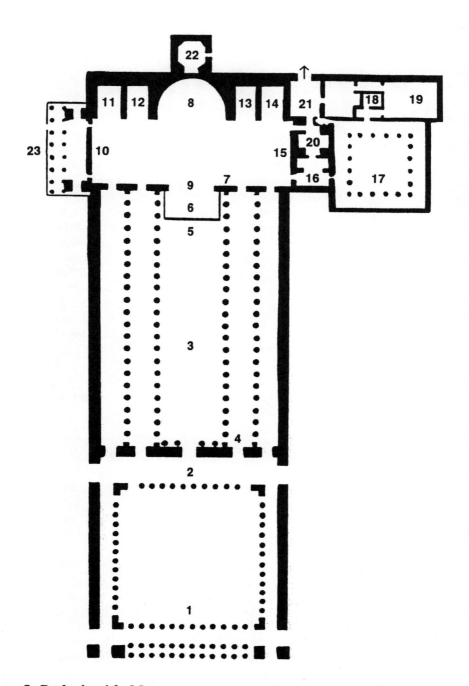

S. Paolo fuori le Mura

4 S. Paolo fuori le Mura***

Via Ostiense

History. St. Paul Outside-the-Walls is the largest church in Rome after St. Peter's and is sometimes referred to as "Basilica Ostiense," because of its location on the Ostian Way; it is one of the five patriarchal basilicas.

The Apostle Paul was brought to Rome as a prisoner and was martyred between the years 64 and 67, during the persecution of Nero (emperor 54–68). Aquae Salviae, today's Tre Fontane, about two miles from the basilica, is traditionally given as the site of Paul's martyrdom. The body was claimed by the Roman matron Lucina, who buried it in her family tomb near a vineyard on the road to Ostia. An oratory was soon erected over it. About 324 Constantine (emperor 306–337) replaced the oratory with a basilica and placed the apostle's body in a bronze sarcophagus with a marble slab over it. Because of the large number of pilgrims a new building was soon needed, and in 386 Valentinian II (emperor 375–392) made plans for a larger building, which Theodosius (emperor 379–395) began and Honorius (emperor 395–423) completed. Pope Leo III (795–816) further embellished it, and in time this became the largest and most beautiful church in Rome, surpassing St. Peter's.

After the Saracens had pillaged (847) the basilica, John VIII (872–882) built a village around it and fortified it. Thus the basilica remained until the fateful night of 15–16 July 1823, when the roof caught fire and crashed into the nave and aisles, destroying most the basilica. The cause of the fire is presumed to have been a hot coal, inadvertently dropped by workers on the roof; it smoldered until the roof burst into flames at about midnight. At the time of the fire Pius VII (1800–1823) was dying, and those attending him thought it better to keep the sad news from him. He died on 20 July.

Leo XII (1823–1829) ordered the basilica's reconstruction and it was financed by donations from the entire world. The work was entrusted to *Pasquale Belli, Pietro Bosio, Pietro Camporese*, and later to *Luigi Poletti*. The transept was consecrated by Gregory XVI (1831–1846) on 5 October 1840. The building was finally completed in 1854 and on 10 December of that year it was consecrated by Pius IX (1846–1878). The present basilica is virtually the same in size and plan as the one that had been destroyed. In 1891 a nearby explosion broke most of the stained glass windows; these were replaced with Egyptian alabaster.

Exterior. (1) The basilica faces the Tiber and is preceded by a *quad-riporticus* (1892–1928), designed by Poletti but modified by *Guglielmo Calderini*. In its center is a statue of St. Paul with the inscription, "To the preacher of truth, the teacher of nations," and in the right corner a statue of St. Luke. The pedestals in the other three corners are still without their statues. As we face the basilica, the ten massive monolithic columns directly in front are of red Baveno granite, while the columns on the other three sides are of Montofarno granite. A head of St. Paul is at the top of the capitals of the columns in front of the facade.

The facade mosaic (1854–1874) is the work of Vatican mosaicists after designs by *Filippo Agricola* and *Nicola Consoni*. In the tympanum Christ is seated in the center giving his blessing, holding his hand according to the Greek manner. On his right is St. Peter and on his left St. Paul. Below, the Lamb of God is seated on a mound, from which flow the four rivers of Paradise. Twelve sheep (apostles) approach the Lamb from the two holy cities of Bethlehem and Jerusalem. This is a modern rendering of a much earlier theme as found, for example, in the apse of Ss. Cosma e Damiano. Between the windows are the four major prophets (Isaiah, Jeremiah, Ezekiel, and Daniel).

(2) Under the portico, the wall niches have statues of St. Peter (left) and St. Paul (right) by *Gregorio Zappalà*, and above are faded fresco portraits of St. Paul's disciples. The central door is of bronze, the work of the sculptor *Antonio Maraini*, and was cast in Florence in 1931. When the door is closed the striking feature is a large cross highlighted in silver, whose horizontal bar bears the names of the evangelists, while the vertical has portraits of the apostles. Five panels on the left depict scenes from the life of St. Peter, and five on the right from that of St. Paul. In both third panels the figure of Christ is in silver and the respective scenes are Christ's giving the keys to St. Peter and St. Paul's conversion. The door on the right is the Holy Door, last opened in 1983–1984.

Interior. (3) The basilica has a "T" shape, that of an Egyptian cross, and is an excellent example of what an early Christian basilica was like. It has one nave (this is entirely from the nineteenth century) with double aisles separated by eighty columns of Montofarno granite. Between the windows, the walls of the nave have twenty-two nineteenth-century frescoes by various artists illustrating episodes from St. Paul's life. Beneath the frescoes and windows is a frieze of mosaic portraits of the popes. The series begins in the right transept, next to the apse, and weaves its way through the basilica. The portrait of Pope John Paul II (1978–) is in the right aisle, near the right transept, and has a light shining upon it. There

Basilica di S. Paolo fuori le Mura (G. Vasi, 1753)

is room for twenty-eight more portraits. The ten niches of the outer walls have statues of the apostles.

The coffered ceiling is in Renaissance style, with much gold stucco work; in the center is the coat of arms of Pius IX, during whose pontificate the basilica was completed and consecrated.

(4) Over the main door two angels hold Pius IX's coat of arms. At the entrance there are six tall splendid columns of Oriental alabaster, the gift of Mohammed Ali, khedive of Egypt, to Gregory XVI in 1843. Two of the columns support the entablature over the main door, the other four are decorative. In the aisle, left of the central door, are the now restored bronze doors that once were the basilica's main doors. They were cast in Constantinople by *Staurachius* of Chios in 1070 and have fifty-four panels with scenes from the Old and New Testaments. The doors were severely damaged by the fire.

(5) The triumphal arch over the main altar rests on two massive granite columns; near the base of the column on the left is a statue of St. Peter, with one of St. Paul on the other side. Neither statue is memorable. The mosaic above is from the fifth century, and is said to have been erected at the expense of Galla Placidia, sister of Emperor Honorius. Since the arch underwent greater damage than did the mosaic, the arch was totally reconstructed in 1853 and the mosaic restored. The inscription at the very top informs us: "Theodosius began [and] Honorius completed the build-

ing made sacred by the body of Paul." The inscription at the bottom of the arch tells us: "Placidia rejoices that, as a result of Pope Leo's concern, the beauty of her father's work is again resplendent." This refers to the repairs that Leo I (440–461) made after a fire or an earthquake had damaged the basilica.

In the mosaic's center is a bust of the Savior, with a rather severe face, in the act of blessing. On either side of him, amid floating clouds, are the symbols of the evangelists. A bit lower and toward the center are two angels with rods in their hands, perhaps pointing to Paul's tomb beneath them; on the sides are the twenty-four elders of the Apocalypse carrying their crowns, and these too look downward reverencing the apostle beneath them. On the next level, on blue backgrounds are Sts. Peter (right) and Paul (left).

(6) Over St. Paul's tomb is the celebrated Gothic **baldachin** of *Arnolfo di Cambio*, resting on four porphyry columns with gilded capitals. The four corner niches above have statues of Sts. Peter, Paul, and Timothy, and Bartholomew, the Benedictine abbot of St. Paul's who commissioned it. In the front abbot Bartholomew (right) offers the baldachin to St. Paul (left). Below the front tympanum, and in the center, is an inscription which recalls that the baldachin was done in 1285 at the request of abbot Bartholomew. There are also inscriptions at both ends; the one on the left reads, "Arnolfo did this work," and it continues on the other, "with his assistant Pietro."

Under the altar is the apostle's tomb. Excavations at the time of rebuilding uncovered a first-century tomb, surrounded by Christian and pagan burials. A marble slab (approximately 7 feet by 3 feet 6 inches) with the inscription "PAULO APOSTOLOMART" is above the bronze sarcophagus containing the apostle's relics. A plaster copy of this slab is in the Pinacoteca off the cloister, and from it we see that the marble slab has a round opening in the center as well as two square openings to the right. On the saint's feast day a censer with burning incense was introduced into the round opening and lowered so as to rest on the sarcophagus; it remained there until the feast day the following year when it was replaced. Pilgrims used the square openings to lower down objects to touch the apostle's tomb.

(7) This superbly carved **Easter candlestick** is approximately 18 feet tall and dates from about 1170; it has figures of animals and scenes from Christ's passion and the ascension on it. The work is signed; on one of the bands near the base there appears, "I Nicolaus de Angelo with Petro Bassaletto produced this work."

(8) The **apse mosaic** dates from about 1220 and survived the fire. It is the work of Venetian artists sent to Rome by Doge Pietro Ziani at the request of Pope Honorius III (1216–1227) to replace a much damaged fifth-century mosaic. A majestic Christ, wearing imperial colors, sits erect on a cushioned throne; his visage is serene and in his left hand he holds a book with the words, "Come blessed of my Father and receive the kingdom prepared for you." His right hand is raised in blessing in the Greek manner. Sts. Paul and Luke are on his right, with Sts. Peter and Andrew on his left. They wear togas of different colors and stand amid flowers. The palm trees at either end are symbols of Paradise. Honorius, who commissioned the work, is the tiny figure kneeling at Christ's right foot; his size indicates his unworthiness to be included among such illustrious personages.

In the center, lower down, is a jewelled cross on a throne with symbols of the passion, flanked by two angels with the other nine apostles as well as Sts. Mathias, Barnabas, and Mark. The figures are separated from each other by trees; they sing the "Gloria" from the Mass, the words of which are written on the scrolls they hold.

The walls of the apse have six marble panels with the names of 187 cardinals and bishops who assisted Pius IX on the day (10 December 1854) of the basilica's consecration. The papal chair is in the center with a relief (by *Pietro Tenerani*) of Christ instructing Peter to feed his sheep. The lunette above the chair has "St. Paul in Ecstasy," by *Vincenzo Camuccini.*

In the mosaic on the arch outside the apse, the Virgin and Child are on the left with St. John the Baptist with a diminutive John XXII (1316–1334) on the right. There are also symbols of two evangelists (Matthew and John). This mosaic is by *Pietro Cavallini* and was originally on the basilica's facade. It was executed during the pontificate of John XXII and, thus, he appears in it. It was relocated here, as was the mosaic on the reverse side of the triumphal arch, in which Christ gives his blessing, with the symbols of the other two evangelists (Luke and Mark), and with St. Peter (right) and St. Paul (left).

To the right of the apse begins the famous series of mosaic roundels with the popes' portraits and continues around the basilica. About forty-two original fresco portraits (from St. Peter to Innocent I) survived the fire; these are now preserved in the adjacent Benedictine monastery.

(9) The magnificent coffered ceiling of the transept has the coats of arms of Pius VII (1800–1823), Leo XII (1823–1829), Pius VIII (1829–1830), Gregory XVI (1831–1846)—the four popes from the time of the fire to the year (1840) when Gregory dedicated the transept—as well as that of the basilica (an arm holding a sword), at the end of the right transept. The walls are covered with rare marbles and the pilasters are made up of fragments from the earlier basilica. Between the windows the frescoes (fourteen) depicting scenes from St. Paul's life continue.

(10) The altar, with Camuccini's uninspired "Conversion of St. Paul," is of malachite and lapis lazuli; the marble was presented to the basilica by Tsar Nicholas I (1796–1855) of Russia. The statue on the altar's left is of St. Gregory the Great and that on the right St. Bernard.

(11) The chapel is dedicated to St. Stephen. The statue on the altar is by *Rinaldo Rinaldi*; the left wall has "Stephen Expelled from the Sanhedrin," by *Francesco Coghetti*, and the right "Martyrdom of Stephen," by *Francesco Podesti*.

(12) The chapel, designed by *Carlo Maderno*, was the only one that was not destroyed in the fire. The crucifix on the altar, attributed to Cavallini and *Tino di Camaino*, is said to be the one that spoke (1370) to St. Brigid of Sweden (ca. 1303–1373). In a niche to the left of the entrance is a statue of a kneeling St. Brigid by *Stefano Maderno*. The mosaic of the Virgin and Child is from the thirteenth century; it was placed here after the chapel in which it was originally located had been destroyed. In a niche on the right is an ancient (fourteenth- fifteenth-century) wooden statue of St. Paul. Cavallini is said to have been buried in this chapel.

(13) The chapel to St. Lawrence was originally designed by Carlo Maderno, but had to be redone because of the fire. The altar has a marble triptych from the fifteenth century. The inlaid choir stalls are due to *Monteneri* of Perugia. The lunettes on the side walls have scenes from the life of St. Lawrence, and above the altar "St. Lawrence Taken to Heaven." The frescoes are by *Arturo Viligiardi*.

(14) In designing this chapel of St. Benedict, Poletti chose to imitate a *cella* of a Greco-Roman temple. The twelve fluted columns came from Veio. The statue of St. Benedict is by Tenerani. Outside the chapel on the right is a holy water font (1860) by *Pietro Galli*; a child reaches up to dip her hand into the holy water as protection against the devil.

(15) The malachite and lapis lazuli in this altar were likewise the gift of Tsar Nicholas I. The altar has a mosaic copy of "Coronation of Mary," by *Giulio Romano* and *Giovanni Francesco Penni*; the original is in the Vatican Pinacoteca. A statue of St. Benedict is on the left and his sister, St. Scholastica, is on the right.

(16) The passage leading to the cloister has thirteenth-century frescoes; the bust of *Luigi Poletti*, the basilica's architect, marks the place where he is buried.

(17) The cloister is a touch of the Middle Ages, and though smaller than that at St. John Lateran, nevertheless, it is more ornate, better preserved, and more beautiful. It was begun by Abbot Pietro de Capua (1193–1208) and completed some twenty years later. It is thought to be the work of *Pietro Vassalletto*, who also worked on the large Easter candlestick in the basilica. Some of the columns, decorated with cosmatesque

work, twist and twine, while others remain their simple selves. The walls have inscriptions and fragments from monuments and sarcophagi; a large fourth-century sarcophagus stands in one of the walkways. A most pleasant and well-kept rose garden is in the center.

(18) This is the chapel of the relics, among which are the chains which once bound the Apostle Paul while a prisoner in Rome. These are in the center, on the lowest level.

(19) The Pinacoteca has two large exhibition cases with prints and engravings illustrating what the basilica looked like prior to as well as immediately after the fire. These are invaluable for an understanding and appreciation of the present building.

(20) Retracing our steps along one side of the cloister, we enter the baptistery (1930), the work of *Arnaldo Foschini.*

(21) The over-sized statue of Gregory XVI is by Rinaldo Rinaldi, and the walls have frescoes from the sixteenth century. A door on the right leads to the sacristy. Another door leads outside to the Ostian Way.

(22) Once outside we may now have a look at the unfortunate campanile that Poletti built; since it looks like a lighthouse it is no wonder that the Romans call it such.

(23) If we continue walking a short distance to the left, we arrive at the northern portico. What is worthy of notice here is that the columns are from the lateral aisles of the ancient basilica; though damaged in the fire, they nevertheless survived. One of them, in the inner row first on the right, bears the inscription "Siricius Episcopus . . ."; it was Pope Siricius (384–399) who consecrated the basilica in 390.

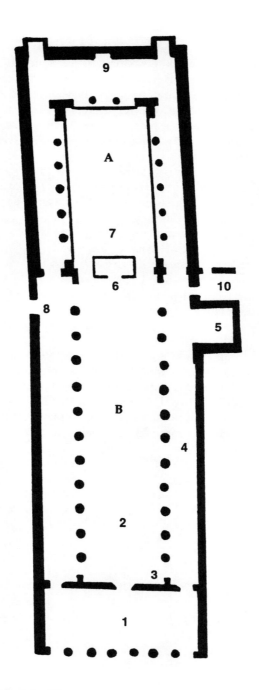

S. Lorenzo fuori le Mura

5   S. Lorenzo fuori le Mura***

Piazzale di S. Lorenzo

History. This is one of Rome's five patriarchal basilicas and is dedicated to St. Lawrence the deacon, martyred (10 August 258) during the persecution of Valerian (emperor 253–259). The present basilica is formed by two churches; each next to the other, but facing in opposite directions. The older **(A)** was built (330) by Constantine (emperor 306–337) on the site of an oratory to the martyr, who had been buried here. It was later totally rebuilt (578) by Pelagius II (578–590). The newer **(B)** was constructed by Honorius III (1216–1227), who joined both churches together by demolishing the apse of the Pelagian church. The basilica was subsequently restored in the fifteenth and seventeenth centuries, and in the nineteenth Pius IX (1846–1878) had *Virginio Vespignani* redo (1862–1865) the interior. Thus, it was cleared of its accumulated baroque additions and the nave was decorated with frescoes by Roman artists. The basilica was severely damaged by aerial bombardment on 19 July 1943, but was rebuilt and reopened in 1949.

Exterior. The basilica is preceded by a portico (1220), the work of *Vassalletto;* six marble columns (the four in the center are spiral), with Ionic capitals, support a trabeation with a frieze of small mosaics and disks of red porphyry and green serpentine. Above is a finely engraved cornice with stylized palms and adorned with lion heads. The plain brick upper facade has three windows. Prior to the bombardment it had frescoes (1855) with figures of Constantine and of the five popes who shared in building or decorating the basilica. The Romanesque campanile is from 1150.

(1) Three of the portico's walls have frescoes from the first half of the thirteenth century (restored in the nineteenth), the work of a certain Paolo and his son Filippo. The front wall, left of the main doorway, has sixteen panels in three rows with scenes connected with St. Stephen the deacon; right of the doorway, the same number of panels representing events in the life of St. Lawrence. The right side wall has eight panels treating legends connected with the death of St. Henry II (973–1024), and the panels on the left wall tell the story of the appearances (1062) of Sts. Lawrence and Stephen to a monk in the monastery adjoining the basilica.

On the left wall is *Giacomo Manzù*'s tomb of Alcide de Gasperi (1881–1954), Italian statesman. Above is a relief of St. Vigilius with the inscription: "May the light of eternal rest shine on him who loved peace and country." The massive seventh-century sarcophagus left of the doorway has pagan reliefs of genii harvesting grapes; there are also flowers, fruit, and a variety of birds.

Right of the main doorway is a huge block of marble, placed here in 1948 by a grateful Rome, recalling the visit of Pius XII (1939–1958) to the piazza the day after the bombardment, and of his successful effort to keep the city safe from further destruction. This is the only church in Rome that suffered during World War II. The old Christian sarcophagus next to the wall on the right has a series of biblical scenes: the resurrection of Lazarus, multiplication of the loaves, sacrifice of Abraham, woman with hemorrhage of blood, and prodigal son. The Good Shepherd is in the center. Near it is an eleventh-century *arca* with pitched roof, which probably marked a floor tomb.

Three entrances lead into the basilica. Two eighth-century Romanesque lions flank the main doorway; the one on the left has a child between its paws, and the one on the right clutches an animal. An eagle holding a snake is above the door.

Interior. (2) This western portion of the basilica has a nave and two aisles, separated by twenty-two columns (sixteen granite, six marble) of various circumferences and coming from different Roman buildings, but with matching twelfth-century Ionic capitals. The church has a severe appearance. Prior to 1943, the nave walls beneath the windows had eight large frescoes (1868); the left side had four scenes from the life of St. Stephen and the right four from the life of St. Lawrence. These were destroyed during the bombardment; the only one preserved, because it was near the front, was "Ordination of St. Stephen and Other Deacons," by *Cesare Fracassini.* This fresco, transferred to canvas, is now on the rear of the facade.

The two pulpits are left over from the thirteenth-century *schola cantorum* that once was in the center of the nave. The pulpit on the viewer's right (for reading the Gospel) is more ornate, with panels of porphyry and serpentine, bordered by mosaic designs by the Cosmati family. Near the top, an eagle holding its prey. The slender spiralling paschal candlestick, resting on two small lions, is likewise the work of the Cosmati. The other pulpit (for reading the Epistle) is smaller and undecorated.

The fresco on the triumphal arch is by Fracassini; an enthroned Virgin and Child is in the center, with angels at her sides. On the viewer's left are Sts. Cyriaca and Stephen, with Sts. Lawrence and Justin on the right. The relics of the last three are preserved here and St. Cyriaca was the Roman matron who buried St. Lawrence on this site. The inscription

Basilica di S. Lorenzo fuori le Mura (G. Vasi, 1753)

below recalls that it was Pius IX who had the church restored (1864); the prophets Daniel (left) and Isaiah (right) are in the spandrels.

The pavement of the nave is *opus alexandrinum*, from the thirteenth century. Halfway down the nave is an eleventh-century mosaic; the center formerly had two armed knights in combat (destroyed during the bombardment), but now has an inscription commemorating the recent rebuilding of the church: "This temple to Lawrence, destroyed by war on 19 July 1943, was, with divine aid, happily restored." The winged creatures in the corner triangles are original, but have been reset. The pavement between the pulpits is of another design—this was the area of the *schola cantorum*.

(3) Tomb of Cardinal Guglielmo Fieschi (d. 1256), nephew of Innocent IV (1243–1254). This is a second-century Roman pagan sarcophagus, placed within a white marble aedicule, whose columns support a cosmatesque-decorated architrave with small columns, which, in turn, support a slanting roof. The sarcophagus depicts a nuptial service; the contracting parties are holding hands on the right, with Cupid between them and witnesses behind them. The two-line inscription above the relief identifies the tomb as that of Guglielmo Cardinal Deacon of St. Eustachio. The inscription on the wall is in praise of the cardinal; above the marble tablet there once was a fresco of saints presenting the cardinal to the Savior, but this too was destroyed in the bombardment.

(4) These three detached frescoes are from the Pelagian church and were discovered during the nineteenth-century restorations.

(5) The painting over the altar, "St. Cyriaca Buries Martyrs" (ca. 1620), is by *Emilio Savonanzio;* beneath the altar is a statue of St. Tarcisius. Statues of St. Lawrence (left) and St. Stephen (right) flank the altar. The painting on the left wall, "Beheading of St. John the Baptist" (1630), is by *Giovanni Serodine.*

(6) Eight steps lead down to the confession. The architrave bears the words: "Here, under the vault, lie the bodies of Blessed Stephen, protomartyr, Blessed Lawrence, deacon, and Justin, presbyter and martyr." Their relics are in a large sarcophagus behind the altar. St. Justin was martyred in Rome about 165; the relics of St. Stephen were brought here from the East and placed, by Pope Pelagius, with those of the other two saints. Eight columns (four of black and white and four of green marble) support the covering over the sarcophagus.

(7) Two staircases lead up to the presbytery; this is the church built by Pelagius. The elevated floor was introduced at the time when both churches were united; it was completed (1254) during the pontificate of Innocent IV. The pavement, however, is probably from the ninth century.

Twelve splendid fluted columns with superb Corinthian capitals (the first two nearest the altar are decorated with war trophies) support a trabeation composed of unmatched but handsomely carved pieces of marble derived from older Roman buildings in ruin. Over these are smaller columns of antique marble with composite capitals, which support the arches of the women's galleries (*matronea*). The cosmatesque throne in the rear is from 1254; the side extensions, with marble panels and mosaic decorations, are possibly from the *schola cantorum* and were placed here as a backdrop for the presbytery. The marble benches at the sides, ending in half lions, are also from 1254.

The sixth-century Byzantine-style mosaic on this side of the triumphal arch originally faced the congregation in the Pelagian church. The Savior is in the center, seated on a globe, giving his blessing in the Greek manner; the other figures are (left to right) Pope Pelagius, Sts. Lawrence, Peter, Paul, Stephen, and Hippolytus. Pelagius, without a halo, offers a model of the basilica to St. Lawrence. Hippolytus was Lawrence's jailer, whom the latter converted; he holds a crown in his hands indicating that he too had been martyred. Beneath the windows are the cities of Jerusalem and Bethlehem. The inscription at the top records Pelagius' concern in restoring the church.

The altar is from 1148; it has four columns of porphyry, supporting a baldachin of white marble, with two tiers of smaller columns and a lantern. It bears the date 1148 and the statement that the altar was commissioned by Abbot Hugh and that it was done by the sons of Paolo, the marble mason.

(8) A staircase leads down to the chapel of St. Cyriaca. The sides have two seventeenth-century reliefs depicting suffering souls in purgatory. The altar is of white marble and has a thirteenth-century cosmatesque-decorated aedicule with two spiral columns supporting a tri-lobed arch. Within is a relief of "Virgin and St. John Hold the Dead Christ." One of the entrances to the Catacombs of St. Cyriaca is here.

(9) Entrance to the Funerary Chapel of Pius IX is from the ends of the side aisles; the chapel occupies the narthex of the Pelagian basilica, and is decorated (ca. 1890) with Ravenna-style mosaics designed by *Ludwig Seitz*. The pope's tomb is in the style of the sixth-century tombs of Ravenna. The vault, walls, and floor have mosaics. The saints depicted on the upper wall are Lawrence, Peter, Paul, and Stephen; on the left wall Sts. Cyriaca and Agnes, and on the right Sts. Francis of Assisi, Joseph, and Catherine of Siena. Below, spread out like a tapestry, are the coats of arms of the many dioceses and institutes that contributed toward the chapel's decoration. On the other wall there are medallions of Sts. Alphonsus Liguori (left) and Francis de Sales (right), both were declared Doctors of the Church by Pius IX. The remaining three mosaics are: "Christianity Offers Homage to Pius IX," in which the five continents present gifts; "Definition of the Immaculate Conception," which occurred 8 December 1854, and "Definition of Papal Infallibility," which took place (18 July 1870) during Vatican Council I.

(10) This leads, through the sacristy, to a quiet Romanesque cloister (1187–1191), whose walls have many marble fragments, Roman sculptures, and medieval inscriptions.

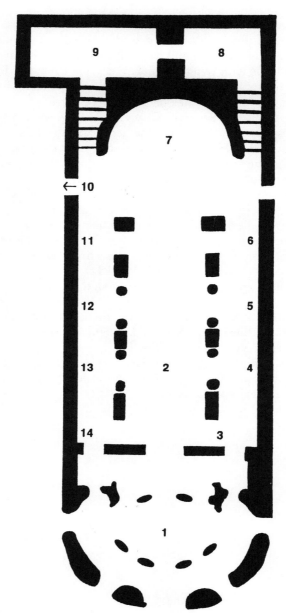

S. Croce in Gerusalemme

6 S. Croce in Gerusalemme***

Piazza di S. Croce in Gerusalemme

History. The basilica of the Holy Cross in Jerusalem is one of Rome's seven pilgrim churches. When St. Helen (d. ca. 328–330), the mother of Constantine (emperor 306–337), returned (about 326) from the Holy Land with a relic of the true Cross, she converted a hall in her residence (Sessorian Palace) into a church as a repository for the relic. This church came to be known as "Basilica Sessoriana." It was likewise known as "Sancta Hierusalem," because, before erecting it, St. Helen spread the soil she had brought with her from Calvary. Thus the church's present name recalls the presence of the relic and that a portion of it is built on Calvary's soil. In 983 Pope Benedict VII (974–983) founded the monastery next door, and a century and a half later Lucius II (1144–1145) remodelled the church, gave it a nave and two aisles, and built a portico and a campanile. Subsequent renovations embellished the interior with frescoes, and in the eighteenth century Benedict XIV (1740–1758) had the church radically transformed (1743–1744) by *Domenico Gregorini* and *Pietro Passalacqua*. This is the church we see today. The Cistercians have been serving the church since 1561.

Exterior. The convex travertine facade, reminiscent of the work of *Francesco Borromini*, dates from 1744. The three doorways are separated by tall pilasters with composite capitals; the middle entrance is arched and supported by two columns; above is an oval window. Windows are likewise over the other two entrances. The inscription on the facade translates: "Pope Benedict XIV, in Honor of the Holy Cross, in the Fourth Year of His Pontificate." Above the main entrance is a segmental pediment and running across the length of the facade, a balustrade with statues of the evangelists, St. Helen, who holds a cross (far left), and Constantine (far right). In the center are two angels pointing toward a cross. The brick campanile is from about 1144.

(1) The atrium is oval with a cupola supported by pilasters and four granite columns. These and the columns flanking the entrance, are from the earlier basilica, perhaps from its portico.

Interior. (2) The church retains the basic plan of Lucius II, that is, a nave, aisles, transept, and apse, but it was redone in the baroque style in the eighteenth century. The nave and aisles are separated by eight granite columns from the earlier basilica, and six pilasters encasing other columns.

The capitals have been redone to achieve uniformity. The gilded-stucco work on the nave walls, including four medallions, are from the eighteenth century and have symbols of the passion. The ceiling is of carved wood with *Corrado Giaquinto's* "St. Helen in Glory" (1744); Benedict XIV's coat of arms is also there. The pavement is cosmatesque, one of the few reminders of the former basilica. The marble holy water stoups are from the end of the fifteenth century; notice the relief of fish within the basins.

(3) Epitaph of Benedict VII, who was buried in the old basilica; the inscription mentions his founding the adjacent monastery.

(4) The altarpiece depicts a miracle of St. Bernard of Clairvaux (1090–1153). The saint successfully extracts a tooth from the skull of St. Caesarius after other monks had failed. The relics of St. Caesarius are in the urn beneath the main altar. The painting is thought to be a copy (1675) of a work by *Giovanni Bonatti.*

(5) The altar has *Carlo Maratta's* "St. Bernard Presents Antipope Victor IV to Pope Innocent II." Bernard, honored as one of the founders of the Cistercian order, convinced Antipope Victor IV to resign (23 May 1138) and submit to the true Pope Innocent II.

(6) *Raffaele Vanni's* "Vision of the Mother of St. Robert of Molesme." The tradition among the Cistercians is that the mother of their founder, St. Robert (1027–1111), had a vision of the child in her womb being espoused to the Virgin.

(7) The apse fresco, "Finding and Triumph of the Cross" (ca. 1495), once attributed to *Antoniazzo Romano*, is now attributed to an anonymous painter of the Umbrian school. The fresco, commissioned by Cardinal Bernardino Carvajal (d. 1522), titular (1495–1522), tells the story of the finding of the cross: St. Helen learns where the three crosses are buried; they are found; a dead youth is brought to life when placed on the true cross; St. Helen holds up the cross for adoration, kneeling before which is the donor, Cardinal Carvajal; Chosroes II (d. 628), king of Persia, conquers (615) Jerusalem and carries the cross away; Heraclius (emperor 610–641) conquers (628) the Persians and returns the cross to Jerusalem. Above is a mandorla with the Savior, surrounded by cherubs; he gives his blessing in the Greek manner.

In the center of the apse wall is the tomb of Cardinal Francisco Quiñones (d. 1540), titular (1528–1540). The tomb (1536) is by *Iacopo Sansovino* and was done while the cardinal was still alive. A tabernacle for the Blessed Sacrament is located in the central niche; statues of Solomon (left) and David (right) are on the sides. To the left is the tomb of Cardinal Carvajal. The apse wall also has two frescoes (1744) by Giaquinto: "Moses Lifting Up the Bronze Serpent" (left) and "Moses Striking the Rock" (right).

Basilica di S. Croce in Gerusalemme (G. Vasi, 1753)

The baldachin over the main altar is from the eighteenth century, but the four columns come from the previous basilica. It is surmounted by undulating volutes that rise to support a cross. Under the altar is a green basalt urn with the relics of Sts. Caesarius and Anastasius. In front of the altar is the burial place of Cardinal Giuseppe Firrao (d. 1744), titular (1740–1744). The ceiling above has Giaquinto's "Apparition of the Holy Cross" (1744) and Benedict XIV's coat of arms.

(8) A passage on the right leads down to the Chapel of St. Helen, built on soil that she had brought from Calvary. The walls of the passage have majolica tiles recalling all that Cardinal Carvajal had done for the basilica. The statue on the altar, an early Roman copy of the statue of Juno, now in the Vatican, was discovered in Ostia, and by adding arms, a head, and a cross, it was transformed into St. Helen. From 1602 to about 1724 *Peter Paul Rubens'* painting of St. Helen was on this altar, and on the side walls were his "Crowning with Thorns" and "Crucifixion"; these are now in France.

Valentinian III (emperor 425–455) is said to have ordered the vault mosaic; it was redesigned (ca. 1484) by *Melozzo di Forlì*, then touched up by *Baldassarre Peruzzi*, and finally redone (1593) by *Francesco Zucchi*. In the center is a bust of the Savior; the ovals have the evangelists and the intermediate spaces have scenes of the finding of the true cross. The underarch near the altar has Sts. Peter (left) and Paul (right), while

71

the other underarch has Sts. Sylvester (who dedicated this chapel in 330) and Helen, at whose foot is the kneeling Cardinal Carvajal. The frescoes (ca. 1590) in the lunettes are by *Niccolò Circignani*, with scenes from the life of St. Helen and allegorical representations of virtues.

The marble plaque on the wall, left of the altar, refers to the floor of the chapel having soil from Calvary. It also states that women are allowed to enter the chapel only on the anniversary of its dedication (20 March). At that time the chapel was within the monastery, and because of the rule of cloister women were allowed in but once a year. Pope Sylvester II (999–1003) died while celebrating Mass in this chapel.

(9) The chapel to St. Gregory the Great was built by Cardinal Carvajal ca. 1520; the cardinal's coat of arms is in the vault. The altar has a seventeenth-century "Pietà." On the left is St. Peter and on the right St. Paul, both fourteenth-century French Gothic statues. The vault above the altar was frescoed (ca. 1640) by *Francesco Nappi* and *Girolamo Nanni.* The Trinity is above, with the Virgin in the center, St. Gregory the Great on the left, and St. Bernard on the right. On the left, nearer the altar, is a scene of St. Gregory celebrating Mass, and on the right St. Bernard celebrating Mass.

Left of the altar is the sepulchral monument to Cardinal Jérôme Souchier (d. 1571), who had been superior general of the Cistercians; on the altar's right the monument to Pompeo Cornazzani (d. 1647), bishop of Parma, also a Cistercian. On the outside wall the large funeral monument of the Cistercian Cardinal Gioacchino Besozzi (d. 1755), who had been abbot of this monastery and titular (1744–1755); he is depicted in prayer. Stone tablets indicate the burial places of other Cistercian abbots.

(10) Chapel of the relics of the passion. The chapel, designed by *Florestano Di Fausto*, dates from 1929–1931 and was built directly over the chapel of St. Gregory the Great. A stairway leads to the chapel; a portion of the Good Thief's cross is on the left wall and a set of bronze stations of the cross (1933) by *Giovanni Nicolini* adorn the walls. In the chapel six relics are in an aedicule behind the altar: three fragments of the true cross (top center); portion of the title from the cross (bottom center); finger of the Apostle Thomas (top left); a nail (bottom left); two thorns (top right); fragments from the Holy Sepulchre, the column of flagellation and the Bethlehem crib (bottom right). The large reliquary (1803) with the fragments of the cross is by *Giuseppe Valadier.*

(11) "St. Sylvester Shows an Image of Sts. Peter and Paul to Constantine" (ca. 1675) by *Luigi Garzi.*

(12) A carved wooden crucifix is on the altar.

(13) The altarpiece (1675) is "St. Thomas the Apostle Touching Christ's Side" by *Giuseppe Passeri.*

(14) The tablet lists the cardinals-titular of this basilica; it was placed here by Cardinal Lucido Parocchi (d. 1903), titular (1884–1889).

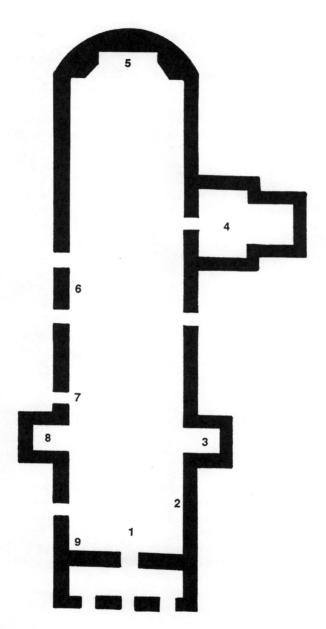

S. Sebastiano

7 S. Sebastiano**
Via Appia

History. In 257 Valerian (emperor 253–259) forbade the Christians in Rome to assemble for religious purposes. Unable to gather at the tombs of St. Peter (in the Vatican) and of St. Paul (on the Ostian Way), the Christians secretly brought (258) the bodies of the apostles to this cemetery outside the city, where they could more easily come and pray. At the time of Constantine (emperor 306–337), since persecution was no longer a threat, the bodies were returned to their former locations, and to new basilicas which Constantine had built for them. Sometime during the first half of that century, perhaps during the pontificate of Julius I (337–352) and the reign of Constans (emperor 337–350), a church was built on this site, dedicated to Sts. Peter and Paul. It was called "Basilica Apostolorum," to recall that the bodies of the apostles had once sanctified this ground. Excavation work done here in 1915 uncovered many third-century graffiti with expressions similar to: "Peter and Paul, pray for. . . ." Such inscriptions corroborate the tradition that the bodies of the apostles had been here.

By the Middle Ages the church's association with the two apostles was forgotten and the church was solely linked with St. Sebastian, a martyr, buried in the same cemetery. Sebastian had been in the emperor's service, an officer in the Praetorian Guard, and when he was denounced for being a Christian, Diocletian (emperor 284–305) ordered the archers to kill him. Sebastian, left for dead, was taken by the widow Irene to her home and there she cared for him. Once recovered, he again went before the emperor, who now ordered him to be clubbed to death (ca. 297–305). Sebastian's cult was popular, especially after he had been successfully invoked during the Roman plague of 680. The church became known as the "Basilica of the Apostles and of St. Sebastian," but by the ninth century it was commonly referred to under his name alone. Early depictions of the saint portray him as a mature man in military dress, but the artists of the Renaissance, with their interest in classical Greek and Roman art, made him into a handsome nude youth.

The fourth-century church was redone in the thirteenth century, but by the end of the sixteenth that too needed repairs. In 1609 Cardinal Scipione Borghese (1576–1633) asked *Flaminio Ponzio* to design and build a new church; after Ponzio's death, it was completed by *Giovanni Vasanzio.*

Exterior. The facade, designed by Ponzio, is of two orders; the lower is a portico with three arches supported by six granite columns, which come from the portico of the previous basilica; the upper order has three windows with Cardinal Borghese's coat of arms over the middle window. The triangular tympanum bears the coat of arms of Paul V (1605–1621). The inscription on the facade records the cardinal's generosity and gives 1612 as the date of the facade's completion.

Interior. (1) The present church has a single nave, with an apse and is baroque in style. The coffered ceiling (1612) is of carved wood, by Vasanzio. In its center is the figure of St. Sebastian; it likewise has two coats of arms, that of Cardinal Borghese is near the entrance, and that of Gregory XVI (1831–1846), who restored it, is near the altar. The pavement is modern, of red Verona marble.

(2) Over the baptismal font is a copy of the inscription which Pope St. Damasus (366–384) placed in the area where the bodies of Sts. Peter and Paul had been located. The text begins: "You, who are looking for the names of Peter and Paul, should know that at one time these saints were here. . . ." Damasus' name is found in the final verse.

Overhead is a painting, attributed to *Annibale Carracci*, of St. Brigid of Sweden (ca. 1303–1373) visiting the catacombs here. There are two other similar paintings. Directly opposite is that of St. Philip Neri (1515–1595), who frequently came here to pray, and toward the front of the church, on the left, is that of St. Jerome (ca. 340–420), who likewise was a frequent visitor to the catacombs.

(3) The chapel of relics was built (1625) at the expense of Maximilian I (1597–1651), duke of Bavaria. Among the objects here: on the lowest level, on the left is an arrow that wounded St. Sebastian, and the column to which he was bound is on the right. Between these are the supposed imprints of Christ's feet when he is said to have met Peter, as the latter was leaving Rome to avoid martyrdom. Seeing Christ, Peter asked: "Lord, where are you going? [*Domine, quo vadis?*]. To this the Lord replied: "I go to be crucified a second time." Peter then turned around and returned to Rome. The place on the Appian Way where this legendary incident is said to have taken place is marked by the *Quo vadis* Church, at the fork in the Appian Way, about a mile from here toward Rome.

Left of the chapel is the tomb of Cardinal Giovanni Maria Gabrielli (d. 1711). Next, there are two altars: the first has a painting of St. Frances of Rome (1384–1440), and the next a fresco of St. Jerome.

(4) This is the Albani Chapel, built (1706–1712) by *Carlo Fontana*; it is in the shape of a Greek cross, with apse and cupola. Clement XI (1700–1721), of the Albani family, erected the chapel to honor Pope St.

Basilica di S. Sebastiano (G. Vasi, 1753)

Fabian (236–250) and as a funerary chapel for his family. Above the altar is a statue (1712), by *Francesco Papaleo*, of St. Fabian in the vestments of a seventeenth-century pontiff. On the left wall is "Election of Pope Fabian" (when a dove landed on his head, the people acclaimed him pope) by *Giuseppe Passeri*, and on the right "Pope Fabian Absolves Emperor Philip the Arab" by *Pier Leone Ghezzi*.

St. Fabian was martyred in 250 during the persecution of Decius (emperor 249–251), and at one time was honored as copatron of this church, with St. Sebastian. Their memorials are still celebrated on the same day (20 January). What is thought to be St. Fabian's body was discovered in 1915 and lies beneath the pavement in the center of the church. His head is in a reliquary behind the altar. Beneath the chapel is the tomb (a fourth-century Christian sarcophagus) of Orazio Albani (d. 1711), Pope Clement's brother. The pope, however, is buried in St. Peter's.

(5) The main altar has four columns of verde antico supporting a broken pediment. The altar was redone in 1676 by Cardinal Francesco Barberini (1597–1679), using material from the catacombs and from an earlier altar. The fresco of the "Crucifixion," a disappointing piece, is by *Innocenzo Tacconi*. The busts (ca. 1600) of Sts. Peter (left) and Paul (right) are by *Nicolas Cordier*.

(6) The painting of St. Francis of Assisi is attributed to *Girolamo Muziano*. Left of the altar is the door which serves as the exit from the cata-

combs. Within are many fragments from the catacombs. The next altar has the fresco "St. Charles Borromeo Prays for Plague Victims."

(7) Entrance to the sacristy; within is a late fourteenth-century wooden crucifix.

(8) The altar to St. Sebastian contains his relics and is placed directly above the area where the saint had been buried in the catacombs. The chapel (1672) is by *Ciro Ferri,* erected at the request of Cardinal Francesco Barberini. Beneath the altar is an exceedingly fine statue of a wounded **St. Sebastian,** by *Antonio Giorgetti.*

(9) On the right wall is a large stone, brought from the catacombs and placed in the church in the sixteenth century. The stone contains a eulogy, composed by St. Damasus, on the martyr Eutychius. It is written in Latin hexameters and describes the saint's martyrdom. Damasus' name appears in the last line. The calligraphy is exceptionally clear and beautiful. Above the tablet is a small fifteenth-century Renaissance tabernacle with Redeemer and angels.

Catacombs. Entrance to the catacombs is on the left of the portico. Though the word "catacombs" today refers to the many early underground burial places in and outside Rome, it was originally used for this particular cemetery. This area was known as *cemoeterium ad catacumbas,* or "cemetery at the hollows" in the road. In time, the name was applied to any and every underground burial place. These catacombs were always known (many of the others were only discovered in the nineteenth century), and when pilgrims came to Rome this basilica was among the seven churches to be visited. A visit to the catacombs is made with a guide.

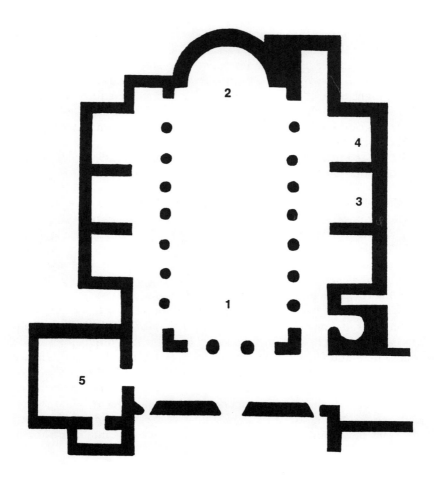

S. Agnese fuori le Mura

8 S. Agnese fuori le Mura**

Via Nomentana, 349

History. After St. Agnes' martyrdom (see S. Agnese in Agone), about the year 304, during the persecution of Diocletian (emperor 284–305), she was buried in the cemetery here. Tradition has it that Constantia (or Constantina), daughter of Constantine (emperor 306–337), came to Agnes' tomb to ask to have her skin ailment cured. While Constantia was spending the night here, Agnes appeared to her and exhorted her to become a Christian. The following morning, when Constantia awoke, she was cured. In gratitude she built (ca. 337–350) a church on the site in honor of the saint. The church was subsequently restored by Pope Symmachus (498–514) and totally rebuilt (ca. 630) by Honorius I (625–638). The last major restoration (1855–1856) was by Pius IX (1846–1878).

Exterior. To enter the basilica from Via Nomentana (the other entrance is from Via di S. Agnese), we walk through a passageway and then a courtyard with a building on the right. Within that building is a hall with a fresco by *Domenico Tojetti*, showing Pius IX with cardinals and prelates, who miraculously escaped injury (12 April 1855), when the floor on which they were standing gave way and fell into the room below. In gratitude for their safety Pius restored the basilica.

The church is below street level; a wide staircase of forty-five white marble steps, dating from the seventh century (restored 1590), leads down into the basilica. The side walls have stone fragments from the catacombs located here and from the earlier church. Near the end of the staircase (second landing from bottom), a bas-relief of St. Agnes, which once decorated the altar over her tomb. At the bottom of the stairs, on the right, a large marble slab with an inscription of ten lines written by Pope Damasus I (366–384) in honor of St. Agnes. Damasus' name appears in the last line. The now faint fresco above the doors leading into the basilica represents St. Agnes appearing to Constantia.

Interior. (1) The church is a good example of an ancient Christian basilica, and apart from lateral altars and nineteenth-century decorations, it is basically the same as when Honorius built it. It has a central nave separated from two aisles by fourteen ancient columns of different marbles (breccia and pavonazzetto) with handsome Corinthian capitals. Over the aisles are women's galleries (*matronea*), also with seventh-century columns.

The coffered ceiling of carved and gilded wood is from 1606, the gift of Cardinal Paolo Camillo Sfondrati (d. 1618), and has three figures, the Virgin Mary, St. Agnes in the center, and St. Cecilia near the main altar. The ceiling was restored in 1855 by Pius IX; his coat of arms has been added.

The large nineteenth-century fresco on the triumphal arch, representing the "Martyrdom of St. Agnes," is by *Pietro Gagliardi*. The decorations (1856) on the walls of the nave (a series of virgin saints is between the windows) and the underarches are by Tojetti and others.

(2) The church's treasure, of course, is the apse mosaic (ca. 630–638), from the time of Honorius I. It is one of the oldest examples of Byzantine-Roman mosaic work in the city. Three stylized figures, clothed in the same colors, are placed on a dark gold background. A stately St. Agnes is in the center wearing the bejewelled dress of a Byzantine empress; she wears a diadem on her head and on her left arm she carries the virgin's veil, embroidered with flowers. On the garment's bottom left is a phoenix, symbol of immortality. At her feet are the fire that did not touch her, when she had been condemned to be burned to death, and the sword that beheaded her. Above her the hand of God reaches down through the starry heavens to place a crown upon her head.

On Agnes' left is Pope Symmachus, holding a book, and on her right Pope Honorius I, who offers her a model of the basilica he built in her honor. Both popes are similarly dressed, with bordered togas, chasubles, and pallia. At the base of the mosaic is a long inscription in gold letters on a blue background praising the popes who had decorated and restored the basilica.

The wall of the apse is faced with cipolin marble and divided by vertical stripes of porphyry. There is also a simple but ancient cathedra or bishop's chair.

Four porphyry columns support the baldachin (1614) over the altar, which is from the time of Paul V (1605–1621). The altar has a statue of **St. Agnes** by *Nicolas Cordier*, who adapted an ancient Oriental alabaster sculpture of Isis by adding (ca. 1600) the gilded bronze head and hands. In her right hand Agnes holds a lamb (in Latin, *agnus*), her usual symbol. Beneath the altar are the relics of St. Agnes and her foster-sister, St. Emerenziana, who was stoned to death because she had come to this cemetery to pray at Agnes' tomb. The relics of both saints were discovered in 1605, at the time of Paul V's restorations, and were placed in a single silver urn provided by the same pontiff. Left of the altar is an early (second-fourth-century?) marble **candlestick** decorated with acanthus leaves.

(3) The chapel has a mosaic altar, after the style of the Cosmati. Over it is a pleasing marble bas-relief diptych (1490) with Sts. Stephen and

Lawrence, said to be by *Andrea Bregno*. The marble bust of the Savior may be by Cordier; at one time it was attributed to *Michelangelo*.

(4) The chapel is dedicated to St. Emerenziana. In the painting over the altar the saint holds the palm of martyrdom in her left hand and, since she had been stoned to death, a stone is in her right. The left wall shows Agnes' body ready for burial, and the right portrays Emerenziana at Agnes' tomb. The paintings (1896) are the work of *Eugenio Cisterna*.

(5) **Catacombs of St. Agnes.** The catacombs date from about 258 to 305, and were discovered in 1865–1866. Entrance is from the left rear of the church and only visited with a guide.

St. Agnes' feast is celebrated on 21 January and on that day two lambs are blessed on her altar and then taken to a convent in Trastevere, where they are raised. On Holy Thursday they are shorn and the wool is then woven into pallia, which are then blessed and placed in the urn in the confession in St. Peter's basilica. The pallia are later given (29 June) by the pope to newly appointed metropolitan archbishops.

Leaving the church from the rear, we enter a quiet courtyard and from there we see the building's simple facade. The pathway directly in front of the courtyard leads to the church of S. Costanza.

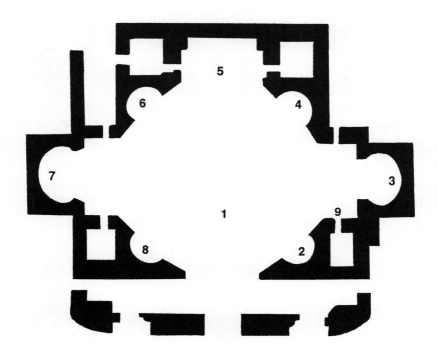

S. Agnese in Agone

9   S. Agnese in Agone**
Piazza Navona

History. The church is dedicated to St. Agnes, a Roman maiden, martyred (304) in her early teens. It is built on the ruins of the Stadium of Domitian (emperor 81–96), and on the site traditionally taken to be the place of Agnes' martyrdom. The church, thus, receives its name *in agone*. When Agnes, according to tradition, acknowledged that she was a Christian and refused to offer incense to idols, she was exposed naked, but her hair grew miraculously to cover her nudity. She was then condemned to be burned to death, but the flames turned from her and went toward her would-be executioners. She was, finally, beheaded and buried on Via Nomentana, where the church of S. Agnese fuori le Mura now stands.

A small church was built on this site in earliest times; Pope Callistus II (1119–1124) enlarged and rededicated it in 1123. It was then totally rebuilt by Innocent X (1644–1655). Innocent had a special interest in it; it was adjacent to his palazzo (now the Brazilian embassy, left of the church), and he wanted it as his burial place. The present building was begun in 1652 by *Girolamo* and *Carlo Rainaldi* (father and son); *Francesco Borromini* succeeded (1653) them as architect and completed the dome in 1654. With Innocent's death (1655) construction was halted, but when it resumed (1657) a committee of six architects took over and brought the building to completion.

Exterior. The church faces Piazza Navona and blends in well with the adjoining buildings. The arresting concave facade is of travertine and by Borromini, who made slight changes in Rainaldi's plans. It has one order, with pilasters and columns and three doorways. The capitals of the pilasters and columns are joined by garlands. A balustrade above has a statue of St. Agnes on the right, but none on the left. The twin bell towers date from 1663–1666.

Interior. (1) The church is in the form of a Greek cross, with a longer transept. The interior was decorated in the 1660s with seven altars; the two in the transept have statues, while the others have reliefs so deeply sculpted that many figures approach being statues. All are powerful pieces and are by pupils or followers of *Gian Lorenzo Bernini*.

The dome is supported by eight columns of red and white cottanello marble and was frescoed by *Ciro Ferri*, completed by *Sebastiano Corbel-*

lini after Ferri's death (1689). It depicts the "Assumption of the Virgin"; Christ and the angelic hosts greet the Virgin Mary in heaven. The attractive pendentives, unveiled in 1672, are by *Giovanni Battista Gaulli*, known as *Baciccia*, and are allegorical representations of the virtues. These frescoes established Baciccia's reputation in Rome and led to his receiving the commission for the vault fresco in the Gesù, his masterpiece. Facing the main altar, Prudence (gazing into a mirror) is on the left, and on the right Justice (with scale) being kissed by Peace (Ps 85:11: "Kindness and truth shall meet; justice and peace shall kiss"). Facing the rear wall, Faith (helmeted) and Charity (with child) on the left, and on the right Temperance (being crowned with flowers). Over the main entrance is the cheerless monument (1729) to Innocent X by *Giovanni Battista Maini*. The pope is buried with other members of the Pamphili family in the crypt below the church.

(2) The altar has *Giovanni Francesco Rossi*'s relief "Death of St. Alessio." The scene depicts the pope and emperor coming to visit the saint after he had died. Those in the background read the document found in Alessio's hand; it reveals his true identity.

(3) *Ercole Ferrata*'s statue (1660) of St. Agnes is an especially outstanding creation; the flames do not envelop her but search out her executioners. It is placed in an illusionistic architectural setting of verde antico marble.

(4) Ferrata likewise did the relief (1660–1661) of the "Martyrdom of St. Emerenziana." Emerenziana was Agnes' foster-sister and was stoned to death because she had prayed at Agnes' tomb. She was buried next to Agnes.

(5) The main altar has *Domenico Guidi*'s "Holy Family." The four columns supporting the pediment over the altar are of verde antico; the angels on the pediment are by Maini.

(6) This "Martyrdom of St. Cecilia" (1660–1667) is one of *Antonio Raggi*'s best works. Cecilia was also a Roman, who miraculously survived an attempt to suffocate her in the bath in her home; she was then beheaded.

(7) To the right of the altar is the entrance to a small chapel with a reliquary over the altar containing the skull of St. Agnes.

The altar in the left transept is dedicated to St. Sebastian. This is an antique statue, adapted in the eighteenth century by *Pietro Campi*; he gave it a new head. The altar matches that of St. Agnes in the right transept. The doorway on the altar's left leads to a chapel containing the font at which St. Frances of Rome (1384–1440) had been baptized; the font comes from the church that formerly stood on this site. A marble relief of St. Frances is over the altar, and the ceiling has a fresco of the saint being received into heaven.

S. Agnese in Agone-Piazza Navona (G. Vasi, 1752)

(8) The relief on the altar is "St. Eustace and Family Exposed to Wild Beasts"; it was begun by the Maltese *Melchiorre Caffà*, but after his death (1667) it was finished by Ferrata. St. Eustace was a Roman general; he, his wife, and two sons were condemned to be killed by the beasts, but the beasts refused to injure them. They were then martyred by suffocation in a brazen bull.

(9) This is the entrance to the subterranean rooms, where, according to tradition, Agnes had been exposed to insult. At the foot of the staircase is an altar, whose bas-relief of "St. Agnes Led to Martyrdom" is attributed to *Alessandro Algardi*. The walls have frescoes (1882) by *Eugenio Cisterna*, his first commission in Rome; they are in deplorable condition because of the dampness. In two back rooms portions of Roman pavement are visible and there are hints of medieval (thirteenth century) frescoes.

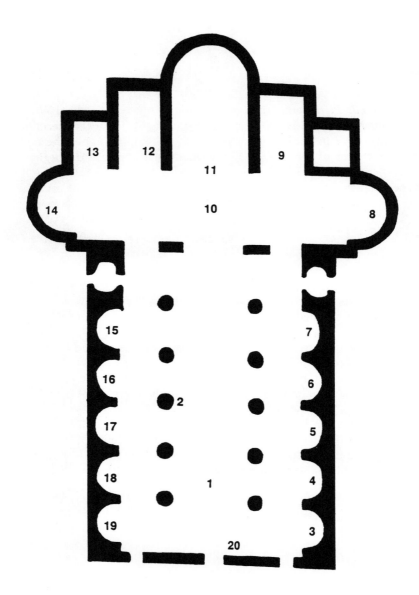

S. Agostino

10 S. Agostino***

Piazza di S. Agostino

History. The church is named after St. Augustine (354–430), bishop of Hippo (North Africa) and Doctor of the Church; it was built (1479–1483) by *Iacopo da Pietrasanta*, thanks to the munificence of Cardinal William d'Estouteville (ca. 1403–1483), protector of the Order of the Hermits of St. Augustine. In 1287 Pope Honorius IV (1285–1287) gave the ninth-century church of San Trifone to the Augustinians, and at the beginning of the fourteenth century they erected a new church to honor their founder. When that church proved too small and the monks thought of constructing a new one, Cardinal d'Estouteville happily bore the expense, as the inscription on the facade states: "William d'Estouteville, Bishop of Ostia, Cardinal of Rouen, Chamberlain of the Holy Roman Church Erected [this building], 1483." The transept of the present church was the nave of the earlier church.

Exterior. The facade (1483), built with travertine taken from the Colosseum, is simple, restrained, and retains its original appearance; it is one of the earliest Renaissance facades in Rome. The faded fresco depicts St. Augustine giving his rule to his monks and nuns. Fifteen steps lead to the church, built high above street level to escape the Tiber's floods.

Interior. (1) The church, Renaissance in style and in the form of a Latin cross, with a central nave and two lateral aisles, was redone (1750–1760) by *Luigi Vanvitelli*. The frescoes in the nave, cupola, and presbytery are the work (ca. 1855) of *Pietro Gagliardi*, except for one important fresco by *Raphael* on the third pillar **(2)**. Raphael painted (1512) his Isaiah at the request of the Luxembourg humanist Johann Goritz (d. 1527), an apostolic protonotary, and when the latter complained to *Michelangelo* that Raphael had overcharged him, Michelangelo merely responded: "The knee alone is worth that price." The prophets (Zechariah, Daniel, Jeremiah, Ezekiel, and Micah) on the remaining pillars are by Gagliardi and imitate Raphael's style. Beneath Isaiah is the remarkably beautiful sculpture group of St. Ann, Virgin, and Child by *Andrea Sansovino*. This too was commissioned by Goritz and was completed in 1512, as the inscription beneath the statue indicates.

Above the arches in the nave is a series of frescoes, six on each side, also by Gagliardi, illustrating the life of the Virgin. The series starts on the left, over Daniel, with Mary's nativity and ends with her death on the opposite side. Above these, and between the windows, are six famous women of the Old Testament: Rebecca, Ruth, Jael on the left, with Esther, Abigail, and Judith on the right. The vault of the nave has Abraham and David (with lyre).

(3) The center painting, "Crowning of St. Catherine of Alexandria," is by *Marcello Venusti*, as are the small side panels of St. Stephen (left) and St. Lawrence (right).

(4) "The Madonna of the Roses" on the altar is a copy, attributed to *Avanzino Nucci*, of a Raphael painting. He likewise did the three oval frescoes on the life of the Virgin in the vault. Flanking the altar are Gagliardi's "Death of St. Joseph" (left) and "Betrothal of the Virgin" (right).

(5) This chapel is dedicated to St. Rita of Cascia (1377-1447), an Augustinian nun. The expressive altar painting by *Giacinto Brandi* depicts the saint in ecstasy; those on the sides by *Pietro Lucarelli* illustrate her death (left) and an incident in her youth when bees would not touch her while she slept (right).

(6) The sixteenth-century marble group "Christ Gives the Keys to St. Peter" is by *G. B. Cotignola*. The two wall frescoes, "Assumption" (left) and "Immaculate Conception" (right) are the work of *Giuseppe Vasconio*; the "Angelic Choir" in the vault is also his.

(7) The carved wooden crucifix dates from the first half of the fifteenth century; the color is that of the natural wood. St. Philip Neri (1515-1595), who made his theological studies in the Augustinian monastery next door, is said to have often prayed before it.

(8) This attractive chapel with its four black marble columns and white Corinthian capitals is dedicated to St. Augustine, the Latin Church's greatest theologian and most prolific author. The altarpiece depicts "St. Augustine with Sts. John the Baptist and Paul, the First Hermit" (1636) by *Guercino*. The two lateral paintings, "St. Augustine Washes the Feet of the Redeemer" (left), and "St. Augustine Overcomes Heresy" (right), are sometimes attributed to Guercino, or to his school, or to *Giovanni Lanfranco*.

Outside the chapel on the left is the baroque monument to Cardinal Giuseppe Renato Imperiali (d. 1737), after the design of *Pier Paolo Posi*; the statues of Charity (left) and Fortitude (right) are by *Pietro Bracci*. A mosaic portrait of the cardinal is held by an angel. Opposite, on the right wall, is Gagliardi's version of "Baptism of St. Augustine." In the pavement in front of the chapel and to the left is the burial place of Venerable Joseph Bartholomew Menochio (1741-1823), an Augustinian bishop.

(9) St. Nicholas of Tolentino (1245-1305) was an Augustinian and the altar painting by *Tommaso Salini* depicts him warding off the flesh and the devil. On the walls Gagliardi illustrated St. Nicholas' intercessory power with regard to the souls in purgatory (left) and the afflicted (right). The other portraits are of four Augustinian blessed: Jerome of Recinato, Anthony of Amandola, Clement of S. Elpidio, and Peter James of Pisauro. The vault has frescoes by *Francesco Conti* and *Giovanni Battista Ricci,* retouched by Gagliardi in 1860.

(10) The cupola has Gagliardi's apostles in its twelve panels, with Christ the Savior in the lantern.

(11) The main altar, adorned with four columns of black marble and gilded capitals, was designed by *Gian Lorenzo Bernini* and erected between 1626 and 1628. In the center is a small Byzantine icon of the Virgin, which is said to have once been in the church of Hagia Sofia in Constantinople and, after the fall of that city (1453), was brought to Rome and given (1482) to this church. The two uppermost angels in adoration are by Bernini.

(12) This is the St. Monica Chapel. St. Monica, the mother of St. Augustine, died in 387 at Ostia, while she and her son were waiting to return to Africa. In 1430, by order of Martin V (1417–1431), her body was brought from Ostia to Rome and placed (1455) in a tomb with a recumbent figure of the saint by *Isaia da Pisa.* That tomb is now on the chapel's left wall. During the restoration of the church in 1760, the saint's remains were put in a new verde antico urn, simpler in design, and placed beneath the altar. On the right wall is the tomb of Pietro Griffi (d. 1516), bishop of Forlì.

The painting over the altar, "Mother of Consolation with Sts. Augustine and Monica" (1765), is by *Gottardi di Faenza.* The ceiling frescoes with scenes from the life of St. Monica are by Ricci. Gagliardi decorated the chapel walls with scenes from the saint's life: the left wall has "St. Monica Consoled by a Bishop" and "St. Monica's Vision," while the right has "St. Monica Receives News of Her Son's Conversion" and "Death of St. Monica." The figures on the altar's sides are of St. Navigius and St. Perpetua, children of Monica.

(13) This is a tiny chapel dedicated to Sts. William and Augustine. It receives very little light. The three paintings (1620) are by Lanfranco. The one over the altar is "Sts. Augustine and William Honor the Virgin"; the right wall has "St. Augustine Meditating on the Mystery of the Trinity," while the left has "St. William Consoled and Healed by the Virgin."

(14) St. Thomas of Villanova (d. 1555), Augustinian archbishop of Valencia, Spain, was famous for his charity toward the poor. The baroque marble group over the altar represents the saint distributing alms; it was begun by *Melchiorre Caffà* but, after his death, completed (1680) by *Ercole Ferrata.* The two groups flanking the altar are of plaster and

are attributed to *Andrea Bergondi;* they depict the saint's healing a cripple (left), and blessing a child (right).

The left wall has Gagliardi's "St. Thomas of Villanova in Ecstasy" and the right the funeral monument to Cardinal Lorenzo Imperiali (d. 1673), by *Domenico Guidi.* The kneeling figure on top is a marble likeness of the cardinal; an angel opens his tomb and an eagle (the Imperiali device) ascends to heaven; Time (left) and Death (right) remain behind.

(15) The chapel is dedicated to St. John of San Facondo (1430–1479), an Augustinian. The painting (1650) of the saint over the altar is by Brandi, while those on the sides showing the saint curing a sick man (left) and healing a mad man (right) are by Brandi's students. The painting in the vault of the saint in glory is likewise by a student.

(16) *Girolamo Muziano's* painting (ca. 1565) of St. Apollonia is the altarpiece. The two on the side (ca. 1650) are by *Francesco Rosa:* an allegorical figure with unicorn (left) and St. John the Evangelist (right).

(17) The painting (1730) of St. Clare of Montefalco (ca. 1275–1308), an Augustinian nun, is by *Sebastiano Conca;* this is one of his better works and shows the saint meeting Christ and receiving the marks of the passion in her heart. The two on the sides are less than mediocre and depict scenes from the saint's life.

(18) Until 1982 this chapel had the marble group now under Raphael's "Isaiah" (see #2); *Ventura Salimbeni's* painting of the crucifixion is currently here.

(19) This chapel contains the church's most valuable painting, "Madonna of the Pilgrims," also known as "Our Lady of Loreto," a particularly charming work by *Caravaggio,* done in 1604. It shows two individuals in pilgrim garb, who have come to the Virgin's house in Nazareth to see the Christ Child. The Virgin and Child look lovingly upon the pilgrims who, in turn, kneel in adoration.

(20) Madonna del Parto (Madonna of Birth). In 1516 the heirs of a certain Giovanni Francesco Martelli commissioned *Iacopo Sansovino* of Florence to sculpt a statue to be placed next to his tomb. It was completed between 1518 and 1521. The statue was always admired by the Romans, but only in the early nineteenth century did it take on a new role. In 1820 a worker, whose young wife was expected to have a difficult delivery, asked the sacristan to burn an oil lamp day and night before the Virgin, seeking her intercession for a successful delivery. His prayer was answered, and ever since lamps and candles have continued to burn before the statue. That the Virgin acts as intercessor in heaven is seen by the great number of *ex votos* surrounding the statue. Above the statue is the inscription: "Virgin, your glory is motherhood."

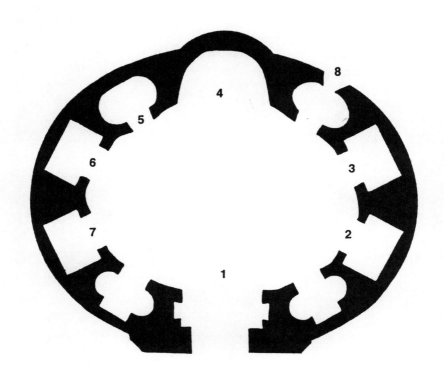

S. Andrea al Quirinale

11 S. Andrea al Quirinale***
Via del Quirinale, 28

History. Since 1566, the Jesuits had a novitiate and a church dedicated to St. Andrew just to the right of the present church. In 1658 they requested permission of Pope Alexander VII (1655–1667) to build a new church; not only was permission granted, but the pope also suggested that the Jesuits could have the services of his architect, *Gian Lorenzo Bernini*. The first stone was blessed on 3 November 1658, and the church was opened for services on 13 November 1670. The expenses of the church were borne by Prince Camillo Pamphili (1622–1666), nephew of Innocent X (1644–1655). Bernini is said to have preferred this church to all his other creations, and his son Domenico attests that he one day found his father in this church and asked what he was doing there all alone. Bernini answered: "I feel a special satisfaction deep in my heart for this one work of architecture, and I often come here to console myself." The church is still served by the Jesuits.

Exterior. Ten semi-circular steps lead to a curved projecting pronaos, whose two columns support a pediment with the coat of arms of the Pamphili family. Since Prince Camillo had built the church, his son, Prince Giovanni Battista, now that the father had died, undertook the expense of the facade (1670). It has a single bay and is exceedingly simple; there is only one portal. Pilasters with Corinthian capitals are at both ends and support a triangular pediment. The concave walls on the church's sides emphasize the facade.

Interior. (1) The church, elliptical in shape with lateral altars, is a magnificent blend of polychrome marbles with a richly decorated gilded dome. The apse, which immediately draws the viewer's eye, is handsomely framed by two pairs of fluted red and white cottanello columns, surmounted by an entablature that curves with the building; the broken segmental pediment above has *Antonio Raggi*'s statue of St. Andrew being taken into heaven. The entire complex forms an attractive aedicule to house the main altar.

The walls have white Carrara marble pilasters, whose upward lines continue into the dome to form eight compartments. The columns' capitals are Corinthian and have the Pamphili dove and olive branch perched on top of them. The arches opening on to the lateral altars are of cottanello marble with friezes and spandrels of Sicilian jasper.

The dome (1662–1665) has a plethora of gilded hexagonal coffers of different sizes with a variety of flowers in the centers. The ribbing in the dome leads to a lantern that has twenty-eight cherub heads flying around it. Eight windows in the drum provide abundant illumination; over the four smaller ones Bernini placed putti playing with garlands and palm branches, while over the four larger ones there are figures of semirecumbent fishermen, whose nets drape over the window frames, under which are decorative curled fish. Since St. Andrew had been a fisherman, these figures are not out of place. The stucco figures in the dome are also by Raggi.

The pavement (1670–1671) of white and grey-blue bardiglio marbles was designed by Bernini's assistant and former student, *Mattia De Rossi;* the latter likewise designed the side chapels. In the pavement directly in front of the entrance is the coat of arms and place of burial of the Jesuit Cardinal Pietro Sforza Pallavicino (1607–1667); the mosaic and marble inlay in the center of the church marks the place of burial of Cardinal Giulio Spinola (d. 1691) and his nephew Cardinal Giovanni Battista Spinola (d. 1719).

Over the entrance door is the Pamphili coat of arms and the inscription: "Prince Camillo Pamphili, son of Innocent X's brother, built this church to St. Andrew the Apostle."

(2) The chapel is dedicated to the great missionary, St. Francis Xavier (1506–1552). The three paintings are by *Baciccia:* the one on the altar depicts the "Death of St. Francis Xavier" on an island several miles off the China coast, 3 December 1552. The painting, now in very poor condition, was done in 1676; the other two were not done until 1705. The left wall has "St. Francis Baptizes a Pagan Queen," and the right "St. Francis Preaching." The fresco (1746) in the vault, by *Filippo Bracci,* represents "St. Francis in Glory."

(3) The altarpiece is *Giacinto Brandi*'s "Christ Taken from the Cross"; on the left is his "Christ Meets Veronica" and on the right his "Christ Scourged at the Pillar." The three paintings date from 1682. The vault fresco, also by Bracci, represents the Eternal Father.

(4) The main altar was designed by Bernini, but executed by others. The painting over the altar, "Martyrdom of St. Andrew" (1668), is by *Guillaume Courtois.* The painting is framed in cottanello marble on a blue mosaic background. The fresco of the Eternal Father in the vault is likewise his. The altar has chiselled and gilded bronze with lapis lazuli panels. Above the painting is a splendid glory; three angels float about the paint-

ing, and nine putti and countless cherubs fly upwards into the cupola. These figures (1668–1670) are by *Giovanni Rinaldi*.

(5) Tomb of Charles Emmanuel IV, king of Sardinia (1796–1802). After the death of his wife, the king abdicated the throne in June 1802 and on 11 February 1815, at age sixty-four, entered the Jesuit novitiate located here; he died on 5 October 1819. The tomb is by *Felice Festa*.

(6) The chapel is dedicated to St. Stanislaus Kostka (1550–1568), a Pole of noble rank, who became a Jesuit in Rome on 25 October 1567, after having walked more than 600 miles from Vienna. He died on 15 August 1586. His relics are in the urn beneath the altar. The altar painting (ca. 1687), by *Carlo Maratta*, is "St. Stanislaus Receives the Child Jesus from the Hands of the Virgin." The two other paintings, by *Ludovico Mazzanti*, illustrate episodes from the saint's life. That on the left is "St. Stanislaus Cools His Breast" because of the ardor that prayer had produced in him; on the right "St. Stanislaus Receives Communion from an Angel." *Giovanni Odazzi*'s fresco, "St. Stanislaus in Glory," is in the vault.

(7) The painting on the altar has three Jesuit saints: St. Ignatius Loyola (1491–1556) founder of the Society of Jesus, St. Francis Borgia (1510–1572), the Jesuit general who established the novitiate here, and St. Aloysius Gonzaga (1568–1591), who was canonized (1726) with St. Stanislaus. The painting is by Mazzanti. The two other paintings are by *Ludovico David:* "Adoration of the Magi" (left) and "Adoration of the Shepherds" (right). The vault has a fresco of angels by *Giuseppe Chiari*.

(8) With the sacristan's permission, one may visit the rooms of St. Stanislaus on the floor above. The saint died in a building that stood on the corner of Via Ferrara, on the church's right. When that building was demolished to make way for the edifice that now stands there, the rooms of St. Stanislaus were reconstructed here (1888–1889).

The first room has a dozen scenes in tempera by the Jesuit artist *Andrea Pozzo*, representing episodes in the saint's life. Begin with those on the wall left of the entrance; the last three on the right wall illustrate miracles. The second room has a photocopy of the letter that Stanislaus carried with him to Rome. It was written (25 September 1567) by St. Peter Canisius (1521–1597), provincial of Germany, to St. Francis Borgia (1510–1572), general of the Society of Jesus, to introduce the young bearer. Above the letter is a portrait of Stanislaus at age 10–12.

In the third room the recumbent polychrome statue of St. Stanislaus is by *Pierre Le Gros*, who used Carrara marble for the face, hands, and feet, black basalt for clothing, and yellow Sienese for the couch. Behind the statue is *Tommaso Minardi*'s painting (1825) of the Virgin coming toward St. Stanislaus; the three saints on the right were Stanislaus' patrons, Sts. Barbara, Agnes, and Cecilia.

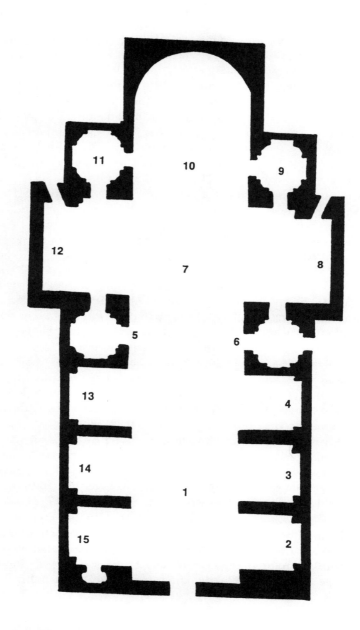

S. Andrea della Valle

12   S. Andrea della Valle**

Piazza di S. Andrea della Valle

History. In 1584 Costanza Piccolomini, duchess of Amalfi, gave her palazzo and the nearby small church of St. Sebastian to the Theatine Fathers for a new church to be dedicated to St. Andrew (patron of the Piccolomini family) and to St. Sebastian. The palazzo and the church were demolished (1590) and, under the patronage of Cardinal Alfonso Gesualdo, construction of the new church began in 1591, according to the plans of *Fra Francesco Grimaldi*, a Theatine, and *Giacomo Della Porta*. With Cardinal Gesualdo's death in 1603 construction halted, but in 1608 Cardinal Alessandro Peretti Montalto (d. 1623) resumed construction with *Carlo Maderno* in charge, and it is to the latter that we owe the dome (1622), the largest in Rome after St. Peter's. The building was completed in 1625 and consecrated in 1650. The "della Valle" in the church's name derives from the area where it is located.

Exterior. The baroque travertine facade (1655–1665), recently and magnificently cleaned (1991), is by *Carlo Rainaldi*, who slightly modified Maderno's original design. It has two orders with four sets of double columns in each; Corinthian capitals in the lower and composite capitals in the upper. The lower order has a single door with two niches with statues on both sides (left to right: Sts. Cajetan [founder of the Theatines], Andrew, Sebastian, and Andrew Avellino [also a Theatine]; the first and third are by *Domenico Guidi* and the other two are by *Ercole Ferrata*). The upper order has one window with a balustrade, giving it the appearance of a loggia or balcony; the two niches are empty. Above the entrance, between the reclining figures of Hope (left) and Prudence (right) by *Giacomo Antonio Fancelli*, is the coat of arms of Cardinal Peretti. In the tympanum at the top, two angels support the coat of arms of Pope Alexander VII (1655–1667). Above on the left, where one would expect a volute, is an angel with outstretched wings by Ferrata, but none on the right. The finials at the ends are Alexander's device of mountains surmounted by a star. The inscription on the facade reads: "Pope Alexander VII, to St. Andrew, Apostle, in the Year of Salvation 1665."

Interior. (1) The church is in the form of a Latin cross; its wide nave and barrel vault create an ambience of spaciousness, further augmented by the tall pilasters rising to a handsome cornice. There are three lateral altars on each side and the church's baroque ornamentation is graceful and restrained.

The vault has large frescoes (1905) in the center: nearest the entrance is "Expulsion from Paradise" by *Salvatore Nobili*, who also did the following one, "Our Lady Appears to Sister Orsola Benincasa" (foundress [1547–1618] of the Theatine Sisters). "Proclamation of the Dogma of the Immaculate Conception," and "Visitation" are by *Virginio Monti*. The apostles and putti over the nave windows are the work of *Silvio Galimberti*; on the rear wall of the facade are *Cesare Caroselli*'s "Holy Family" (left) and "Annunciation" (right).

(2) The chapel (ca. 1670) was designed by *Carlo Fontana* for the Ginnetti family. The eight columns of verde antico marble harmonize well with the black africano and red Sicilian jasper. The altar has a marble relief (ca. 1675) depicting "Angel Instructs Joseph to Flee to Egypt." This is one of *Antonio Raggi*'s better achievements; the Virgin is especially attractive. Over the doorway on the left, the monument to Cardinal Marzio Ginnetti (d. 1671); the statue of the kneeling cardinal is likewise by Raggi, as is the bust of Marquis Marzio Ginnetti on the altar's right. The statue of Cardinal Giovanni Francesco Ginnetti (d. 1691) on the right wall is by *Francesco Rondone*, who also did the bust of Marquis Giovan Paolo Ginnetti on the altar's left. The Ginnetti coat of arms is in the pavement.

(3) The Strozzi Chapel, though not the work of *Michelangelo*, was inspired by his chaste simplicity. The altar and side walls have fluted columns with gilded bronze capitals; the Pietà (1616) in the center is a bronze copy of Michelangelo's work in St. Peter's, and the Leah (left) and Rachel (right) are bronze copies of his work in S. Pietro in Vincoli. The black marble cenotaphs on the sides are in memory of the four sons of Filippo Strozzi.

(4) The image on the altar is *Silverio Capparoni*'s "Our Lady of the Sacred Heart" (1889). The cold neoclassical monument (1824) on the left wall to Countess Praxedes Tomati Robilant (d. 1824) is by *Rinaldo Rinaldi*, a follower of *Antonio Canova*. A bust of the deceased is at the top; lower down, a grieving genius (left) and Charity (right).

(5) Two members of the Piccolomini family were popes and their tombs are in this church. Over the arch on the left is that of the great humanist, Enea Silvio Piccolomini, who became Pius II (1458–1464); it is probably the work (1470–1475) of *Paolo Taccone*, a follower of *Andrea Bregno*. The tomb has four levels: above is the Virgin and Child, to whom St. Peter on the left presents Pius II, while on the right St. Paul presents him as a cardinal; next is the recumbent figure of the pope in death; there follows a relief of the arrival (12 April 1462) of the relic of

S. Andrea della Valle (G. Vasi, 1756)

St. Andrew's head in Rome; and finally an inscription describing the pope's accomplishments.

(6) Over the arch on the right is the tomb of Francesco Todeschini-Piccolomini, nephew of Pius II, who became Pius III. He was pope for only twenty-seven days (22 September to 18 October 1503). The tomb is probably the product of *Francesco Ferrucci* and his son *Sebastiano;* though modelled after that of Pius II, it is richer in its decorations. Above, Sts. Peter and Paul present the pope to the Virgin and the relief beneath the urn depicts Pius III's coronation as pope. Both popes were first buried in St. Andrew's chapel, next to old St. Peter's, but when that was demolished to make room for the new basilica, Cardinal Peretti had the tombs brought here (1614), because the present church is built on the site of Pius II's palazzo, at the time he was a cardinal. The tombs were reconstructed by Maderno.

(7) The **dome fresco** (ca. 1625–1628), "The Glory of Paradise," is one of *Giovanni Lanfranco*'s great creations; he here sets the pattern for all future dome frescoes in Rome. The pendentives (1624–1628) have *Domenichino*'s evangelists; these are among his best works.

(8) The painting (1625) over the altar in the right transept is "St. Andrew Avellino Suffers a Stroke of Apoplexy" by Lanfranco and is set within an elegant architectural setting. The painting, however, is not up to the artist's usual standard; the tradition is that he did it in eight days so that something could be in place at the time of the altar's consecration. St.

Andrew Avellino (1521–1608) was a Theatine and suffered this attack on 10 November 1608, as he was about to begin Mass; he died that evening. He was beatified in 1624, the year before the painting was done. Right of the altar is the monument to the famous Theatine preacher, Gioacchino Ventura (1792–1861).

(9) The beauty of this tiny polygonal chapel (mid-seventeenth century) derives from the eight black marble columns with white Corinthian capitals and the surrounding Sicilian jasper and alabaster. A finely carved wooden crucifix is on the altar. On the right the portrait and body of the Theatine cardinal, St. Joseph Mary Tomasi (1649–1713) of the princely house of Lampedusa. He was canonized in 1986.

(10) The apse wall is dominated by three frescoes (1650–1651) by *Mattia Preti*; on the left is "St. Andrew Being Raised on the Cross," in the center "Crucifixion of St. Andrew," and finally "Burial of St. Andrew." Outside the presbytery on the left is *Carlo Cignani*'s "St. Andrew's Condemnation" (ca. 1660) and on the right his "Cardinal Bessarion Arrives in Ancona with the Head of St. Andrew."

The upper part of the apse has frescoes (1624–1627) also by Domenichino. In the center of the underarch is the remarkably beautiful "St. John the Baptist Points Out Jesus to the Apostles John and Andrew." The canopy of the apse has three frescoes, also depicting episodes in the life of St. Andrew: "Call of Sts. Andrew and Peter" is in the middle, with "Scourging of St. Andrew" (left), and "St. Andrew Led to Martyrdom" (right). In the center, where the three panels meet, is "St. Andrew in Glory." The ornate white ribbing and gold stucco work between the frescoes is by *Alessandro Algardi*. The six female figures next to the windows are (left to right): Prayer, Fortitude, Hope, Religion, Charity, and Faith. These are also by Domenichino.

(11) An image of the Virgin Mother of Purity (1647) by *Alessandro Francesi* is on the altar; the small wooden statue of the Christ Child is known as "St. Cajetan's Bambino." Behind is the burial place of Cardinal Giovanni Francesco Stoppani (1695–1774), bishop of Palestrina.

(12) The altar in the left transept is dedicated to St. Cajetan (1480–1547), founder of the Theatines. The heavy baroque altar dates from 1912; it was designed by *Cesare Bazzani* and replaces an earlier altar. The mediocre painting (1770) of "Our Lady Offers the Christ Child to St. Cajetan" is by *Mattia De Mare*, and was over the earlier altar. The painting recalls a special event in St. Cajetan's life: while praying in Rome's Basilica of St. Mary Major on Christmas Eve 1517, our Lady appeared to him and gave him the Christ Child to hold. The statues on the balustrade representing Abundance (left) and Wisdom (right), are by *Giulio Tadolini*. The walls have four scenes (1770) from St. Cajetan's life, by *Alessio D'Elia*.

(13) The altar painting (1614) is of St. Sebastian, by *Giovanni De Vecchi*. A chapel to this saint is included in the church because there once had been, on this site, an earlier church dedicated to him. That church is said to have stood over the drain into which the saint's body had been thrown after his martyrdom. The body was then taken and buried in the catacombs. In 1869 Pope Pius IX (1846–1878) redecorated the chapel and dedicated it to Sts. Sebastian, Roch, and Martha, three saints invoked in times of plague. The frescoes (1869) on the walls are by the Roman *Guido Guidi* and replace the lost sixteenth-century frescoes; the one on the left represents Christ healing the sick at the request of St. Martha, and on the right, St. Roch, ill from the plague, is found in the woods by a wealthy noble, who takes him home and cares for him.

(14) The altarpiece by *Francesco Manno* represents three Theatine blessed: Cardinal Paul Burali (1511–1578), who was archbishop of Naples, Cardinal Joseph Mary Tomasi (1649–1713), and John Marinoni (1490–1562). Cardinal Tomasi has since been canonized and his body rests elsewhere in the church (see #9). The wall paintings are by an anonymous seveteenth-century Roman artist: St. Sebastian (left) and St. Lawrence (right).

(15) This is the Barberini Chapel, erected (ca. 1610) most probably by *Matteo Castelli*, at the request of Cardinal Maffeo Barberini, who later became Urban VIII (1623–1644). The paintings (ca. 1616) in the chapel are by *Passignano*; "Assumption" is on the altar and on the left wall "Nativity of Mary" (in lunette) and "Visitation," while on the right are "Annunciation" (in lunette) and "Presentation in the Temple." The statues on the left wall are of Mary Magdalene by *Cristoforo Stati* and St. John the Baptist by *Pietro Bernini*. Those on the right are of St. John the Evangelist by *Ambrogio Buonvicino* and St. Martha by *Francesco Mochi*. Standing in the archway on the left is the bust of Urban Barberini (1923–1947), who died at age twenty-three with a reputation for holiness.

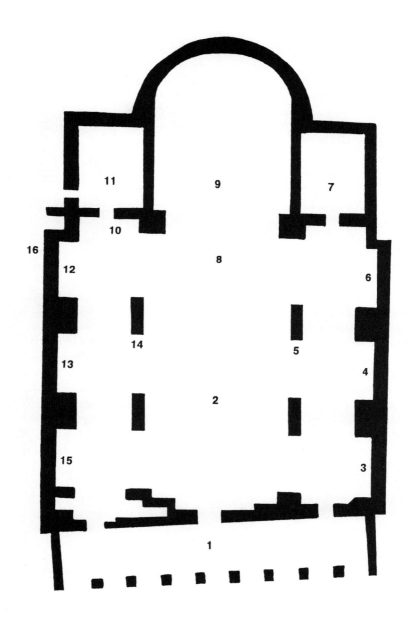

Ss. Apostoli

13   Ss. Apostoli**

Piazza dei Ss. Apostoli

History. The first church on this site was begun in 560 by Pope Pelagius I (556–561) to commemorate General Narses' (478?–573?) triumph (553) over Totila and the Ostrogoths, and was completed by John III (561–574). John placed the bones of the apostles Sts. Philip and James the Less, recently brought from the East, in this church and dedicated (570) it to them and to all the apostles. The church was restored in succeeding centuries. After the earthquake of 1348, it remained abandoned for some eighty years until Martin V (1417–1431), a Colonna, whose palazzo was adjacent, restored it in 1421. Pius II (1458–1464) then gave it (1463) to the Conventual Franciscans, who still minister here. Sixtus IV (1471–1484) renovated it in 1475; it was again almost completely redone (1702–1714) by *Carlo* and *Francesco Fontana* during the pontificate of Clement XI (1700–1721).

Exterior. The church has a fifteenth-century portico, a seventeenth-century enclosed loggia, and nineteenth-century facade. The portico, by *Baccio Pontelli*, was erected (1474–1481) by Cardinal Giuliano Della Rovere, later Julius II (1503–1513). It has nine arches and the capitals of its octagonal pillars bear the heraldic oak tree of the Della Rovere family. The iron grille dates from 1672. The loggia above the portico was closed in with baroque windows by the beginning of the seventeenth century, and in 1675 *Carlo Rainaldi* added the balustrade with statues of Christ and the twelve apostles. The upper facade was then completed (1827) in the neoclassical style by *Giuseppe Valadier*, thanks to the beneficence of Prince Giovanni Torlonia (1775–1829). The facade was cleaned in 1990.

(1) Under the portico, on the far left wall, is a monument (1807) commemorating the Venetian engraver Giovanni Volpato (1740–1803); this is the work of his student and friend, *Antonio Canova*. The weeping figure is Friendship. On the far right wall an imperial eagle holding an oak-wreath in its claws; it comes from the Forum of Trajan (emperor 98–117). Beneath this is a well-worn lion (thirteenth century) bearing, on its base, the name of the *Vassolletti* family. A Byzantine lion is on either side of the main entrance.

Interior. (2) The church, in the baroque style, has a wide nave and two aisles with six lateral altars, each with a cupola; massive piers separate the aisles from the nave. The vertical lines of the pilasters continue into the vaulting, and the thrust of the vault leads into the apse. The pavement is from 1874–1878.

The vault has "Apotheosis of the Franciscan Order" (1707) by *Baciccia*. Sts. Philip and James present St. Francis of Assisi (left) and St. Anthony of Padua (right) to the Savior; other Franciscan saints are also represented. Baciccia finished the fresco within two months. The other frescoes (1872–1875) in the vault (angels, apostles [next to windows] and evangelists [between windows]) are by *Luigi Fontana*. Over the central door is the coat of arms of Clement XI and the large tablet beneath records his renovations begun in 1702.

(3) The altarpiece (1775) by *Nicola La Piccola* depicts our Lady and St. Bonaventure (1221–1274), who was the seventh master general of the Franciscans. The large fifteenth-century Madonna (school of *Antoniazzo Romano*) beneath was once in the private chapel of Cardinal Bessarion (1403–1472); on his death he left it to the church. This had been his titular church. The two statues (1775) are of Faith (left) and Divine Wisdom (right) by *Bartolomeo Cavaceppi*.

(4) "Immaculate Conception" (1749) is by *Corrado Giaquinto*. The altar is flanked by two angels holding Marian symbols from the Litany of Loretto: Ark of the Covenant (left) and Mother Most Pure (right). They date from 1859–1860.

(5) The monument (1737) on the pillar is to Maria Clementina Sobieska (1702–1735), wife of the Old Pretender, James Stuart ["James III"] (1688–1766). The urn contains her heart; she is buried, however, in St. Peter's basilica. The Stuarts lived in a palazzo near the church. The monument is by *Filippo Valle*.

(6) This is the Odescalchi chapel, designed in 1703; the altarpiece, "St. Anthony of Padua with the Christ Child" (1723), is by *Benedetto Luti*. The altar likewise has a portrait of St. Maximilian Kolbe (1894–1941), martyr of charity at Auschwitz, canonized in 1982. St. Maximilian lived in the adjoining monastery during his years (1912–1919) in Rome. The fresco in the cupola shows "St. Anthony in Glory" by *Giuseppe Nasini;* his are also the pendentives with the four cardinal virtues (Prudence, Fortitude, Temperance, and Justice). The pavement in front of the altar has the Odescalchi family's coat of arms (1723), surrounded by military banners, cannons, etc., recalling the liberation (1683) of Vienna from the Turks, in which Prince Livio Odescalchi had heroically participated. The Odescalchi palace is directly across from the church.

(7) The chapel of the crucifix was constructed in 1721 (redone in 1858) and has eight spiral fluted columns (fourth century) that had once been part of the earliest basilica on the site. The carved-wooden crucifix is from the sixteenth century.

(8) A double staircase leads down to the crypt or confession, the work (1871–1879) of *Luca Carimini*. Behind the grating in the chapel beneath the main altar is a marble sarcophagus containing the bones of the apostles Philip and James the Less. They were placed here (1 May 1879) after they had been discovered (January 1873) under the main altar. The entire crypt area is painted with figures, symbols, and inscriptions to simulate the catacombs. The cubicle to the left, in the form of a Greek cross, has on the right the monument to Raffaele Della Rovere (d. 1477), brother of Sixtus IV and father of Julius II, and on the left an early Christian sarcophagus with the remains of Cardinal Alessandro Riario (d. 1585).

In the area of the crypt extending beneath the central nave, there is a large green oval stone on which stands an altar. Beneath the altar is the "well of martyrs" into which Stephen V (885–891) is said to have placed many relics collected from the early Christian cemeteries.

(9) The painting (1715) on the main altar, the largest altarpiece in Rome, is "Martyrdom of Sts. Philip and James" by *Domenico Muratori*. The artist combines two disparate scenes: St. Philip being crucified in Hierapolis, and St. James being clubbed to death (upper left) after he had been thrown from the temple in Jerusalem. The large allegorical figures (1727) standing on the columns, two on each side of the altar, are the four cardinal virtues, and higher still, the frescoes (eight) next to the windows are of the Doctors of the Church.

On the left wall is the monument (1475) to Cardinal Pietro Riario (d. 1474), nephew of Sixtus IV, by *Andrea Bregno* and assistants. The Virgin and Child above the urn is by *Mino da Fiesole*. On the right wall, the tomb of Count Giraud d'Ancezune [Ansedun] (d. 1505), brother-in-law of Julius II, by Bregno's followers. Above is the tomb of Cardinal Raffaele Riario (d. 1521), grand-nephew of Sixtus IV.

The fresco (1709) in the apse, "Fall of the Rebel Angels," is by *Giovanni Odazzi;* he has the rebels cast from the frame and cascading down to the lower regions. Odazzi was Baciccia's student. The apse formerly had *Melozzo da Forlì*'s fresco of the Ascension, but because of its deteriorated state it was removed at the time of the eighteenth-century renovations. Fragments of it are in the Quirinal and the Vatican Pinacoteca.

The marble slab marking the place of burial of the great organist and composer Girolamo Frescobaldi (1583–1643) is in the pavement on the left outside the presbytery.

(10) Above the door leading to the sacristy is the monument to the Conventual Franciscan who became Clement XIV (1769–1774); his remains are in the wall on the left. The monument (1783–1787) is by Canova; this was the sculptor's first commission in Rome and the earliest example of the neoclassical style in the city. Temperance (left) leans on the urn and Meekness (right) sits pensively with a lamb at her right.

(11) The sacristy has fine oak wardrobes (1697–1699). The ceiling has a painting (1701) of the Ascension by *Sebastiano Ricci*, and the walls have frescoes (1882) by *Domenico Bruschi*: "Conversion of Constantine" (right), "St. Bonaventure Proclaimed a Doctor of the Church" (left), and medallion portraits of popes.

(12) The painting (1726) of "St. Francis in Ecstasy" is by *Giuseppe Chiari*. This is the Colonna chapel; in the urn (1753) on the left wall are the entrails of Cardinal Carlo Colonna (d. 1739), and on the right the monument (1749) to Maria Lucrezia Rospigliosi-Salviati. In the pavement in front of the chapel is a tablet marking the place of the ashes of Cardinal Marcantonio Colonna (1724–1793), together with his accomplishments and honors. Between this chapel and the next, is the funerary monument (1822) to Prince Filippo Colonna (1760–1818) and his wife, Catherine of Savoy Carignano (d. 1823). The medallion bears a portrait of the prince, and above is a statue of Charity.

(13) The altarpiece (1777) depicts St. Joseph of Cupertino (1603–1663) and is by *Giuseppe Cades*. The painting shows the saint raised in ecstasy while celebrating Mass. The two columns of verde antico marble on the altar are said to be the largest in Rome. The frescoes (1865) in cupola and pendentives are by Luigi Fontana.

(14) Monument to Cardinal Bessarion (1403–1472); the remains of this outstanding Greek humanist were transferred here from the monastery cloister in 1957; his portrait (sixteenth century) is in the medallion.

(15) "Christ Being Taken from the Cross" (1815) is by *Francesco Manno*. The cupola has frescoes of scenes of the passion done in 1971 by the Franciscan *Giovanni Lerario*. The pendentives, also by Lerario, have portraits of the four Conventual Franciscans who became popes: Sixtus IV, Julius II, Sixtus V, and Clement XIV.

(16) Next to the church, on the left, is the entrance (no. 51) to the monastery and, with the porter's permission, one may visit the two cloisters, both of which date (1480–1512) from the Renaissance. In the first cloister, on the wall parallel to the piazza outside, there is a striking relief with three nativity scenes, attributed to the school of *Arnolfo di Cambio*. In the second cloister, on the right wall, near the entrance to the sacristy, a marble tablet commemorating the transfer (1802) of the body of Clement XIV from St. Peter's basilica to this church. Next, on the right, stone tablets with Latin and Greek inscriptions, which once had been part of Cardinal Bessarion's tomb. Following this is the tomb of an unknown individual in which *Michelangelo's* body (d. 18 February 1564) was placed for seventeen days before being secretly taken to Florence to

be buried in the church of Santa Croce. The tomb had been in the church but was removed during the renovations of 1702–1714. It was placed here in the second half of the nineteenth century in memory of the great artist, whose parish this was.

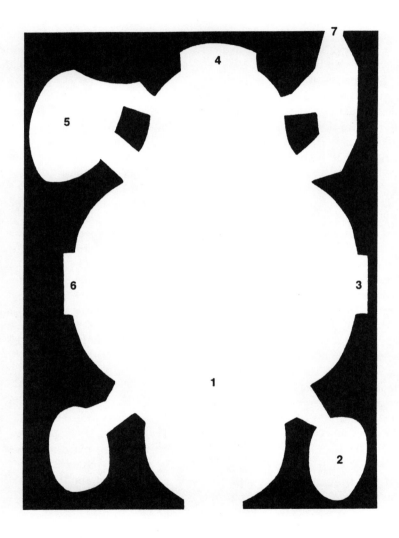

S. Carlo alle Quattro Fontane

14   S. Carlo alle Quattro Fontane***

Via del Quirinale, 23

History. The church is dedicated to the Most Holy Trinity and to St. Charles Borromeo (1538–1584), the renowned bishop of Milan. Its name is "St. Charles at the Four Fountains," but because of its size, it is more frequently referred to as "San Carlino," the "Little St. Charles." In 1634 the Spanish Discalced Trinitarians (Order of the Most Holy Trinity for the Redemption of Captives) asked *Francesco Borromini* to build them a monastery. This was the architect's first independent commission. Then in April 1638 he began work on the church, adjacent to the monastery. It was completed in 1641 and is one of his most original creations.

Exterior. Borromini began the baroque facade, recently restored, in 1664 and completed it in 1667, the year of his death. The architect's love for convex and concave linear movement is in evidence. The facade is tall and narrow, divided into two orders, each having two tiers. The four columns of the lower order are repeated in the upper. The portal is surmounted by a niche containing *Antonio Raggi's* statue (1680) of St. Charles; the niche is framed by two seraphs, whose outstretched wings meet to form an arch. The niches over the windows have statues (1682) of the two Trinitarian founders, St. John of Matha (1160–1213 [left]) and St. Felix of Valois (1127–1212 [right]). The upper order has a window in the center, enclosed in a strange aedicule, and two empty niches. Above the window is an oval medallion, supported by two angels in flight; the medallion once had a fresco, now totally lost. The church bears the inscription: "In honor of the Most Holy Trinity and of St. Charles, 1667." The Trinitarians still minister in the church, and their monastery is to the right.

Since the church is flush with the street, a good place to view the facade is on the corner diagonally across from the church. From this position the campanile is in better view; it dates from about 1670 and is by *Bernardo Borromini*, nephew of the architect.

Interior. (1) The church is elliptical in shape, with a main altar and two lateral altars. The predominant color is off-white, with abundant light flowing in from the windows in the dome. The walls have a Borrominian undulation and sixteen columns support the dome; over the altars are tympani upon which the honeycombed dome rests. The most important archi-

111

tectural feature in the church is the dome. Within it are geometric designs (crosses, octagons, hexagons) and a lantern with the symbol of the Holy Spirit. Stucco medallions in the pendentives illustrate episodes in the lives of the order's founders. Beginning with the medallion on the back left wall: "Sts. John of Matha and Felix of Valois Meet," "Pope Innocent III Approves the Order," "The Founders Receive the Habit," "The Ransoming of Captives." The order was founded to ransom Christians held in slavery by the Turks. The stucco work in the dome, including the medallions, is by *Giuseppe Bernascone.*

(2) The three modest, devotional paintings in this tiny chapel are attributed to *Giuseppe Milanese.* The "Crucifixion" is over the altar, with "Scourging of Christ" on the left and "Crowning with Thorns" on the right.

(3) The altar is dedicated to the Trinitarian St. Michael of the Saints (1591–1625). The painting (1847) by *Amalia De Angelis* shows the saint in ecstasy, during which the Savior exchanges hearts with him.

(4) The painting over the main altar is *Pierre Mignard*'s "St. Charles Borromeo Contemplates the Trinity with Sts. John of Matha and Felix of Valois." Above is the order's symbol, a cross formed by a red vertical and a blue horizontal bar. This symbol is also found on the tabernacle, on the front of the altar and on the Trinitarian habit. The statues in the niches above the doors on the sides of the main altar are of Sts. John of Matha (left), and Felix of Valois (right).

(5) This small chapel has a pleasing altarpiece (1642), "Rest on the Flight into Egypt," by *Giovanni Francesco Romanelli.*

(6) The altar is dedicated to St. John Baptist of the Conception (1561–1613), reformer of the Trinitarian order and founder of the discalced branch. The painting, by an anonymous eighteenth-century artist, shows the saint in ecstasy, while looking upon a crucifix.

(7) This leads to the cloister and sacristy. The cloister is to the right. Begun by Borromini in 1635, it is small, but remarkable for its sense of proportion. It has two orders; the lower has paired columns with Doric capitals and supports the colonnade and upper order. The corners are slightly convex. Borromini was being innovative.

The sacristy, to the left, is elegant in its stucco work and has *Orazio Borgianni*'s famous painting (1612), "St. Charles Borromeo Adores the Most Holy Trinity." The saint, in his cardinal's robes, stands next to Roman architectural fragments and gazes meditatively on the Trinity. Several tombstones are in the pavement.

In the small room off the sacristy there is, over the door, a portrait of the architect, *Francesco Borromini* (1599–1667), with the inscription: "Knight Francesco Borromini of Como, illustrious architect of this church and convent of St. Charles at the Four Fountains, and outstanding benefactor, died in Rome 1667." He is not buried here, but in S. Giovanni dei Fiorentini; he requested to be buried with his uncle *Carlo Maderno* (1556–1629), the architect who had completed St. Peter's basilica.

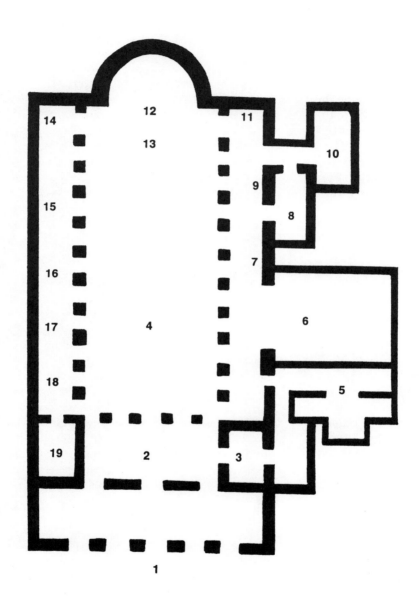

S. Cecilia in Trastevere

15 S. Cecilia in Trastevere***

Piazza di S. Cecilia

History. The church is dedicated to St. Cecilia (d. ca. 230) and is believed to be on the site of her home, where she suffered martyrdom. She was married to the patrician Valerian, whom she had converted to Christianity; she had also converted Valerian's brother Tiburtius. Because both brothers had buried the bodies of martyrs, forbidden during times of persecution, they were arrested. On their way to execution they converted Maximus, one of the Roman officers. The three were martyred together and Cecilia had their bodies taken to the cemetery of Callistus on the Appian Way. When Cecilia refused to abandon her Christian faith by sacrificing to pagan gods, she was enclosed in the bath of her home to die by suffocation from the steam. Since she survived, she was ordered to be beheaded; she endured three strokes of the sword, died three days later, and was likewise buried in the cemetery of Callistus.

The tradition is that after Cecilia's martyrdom, Pope Urban I (222–230) adapted her and Valerian's home into a place of worship. When the first church was actually built here is unknown, but by 499, the year of a Roman synod, the church of St. Cecilia was numbered among Rome's more important churches. Paschal I (817–824) rebuilt the church in basilican style and had the bodies of Cecilia, Valerian, Tiburtius, Maximus, and of popes Urban I and Lucius I (253–254), brought (822) from the cemetery of Callistus to the new church. These he placed in three urns beneath the main altar. He also built a monastery next door and named it after Sts. Cecilia and Agatha. The church and monastery were later given (1530) by Clement VII (1523–1534) to Benedictine nuns. Nuns still live in the convent and care for the church. In 1599–1600 Cardinal Paolo Sfondrati (1561–1618), titular (1591–1618), had the church's structure transformed to basically what we see today, and in 1823 Cardinal Giorgio Doria (d. 1837), titular (1818–1837), made further changes in the nave.

Exterior. The imposing entrance leading into the courtyard and to the church is the work (1725) of *Ferdinando Fuga*, done at the request of Cardinal Francesco Acquaviva d'Aragona (1665–1725), titular (1709–1724). His coat of arms is above the entrance. The courtyard is large, has a garden, and in its center a massive ancient vase (*cantharus*).

(1) The church's facade is from the eighteenth century, also by Fuga. In redoing the facade he preserved the old portico with its four ancient columns (the two in the center are of red granite, the other two are of africano marble), as well as the twelfth-century mosaic frieze, whose medallions have portraits of the saints, whose relics are preserved in the basilica. The inscription over the portico bears the donor's name: "Francesco Acquaviva, Titular Cardinal of St. Cecilia." The facade's upper portion has three windows with Acquaviva's coat of arms in the tympanum. The large Romanesque campanile on the right dates from about 1113.

The portico's walls have numerous fragments and tombstones. To the right is a monument to Cardinal Sfondrati. It was he who renovated the church at the end of the sixteenth and the beginning of the seventeenth century. The monument, with a bust of the deceased, was designed (1618) by *Carlo Maderno*. The relief near the top recalls the cardinal's official recognition of St. Cecilia's body, when her sarcophagus was opened in 1599 (see #13); in the relief the cardinal shows the saint's body to Pope Clement VIII (1592–1605). The two statues on the monument are of St. Agnes (left) and St. Cecilia (right). The cardinal is buried in the church; the monument was originally in the church's right aisle.

Interior. (2) On the rear wall are two early tombs; they were once elsewhere in the church, then demolished, but in 1891 were reconstructed and placed here. As one faces the doorway, to the left is the tomb of the Englishman, Cardinal Adam Easton of Hertford (d. 1398). He had been titular of S. Cecilia (1389–1398); the tomb, by *Paolo Romano*, bears England's coat of arms in the center and the cardinal's on the sides. To the doorway's right is the tomb of Cardinal Niccolò Fortiguerra (d. 1473), who was also titular (1460–1473). His tomb is by *Mino da Fiesole*. The narthex and side aisles have seventeenth-century frescoes.

(3) Over the altar a fifteenth-century fresco of the "Crucifixion."

(4) The church has a wide nave with two narrow aisles divided by pilasters; it once had twelve columns on each side, but in 1823 they were enclosed, better to support the walls of the building. The ceiling was redone by Cardinal Acquaviva; his coat of arms appears twice. In the center is *Sebastiano Conca*'s "St. Cecilia in Glory" (1721–1724). An organ is in the fresco and in the decorations on the nave walls. St. Cecilia is the patron of Church music, and since the fifteenth century she is frequently portrayed as playing an organ. The Cecilia of Rome was not a musician and this attribution to her is based on a misreading. The *Acts* of her martyrdom (fifth century) states that on her wedding day "amid the songs of the instruments (*cantantibus organis*), she sang within her heart to God alone." This phrase from the *Acts* was used as the first antiphon for vespers on her feast day, 22 November. This was then misunderstood by the

S. Cecilia in Trastevere (G. Vasi, 1758)

people to mean that it was Cecilia who was singing and playing the instrument. Cecilia and the organ have been joined ever since.

(5) The corridor leads to the *calidarium*, the room, now a chapel, where Cecilia was kept for three days, having been condemned to die by suffocation. The landscape frescoes are by *Paul Bril*; the frescoes depicting scenes from the saint's life are by *Niccolò Circignani*. The early sixteenth-century marble statue of St. Sebastian is by *Lorenzo Lotti*. The large tondo on the corridor wall, facing the altar, is *Guido Reni's* "Coronation of Sts. Cecilia and Valerian" (1600). Reni's "Beheading of St. Cecilia" (1601) is on the altar. Steam conduits are still visible in the chapel. This area was restored (1600) by Cardinal Sfondrati.

(6) This is the Ponziani chapel, to which family the husband of St. Frances of Rome (1384–1440) belonged. St. Frances' two children, Evangelista and Agnes, are buried here. The vault frescoes of the Eternal Father and evangelists are by the school of *Pinturicchio*. The left wall has Sts. Sebastian (left) and Jerome (right); the right has Sts. George (left) and Catherine of Alexandria (right). A fresco of the "Crucifixion," in which St. Frances of Rome appears, is over the altar. These sixteenth-century frescoes are attributed to *Antonio da Viterbo*. The altar has a fine cosmatesque front. The pavement is recent.

(7) The names over the side altars do not always agree with the saint portrayed in the painting; over the years the paintings have been switched. The altarpiece here is of St. Augustine.

(8) This handsome Chapel of the Relics, separated from the nave by a grille and flanked by two white spiral fluted columns, was designed by *Luigi Vanvitelli*. The altar has a small painting of the Virgin, with reliquaries as a backdrop. The painting of angels in the vault and of "An Angel Crowning Sts. Cecilia and Valerian" on the right are said to be by *Gaspare Vanvitelli*, father of the chapel's designer.

(9) The painting of Mary Magdalene is attributed to *Giovanni Baglione*. Left of the altar is the tomb of Cardinal Giuseppe Maria Feroni (d. 1767), titular (1764–1767).

(10) The corridor leads to the tomb of Cardinal Mariano Rampolla del Tindaro (1843–1913), who was secretary of state to Leo XIII (1878–1903), and titular (1887–1913). The dramatic tomb is the creation (1929) of *Enrico Quattrini;* the cardinal is depicted looking into the crypt, which he had constructed beneath the main altar in this church. In the niche to the left is the tomb (1936) of Cardinal Bonaventura Cerretti (1872–1933), titular (1926–1933). It is by *Carlo Quattrini*, son of the above-mentioned sculptor.

(11) The altar has a statue of St. Thérèse of Lisieux. On the right is a fragment of a twelfth-century fresco, "Paschal I Is Encouraged To Continue Searching for the Body of St. Cecilia." The fresco was formerly on a wall under the portico; it was placed here in 1785. On the left are stairs leading to the crypt.

(12) The ninth-century **apse mosaic** is from the time of Paschal I. The tall, slender figures bear the stamp of Byzantine influence. The Savior, robed in a red-bordered golden robe, stands on clouds and gives a blessing after the Greek manner. Above him is the hand of the Father, holding a crown. On the Savior's left are Sts. Peter, Valerian, and Agatha, and on his right, Sts. Paul, Cecilia, and Pope Paschal. Cecilia has her right hand on the pope's right shoulder; the pope holds a model of the basilica in his hands, and St. Cecilia is either pointing to it or accepting it with her left hand. The square nimbus indicates that Paschal was alive when the mosaic was executed. Palm trees are on the sides; a phoenix, symbol of the resurrection, perches on a palm branch on the left. Beneath the figures is the usual depiction of the twelve lambs leaving Jerusalem and Bethlehem and approaching the Lamb of God in the center. The inscription at the base of the mosaic tells of Paschal constructing the church and placing the bodies of St. Cecilia and companions in the crypt.

In the niches on the sides of the apse are busts of Innocent XII (1676–1689) on the left and Clement XI (1700–1721) on the right. Both are by *Giuseppe Mazzuoli*.

An Italian Gothic marble baldachin (1283) stands over the altar, resting on four columns of black and white marble, with gilded capitals. The baldachin has trilobed arches, decorated with gilded reliefs of angels, statues of saints, and spires. It is a signed work of *Arnolfo di Cambio*.

(13) Beneath the altar is *Stefano Maderno*'s statue of St. Cecilia. During Cardinal Sfondrati's remodelling of the presbytery and crypt, three sarcophagi were discovered (20 October 1599) beneath the main altar. These had been placed here by Paschal I in the ninth century. The cardinal had them opened for official recognition. One had a cypress box in which was the body of St. Cecilia, wrapped in a darkish silk veil, and beneath it was a dress of gold cloth, stained with blood, which she was wearing when Paschal found the body in the cemetery of Callistus. Maderno, then twenty-three years old, was present at the opening of the sarcophagus and noted the position of body, head, and hands. Later (1600) he sculpted the statue exactly as he had seen the body. The second sarcophagus contained the bodies of Sts. Valerian, Tiburtius, and Maximus, and the third the bodies of Sts. Urban I and Lucius I. After this discovery, the relics were exposed for the faithful's veneration for a month, then resealed by Clement VIII and replaced in the crypt on St. Cecilia's feast, 22 November 1599.

The two gilded reliefs on the sides of the statue depict the six saints buried here. Directly in front of the statue is a round porphyry disk in the floor; this marks the place where Cardinal Sfondrati is buried.

The crypt, directly beneath the presbytery (ask the sacristan to visit it), is the work (1899–1901) of *Giovanni Battista Giovenale*, undertaken at the request of Cardinal Rampolla and decorated in Byzantine style. Thirty-five highly polished grey granite columns support the presbytery above; the vault is highly ornamented. In the center of the main wall is an altar, over which a latticed window permits the viewer to see the sarcophagus containing St. Cecilia's body. Two other sarcophagi are there as well; one contains the bodies of Sts. Valerian, Tiburtius, and Maximus, the other the bodies of popes Urban I and Lucius I. The mosaic over the altar is "St. Cecilia Taken to Heaven by Angels"; the medallions in the underarch have St. Tiburtius (left) and St. Valerian (right). The mosaic on the altar's left is "Angel Appears to Sts. Cecilia and Valerian" and on the altar's right "Sts. Cecilia, Valerian, and Tiburtius." On the right wall is a mosaic of St. Agnes and on the left one of St. Agatha. The mosaics are by *Giuseppe Bravi*. Opposite the altar is *Cesare Aureli*'s statue of St. Cecilia. The pavement, though recent, is in the cosmatesque style.

A passage leads behind the altar and offers a different view of the area where the sarcophagi are kept. Above is a mosaic with the portraits of Sts. Urban I, Lucius I, and Maximus.

(14) Baglione's "Sts. Peter and Paul" is the altarpiece; the painting is framed by two columns of verde antico marble.

(15) The painting of St. Agatha on the altar is by an unidentified artist. Right of the altar is a grille, through which the nuns may participate in the services in the church.

(16) "St. Andrew" is by Baglione.

(17) Tomb of Bishop Gregorio Magalotti of Chiusi (d. 1537), with a figure of the deceased and statues of Faith (left) and Justice (right). The bishop was a benefactor to the nuns in the adjoining convent. His sister Maura had been the first abbess here; she is buried at the foot of his tomb.

(18) The altar has a painting of the deacons Sts. Stephen and Lawrence by *Giuseppe Ghezzi*.

(19) This is the entrance to the excavations beneath the basilica; the constructions (several early Roman houses) are of different periods. Portions of mosaic pavement are visible and there is a room with seven silos. Collected in the largest room are epigraphs, fragments, and Christian sarcophagi.

In the convent, in the nun's choir upstairs, is *Pietro Cavallini's* splendid **Last Judgment**, dating from 1293. It was painted on what was once the facade's inside wall. The fresco, of which large fragments remain, was discovered in 1900 and has been restored. An enthroned Savior is in the center, surrounded by brightly winged angels; the Virgin and John the Baptist are at his sides, with twelve seated apostles. This is one of the great but hidden wonders of Rome. Visits are on Tuesday and Thursday 10–11 and Sunday 11–12.

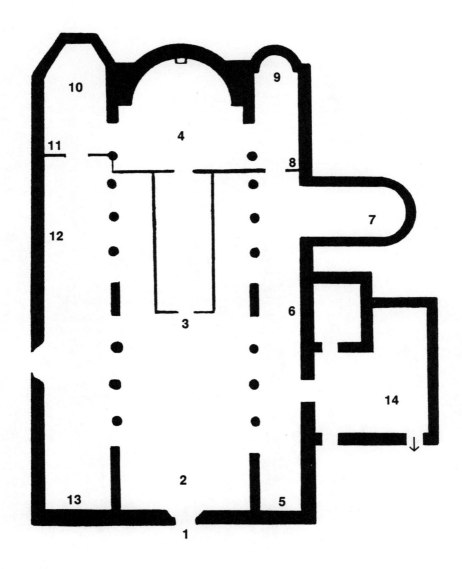

S. Clemente

16 S. Clemente***

Piazza di S. Clemente

History. The church is dedicated to Pope St. Clement (ca. 91–ca. 101), third successor to St. Peter. Legend has him banished to the Crimea by Trajan (emperor 98–117), where he was martyred by being thrown into the sea. By the year 200 there was a place of worship on this site, but the first church was from about 384, dedicated by Pope Siricius (384–399). That church continued on into the eleventh century but was severely damaged, if not destroyed, when the Normans sacked (1084) Rome. In 1108 Paschal II (1099–1118) built a new but smaller church on the ruins of the former. This is the church we see today. In 1645 the church was given to the Dominicans to service, and Irish Dominicans have been here since 1677. In the eighteenth century Clement XI (1700–1721) had *Carlo Stefano Fontana* introduce some renovations (1715–1719).

Exterior. The principal entrance to the basilica is from Piazza di S. Clemente. A twelfth-century porch (*prothyron*) leads into the atrium. The porch's baldachin rests on four granite columns and a carved cornice surrounds the door. This entrance is usually closed. The one more frequently used is on Via di S. Giovanni in Laterano, where a baroque doorway (1719) leads into the left aisle. Clement XI's heraldic device of mountains is on the sides, and the inscription above the door records Clement's munificence.

(1) The atrium dates from the twelfth century. The fountain in the center is from the eighteenth century. The church facade is also from the eighteenth century and is of two orders. The lower is a portico with five arches formed by four ancient granite columns. The upper is of three bays with a large window in the middle bay. A triangular pediment surmounts the facade.

Interior. (2) The basilica has a wide nave with two narrow aisles. The nave is separated from the aisles by sixteen ancient columns (one is walled in and one partially) and two piers. The columns differ: some are marble, others granite; some fluted, others plain. The capitals are all Ionic and have been uniformly restored. The pavement is twelfth-century cosmatesque. The exuberantly baroque ceiling dates from the time of Clement XI's renovations; that pope's coat of arms appears twice in the ceiling.

123

The painting (1714–1719) in the center of "St. Clement in Glory" is by *Giuseppe Chiari.*

The frescoes in the nave's upper portion are also from the time of Clement XI. His device (mountains) is several times found on the nave's walls. On the rear wall, as we face it, St. Cyril is on the left and St. Methodius on the right; both are by *Pietro Rasina.* St. Cyril is vested in Byzantine episcopal robes; he was a monk, but not a bishop. The left nave wall, as we face the altar, has four scenes from the legendary life of St. Clement, starting from rear: "St. Clement Gives the Veil to Flavia Domitilla" (*Pietro di Pietri*), "St. Clement Performs a Miracle" (*Sebastiano Conca*), "Martyrdom of St. Clement" (*Giovanni Odazzi*), "Burial of St. Clement's Remains in Rome" (Odazzi). The right wall, in the rear, has "Death of St. Servulus" (Chiari). Servulus (d. before 593) was a paralytic who regularly begged under the church's portico; Pope Gregory the Great (590–604) delivered a homily on him in 593. Servulus was also buried here. The other three frescoes deal with the life of St. Ignatius of Antioch (ca. 35–ca. 107), who was martyred in Rome. His bones were taken to Antioch, but at the time of the Saracen invasion they were returned to Rome (ca. 638) and preserved in this basilica. The frescoes are: "St. Ignatius of Antioch Is Condemned to Death" (*Giovanni Domenico Piastrini*), "St. Ignatius Bids Goodby to St. Polycarp" (*Giacomo Triga*), "Martyrdom of St. Ignatius" (*Pier Leone Ghezzi*).

(3) A good portion of the *schola cantorum* dates from the sixth century. After his election as pope, John II (533–535), who had been parish priest here, donated the *schola cantorum* to the church. It was later reconstructed in the new basilica; several panels still bear John's monogram, for example, the first panel facing the right aisle. The paschal candle on the left and the adjoining pulpit are twelfth-century additions.

(4) The **apse mosaic** is from the first half of the twelfth century and a product of the Roman school. The dominant theme: Christ's Cross is the Tree of Life. The cross blooms forth from an acanthus plant, and because the Savior had died on it (Virgin and John at sides), the waters of life flow beneath it, permitting the animals of creation to slake their thirst from its abundance. The twelve doves, symbols of the apostles and of the faithful, perch peacefully on the cross, for it is in the cross that they find their salvation. The branches of the plant grow luxuriantly and fill the entire apse, from the water below to the empyrean at top center, in which the hand of the Father holds a crown of victory for his Son. The fruitfulness of the cross is indicated by the personages, exotic animals, flowers, and fruit placed amid the foliage. The figures in black and white are the four Doctors of the Western Church (Augustine, Jerome, Gregory, and Ambrose), and are identified by name. Below is the Lamb of God

S. Clemente (G. Vasi, 1753)

in the center, with the twelve lambs approaching from the cities of Bethlehem and Jerusalem.

The triumphal arch also has a mosaic. In the center at the top is Christ, raising his hand in blessing, with the symbols of the evangelists. Lower down on the left is St. Paul (his name is in Greek) with St. Lawrence, and below them the prophet Isaiah. On the right is St. Peter (name also in Greek) with St. Clement, and further down Jeremiah. The Latin inscription that runs along the edge of the arch translates: "Glory in the highest to God, who sits on the throne, and peace on earth to men of good will."

Below the cornice that horizontally divides the apse, there is a fourteenth-century fresco of the Savior, Virgin, and apostles. The bishop's chair in the center, against the wall, is from the twelfth century; on its backrest is the word MARTYR, written vertically, indicating that in constructing the chair the masons used marble that had once been part of some inscription. On the back of the chair the following is also found: "Anastasius Cardinal Priest of this title began and completed this work." Anastasius was titular from ca. 1099 to 1125.

The present altar was dedicated in 1726, and the confession beneath with the relics of Sts. Clement and Ignatius was redone in the nineteenth century. The baldachin over the altar may possibly be from the sixth century, but the pavonazzetto columns are from the fifteenth or sixteenth.

On the right wall is a magnificent tabernacle (1299), perhaps the work of *Arnolfo di Cambio*, and the gift of Cardinal Giacomo Gaetani (d. 1300), titular (1295–1300) and nephew of Boniface VIII (1294–1303). In the lunette Boniface presents his kneeling nephew to the Virgin and Child and to St. Clement.

(5) The chapel dedicated to St. Dominic (1170–1221), founder of the Order of Preachers, was decorated in 1715 at the expense of the Dominican Cardinal Tommaso Ferrari (d. 1716), titular (1696–1716). The paintings are by Conca. The altarpiece is "St. Dominic in Ecstasy"; the left wall has "St. Dominic Raises Napoleon Orsini to Life," and on the right is "St. Dominic's Miracle at Old S. Sisto."

(6) Handsome modern monument to Frederick Ambrose Ramsden (1793–1859) and his wife, Catherine Teresa (1793–1880). In the center of the ceiling above, "St. Servulus Taken to Heaven," by Rasina.

(7) This chapel, built (1882–1886) by Leo XIII (1878–1903) honors the brothers Sts. Cyril (827–869) and Methodius (826–885), Apostles of the Slavs. St. Cyril invented the Glagolithic alphabet (more commonly known as Old Cyrillic), and by translating the Gospels and liturgical books into Old Slavonic became the father of Slavonic literature. On his way from the Crimea to Rome, he brought (868) with him the remains of St. Clement, which were then placed beneath the altar in the basilica. When Cyril died in Rome he was buried near St. Clement. It is known that from 1600 to 1798 St. Cyril's relics were beneath the altar in the chapel now dedicated to St. Dominic, but with the church's suppression at the time of the occupation of Rome by Napoleonic forces (1798) the relics were removed and eventually lost. They were partially recovered in 1963 and placed within the present altar in November of that year.

The frescoes (1886) by *Salvatore Nobili* are cold and academic. In the apse is "Leo XIII Offers St. Clement's Basilica to the Savior." Sts. Cyril and Methodius, in episcopal vestments, stand at the Savior's sides. Right wall: "Sts. Cyril and Methodius Discuss with Pope Hadrian II the Need for a Vernacular Liturgy for the Slav Peoples." Left wall: "Burial of St. Cyril in St. Clement's." The cupola has angels and the pendentives the symbols of the evangelists.

(8) The first tomb on the right is that of Giovanni Francesco Brusati (d. 1485), archbishop of Nicosia; the tomb is the joint work of *Giacomo di Domenico* and *Luigi Capponi*. The next and larger Renaissance tomb is that of Cardinal Bartolomeo Roverella (d. 1476), titular (1461–1476). It is the work of *Andrea Bregno* and *Giovanni Dalmata*. Above is the figure of Virgin and Child with angels; on left St. Peter presents Cardinal Roverella to the Christ Child, and on the right St. Paul. Higher still, the Eternal Father looks down on the cardinal's recumbent figure. The tombs

have been placed next to each other because the archbishop was the cardinal's nephew.

(9) The statue of St. John the Baptist is perhaps from the sixteenth century and by an unknown artist. The vault has a fresco of the Eternal Father. The chapel was restored in 1960 by Cardinal Amleto Cicognani (1882–1973), titular (1958–1962). The modern altar (1960), whose frontal has scenes from the life of John the Baptist, is by *Raoul Vistoli*. Cardinal Cicognani's tomb is directly below the chapel; it will be seen when visiting the lower church.

(10) The altarpiece (1714) is "Madonna of the Rosary," by Conca. The left wall has "St. Francis of Assisi Receives the Stigmata" and the right, "St. Charles Borromeo." The artists are said to be of the Carracci school. Outside the chapel on the right wall is a painting from the late sixteenth century, "Virgin with Child and St. John," by *Iacopo Zucchi*.

(11) The Renaissance tomb of Cardinal Antonio Venerio (d. 1479), titular (1476–1479). His figure lies beneath a relief of the Virgin and Child with St. Clement (left) and St. Peter (right). The tomb is attributed to the school of *Mino da Fiesole*; the two columns used in decorating the tomb are from the sixth century, and were once part of the ciborium over the main altar in the earlier basilica.

(12) The modern monument to Bartholomeu Conte de Basterot (1800–1887) and his wife Marie Pauline (1816–1839). The monument bears the signature of *Teodoro Forlivesi* with the date 1874. The epitaph reads: "Human weakness weeps; immortal hope smiles." In the center of the ceiling above is "Coronation of the Virgin," by Rasina.

(13) This Gothic **Chapel of St. Catherine of Alexandria**, with its fifteenth-century frescoes, is one of the glories of the basilica. The frescoes (1428–1431) are the work of *Masolino da Panicale*, and perhaps with some assistance from *Masaccio*. The chapel was erected by Branda di Castiglione (d. 1443), Cardinal of St. Clement's (1411–1431); his arms are on the arch over the entrance to the chapel. The "Crucifixion" on the rear wall was probably done first, and Masaccio may have helped with it.

The left wall has scenes (not in chronological order) from the life of St. Catherine of Alexandria (d. ca. 307). Upper level: St. Catherine protests to Maxentius (emperor 306–312) the persecution of Christians; while in prison she converts the empress to Christianity and the empress is subsequently beheaded; after Catherine's death, her body is carried by two angels to Mount Sinai. Lower level: St. Catherine defends Christianity before philosophers; she is condemned to be martyred on a spiked wheel, but is saved by an angel; finally, she is beheaded.

The right wall has three scenes from the life of St. Ambrose (339–397): his birth (left); a child proposes him as bishop of Milan (right); his death (center). The vault has evangelists and Doctors of the Church. The outside arch has an "Annunciation"; the underarch has apostles, and outside on the left a fifteenth-century St. Christopher.

When the frescoes were being restored in 1954–1956, some ("Crucifixion" and "Beheading of Catherine") were removed and placed on frames. At that time, the artist's original sketches (*sinopia*) were discovered below. These sketches now hang on either side of the door leading to Via di San Giovanni in Laterano.

(14) Excavations (1857–1870) beneath the basilica uncovered, not only the earlier fourth-century basilica, but beneath this, the ruins of first-century buildings. Later excavations (1912–1914) discovered still a lower level, the ruins of buildings that suffered during Nero's burning of Rome (A.D. 64). The entrance to these excavations is through the vestibule of the sacristy. The area is well illuminated and the wall frescoes are identified.

The stairs lead down to the narthex of the fourth-century basilica, with four aisles facing the visitor. The first aisle, nearest the stairs, was the right aisle of the original basilica; the wall on the right was the building's north (outside) wall and that on the left was built in 1100 to support the present basilica's north (outside) wall. Halfway down on the right is a niche with a sixth-century Madonna, and further down a pagan sarcophagus discovered in 1937, whose relief depicts scenes from the story of Phaedra and Hippolytus.

The second aisle was part of the fourth-century nave and now corresponds to the right aisle of the upstairs church. The wall on the left was constructed in 1100 to support the columns of the nave of the upper basilica.

The third aisle corresponds to the nave area of the present basilica and the wall on the left supports the nave columns in the above basilica. The supports in the center were erected between 1862–1870 to sustain the upstairs church, once the rubble beneath had been removed. There are four frescoes on the left. The altar is modern (1866–1867).

The fourth aisle is directly beneath the upper basilica's left aisle. At the end of the aisle on the left is the presumed burial place of St. Cyril (d. 869); the walls have monuments and plaques from Slavic nations and an attractive modern mosaic of Sts. Cyril and Methodius.

The door on the left leads down to another level, to the Mithraic temple (first-century buildings). To the right of the entrance is a bust of Cardinal William O'Connell (1859–1944), archbishop of Boston, titular (1911–1944) of St. Clement's and benefactor. The room on the left, with an altar in its center, is the Mithraic banquet room (*triclinium*), and the area in front is the vestibule where sect members sat. It was probably here that the altar had been originally located. The second-century altar has a relief of Mithras slaying the bull. In proceeding toward the exit, one passes through a series of first-century rooms.

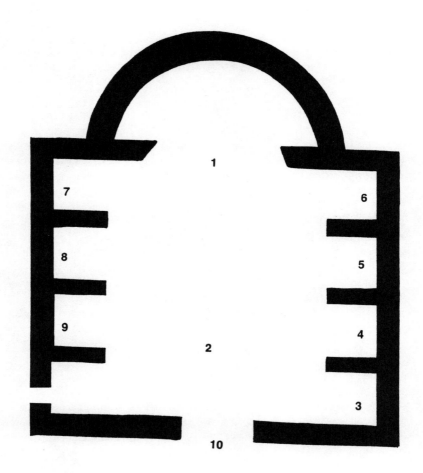

Ss. Cosma e Damiano

17 Ss. Cosma e Damiano***

Via dei Fori Imperiali

History. The church is dedicated to Sts. Cosmas and Damian, brothers, who are said to have been physicians and were known as "silverless," because they never charged their patients. Both were martyred in ancient Cyrus in northern Syria during the persecution of Diocletian (emperor 284–305). In 527 Pope St. Felix IV (526–530), with the permission of Queen Amalasuntha (498–ca. 535), converted two buildings in the Roman Forum into a Christian church, the first time that this had been done. He transformed the library in the Forum of Peace, built (70) by Vespasian (emperor 69–79), by adding an apse to it, and for the church's vestibule he used the so-called Temple of Romulus, which may have been erected by Maxentius (emperor 306–312) for his son Romulus, who had died ca. 307. The church's original entrance was from the Roman Forum.

The church was restored in 780 by Hadrian I (772–795). In 1632 Urban VIII (1623–1644) had the church fully renovated after the design of *Luigi Arrigucci.* Since the church was, at one end, below ground level and always damp, a floor was added, dividing the church into an upper level, even with the soil at one end, and a lower level (now known as the crypt).

Entrance to today's church is by walking through the quiet seventeenth-century courtyard of the monastery of the Franciscans of the Third Order Regular, who service the church. The courtyard once had seventeenth-century frescoes by *Francesco Allegrini,* of which only four remain, illustrating scenes from the life of St. Francis of Assisi (1182–1226).

Interior. (1) The church is rectangular in shape and has a single nave with lateral altars. What we see is the church as redone by Urban VIII.

The glory of the church is the **apse mosaic.** The mosaic, cleaned in 1988, dates from the sixth century, the time of Felix IV, and was executed by Byzantine artists. It is among the earliest in Rome and because of its extraordinary beauty it has served as a model for later mosaics in other Roman churches. A majestic Christ, on a resplendent blue background, wears a Roman-style toga of brilliant gold and approaches on clouds as the Sun of Justice, whose radiance is reflected in the clouds that bear him up. In his left hand he holds a scroll, and with his right he welcomes Sts. Cosmas and Damian, who carry crowns of martyrdom and are being presented by Sts. Peter (the older one on Christ's left) and Paul, both garbed in the white robes of heaven. Cosmas and Damian not only wear similar clothing and of the same color, but their faces are also similar, no doubt, to indicate that they are blood brothers.

On the viewer's right is the Roman soldier-martyr St. Theodore, wearing a handsome chlamys, or short mantle of Byzantine origin, and on the left Felix IV, holding a model of this church. The figure of Felix is greatly restored; the execution of face and vestments reveals a baroque artist's hand. Hovering over the cluster of flowers at Felix's feet are three bees, the telltale sign that the restoration was done during the pontificate of Urban VIII, whose coat of arms has three bees. Glittering palm trees are at the ends, symbols of Paradise; the tree on the left (also restored) has a phoenix, a sign of the resurrection (or immortality), on one of its branches.

Below is a mosaic frieze of the Lamb of God with the four rivers of Paradise flowing beneath, with twelve sheep (apostles), six on each side, emerging from Bethlehem and Jerusalem. The central portion of the frieze is, unfortunately, blocked from vision because of the altar. The three sheep and the city on the left were likewise restored.

The **mosaic** on the triumphal arch is from the seventh century. In the center is the enthroned Lamb of God. On the sides of the Lamb are candlesticks, a total of seven, and two angels on either side. On the right is the symbol of John the Evangelist and on the left that of Matthew. The symbols for Mark and Luke, as well as the figures of the twenty-four elders of the Apocalypse, were covered over (?) at the time when the side altars were built. The only parts of the elders now visible (at both ends of the arch) are draped hands offering crowns to the Savior.

The baroque altar (1628) has four black and white marble columns; these are from the original altar in the crypt. In the center is the thirteenth-century "Our Lady of Grace." Portraits (seventeenth-century) of Franciscan saints and blessed are in medallions above the choir stalls (1635).

(2) The painted ceiling is from 1632 and has a mediocre fresco by *Marco Tullio Montagna* of Sts. Cosmas and Damian being greeted in heaven by the Virgin and Child. Montagna gave the saints similar features and garbed them in robes similar in style and color as in the apsidal mosaic. Each end of the ceiling has the coat of arms of Urban VIII, where the Barberini bees are more noticeable. The nave's upper portion has a total of eight frescoes depicting episodes in the lives of Sts. Cosmas and Damian; in these the brothers also wear the same colored garb as in the mosaic. The series is usually attributed to Montagna. The pilasters between the frescoes have full-length representations of other saints, most of them martyrs.

(3) This is a remarkable crucifix; the living Christ, wearing a crown and robes (sacerdotal? regal?), is nailed to a cross. The fresco is perhaps

from the thirteenth century with seventeenth-century repainting. The scenes of the passion (1636) in the vault are by *Giovanni Battista Speranza*.

(4) The chapel has three paintings (ca. 1638) by *Giovanni Baglione:* "Sts. Peter and John Heal the Paralytic at the Gate 'Beautiful' " is on the altar, while the left wall has "Presentation in the Temple" and the right, "Adoration of the Magi." These are among his latest and best works. The chapel was his family's chapel, and the stone marker on the left wall lists the members of the family buried here.

(5) The seventeenth-century painting of Saint Anthony of Padua on the altar is thought to be by *Carlo Saraceni.* The wall painting on the left depicts St. Louis of Anjou (1274–1297), who renounced his right to the throne of Naples and, though named bishop of Toulouse, preferred to be a Franciscan. The painting on the right is of St. Clare of Assisi (1194–1253) with her nuns.

(6) The altarpiece is "St. Francis Receives the Stigmata," a copy of *Girolamo Muziano*'s famous version. The left wall has "Immaculate Conception" and the right St. Louis of France, patron of the Franciscan Third Order.

(7) The painting on the altar is of St. Rose of Viterbo (1235–1252) and St. Rosalia of Palermo (d. 1160), by an unidentified artist. The fresco on the left represents St. Rose carrying roses in her mantle, and on the right St. Rosalia, who was often invoked in times of plague. In the background are the Bay of Palermo and Monte Pellegrino, where she lived.

(8) The "Crucifixion" here is said to be of the school of *Peter Paul Rubens.* The altar originally had a painting of St. Alexander; the fresco on the left depicts St. Alexander's condemnation and that on the right his martyrdom. Both frescoes (1640) are by Allegrini.

(9) The altarpiece (1642) depicting St. Barbara is by *Bernardino Cesari;* this is his copy of the painting by his father, *Cavalier d'Arpino*, in S. Maria in Traspontina. The wall frescoes are late works (ca. 1660) by Allegrini based on episodes in the life of St. Barbara. On the left, because she refused to marry, she was tortured, and on the right her father has the governor condemn her to death. Her martyrdom is in the background.

(10) This is the area of the Temple of Romulus.

The church has a magnificent eighteenth-century Neapolitan *prese-pio*, whose figures are all hand-crafted, in wood, terra-cotta, and porcelain, and wear costumes reproducing in minute detail styles of earlier periods. Until recently it was exhibited in a side altar on the right. However, on the night of 29–30 November 1988, thieves broke into the church and made away with many of its pieces. It is hoped that the pieces can be replaced so that the *presepio* can again be on display.

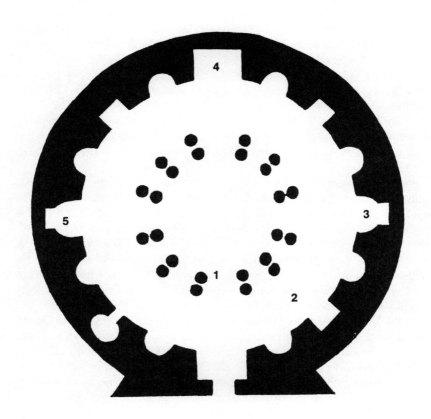

S. Costanza

18 S. Costanza***

Via Nomentana, 349

History. The church was built before 350 as a mausoleum for Constantia (or Constantina), daughter of Constantine (emperor 306–337). In 335 Constantia married Annibaliano, and after his death (337), she continued to live in Rome until 350, when she married Gallo, half-brother of Julian "the Apostate," her sister Helena's husband. Constantia died at Antioch in 354, but was buried here in the mausoleum she had built for herself. In time the building was used as a baptistery and by the ninth century the Romans were accustomed to refer to Constantia as a saint. About 1256 Pope Alexander IV (1254–1261) transformed it into a church honoring St. Constantia.

Exterior. The building is preceded by an atrium and the remains of ruins from the earlier cemetery.

Interior. (1) The church is unique in Rome; it is a superb example of an imperial mausoleum and is an important witness of an early Christian building. It is circular in shape with a cupola, and is surrounded by an ambulatory with apses and niches. The cupola, with a diameter of approximately 74 feet, is supported by twelve double columns of granite with marble Corinthian capitals, linked together by arcades. The building is illuminated by the windows in the cupola's drum. The cupola at one time had mosaics; the relatively recent mediocre fresco that is now there is more a distraction than a decoration.

The frontal of the altar in the center bears an inscription telling us that the bones of Sts. Constantia and her companions Attica and Artemia are enclosed within.

(2) The ambulatory's vault is covered with magnificently preserved fourth-century **Roman mosaics**, which are among the earliest in Rome. The colors white (background) and green dominate. There are eleven panels in all; the panel near the entrance serves to introduce the others which are then paired (right with left sides). The mosaic patterns vary: geometric designs; circular motifs with figures and animals; vintage scenes with carts carrying grapes to workmen making wine; tree branches bearing fruit, amphorae, exotic birds, etc. The central figures in two of the panels are presumed to be Constantia (left of entrance) and her first husband Annibaliano (right).

Some of the niches in the wall still bear the remains of more recent frescoes of the Savior and apostles.

(3) The apse on the right has a fifth-century mosaic which probably depicts Christ giving the keys to Peter. The stylized palm trees are a symbol of Paradise. The mosaic is outlined with garlands of vividly colored fruit.

(4) The large apse opposite the entrance has a reproduction of the porphyry sarcophagus that once contained Constantia's body. The figures on it are varied: harvesting cherubs, peacocks, spiraling acanthus, etc. The original, which has been in the Vatican Museum since 1791, taken there by Pius VI (1775–1799), was first located in the center under the cupola. The top portion of the apse has a fragment remaining of a mosaic with a star design. Constantia's sister Helena was also buried in the building.

(5) The apse on the left also has fifth-century mosaics. A youthful Christ stands on a mound from which the waters of salvation flow, and toward which lambs advance. On Christ's sides are two figures, perhaps Peter (right) and Paul (left). The figure on the right holds a scroll upon which is written "The Lord gives peace." The mosaic is outlined by charming garlands of fruit.

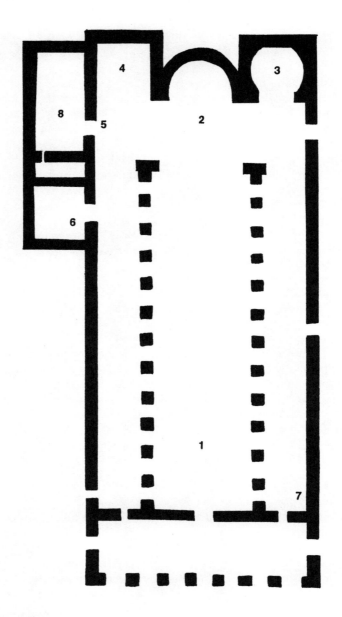

S. Crisogono

19 S. Crisogono*

Piazza Sonnino

History. The church is dedicated to St. Chrysogonus, Roman military officer, martyred ca. 304 near Aquileia in northern Italy, during the persecution of Diocletian (emperor 284–305). The first church on this site was in existence by 499; it is mentioned in the records of the Roman synod held that year. The church was later embellished by Gregory III (731–741), and subsequently totally reconstructed ca. 1122–1124 by Cardinal Giovanni da Crema. Five centuries later it was radically restored (1626) by *Giovanni Battista Soria* for Cardinal Scipione Borghese (1576–1633), the church's titular (1605–1633). The last major restoration was done in 1866 under Pius IX (1846–1878), who gave (1847) the church to the Order of the Most Holy Trinity for the Ransom of Captives, more commonly known as Trinitarians, who still serve it.

Exterior. The simple facade is Soria's design and is preceded by a large portico (1626) with four free standing red granite Doric columns and four brick pilasters, the latter flanking two arches. The inscription on the architrave bears Cardinal Borghese's name and the date 1626. Above the portico is an attic with a row of decorative vases, winged dragons, and eagles; the latter two are devices from the cardinal's coat of arms. In the tympanum, cradled between two cornucopias, is a red and blue cross, the symbol of the Trinitarian order. The facade was cleaned in 1989. At the right is a tall Romanesque campanile (1124), with a spire added in the sixteenth century. Under the portico, the center doorway is elegant in its simplicity; all five doorways bear the cardinal's name.

Interior. (1) The present church retains the structure of that of the twelfth-century church, but the decorations are from the seventeenth. It is basilican in style, having a wide nave with two aisles, separated by twenty-two antique Egyptian granite (red and grey) columns, taken from earlier Roman buildings (perhaps from the baths of Septimius Severus [emperor 193–211] in Trastevere). The Ionic capitals, however, have Soria's stucco embellishments. Over the columns is an ornate gilded stucco trabeation that includes the Borghese devices. Two gigantic porphyry columns with marble Corinthian capitals support the triumphal arch; because of their size, they are most rare.

The magnificent coffered ceiling, with its gilded, carved compartments with a blue background, is from 1620; the painting in the center is "Triumph of St. Chrysogonus," a copy of *Guercino*'s original, which is now in London. The coat of arms is that of Cardinal Borghese. The windows in the upper portion of the nave were added by Soria; the cardinal's eagle is used as a decorative motif above the window, and his winged dragon beneath.

The handsome cosmatesque pavement dates from the thirteenth century and covers the entire church. It has been restored over the years. In the center aisle leading to the main altar, Soria has added mosaic designs from the Borghese coat of arms.

(2) Over the main altar is Soria's restored baldachin, which rests on four dark yellow alabaster columns with Ionic capitals. In the half-dome of the apse there are three gilded stucco bas-reliefs depicting the trial and martyrdom of St. Chrysogonus; beneath these is the late thirteenth-century mosaic "Enthroned Madonna and Child with Sts. Chrysogonus and James," attributed to the school of *Pietro Cavallini*. St. Chrysogonus is on the left wearing a military uniform; St. James (the Less) is included because his relics are likewise under the main altar together with those of the church's patron. The handsome choir stalls were carved by various artists ca. 1865; running along the top are angels with ransomed captives. The ceiling above is coffered, and in its center a canvas of the Virgin and Child by *Cavalier d'Arpino*.

(3) At the end of the right aisle is a charming chapel designed (1641) by *Gian Lorenzo Bernini*. The altarpiece is an anonymous work from the seventeenth century with both founders (1118) of the Trinitarians; on the left is St. John of Matha (1160–1213) and on the right St. Felix of Valois (1127–1212), while above is the Trinity. The vault has *Giacinto Gemignani*'s "Holy Trinity" fresco. On the left is the funerary monument of Cardinal Fausto Poli (d. 1653) and on the right, that of his brother Bishop Gaudenzio Poli (d. 1679). The busts were sculpted (ca. 1680) by *Giuseppe Mazzuoli*. The variety of marbles makes for a harmonious whole.

(4) This chapel (1865), at the end of the left aisle, has a statue of the Savior as "Ecce Homo," clothed in a red robe and wearing the Trinitarian scapular about its neck. The oval reliquary beneath the altar contains a relic of St. John of Matha. The chapel was faced with marble in 1962.

(5) The two ancient inscriptions imbedded in the wall on the right of the sacristy door are from the time of the church's dedication and consecration (1127). On the door's left an attractive tabernacle (ca. 1200) with spiral columns decorated with mosaics.

(6) The chapel is dedicated to Blessed Anna Maria Taigi (1769–1837), a Trinitarian tertiary, who lived in the building next to the church. She

S. Crisogono (G. Vasi, 1756)

was beatified in 1920; her relics are beneath the altar. Over the altar is a nineteenth-century painting of "Mother of God, Refuge of Sinners"; the gold mosaic surrounding the painting (with symbols of the evangelists), as well as the vault depicting "Trinitarian Saints in Glory," is by *Aronne Del Vecchio*. The canvas on the left wall represents the Virgin Mary reciting matins with St. Felix of Valois and angels, an incident said to have happened in France on 8 September 1212. That on the right shows the Our Lady of Good Remedy supplying St. John of Matha with purses of money to ransom captives. Both paintings are from the nineteenth century.

(7) This tiny shrine, dedicated to Our Lady of Good Remedy, is the result of a vow made in 1944 for the liberation of Rome from the occupying German army. The Child holds the Trinitarian scapular in his hands, and the Virgin holds purses, symbolizing the ransoming of captives. The painting is by *Giovanni Battista Conti*.

The paintings on wall of the left aisle (rear to front) are: St. Adalbert (956–997) rescuing a Turk (seventeenth century), Holy Family (nineteenth century), St. Michael of the Saints (1591–1625) (nineteenth century) and St. John Baptist of the Conception (1561–1613) (nineteenth century). The latter two were members of the Trinitarian order. The paintings on the wall of the right aisle (front to rear) are: Crucifixion (seventeenth century), St. Frances of Rome (1384–1440) (eighteenth century), Archangels Michael, Gabriel, and Raphael (seventeenth century) and Sts. Catherine of Alexandria and Barbara (eighteenth century).

(8) Entrance to the subterranean fifth-century church, about twenty feet below, is through the sacristy. Excavations were carried out in 1907 and the early church was discovered. It was a large rectangular hall, with an apse. The walls still retain traces of early frescoes.

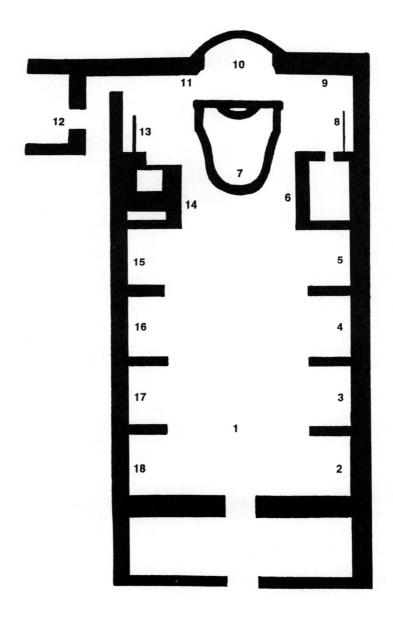

S. Francesca Romana (S. Maria Nova)

20 S. Francesca Romana (S. Maria Nova)*
Via dei Fori Imperiali

History. The church is located at the edge of the Roman Forum and at the head of the ancient *Via Sacra*. Pope Paul I (757–767) erected a church in honor of Sts. Peter and Paul in the western portico of the Temple of Venus and Rome, built by Hadrian (emperor 117–138), and into it he incorporated an earlier oratory to the same saints. This oratory had been constructed near the spot where Simon Magus, in an attempt to demonstrate his magical prowess, flew into the air through demonic aid, but because of the prayers of both apostles, crashed to earth. Simon Magus is mentioned in Acts 8:9-24, but this incident derives from the apocryphal *Acts of Peter*. When the church of "S. Maria Antiqua" (sixth century), at the foot of the Palatine in the Forum, had to be abandoned in the tenth century because of structural damage, the diaconate of that church was transferred to the one built by Paul I and, thus, it became known as "S. Maria Nova." The church was subsequently destroyed (1216) by fire, but was rebuilt (about 1220) by Honorius III (1216–1227). In 1352 Clement VI (1342–1352) entrusted the church to the Olivetan Benedictines, who still serve it. After the canonization (1608) of St. Frances of Rome (1384–1440) the church became more commonly known as "S. Francesca Romana."

Exterior. The stately facade is of travertine by *Carlo Lombardi* and dates from 1615. The elegant campanile, among Rome's finest, dates from about 1160 and is one of the few reminders of the church's earlier period. It has five storys, is decorated with majolica tiles, and is 140 feet tall. It was restored in 1916–1917. One enters the church through a portico.

Interior. (1) The building is in the form of a Latin cross, a single nave with side altars. The interior underwent a baroque restoration (1600–1615) and is now faced with polychrome marbles and gilded stucco work. The coffered ceiling, in which blue and gold dominate, is from 1612 (restored 1867); nearest the entrance is the figure of St. Benedict, then the coat of arms of Cardinal Paolo Camillo Sfrondrati, protector (1591–1618) of the Olivetan Benedictines; in the center is the Virgin Mary with Sts. Agnes and Cecilia; then the coat of arms of the Order of Mount Olivet; finally St. Frances of Rome with her guardian angel, whom she always saw near her.

In the center of the nave's floor, toward the front, is an area (approximately thirteen feet square) of mosaic cosmatesque work indicating where the *schola cantorum* was once located. Immediately to the right, imbedded in the floor, is a tablet, whose inscription informs us that the Italian artist *Gentile da Fabriano* (1370–ca. 1427) had died in the adjoining monastery and had been buried in the church. Since his tomb disappeared during the seventeenth-century renovations, the monks wanted to preserve some memorial to him, and thus they placed the tablet here in 1952.

(2) The painting, "Crucifixion," is an anonymous work of the eighteenth century. On the left wall is "Repose in Egypt," by an unidentified artist; on the right, "Blessed Bernard Tolomei at Prayer," by the same. Blessed Bernard (1272–1348) was the founder of the Olivetan branch of the Benedictines and, hence, there are several paintings of him in the church.

(3) This was once a vestibule for the entrance from the Roman Forum. On the left is a monument by *Mino del Reame* to Antonio da Rio [Rido] (d. ca. 1450), a Paduan. Rio, who was castellan (1434–1447) of Castel S. Angelo under Eugenius IV (1431–1447) and head of papal troops under Nicholas V (1447–1455), wears armor and rides a steed. The other wall has a monument, attributed to *Paolo Romano*, to Cardinal Marino Vulcani (d. 1394), titular, and onetime protector of the Olivetans.

(4) A modern painting of Sts. Benedict, Frances of Rome, Henry, and an Olivetan monk adorns the altar. The left wall has Blessed Bernard Tolomei freeing a possessed person, and the right has him assisting a dying monk. The paintings are by anonymous artists.

(5) "Virgin and St. Frances of Rome," a copy of a painting by *Carlo Maratta*.

(6) "St. Andrew Adores the Cross," a copy after *Guido Reni*.

(7) St. Frances of Rome was known for her charity toward the sick and poor. In 1425 she and several other ladies dedicated themselves in this church as oblates to God's service. When she died (1440) she was buried at the foot of the main altar. After her canonization (1608), this confession, designed by *Gian Lorenzo Bernini*, was constructed (1638–1649). The statues of the saint and angel (1866) are by *Giosuè Meli*. Stairs on either side lead to the transept, about 4½ feet higher than the nave's floor.

(8) Next to the stairs leading down to the crypt are two basalt stones imbedded in the wall and protected by metal gratings. The inscription informs us, "St. Peter knelt on these stones when the demons carried Simon Magus through the air." They are from the original oratory on the site. On the floor, to the left, is the tombstone of Cardinal Francesco Uguccioni Brandi of Urbino (d. 1422).

Proceeding down to the crypt we see the urn containing what remains of the body of St. Frances of Rome. The lunette above depicts Mary Magdalene with Sts. Paul and Benedict. The restoration work done in the crypt dates from 1867. The bas-relief on the opposite wall, "St. Frances and Her Angel," is by *Ercole Ferrata*.

(9) Tomb of Gregory XI (1370–1378). The monument was erected here in 1584 by the Roman senate and people, in gratitude to Gregory, the last French pope, for returning the papacy to Rome, after it had been in Avignon, France, for almost seven decades. The relief is the work of *Pier Paolo Olivieri* and represents Gregory entering Rome (17 January 1377) through the S. Paolo gate. St. Catherine of Siena (1347–1380), who was instrumental in convincing the pope to return to Rome, walks in front. The breach in the wall symbolizes the ruinous state into which Rome had fallen during the pope's absence. The figure on the left, dressed as Minerva, coming forth to welcome the pope, is Rome. Above the city an angel carries the papal tiara and keys and Peter's chair is seen floating back to Rome. The marble urn beneath contains the pope's ashes. When Gregory died in 1378, he requested to be buried in the church, since this had been his church as a cardinal. The tomb was originally next to the main entrance.

(10) The **apsidal mosaic** is Byzantine in style and is from about 1160; it fortunately escaped damage during the fire (1216) that destroyed the church. The Virgin sits on a lyre-shaped jewelled throne and holds the Child on her knee. On her right are the apostles John and James, on her left Peter and Andrew. The outside arch has figures of David (left) and Moses (right), painted (1870) by *Cesare Maccari.*

The two frescoes beneath the mosaic depict the martyrdom of Sts. Nemesius, Olympius, Sempronius, Lucilla, Esuperia, and Theodulus, and are attributed to *Domenico Canuti.* The relics of these saints are beneath the main altar; they were brought here from Via Latina by Gregory V (996–999).

The icon of the Virgin and Child on the altar also survived the fire. Tradition maintains that it was brought from the East by Angelo Frangipani about 1100. In 1950 the painting of the Virgin and Child that was then on the altar was carefully examined, and it was found that beneath the nineteenth-century Virgin there was an under-painting. When the over-painting was removed, a thirteenth-century Virgin by a Tuscan artist was revealed. Below this thirteenth-century painting another painting from the fifth century was then discovered. The fifth-century painting is now in the sacristy and the thirteenth-century painting is on the altar.

The two angels carrying cornucopias at either end of the presbytery are of the school of Bernini; the one on the left is the more successful effort.

(11) "Blessed Bernard Tolomei among the Plague-stricken," school of *Pierre Subleyras*.

(12) Several paintings hang on the sacristy's walls, for example, the fifth-century "Virgin and Child," the under-painting of the icon presently on the main altar; also "St. Benedict Restores a Child to Life," by Subleyras, done in Rome in 1744, and one of the artist's better works; opposite is the "Trinity," by *Giacinto Brandi*. There is another worthy work, namely, that of Pope Paul III (1534–1549) and the Englishman Reginald Pole (1500–1558) in conversation, and attributed to *Perin del Vaga*. Paul III made Pole a cardinal in 1536, but since the latter is not wearing cardinal's robes, it is thought that the painting might have been executed before that date.

(13) Tabernacle taken from the apse in 1612 and placed here; it is attributed to *Mino del Reame*. The bronze door with the coat of arms of the Olivetan Benedictines is of a later date.

(14) "Scourging of St. Andrew," school of *Domenichino*.

(15) "Blessed Bernard Tolomei Ministers to the Plague-stricken," by *Giuseppe Pirovani*, a mediocre painting.

(16) "St. Emidio," bishop and martyr, by *Pietro Tedeschi*.

(17) "St. Gregory the Great Celebrates Mass," by *Angelo Caroselli*.

(18) The "Nativity" is on the altar, with two scenes from the life of Blessed Bernard Tolomei on the walls. On the left he overcomes temptation and on the right he contemplates his crucified Lord.

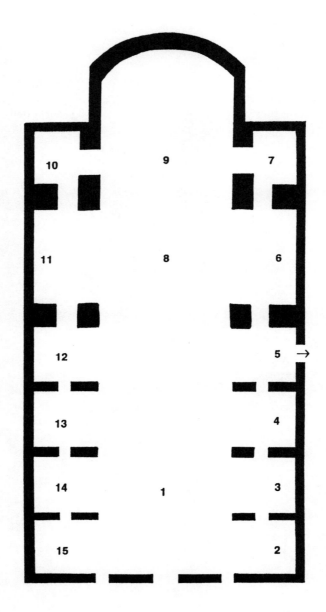

Il Gesù

21   Il Gesù***

Piazza del Gesù

History. When St. Ignatius of Loyola (1491–1556), founder of the Society of Jesus (Jesuits), came (1537) to Rome with his first companions,
they carried on their ministry in a church named S. Maria della Strada.
When that church proved too small, they decided on a new building. The
first laying of the foundation stone was at the end of 1550 or early 1551,
but construction soon came to a stop. *Michelangelo* then submitted his
design for the church and another foundation stone was laid (6 October
1554), but less than a month later work again came to a halt. It was only
with the laying (16 June 1568) of the third stone that the building went
ahead to completion. The church was the gift of Cardinal Alessandro Farnese (1520–1589) to the Society; the architect was *Vignola*, who oversaw
the work until his retirement (1571), when he was succeeded by the Jesuit
Giovanni Tristano. When the latter died (1575), he was followed by another Jesuit, *Giovanni De Rosis*. The church was consecrated 25 November 1584. The Jesuits have served the church from the beginning, except
for the period 1773–1814, when the Society was suppressed.

Exterior. The travertine facade (1571–1575) was designed by *Giacomo
Della Porta*. It has two orders; the lower is divided into five bays by double
pilasters with Corinthian capitals. The main doorway has semicolumns,
surmounted by a double pediment. Above is IHS, monogram of the Holy
Name of Jesus. Above the two side doors are niches with statues of St.
Ignatius (left) and St. Francis Xavier (right). The second order has three
bays, formed by double pilasters, with a large window in the center and
niches in the other two. Volutes are on the sides. At the very top is the
Farnese coat of arms, now unrecognizable. The inscription on the facade
reads: "Cardinal Alessandro Farnese, Vice-Chancellor, erected [this church]
1575." The Gesù facade forms the transition from the Renaissance to the
baroque, and was soon imitated throughout Europe.

Interior. (1) The church has the form of a Latin cross, with a nave,
transept, presbytery, and three interconnecting chapels on each side.
Pilasters with composite capitals support an entablature with a frieze of
grape clusters. The side chapels have marble balustrades and above their
arches are panels with cherub heads and garlands of fruit and flowers.
Until 1858 the lower portion of the nave was undecorated. Prince Ales-

sandro Torlonia (1800–1886) undertook its decoration (1858–1861); the pilasters were covered in giallo antico and Egyptian alabaster was used in between. He likewise placed the two marble columns with pediment near the main entrance. In memory of his beneficence, his name appears over the side doors as well as over the doorways at the end of the nave; above these last doorways is the Torlonia coat of arms.

The fresco in the vault, "Triumph of the Name of Jesus," is *Baciccia*'s undisputed masterpiece and the most important piece of art of the Roman high baroque. Baciccia began the ceiling (mid-1676) after he had completed the cupola and pendentives; it was unveiled on 31 December 1679. A monogram of the Holy Name is toward the center, enveloped in golden yellow light and surrounded by angels. A good part of the fresco is contained within its rich frame; the blessed outside appear to be drawn within it by the light, while that same light repels the damned, whose writhing and contorted bodies visibly fall beyond the frame.

The elaborate stucco decorations and coffers with rosettes, in the vault and throughout the church, are by *Antonio Raggi* and *Leonardo Reti*, who followed Baciccia's drawings. Raggi and Reti likewise did the allegorical figures at the sides of the nave windows, the putti above and the panels of playing putti beneath. The pulpit on the left, with its inlaid marble, is from the first half of the seventeenth century.

(2) The chapel is dedicated to St. Andrew the Apostle, and was fully decorated by *Agostino Ciampelli*. The altar has "St. Andrew Greets His Cross," and the side walls the martyrdoms of St. Lawrence (left) and St. Stephen (right). The vault has "Virgin Mary Surrounded by Martyrs"; the pendentives have bishop martyrs, and the lunettes depict the martyrdoms of Sts. Agnes (left) and Catherine (right).

(3) Christ's passion is this chapel's theme. The left wall has "Way to Calvary" and the other "Christ Nailed to the Cross"; "Adoration of the Cross" is in the vault. These are by *Giuseppe Valeriano* and *Gaspare Celio*. Evangelists are in the pendentives. The left lunette has "Kiss of Judas" and the right "Christ in the Garden." The painting over the altar is by *Pietro Gagliardi* and depicts "Our Lady with Jesuit Saints." The urn beneath the altar contains the relics of the Jesuit St. Joseph Pignatelli (1737–1811).

(4) This chapel is dedicated to the angels. *Federico Zuccari*'s "Archangel Michael and Angels Adore the Trinity" (ca. 1590) is the altarpiece. The walls have his "Angels Free Souls from Purgatory" (left) and "Expulsion of Rebel Angels from Heaven" (right); the vault has "Coronation of the Virgin." *Ventura Salimbeni* did the pendentives ("Jacob's Dream" [front left], "Tobias and the Angel" [front right], "Angel Transports Habakkuk to Daniel" [rear right], and "Three Angels Visit Abraham" [rear left]) and lunettes ("Angel Ministering to the Prodigal Son" [left] and "Angels Offer-

Il Gesù (G. Vasi, 1756)

ing the Prayers of the Faithful to God" [right]). Beneath the wall paintings are four marble panels with fruit and flower festoons; these were discovered (1594) in the ruins of the Baths of Titus (emperor 79–81). The cherub heads were added in the seventeenth century. The four niches have statues of angels.

(5) This passage leads to the sacristy. Several paintings are on the walls of the ante-sacristy, most by anonymous artists. Over the entrance door, "Canonization of St. Francis Borgia by Clement X"; left of the sacristy entrance, "Pope Paul III Approves the Society of Jesus"; right of the entrance, "Cardinals Alessandro and Odoardo Farnese"; over the door on the right, "Canonization of Sts. Ignatius and Francis Xavier by Gregory XV." In the right corner is "St. Francis of Assisi Receives the Stigmata," by *Giovanni De Vecchi* or *Durante Alberti*; this had been on the altar of #7 until 1920.

The name of Cardinal Odoardo Farnese (1574–1626), nephew of Cardinal Alessandro Farnese, appears over the sacristy door. He added the sacristy at the time the Jesuit residence next door was being built (1599–1623). The sacristy's walls are lined with walnut wardrobes (1609–1611). Ciampelli's "Adoration of the Blessed Sacrament" is in the vault; the altar at the end has a painting of St. Ignatius attributed to *Annibale Carracci*. On one wall there are four canvases by anonymous artists.

(6) The chapel is dedicated to St. Francis Xavier (1506–1552), one of St. Ignatius' first companions and the modern Church's greatest mission-

ary. The chapel was designed (1674–1678) by *Pietro da Cortona* and has *Carlo Maratta*'s "Death of St. Francis Xavier" (1679) as the altarpiece. St. Francis died on the island of Sancian, off the China coast, 3 December 1552. The painting is flanked by four columns of Sicilian jasper with gilded Corinthian capitals. On the pediment above is "St. Francis Taken into Heaven." The three vault frescoes were done by *Giovanni Andrea Carlone:* "St. Francis Xavier Finds His Lost Crucifix" (left), "St. Francis in Glory" (center), and "St. Francis Baptizes an Indian Princess" (right). The reliquary on the altar contains the saint's right forearm, brought here in 1614. On the plinths beneath the columns, the founder of the chapel, Giovanni Francesco Negrone (1629–1713), placed the coat of arms of Clement IX (1667–1669) on the left, and that of Innocent XI (1676–1689) on the right, in appreciation for their kindnesses toward him. Later (1686) Innocent XI made Negrone a cardinal; he is buried in front of the altar. Cardinal Jerzy Radziwill (1556–1600) of Cracow is buried on the chapel's left.

High on the left wall is one of the two baroque organ lofts, carved (1633–1635) by Flemish craftsmen. The other is in the left transept.

(7) St. Francis Borgia (1510–1572), the Society's third general, dedicated this small intimate chapel, with its polychrome marbles, to his patron, St. Francis of Assisi (1182–1226). The seven paintings on the walls depict scenes from that saint's life and are by *Joseph Peniz* and *Paul Bril.* During the early years of the twentieth century the chapel was rededicated to the Sacred Heart of Jesus; *Pompeo Batoni*'s famous painting (1760) of the Sacred Heart is now over the altar. *Baldassarre Croce* did (1599) the evangelists and Doctors of the Church in the cupola.

(8) The drum of the cupola has four windows and four niches, with paired pilasters between. Statues of the cardinal virtues (Prudence, Fortitude, Justice, and Temperance) are in the niches. The fresco is Baciccia's "Vision of Heaven," his first work (1672–1675) in the church. The fresco, unfortunately, has somewhat deteriorated and the figures of God the Father, with Christ on his left and the Virgin Mary on his right, are the only ones easily recognizable. The remaining figures are of saints. The Holy Spirit is in the lantern. The fresco was unveiled on Easter Sunday, 14 April 1675.

After completing the cupola Baciccia began the pendentives. Each has four personages: the "Evangelists" are on the viewer's left rear, when facing the main altar, "Lawgivers and Leaders of Israel" are on the left of the main altar, "Prophets of Israel" on the right, and "Doctors of the Western Church" on the viewer's right rear. These were begun in early 1675 and completed by July 1676. Beneath each is the Farnese coat of arms.

(9) The presbytery was decorated (1841–1843) by *Antonio Sarti.* The altar is chaste in comparison to the exuberance that surrounds it. It stands

against the apse wall and the four giallo antico columns that support the triangular pediment come from the earlier altar. The inscription on the altar's architrave reads: "Dedicated to the Most Holy Name of Jesus." Above is an aureole with the sacred monogram. The painting (1842) over the altar, by *Alessandro Capalti*, is of the "Circumcision"; this replaces the painting (1587) of the same theme by *Girolamo Muziano*. Behind the painting is a niche with a polychrome statue of the Sacred Heart of Jesus; at times the painting is removed and the statue is open to view. Over the doorway on the altar's left is a bust (1622) of Cardinal Robert Bellarmine (1542–1621) by *Gian Lorenzo Bernini*, and over the door on the right a bust of St. Joseph Pignatelli (1737–1811) by *Antonio Solà*. Cardinals Alessandro and Odoardo Farnese are buried directly in front of the presbytery; red porphyry markers indicate the places.

The **fresco** in the half-dome is Baciccia's "Adoration of the Lamb." The artist began this in early 1680, after he had completed the nave; it was unveiled on 30 July 1683. On the vault separating the apse from the crossing is his "Angelic Concert" (ca. 1683).

(10) This is the Chapel of our Lady della Strada and was the first chapel to be finished. The altar has a fifteenth-century fresco of the Virgin and Child, which had been in the small church of S. Maria della Strada on this site. The chapel was designed and decorated by Valeriano; the walls have seven scenes from the Virgin's life; in these Valeriano was assisted by *Scipione Pulzone*. The dome, supported by eight columns, has angels by *Giovanni Battista Pozzi*. The St. Joseph on the altar is by *Francesco Podesti*.

(11) St. Ignatius Chapel. This chapel is dedicated to St. Ignatius of Loyola. He was canonized on 12 March 1622 and his body had been placed under the altar in this transept, thirteen days prior to the canonization. Seventy years later, the Jesuit *Andrea Pozzo* began (1695) work on the present altar, which was completed in 1699. The altar is convex; double columns (travertine), whose flutes are filled with lapis lazuli and strips of gilded bronze, flank the large niche (laminated with lapis lazuli and alabaster panels separated by gilded bronze decoration), in which stands an ornate statue of the saint on a pedestal. The first statue here was modelled by *Pierre Le Gros* and cast by *Federico Ludovici*; its head, hands, and feet were of pure silver, the rest a mixture of bronze and silver. The chasuble was decorated with semi-precious stones. During the French occupation of Rome (1798), the silver parts of the statue and the three silver angels surrounding it were melted down to meet the reparations demanded by Napoleon. The niche remained empty until the beginning of the nineteenth century when *Adamo Tadolini*, under *Antonio Canova*'s supervision, replaced the statue's missing parts with new ones made of stucco

and covered in silver. The missing silver angels were redone in stucco. The "new" statue was unveiled on Easter Sunday, 14 April 1804. The altar was at the same time cleaned; its most recent cleaning was in 1989.

The composite capitals of the columns are of gilded bronze and the two marble angels holding the sacred monogram over the niche are by *Étienne Monnot*. The Trinity is on the pediment; the marble figure of God the Father (right) is by *Bernardino Ludovisi* and that of Christ (left) by *Lorenzo Ottoni*. Christ points to a globe made of lapis lazuli.

At the base of the columns, imbedded into the verde antico, are seven gilded bronze reliefs, designed and cast by various artists. The large one in the center depicts "St. Peter Appears to St. Ignatius during His Convalescence." The other six represent miracles and events associated with the saint. Above the relief in the center there are two silver-covered putti next to a medallion with a cherub's head, under which is the motto of the Society of Jesus: "To the Greater Glory of God." Beneath the altar is a bronze urn by *Alessandro Algardi* with the saint's relics; the relief has St. Ignatius and other Jesuit saints and martyrs.

The marble group on the altar's left is "Faith Triumphs over Idolatry" by *Jean-Baptiste Théodon*; kneeling before faith is a barbarian king. The group on the altar's right, more Bernini-like than its partner, is "Religion Overcomes Heresy," by Le Gros. The putto on the left is busy destroying heretical books. Both groups were completed in 1702. The marble relief above the group on the left represents "Paul III Approves the Society of Jesus," by *Angelo De Rossi*, and the bas-relief on the right by *Bernardino Cametti* depicts "Gregory XV Canonizes St. Ignatius." The bronze balustrade in front of the altar, one of the more admirable creations of the baroque, was designed by Pozzo, but modelled and cast by various artists. The vault above the altar has Baciccia's "St. Ignatius in Glory," done in 1685, his last work in the church.

(12) This area was once a vestibule with a side entrance to the church; it was converted into a chapel in 1950. The wooden crucifix had been over the altar in #11 until 1695. When that chapel was redone to honor St. Ignatius, the crucifix was moved to the ante-sacristy. It was brought here in 1950.

(13) The altar has *Francesco Bassano*'s "Most Holy Trinity"; the painting was done in Venice and sent to Rome in 1592. Durante Alberti did the other decorations in the chapel: "Creation" (vault), "Eternal Father with Angels" (left lunette), "Abraham Visited by Three Angels" (right lunette), and the putti in the pendentives. His is also the "Transfiguration" on the left wall; the "Baptism of Christ" on the right, however, is by Salimbeni.

(14) Pietro Gagliardi's painting, "Holy Family of Nazareth," was

placed here ca. 1890. *Niccolò Circignani*'s "Joy of the Angels at Christ's Incarnation" is in the vault, and his prophets are in the pendentives. He likewise did "Slaughter of the Innocents" (left lunette) and "Annunciation to the Shepherds" (right lunette). The "Presentation in the Temple" (left wall) and "Adoration of the Magi" (right) are by *Giovanni Francesco Romanelli.* The niches have statues of the cardinal virtues.

(15) The altarpiece is Pozzo's "St. Francis Borgia in Prayer." After the canonization (1862) of the Japanese Martyrs, of whom three were Jesuits, the figures of these three were added to the painting by Gagliardi. The walls have *Pier Francesco Mola*'s "St. Peter Baptizes Sts. Processus and Martinian" (left) and "Conversion of St. Paul" (right). "Pentecost" in the vault is by Circignani; his are also the lunettes "Crucifixion of Peter" (left) and "Beheading of Paul" (right), and the four medallions (Faith, Hope, Charity, and Religion) in the pendentives.

The rooms where St. Ignatius lived (1544–1556) may be visited. Entrance is through the building on the right of the church, number 45. When Cardinal Odoardo Farnese was building (1599–1623) the Jesuit residence, the Jesuits were intent on preserving the rooms of the old house in which St. Ignatius had worked and died. These rooms were transformed into chapels in 1605, and over the years they had been decorated. On the occasion of the fifth centenary (1991) of St. Ignatius' birth, the rooms were restored to their original state. Since an excellent descriptive booklet is available inside, the following is merely for the sake of orientation.

The corridor leading to the upstairs rooms has paintings and reproductions of engravings touching on the life of St. Ignatius and the early Jesuits in Rome. The frescoed corridor outside the rooms (of a later date than the rooms) was decorated toward the end of the seventeenth century by two Jesuit brothers, *Jacques Courtois* and Pozzo. The first room served as St. Ignatius' waiting room or ante-camera, the second was his study and private room, the third was his private oratory and reception room, and the fourth was the room of his attendant.

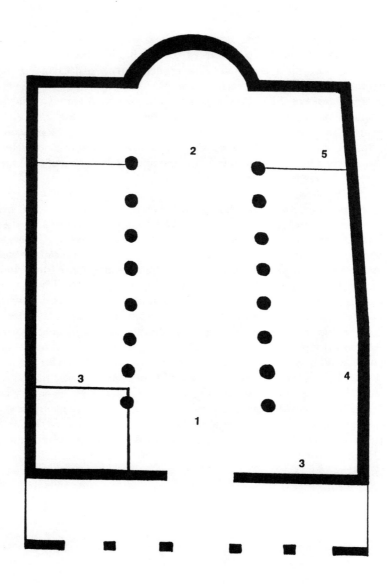

S. Giorgio in Velabro

22   S. Giorgio in Velabro**

Via del Velabro

History. A fifth- or sixth-century oratory occupied this site; it was then reconstructed by Pope Leo II (682–683), who gave the church its present general structure. The church was, at that time, dedicated to St. Sebastian, the Roman military officer martyred (between 297 and 305) during the persecution of Diocletian (emperor 284–305). According to tradition, the saint's body was here thrown into the *cloaca maxima,* the city's main sewer. The church was dedicated to St. George in the eighth century, when Pope Zacharias (741–752) transferred a relic of the saint (a portion of the skull), from the Lateran to this church. St. George, likewise a military man, was martyred (about 303) in Lydda (today's Lod, Israel), also during the persecution of Diocletian. In the ninth century Gregory IV (827–844) restored (831–833) part of the church and added the apse. Subsequent centuries witnessed additional renovations and restorations, but the most important was carried out (1924–1926) by *Antonio Muñoz* at the request of Cardinal Luigi Sincero (1870–1936), titular (1923–1936). At this time the church was given the appearance it had during the Middle Ages.

The church is said to be in the Roman district known as *Velabro;* it has been suggested that the word comes from the Etruscan word *velum* for "marsh" and the Latin *aurum,* meaning "gold." The area was, thus, marshy with yellow colored sand. The church had been served by the Crosier Fathers (Canons Regular of the Holy Cross) since 1941.

Exterior. The present portico is from the thirteenth century and is formed by four granite columns with Ionic capitals and two sturdy seventh-century pillars at the ends. At the top of the pillars are marble decorative pieces with lions' heads, which probably came from some earlier building. A thirteenth-century inscription runs along the architrave and tells the reader that it was Stefano da Stella, prior of the church, who renovated the portico. The Romanesque campanile is at least from the thirteenth century (before 1259); after it had been struck by lightning (1836), it was reconstructed (1837) by Gregory XVI (1831–1846). To the left, and attached to the portico, is the Arch of the Money-changers, built by them in 204 to honor Septimius Severus (emperor 193–211) and his wife, Julia Domna. Within the portico, various ancient inscriptions are imbedded into the facade; the marble used as a cornice around the portal seems to have been a frieze taken from some previous structure.

Interior. (1) The church is basilican in style, with nave and two aisles separated by sixteen non-matching columns, taken from older Roman buildings. The walls of the nave rest directly on the columns. The building has an irregular shape and narrows as it approaches the apse; this is probably due to the fact that in reconstructing the church, the builders merely followed the foundations of an earlier edifice. During the restorations in the early part of this century, the pavement was lowered to its original level; the bases of the columns are now visible. On some columns to the left, a line (about 18 inches from the base) is still visible indicating the pavement's former level. The windows in the nave, closed since the Middle Ages, were reopened; the window frames are new but reproduce the design and material (selenite) of the earlier ones. The ceiling is from 1704.

(2) The fresco in the apse (about the end of thirteenth century) was commissioned by Cardinal Giacomo Caetani Stefaneschi (1270–1343), titular (1295–1343), and is said to be by *Pietro Cavallini*. It has been heavily repainted over the years. Christ is in the center and on his right the Virgin Mary and St. George with his horse; on Christ's left are Sts. Peter and Sebastian, the latter in Roman military garb. This is the only color in the church. The wall beneath the apse windows has grey marble panels with eight white fluted pilasters.

The baldachin over the altar is from the end of the twelfth century; the columns supporting it, however, are modern replacements. Two tiers of small columns rest on a cosmatesque-decorated architrave, and these, in turn, support a cupola surmounted by a cross. Beneath the baldachin is a marble altar with elegant cosmatesque work at the edges. Below the altar is a grille, behind which is the relic of St. George. The area surrounding the grille also has mosaic ornamentation.

(3) The walls at the rear of the left and right aisles have marble fragments; these are from the eighth or ninth century and were found beneath the pavement at the time of the modern restoration. It is thought that they were part of the *schola cantorum*, which had been dismantled in the thirteenth century.

The rear wall of the church has several commemorative tablets. The one on the top left tells us that Leo XII (1823–1828) had the walls of the church strengthened in 1828. The center one refers to an interior restoration sponsored by Pius IX (1846–1878) in 1869. The one on the right speaks of Gregory XVI's repairing the left wall and reconstructing (1837) the bell tower. The marker below recalls the fiftieth anniversary of the founding of the Italian Catholic Scouts. The large tablet on the left of the doorway commemorates the changes given (1926) the church by Cardinal Sincero and Antonio Muñoz.

S. Giorgio in Velabro (G. Vasi, 1753)

(4) There are also several marble tablets in the right aisle. The more important ones, from the rear to the front, are the monuments marking the burial places of Cardinal Giovanni Mercati (1866–1957), titular (1936–1957), on the left, and his brother, Msgr. Angelo Mercati (1870–1955), head of the Vatican archives, on the right. The following marker is in memory of Cardinal John Henry Newman (1801–1890), titular (1879–1890).

(5) Up the stairs at the end of the right aisle, a stone in the floor reads, "This is the resting place of the Cardinals Titular of San Giorgio, awaiting eternity." On the right wall are various tablets: the grey one recalls Cardinal André Julien (1882–1964), titular (1958–1964), and buried here; the black one recalls Cardinal Benno Gut (1897–1970), titular (1967–1970), but buried in Switzerland, and the one below is for Cardinal Sergio Pignedoli (1910–1980), titular (1973–1980), buried here.

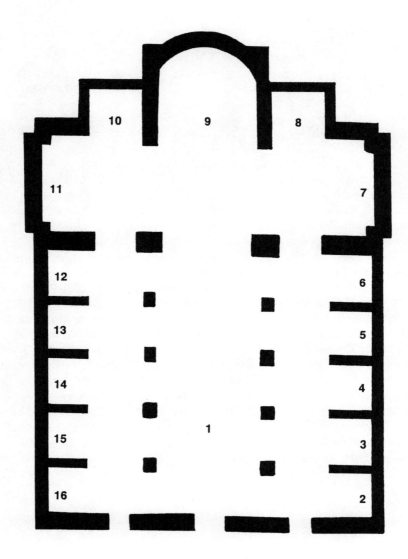

S. Giovanni dei Fiorentini

23   S. Giovanni dei Fiorentini**
Piazza dell'Oro

History. At the time of the 1448 plague, a group of Florentines in Rome formed a confraternity to bury their dead. The confraternity took St. John the Baptist, patron of Florence, as its own. In 1484 it obtained the small church of S. Pantaleo for its center of operation and later, with the election of the Florentine Giovanni de' Medici as Pope Leo X (1513–1521), it received permission (1519) to erect a worthy edifice to their patron on the site of S. Pantaleo. Leo asked the leading Renaissance artists in the city to submit plans, and though *Michelangelo, Raphael*, and *Baldassarre Peruzzi* had done so, the commission was given to *Iacopo Sansovino*. Michelangelo's project was rejected because it would have been too costly. The new church was begun, but because of Sansovino's fall (1520) from a scaffold, *Antonio da Sangallo the Younger* was placed in charge. Construction came to a halt with Leo's death (1521); work was later resumed (1584) under *Giacomo Della Porta. Carlo Maderno* completed (1620) the church, having added the transept and cupola.

Exterior. The impressive facade by the Florentine *Alessandro Galilei* was built (1733–1734) under another Florentine, Pope Clement XII (1730–1740). It is of travertine, has two orders, with six sets of double columns. Over the pediment of the central door are statues of Charity (left) and Fortitude (right) by *Filippo Valle* and in between is Clement's coat of arms. The four bas-reliefs (1735) over the niches are scenes from the life of the Baptist and beneath are fleurs-de-lis, the symbol of Florence.

Interior. (1) The church, a good example of Renaissance architecture, is in the shape of a Latin cross, with a nave and two aisles separated by pillars. Since the nave is without decoration (paintings or frescoes), it has the appearance of being unfinished. The pavement was restored in 1852 and in 1893 as a result of damages caused by the Tiber's flooding. The baroque organ was placed over the main entrance in 1673.

(2) The altar painting, attributed to *Passignano*, depicts the Dominican St. Vincent Ferrer (1350–1419) preaching to the poor. The chapel's floor has the coats of arms of thirteen Florentine families.

(3) The painting over the altar, by an unidentified artist, is of St. Philip Benizi (1223–1285), a native of Florence. Flanking the altar are two frescoes, attributed to *Stefano Pieri*, illustrating episodes in the lives of the apostles Simon and Jude, to whom this chapel was first dedicated. That on the left shows the apostles baptizing the king of Persia, and the one on the right illustrates a story from *The Golden Legend*. A deacon (on the left) was falsely accused of being the father of a new-born infant. The two apostles ask the child whether the deacon was in fact its father, and the infant responded that he was not, because "he was chaste and holy and would never have defiled his body with any kind of impurity."

(4) In a niche above the entrance to the sacristy is a remarkably beautiful statue of a youthful John the Baptist attributed by some to *Donatello*. It was brought here (1889) after it had been found in the Church of S. Orsola della Pietà, which was being demolished to make way for the present Via Vittorio Emanuele II. On the left wall is a bust of Clement XII by Valle, and placed here (1750) to commemorate his erection of the church's facade. On the pilasters are two busts by *Gian Lorenzo Bernini*, discovered in 1967; the one on the left was done in 1612 (when Bernini was about fourteen) and the other in 1622/1623. They portray benefactors of the hospital that was once attached to the church.

(5) The altar painting (1599) portrays St. Jerome in the desert; it is by *Santi di Tito* and surely one of his better works. The left wall has Passignano's "Building of S. Giovanni dei Fiorentini" (1599) and in it he has, on the right, what looks like a portrait of Michelangelo. On the opposite wall is "St. Jerome Translating the Bible" (1599) by *Ludovico Cardi*.

(6) St. Philip Neri (1515–1595) had once been rector (1564–1575) here, and it was with the Florentine priests working in this parish that he began the Congregation of the Oratory. The altar has a faithful copy of a painting of "Virgin Appears to St. Philip" by *Carlo Maratta*. The original was taken to Florence by order of Grand Duke Ferdinand III and is now in the Pitti Palace. On the pilaster on the left of chapel #2 is a wooden cross before which St. Philip had often prayed.

(7) The altarpiece (1669) is by Salvator Rosa and depicts Sts. Cosmas and Damian. When the angel saves the saints from the fire that was meant to kill them, the soldiers cower in fear and the would-be executioner flees in terror. With reference to the fleeing executioner, Rosa vaunted: "Let Michelangelo come and do a better job on that nude than I have—if he can!" Cosmas and Damian were then beheaded. Beneath the altar are the relics of St. Protus, a Roman martyr, brought from the catacombs in 1552.

(8) This is Our Lady's Chapel. The fresco, set into a polychrome altar, is of "Mary, Mother of Grace and Mercy," brought here in 1648 from an outside wall in the nearby Vicolo delle Palle. Some would like to attribute it to *Filippino Lippi*. The "Birth of Mary" on the left wall, together with "Annunciation" and "Visitation" in the lunettes and the "Corona-

tion of the Virgin" in the vault, are by *Agostino Ciampelli;* the "Death of Mary" on the right is by *Anastasio Fontebuoni.*

(9) The baroque main altar and presbytery were designed and begun (1634) by *Pietro da Cortona,* but largely executed by *Francesco Borromini,* and after his death (1667) completed (1673–1676) by *Ciro Ferri.* The marble group of the "Baptism of Christ" is by *Antonio Raggi;* the reclining figures above the altar are of Justice (left) and Fortitude (right). Borromini also designed the two Falconieri monuments with verde antico columns. On the left is the tomb of Cardinal Lelio Falconieri (1599–1648), with Faith by *Ercole Ferrata* in the niche. On the right is the monument and tomb of Orazio Falconieri and his wife, Ottavia Sacchetti; the statue above is Charity by *Domenico Guidi.* Beneath the main altar (entrance is behind the altar), is the oval funeral crypt (also by Borromini) of the Falconieri family, to whose munificence the main altar is due.

Both Maderno and Borromini are buried in the church. The stone marking the place is beneath the cupola, toward the left transept. Borromini requested to be buried with his uncle and that his name not appear on the marker, perhaps because he had attempted suicide. Thus the stone, now largely worn away, only bears Maderno's name. However, on the third pillar (from the altar) in the left aisle, there are two marble tablets commemorating both architects.

(10) The crucifix is bronze and is usually attributed to *Prospero Bresciano.* The paintings on the walls (1621–1623), "Christ in the Garden" (right) and "Christ on the Way to Calvary" (left) are by *Giovanni Lanfranco.* The same artist's vault fresco of the "Ascension," which must have been superb in its day, is now in deplorable condition. The right lunette has "Crowning with Thorns" and the left "Capture of Jesus"; these are also by Lanfranco.

(11) The painting of Mary Magdalene taken to heaven by angels is by *Baccio Ciarpi,* an unimaginative effort.

(12) The altarpiece by Santi di Tito depicts "St. Francis of Assisi at Prayer." The left wall has a fresco of "St. Francis Requests Approval of His Rule from Honorius III," and on the right is "St. Francis before the Sultan of Egypt." Both (1583–1585) are by *Niccolò Circignani.*

(13) "Death of St. Anthony the Abbot" (1612), by Ciampelli, is over the altar; note the saint's soul being carried by angels to heaven. The seventeenth-century paintings on the sides: "Risen Lord Appears to St. Peter" (left) and "Conversion of St. Paul" are by *Giovanni Angelo Canini.* The vault frescoes on the life of St. Lawrence are by *Antonio Tempesta.*

(14) Behind the baptismal font is a painting, in mannerist style, of "John the Baptist Preaching" by *Salvio Salvini.* The two small tabernacles

of white marble in the wall beneath the painting come from the now demolished (1889) church of S. Orsola.

(15) The altar has *Francesco Curradi*'s depiction of St. Mary Magdalene de' Pazzi. The saint kneels before the Virgin Mary and receives the virgin's white veil. The left wall has a large fresco of "Vesting of Carloman" by *Giovanni Balducci*. Carloman (d. 754), the son of Charles Martel, after abdicating (747) his part of the Frankish kingdom, founded a monastery at Mount Soracte and three years later went to Monte Cassino. In the fresco he is receiving the Benedictine habit. On the right is Balducci's "The Virgin Mary Tells St. Luke about Jesus' Infancy." St. Paul is likewise listening to the details.

(16) "St. Sebastian Cared For by Women" is the work of *Giovanni Battista Vanni*. A large painting (early seventeenth century) of Pope St. Stephen I, martyr, is on the right wall. The pavement has the coats of arms of twelve Florentine families.

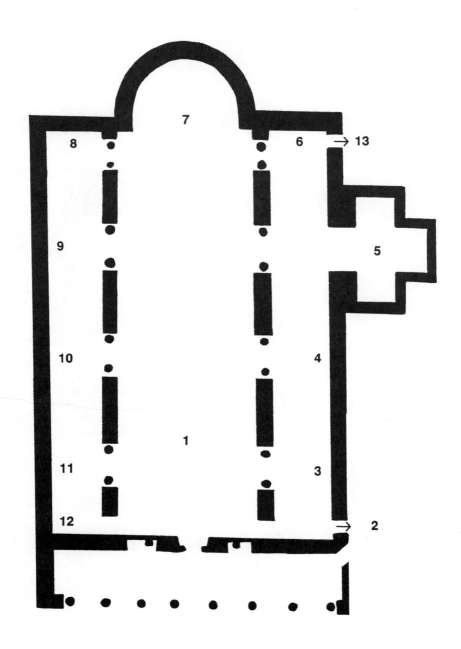

Ss. Giovanni e Paolo

24 Ss. Giovanni e Paolo***

Piazza dei Ss. Giovanni e Paolo

History. The church is dedicated to the two brothers, Sts. John and Paul, officers in the service of Julian "the Apostate" (emperor 361-363). Because they preferred to remain faithful to their Christian faith, the brothers were, by imperial order, martyred (26 June 362) in their home on Rome's Coelian Hill and buried within it. About 398 Senator Byzantius and his son St. Pammachius (ca. 340-410) built a basilica over the house and dedicated it to the two martyrs. The basilica was then sacked (410) by Alaric, and after it had suffered (442) damage from an earthquake, Leo I (440-461) reconstructed it. After the Norman sack of Rome (1084), Cardinal Teobaldo had it rebuilt and also began the Romanesque campanile, completed (ca. 1150) by Cardinal Giovanni Conti of Sutri. Successive centuries saw subsequent restorations, but those (1715-1718) sponsored by Cardinal Fabrizio Paolucci (d. 1726), titular (1699-1719), transformed the basilica into the baroque church we see today. In 1773 Clement XIV (1769-1774) gave the church to the Passionists (Congregation of the Passion of Our Lord Jesus Christ), who still serve it.

Excavations done (1887-1889) beneath the church uncovered three Roman buildings, among them the house in which the martyrs had lived and an early oratory. Cardinal Francis Spellman (1889-1967), titular (1946-1967), underwrote the cost of opening the excavations to the public.

Exterior. The portico is from the twelfth century and replaces the narthex of the earlier basilica. Eight columns support an architrave bearing an inscription informing us that the portico was erected by Cardinal Giovanni Conti of Sutri. The six columns in the center, with Ionic capitals, are of African granite, while those at the ends, with Corinthian capitals, are of marble. The gallery above the portico is from the early thirteenth century. Further up, the facade with its elegant five arches, formed by four marble columns from the Roman imperial period, is that of the original basilica. The facade and portico, much of which had been walled in, were returned (1949-1952) to their former splendor, thanks to the munificence of Cardinal Spellman.

The campanile (1150, restored 1951) is one of Rome's finest; it rests on huge blocks of travertine, formerly part of the Temple of Claudius (emperor 41-54). Its upper stories are decorated with polychrome ceramic plates and porphyry and serpentine marble panels. The exterior of the apse, with its Lombard-style open arcades, the only one in Rome, is also worth viewing.

The doorway has a border of cosmatesque mosaic decoration, with an eagle in the center. The lions at the entrance are from the twelfth century; the one on the left appears to have a human figure straddling its left paw, while that on the right is eating a boar. The columns flanking the doorway, still in their original location, once separated the nave from the narthex.

Interior. (1) The church has a nave and two aisles, separated by pilasters and arches, each of the latter supported by two granite columns from the earlier basilica. On the right, less than halfway down the nave, is a raised marble slab, surrounded by a brass railing, with the inscription: "This is the place of martyrdom of John and Paul in their own house." The actual site of the martyrdom is on the level below; in the sixteenth century an altar had been erected here. The coffered ceiling has the martyred brothers in the center, with the coat of arms of Cardinal Agostino Cusani (d. 1598). Portions of the pavement are restored thirteenth-century cosmatesque work.

(2) The octagonally shaped vestibule, leading to the sacristy, has the busts of several of the church's benefactors: (left to right) Cardinal Fabrizio Paolucci, Clement XIV, Pius IX, Pius VI (1775–1799), and Innocent XII (1691–1700).

(3) The altar has *Marco Benefial's* "St. Saturninus Condemned to Death" (1716). The saint was martyred in Rome toward the end of the third or the beginning of the fourth century. His relics are beneath the altar.

(4) The painting (eighteenth century) by *Aureliano Milani* over the altar is of St. Pammachius, founder of the church.

(5) The chapel, dedicated to St. Paul of the Cross (1694–1775), founder of the Passionists, was built immediately after the saint's canonization (1867). The walls are covered with marble and alabaster. The altarpiece is "St. Paul of the Cross Embraced by the Crucified Lord," by *Luigi Cochetti;* the saint's body is beneath the altar. The columns in front of the altar are of Egyptian alabaster, given the church by Pius IX, who had received the alabaster from the Sultan of Egypt. The cupola has Cochetti's "St. Paul of the Cross in Glory," and the pendentives have his angels with symbols of the passion. The paintings on the side walls are by *Francesco Grandi:* "Christ in the Garden" (left) and "Pietà" (right). The frescoes in the vault above the altar and the side paintings depict scenes from the life of St. Paul of the Cross.

Ss. Giovanni e Paolo (G. Vasi, 1753)

(6) "St. Gabriel of the Sorrowful Mother," by *Giovanni Battista Conti*, is over the altar. St. Gabriel (1838–1862) was twenty-four years old at the time of his death; he was canonized in 1920.

(7) The apsidal fresco (1588), by *Niccolò Circignani*, is "Trinity in Glory." In the center of the presbytery wall is *Giacomo Triga*'s "Martyrdom of Sts. John and Paul." To the viewer's left is *Giovanni Domenico Piastrini*'s "Sts. John and Paul Distribute Their Belongings to the Poor" and on the right is "Conversion of Terentianus." Terentianus, the imperial official who supervised the martyrdom, was converted when his son was healed through the martyrs' intercession.

Beneath the main altar, in a porphyry urn, are the relics of the two saints. The relics were brought up from the lower level in 1558, and later (1677) placed under the main altar. In 1724 Cardinal Paolucci had them put in the urn.

(8) "Assumption" is the altarpiece. Behind the altar there is a small room (see sacristan) on whose wall is a 1255 Byzantine-style fresco, discovered in 1887. Against a backdrop of an arcade, the Savior is enthroned, giving his blessing and holding a book in his left hand. Three apostles are on each side of him.

(9) The altar has *Tommaso Conca*'s "Crucifixion."

(10) Milani's "St. Joseph" is over the altar.

(11) The altar is dedicated to the Scillitan martyrs. Twelve Christians (five women, seven men) from Scillium in North Africa, were martyred

(17 July 180) in Carthage for refusing to hand over a letter of St. Paul. These are the first recorded martyrdoms in North Africa. Their relics were taken to Arles in France in 806; the relics of one of them, St. Speratus, were kept in Lyons but those of the other eleven were brought to Rome and placed in this basilica. These are now beneath the altar. The painting is by Milani.

(12) The stained glass window over the altar represents St. Gemma Galgani (1878–1903), an Italian mystic. The altar was the gift of Pius XII, who canonized St. Gemma in 1940.

(13) The entrance to the **excavations** is at the end of the right aisle. Below are more than twenty rooms from three different buildings (a two-story Christian house, a large public building, and an oratory); some of the rooms have early Roman frescoes. Fr. Germano, a Passionist priest residing in the monastery, suspecting a lower level to the church, began excavating in 1887 and within two years discovered the original oratory built over the tomb of Sts. John and Paul. Since there are many rooms and two levels, any orderly discussion here is impossible. The following are merely the highlights; for those with a greater interest in such matters, booklets with detailed explanations are available in the sacristy.

After descending the stairs, the first room is the *nympheum* with its wonderful, large pagan second-century fresco, probably depicting Persephone's return from Hades. Of the frescoes, this is the best preserved; it was covered over in the fourth century and repainted with festoons and flowers when the house, it seems, came into the hands of a Christian family. The room had a mosaic floor. The next room is the *triclinium* or dining room, with second- or third-century frescoes of youths holding festoons, together with peacocks, birds, cupids, and vine tendrils in the vault. The following room has an altar placed there by Leo XIII (1878–1903). The *tablinum*, or reception room, is an arched room with third-century decorations of animals and flowers. Further up, in a corner, there is a figure in a tunic with arms outstretched, usually identified as an *orante*, a Christian in prayer.

To reach the oratory, ascend the staircase; at the end is a narrow *confessio*, frescoed in the late fourth century. The bodies of the two martyrs were originally buried in a well, behind and below. None of the frescoes on the walls here have been identified with any certainty; the following are mere educated guesses of the experts. The single figures on the sides of the opening are thought to be Sts. John and Paul, and below, the figure with arms outstretched is said to be the Savior being adored by two individuals bowing deeply. On the upper left, the three figures are said to be Sts. Crispus, Crispinian, and Benedicta being led to judgment, while on the upper right the same, now blindfolded, are about to be martyred by beheading. On the lower left is the presbyter Crispus and the second male figure may be the cleric Crispinian; on the lower right is St. Benedicta. Legend has it that since these three were close friends of the brother martyrs, they too were arrested, beheaded, and buried near them. This could explain why they appear on the walls of the *confessio*.

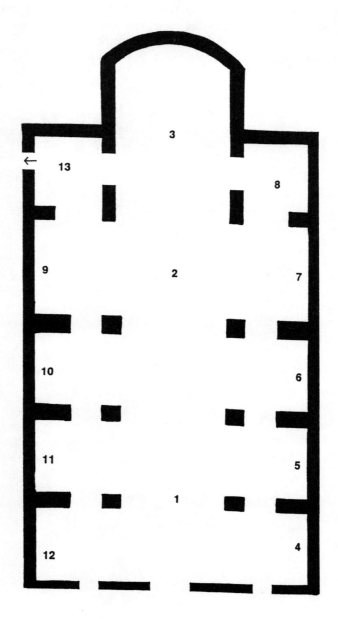

S. Ignazio

25 S. Ignazio***
Piazza di S. Ignazio

History. The church is dedicated to St. Ignatius of Loyola (1491–1556), founder of the Society of Jesus (Jesuits). A portion of the Roman College, an institution operated by the Jesuits, first occupied this site. When the college church, dedicated to the Annunciation, proved too small, Gregory XV (1621–1623), who had canonized St. Ignatius in 1622, suggested to his nephew, Cardinal Ludovico Ludovisi (1595–1632), that he erect a new church and in the saint's honor. Construction began in 1626 with *Orazio Grassi*, professor of mathematics at the college, as architect.

Exterior. The travertine facade, designed by Grassi, is modelled after that of the Gesù. It has two orders; the lower is divided into five bays, with columns flanking the main doorway and double pilasters framing the other two. Festoons, placed over blind windows and niches, link the Corinthian capitals. The second order, with a window and two niches, continues the upward sweep of the lower. A triangular pediment, whose tympanum bears the Ludovisi coat of arms, supports six marble candlesticks and a cross. The inscription is Cardinal Ludovisi's dedication to St. Ignatius, with the date 1626.

Interior. (1) The church is in the form of a Latin cross, with a single nave, and three chapels on each side. The nave is wide and has abundant light. The large archways, leading to the side chapels, are supported by piers and have free-standing marble covered columns with Ionic capitals; the piers, in turn, have two fluted pilasters with Corinthian capitals that rise to *Alessandro Algardi*'s frieze in which the Ludovisi coat of arms is displayed and in which putti play with fruit festoons. Over the main door, Religion (left) and Magnificence (right), also by Algardi, hold an inscription commemorating the church's opening in 1650. The pavement was redone in 1916.

The vault of the nave has Rome's **most famous baroque fresco** (1693–1694). The artist, *Andrea Pozzo*, a Jesuit, was a master of perspective. By using trompe d'oeil architecture, he extends the height of the building and opens it to the heavens. The fresco depicts the Society of Jesus' missionary activity throughout the world; the Savior sends a ray of light into the heart of Ignatius; this, in turn, is transmitted to the then four

175

known continents (Africa, America, Asia, and Europe), where Jesuit missionaries were active.

(2) The best view of the cupola is from the small yellow marble disk in the center of the nave, in line with the first pilaster. A cupola had been planned for the church, but never realized because of lack of funds. *Carlo Maratta*, a successful artist in Rome, suggested a painted cupola, and recommended Pozzo, then working in northern Italy, as the one best suited to do it. The latter came to Rome and completed (1685) it within several months. It is 56 feet in diameter and 112 feet from the floor. This was Pozzo's first commission in the church and because of his success he was asked to do the frescoes in the apse and nave. The Judith, Jael, David, and Samson in the pendentives are also his.

(3) Three of Pozzo's frescoes are in the apse; the middle one serves as the altarpiece. It represents the "Vision at La Storta," which St. Ignatius had (November 1537) while praying in a small chapel several miles north of Rome. The words that Ignatius heard Christ say: "I will show you favor in Rome," are in the oval above the altar. The fresco on the left depicts "St. Ignatius Sends St. Francis Xavier to the Indies," and on the right, "St. Ignatius Receives St. Francis Borgia in Rome." The half-dome has his "St. Ignatius Liberates a City Devastated by the Plague," and the vault his "Siege of Pamplona," during which battle (May 1521) Ignatius was wounded.

(4) Two columns of giallo antico flank the painting of the Jesuit saints Stanislaus Kostka (1550–1568) and John Francis Regis (1597–1640) by an unidentified eighteenth-century artist.

(5) This is the Sacripante Chapel, named after its donor, Cardinal Giuseppe Sacripante (d. 1727). The altar has two verde antico columns, which support a broken pediment with angels. The painting, "Death of St. Joseph," is by *Francesco Trevisani*. The cardinal's coat of arms appears on the base of the columns and he is buried in front of the altar. The right lunette has "Last Communion of St. Aloysius Gonzaga," also by Trevisani. St. Aloysius died in the infirmary of the Roman College, and the room in which he died, prior to its being torn down for the present church, was located about where the painting is now situated. The left lunette is "Blessed Lucia of Narni Receives the Stigmata," by *Giuseppe Chiari*. Cardinal Sacripante was a native of Narni and had sponsored Blessed Lucia's beatification (1710). The cupola has *Luigi Garzi's* "St. Joseph in Glory"; the pendentives, by Trevisani, have scenes from the life of St. Joseph.

(6) The altarpiece is *Stefano Pozzi's* "St. Joachim Presents Mary to the Father." Beneath is the body of the Jesuit cardinal St. Robert Bellar-

S. Ignazio (G. B. Falda, 1669)

mine (1542–1621), canonized in 1930; he once had been a professor at the Roman College. The columns framing the painting are painted.

(7) Chapel of St. Aloysius Gonzaga. This chapel (1697–1699) is dedicated to St. Aloysius Gonzaga (1568–1591), who died while a student at the Roman College. Four twisted columns of verde antico, with entwining gilded vine wreaths, support an elaborate pediment on which rest *Bernardino Ludovisi*'s allegorical figures of Purity (left) and Mortification (right). The **marble relief** in the center is *Pierre Le Gros*'s masterpiece, "St. Aloysius in Glory." The coat of arms at the base of the columns is that of the chapel's donor, Marquis Scipione Lancelotti, who had twice been cured by the saint. The saint's relics are in the lapis lazuli urn beneath the altar and the silver plate on the urn depicts the saint's last Communion. The two splendid angels on the balustrade are also by Ludovisi; they hold lilies, symbols of purity and innocence.

The vault has Pozzo's "St. Aloysius Taken to Heaven"; left of the above window is his "Virgin Appears to St. Aloysius," and to the right, "St. Aloysius Receives His First Communion from St. Charles Borromeo."

(8) This is the tomb (1717) of Gregory XV, who canonized St. Ignatius in 1622. The tomb of Cardinal Ludovico Ludovisi, who built the present church, is at its base. Thus the inscription immediately below the pope's statue, "One raised Ignatius to the altars, the other raised altars to Ignatius." The tomb is by Le Gros. The two figures at the side are Religion (left) and Munificence (right), both by *Étienne Monnot*. The four statues

in the niches, by *Camillo Rusconi*, are the cardinal virtues: Temperance (with vases), Prudence (with serpent and mirror), Fortitude (with shield), and Justice (with sword).

(9) The chapel, architecturally identical with that in the right transept, is now dedicated to St. John Berchmans (1559–1621), a Jesuit scholastic who died while studying at the Roman College. His remains were placed under the altar in 1873; he had been beatified in 1865 and was canonized in 1888. The relief (1750), by *Filippo Valle*, depicts the "Annunciation." The two seated figures above the altar are by *Pietro Bracci*. The two angels on the balustrade are also his. The one on the left holds a serpent and an apple, a reference to Mary's immaculate conception, and the other holds a crown of stars. The vault has *Lodovico Mazzanti*'s fresco of the "Assumption"; next to the window above his "Nativity" (left) and "Presentation in the Temple" (right).

(10) The crucifix, an eighteenth-century carving, is surrounded by relics and flanked by columns of giallo antico. The cupola has nineteenth-century panels referring to Christ's passion. The lunette on the left, as you face the altar, records St. Aloysius' cure (February 1765) of Niccolò Carlestini. On that occasion the saint told Carlestini to have devotion to the Sacred Heart of Jesus and, thus, the opposite lunette has Jesus appearing to St. Margaret Mary Alacoque (1647–1690).

(11) The altar painting is by *Pierre De Lattre*, a Jesuit coadjutor brother; it depicts St. Francis Xavier (1506–1552) on the left and St. Francis Borgia (1510–1572) on the right, both Jesuits. Once again, the columns flanking the painting are painted.

(12) Pope St. Gregory the Great (590–604) and St. Gregory Nazianzen (ca. 330–ca. 390) figure in De Lattre's altarpiece; Gregory the Great is on the left.

(13) On the way to the sacristy is Rusconi's model for his statue of St. Ignatius in the nave of St. Peter's. The statues in the niches are Religion (with keys and a book), Charity (breast-feeding a child), Faith (holding a chalice), and Hope (with an anchor).

The sacristy frescoes are by De Lattre. The ceiling has "St. Ignatius Celebrates Mass"; in the three lunettes opposite the windows, scenes from the life of St. Ignatius. The vault above the altar has "Virgin and Child with Angels," and opposite is an "Annunciation" flanked by "Adam" and "Eve." A painting of Ignatius is over the altar; the other smaller paintings are by De Lattre and Pozzo.

The rooms of St. Aloysius Gonzaga and St. John Berchmans have been preserved in a portion of the former Roman College and may be seen with the sacristan's permission. The rooms visited are: (a) the scholastics' recreation room; (b) the room in which Aloysius lived (1587–1590) when he was a student here; (c) the room used (1617–1618) by St. John Berchmans; (d) house chapel; (e) room in which Blessed Anthony Baldinucci (1665–1717) lived (1693–1697).

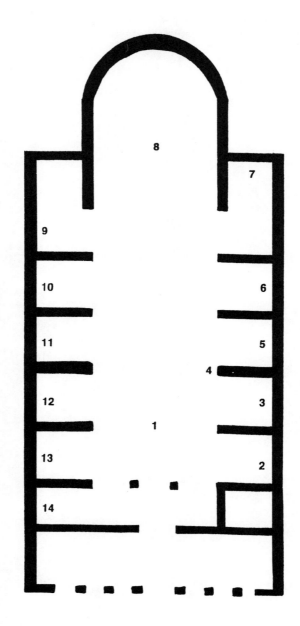

S. Lorenzo in Lucina

26 S. Lorenzo in Lucina**

Piazza di S. Lorenzo in Lucina

History. The church is dedicated to St. Lawrence, martyred in 258, during the persecution of Valerian (emperor 253–259). It is called *in Lucina* because of the tradition that this had been the site of the home of the Roman matron Lucina, who gave hospitality to Pope St. Marcellus I (306–308) when he was being pursued by Maxentius (emperor 306–312). The first oratory or church here was in the fourth century; Damasus I (366–384) was elected pope in it. It was later restored (780) by Hadrian I (772–795) and then totally rebuilt by Paschal II (1099–1118), after the Normans had sacked Rome (1084). In 1606 Paul V (1605–1621) gave the church to St. Francis Caracciolo (1563–1608), cofounder of the Clerks Regular Minor. The church subsequently underwent a radical transformation, especially the interior (1650), under *Cosimo Fanzago.* Further restoration was done (1856–1860) by *Andrea Busiri Vici* under Pius IX (1846–1860) and more under Benedict XV (1914–1922). Finally, in 1927, the portico was returned to its original medieval appearance.

Exterior. The church's portico, with its six granite Ionic columns and its six-story Romanesque campanile, are from the time of Paschal II. The facade is uncommonly simple; a round window in the center with rectangular windows on the sides. The whole is surmounted by a triangular pediment. The church wall, beneath the portico, has imbedded architectural fragments and inscriptions. On the far right is the large relief-monument to Clelia Severini (d. 1822), by *Pietro Tenerani.* To the right, on the outside wall, is a well-executed prelate's tombstone. The entrance door to the church is flanked by two undersized Romanesque lions.

Interior. (1) The church has a nave with lateral altars. The coffered ceiling was restored in 1857 during the pontificate of Pius IX (1846–1878); thus, his coat of arms is there. The painting (1857) in the center is by *Roberto Bompiani* and depicts the "Gloriously Risen Christ" with saints connected with the church: on the left are Sts. Lawrence and Lucina, on the right St. Francis Caracciolo (kneeling) and Pope Paschal II, who, because he had built the church, is portrayed with a church in his hands. The nave's upper walls, next to the windows, have painted banners with Roman saints of the second and third centuries; the ten monochrome medallions above the pilasters illustrate events and miracles in the life of St. Francis Caracciolo.

(2) The chapel is dedicated to St. Lawrence with "St. Lawrence in Glory" (1716), by *Sigismondo Rosa,* as the altarpiece. The artist included the church's facade and has putti holding the church's floor plan; on the right St. Lucina offers the plan to the saint. The nineteenth-century paintings on the sides are by *G. Creti:* "St. Lawrence Points to the Poor as the Church's Treasury" (left) and "Martyrdom of St. Lawrence" (right). Beneath the altar, in an eighteenth-century reliquary, is part of the gridiron on which the saint is said to have been martyred.

(3) A rather poor painting of the Sacred Heart of Jesus is on the altar. In the tympanum over the altar is a small but striking "Holy Family" by *Domenico Rainaldi.* The side walls have scenes from the life of St. Anthony of Padua (1195–1231): on the left, "St. Anthony Heals a Child," and on the right, "An Ass Kneels before the Blessed Sacrament." Both are by *Jan Miel.*

(4) The monument is to the French artist *Nicolas Poussin* (1594–1665), who is buried in the church. The monument was commissioned (1830) by René de Chateaubriand, French ambassador to Rome, and done by *Louis Desprez.* The relief on the monument reproduces one of Poussin's most famous paintings, *Et in Arcadia Ego;* the bust (1829) of the artist is by *Paul Lemoyne.* The epitaph below tells us that though the artist is now silent, his paintings still speak for him.

(5) The altar originally had "St. Francis Caracciolo Adoring the Eucharist," by *Lodovico Stern,* but this has been covered by a sunburst arrangement with an image of the Virgin. Stern and his family are buried in the church; a marker on the left wall recalls that fact. Beneath the altar is the skull of Pope St. Alexander I (105–115).

(6) The chapel was designed by *Gian Lorenzo Bernini.* The large oval "Annunciation" is often attributed to *Guido Reni,* but it may be another's copy of Reni's painting in the Quirinal. The left wall has *Gaicinto Gemignani's* "Madonna Salus Populi Romani" (1664). Below, the bust nearer the altar is Bernini's remarkable portrait of Gabriele Fonseca (d. 1668), physician to Innocent X (1644–1655). *Guillaume Courtois's* "Miracle of the Prophet Elisha" is on the right.

(7) The crucifix is from the sixteenth century. The right wall has a memorial to Umberto II of Savoy, who was king of Italy (9 May to 13 June 1946) until he was forced into exile.

(8) The main altar dates from 1675 and was designed by *Carlo Rainaldi.* Reni's "Crucifixion" is the altarpiece (1639–1642), flanked by fluted columns of nero antico. The painting was given to the church by Marchioness Cristina Duglioli Angelelli, who is buried in front of the presbytery. At the altar's top is an image of the Virgin known as "Madonna della Sanità." On the left wall are two large reliefs with scenes from the life of St. Lawrence, and on the right are reliefs with scenes from the life of St. Lucina. Behind the altar is a twelfth-century episcopal chair of Paschal II; the wooden choir stalls are from the early part of the eighteenth century.

(9) Tomb of Cardinal Gabriele Della Genga Sermattei (1801–1861).

(10) *Marco Benefial*'s "Death of Blessed Giacinta Marescotti" is over the altar; she was beatified in 1726, and canonized in 1807. The vault has *Simon Vouet*'s scenes from the life of the Virgin. His are also the side paintings: "Temptation of St. Francis of Assisi" (left) and "Vesting of St. Francis of Assisi" (right).

(11) The altar has *Alessandro Turchi*'s "Holy Family." On the right is the tomb of Cardinal Carlo Cremonesi (1866–1943), titular (1935–1943).

(12) The chapel is dedicated to St. John Nepomucene (ca. 1350–1393). The saint's statue is by *Gaetano Altobelli*, and the walls have scenes from the saint's life. On the left the saint, in the presence of Wenceslaus IV (king 1378–1419), refuses to break the seal of confession, and on the right the monks come to take the saint's martyred body and bury it in their church. Beneath the altar is the tomb of the Czech composer Josef Myslivecek (1737–1781).

(13) The altarpiece (1618) is "St. Charles Borromeo Carries the Holy Nail in Procession" by *Carlo Saraceni*. The side walls have works by his students: "St. Charles Gives Alms" (left) and "St. Charles Cares for the Plague-Stricken" (right).

(14) The well-lit baptistery has an attractive "Baptism of Christ" by *G. Masini*. Scenes of baptisms are on the walls; St. Lawrence is depicted baptizing on the left, and St. Peter on the right. Both are by *Antonio Grecolini*. The font's cover is somewhat different.

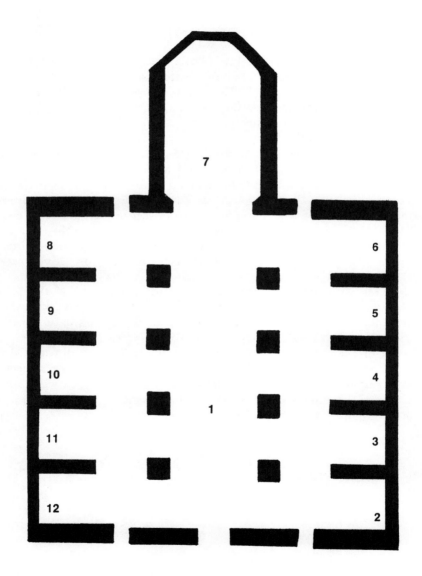

S. Luigi dei Francesi

27 S. Luigi dei Francesi***
Piazza di San Luigi dei Francesi

History. The church is dedicated to St. Louis IX (1214–1270), king of France (1226–1270), and is the national church of the French in Rome; it is, thus, known as "St. Louis of the French." In 1518 Pope Leo X (1513–1521) gave permission to the French community in Rome to erect a church. Building was begun that year under the French architect *Jean de Chenevières*, but construction came to a halt in 1524, when financial problems arose. Then followed the Sack of Rome (1527). Building resumed, thanks to subsidies received from the French monarchs Henry II (king 1547–1559), Charles IX (king 1560–1574) and Henry III (king 1574–1589). The church was completed and consecrated in 1589.

Exterior. The late Renaissance facade is by *Giacomo Della Porta*; it has two orders with a triangular pediment crowning the building. The lower order has pilasters forming five bays; there are three portals and two niches. The left niche has a statue of Charlemagne (742–814) and the right St. Louis IX. Beneath each is a salamander, the device of Francis I (king 1515–1547), during whose reign the church was begun. The upper order has a central window with two niches; St. Clotilde (ca. 474–545), wife of King Clovis, is on the left with St. Joan of Valois (1464–1505) on the right. These statues of French kings and queens are by *Pierre Lestache* and date from 1758. The coat of arms in the tympanum is that of France.

Interior. (1) The church has a main nave with two aisles and five altars on each side. It was over-decorated in the eighteenth century with Sicilian jasper, pavonazzetto, and giallo antico. The white and gilded stucco work (1756–1764) in the coffered ceiling of the nave, cupola, and apse is by *Antoine Dérizet*. The ceiling fresco (1756), "Death and Apotheosis of St. Louis," is by *Charles-Joseph Natoire*. In the fresco's lower portion France kneels at the dead king's bier, while a weeping knight stands in front of a background of crusaders' tents in Tunis, where St. Louis died while on a crusade.

(2) The painting (1630) on the altar is "St. Denis Restores Sight to a Blind Man" by *Renaud Levieux*. St. Denis (d. ca. 258) was the first bishop of Paris. The church has an overabundance of memorials and plaques to the French who had died in Rome. On the pillar immediately opposite the next chapel is a tall memorial "To the French soldiers who died at the walls of Rome in 1849," placed here "by their brothers in arms." They had participated in the siege of Rome.

(3) The Chapel of St. Cecilia has magnificent frescoes (1615–1617) by *Domenichino*. The right wall has "St. Cecilia Distributes Clothing to the Poor" and the left "Martyrdom of St. Cecilia." In the vault is "St. Cecilia in Glory" (center) with "St. Cecilia Refuses to Sacrifice to Idols" (left) and "An Angel Crowns Sts. Cecilia and Valerian" (right). *Guido Reni's* copy (ca. 1600) of *Raphael's* "St. Cecilia and Saints," now in Bologna, is on the altar.

(4) The chapel is dedicated to St. Joan of Valois (1464–1505), daughter of Louis XI (king 1461–1483) and wife of Louis XII (king 1498–1515). After Louis XII had their marriage annulled, Joan founded the religious congregation of Franciscan Annunciades. The painting by *Étienne Parrocel* depicts "St. Joan of Valois Taken to Heaven"; it was done after 1742, the date of her beatification.

(5) The decorations in this chapel, dedicated to St. Remigius of Rheims (ca. 437–ca. 533), depict the Christianization of the Franks. The altarpiece by *Iacopone Del Conte* shows Clovis (465–511), king of the Franks, destroying idols while St. Remigius baptizes soldiers. The right wall's fresco (ca. 1550) shows Clovis preparing his attack at the battle of Tolbiac (496); a deer appears and leads the army to a ford in the river, thus permitting the Franks to cross and gain a victory over the Alamanni. Clovis, as a result, became a Christian. The fresco is by *Pelegrino Tibaldi*, as are those in the vault depicting scenes from Clovis' life. *Sermoneta's* fresco on the left wall represents St. Remigius about to anoint Clovis prior to the latter's baptism (498/499).

(6) The large monument (1836), by *Paul Lemoyne*, in the center on the left wall is to the French painter *Pierre-Narcisse Guérin* (1774–1833), who died in Rome. He had been the teacher of Géricault (1791–1824) and Delacroix (1799–1863), and director (1822–1828) of the Académie de France in Rome.

(7) The apse is faced with marble. The large painting of the "Assumption of the Virgin," in a marble frame of giallo antico over the main altar, is by *Francesco Bassano*. It dates from about 1585–1590, late in his career. The "Trinity" in stucco (1753–1754) above the altar's pediment is by *Jean-Jacques Caffieri*; Jesus holds a crown in his left hand and is about to place it on the Virgin.

The ornately decorated cupola is the work of Dérizet. The pendentives have statues in stucco of four Doctors of the Church; as one faces the altar, St. Gregory the Great (*Giovanni Battista Maini*) is on the left with St. Jerome (*Filippo Valle*) on the right. The other two, partially hidden from view, are St. Augustine and St. Ambrose (*Augustin Pajou*).

(8) Contarelli Chapel. This is the most important chapel in the church because of *Caravaggio's* three paintings. The French cardinal Matthieu

Cointerel (1519–1585), known in Italy as Contarelli, procured this as a funerary chapel and in 1565 asked *Girolamo Muziano* to paint three scenes from the life of his patron, St. Matthew. When the cardinal died in 1585, nothing had been done; the executor of the cardinal's will then gave the commission (1591) to *Cavalier d'Arpino*, who did the frescoes in the vault, now hardly recognizable. The artist, however, never got around to do the paintings for altar or walls. The commission was withdrawn and given (1599) to Caravaggio, who once had worked in Cavalier d'Arpino's studio. The first painting done was "Calling of St. Matthew" (left), a dramatic piece in which Christ indicates by his extended hand that it is Matthew whom he wants, and Matthew, in turn, keeps his head down in astonishment that the Lord should be calling him to follow him. The "Martyrdom of St. Matthew" on the right wall is a violent painting in comparison to its pendant. The apostle has been dragged from the altar and is about to be slain, while onlookers express their horror. Both paintings were done about 1600–1601. The last to be painted (1602) was the altarpiece, "St. Matthew and Angel." This is the second painting that Caravaggio executed for the altar; the first had been rejected. The angel appears to be dictating to Matthew what he is to write in his Gospel.

(9) The "Nativity" (ca. 1630) by *Charles Mellin* is on the altar. The fresco of the "Annunciation" on the right is also by Mellin; that of "Adoration of the Magi" on the left is by *Giovanni Baglione.*

(10) This somewhat theatrical chapel is dedicated to St. Louis IX and is the creation of *Plautilla Bricci.* The outside arch is decorated with stucco drapery, with gold fleurs-de-lis on a blue background. Above the arch are Faith (left) and Religion (right). The altar has two columns of giallo antico; the painting of St. Louis IX is also by Bricci. The right wall has *Ludovico Gemignani's* "St. Louis Gives the Crown of Thorns to the Archbishop of Paris." St. Louis secured (1238) the relic of the crown of thorns from Baldwin II (1217–1273), Latin emperor of Constantinople, and to house it he built (1243–1248) the magnificent Sainte Chapelle in Paris. On the left wall is *Nicolas Pinson's* "Catherine de' Medici Presents the Plans of the Church to St. Louis." Catherine was the wife of Francis I, who started the church.

(11) The painting of St. Nicholas of Bari by Muziano is on the altar. The paintings on either side of St. Catherine of Alexandria (left) and St. Marguerite (right) are by *Girolamo Massei.* The left wall has "Birth of St. Nicholas" and the right, "Death of St. Nicholas," both by *Baldassare Della Croce.* The statue of St. Joan of Arc is by *André-César Vermare.*

(12) The altar has Massei's St. Sebastian. On the pilaster facing this chapel is Lemoyne's monument (1836) to *Claude Lorrain*, France's greatest landscape painter, who died in Rome in 1682.

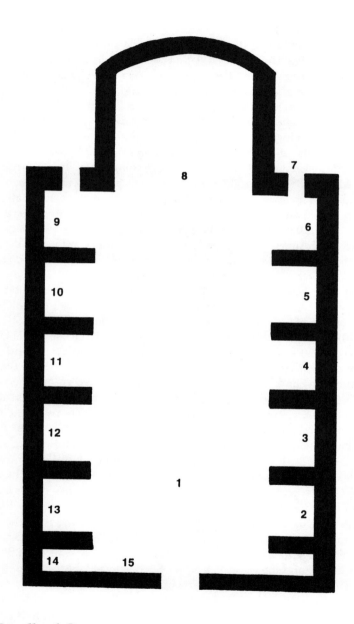

S. Marcello al Corso

28 S. Marcello al Corso*

Piazza di S. Marcello

History. The church is dedicated to St. Marcellus, who was elected pope in May 308. Because he is said to have refused to sacrifice to pagan gods, he was sentenced by Maxentius (emperor 306–312) to do menial work in the stables of the imperial post once located on this site. Exhausted from labor and mistreatment, he is supposed to have died here on 16 January 309. The first recorded mention of a church honoring St. Marcellus on this site is in 418, when Boniface I (418–422) was consecrated pope here on 29 December. Hadrian I (772–795) completely rebuilt the church, but it was centuries later destroyed by fire, on the night of 22 May 1519. The present church, built by the architects *Iacopo Sansovino* and *Antonio da Sangallo the Younger,* was completed in 1592. The Servants of Mary (Servites), a congregation founded in 1233, have served this church since 1369.

Exterior. The baroque travertine facade was begun by *Carlo Fontana* in 1682 and completed in 1686; it is concave and has two orders with a single portal. The entrance is flanked by Corinthian columns. Above is the relief (1686) "St. Philip Benizi Refuses the Papal Tiara" by *Antonio Raggi;* this is supported by two angels and is surmounted by a broken pediment bearing an empty frame (which was to have a relief of the Annunciation), and the figures of Faith and Hope. The left niche has a statue of St. Marcellus and that on the right has one of St. Philip Benizi (1223–1285), the most famous of Servite saints. The second order continues the vertical lines of the columns in the first. Where one expects to have volutes on the sides, there are palm branches: the statues are of Blessed Gioacchino Piccolomini (1258–1306) and Blessed Francesco Patrizi (1266–1328), both Servites. The facade of the present church is where the apse of the earlier church had been. From that apse hung the body of the Italian patriot Cola di Rienzo (1313–1354), after his brutal murder in a riot on 8 October 1354.

Interior. (1) The church is baroque in style and has a single nave with five chapels on each side. The gilded coffered ceiling dates from 1592, the gift of Mons. Giulio Vitelli, whose family coats of arms are depicted there. An image of the Virgin is in the center; other compartments have Marian symbols derived from the Litany of Loreto. The fourteen frescoes next to the windows in the nave depict scenes from our Lord's passion and resurrection and are by *Giovanni Battista Ricci*. His is also the huge "Cruci-fixion" (1613) on the rear wall over the entrance. Beneath the fresco, and left of the entrance door, is the monument to Cardinal Francesco Cenini (d. 1645), titular (1621–1645).

(2) *Lazzaro Baldi*'s "Annunciation" is on the altar. The fresco in the oval frame above the altar contains a fifteenth-century Virgin and Child, which may be from the earlier church.

(3) The altar has "Martyrdom of Sts. Degna and Merita" (1727), early Roman martyrs, by *Pietro Barberi*. The chapel houses the fine tombs of Giovanni Muti (left) and his wife, Colomba (right), who are shown in prayer. The tombs (1725) are by *Bernardino Cametti*.

(4) A fourteenth-century fresco of the Virgin and Child in a hand-some fifteenth-century marble Renaissance frame is over the altar. Sur-rounding the fresco are five scenes from the Virgin's life by *Francesco Salviati*. The walls have "Adoration of the Shepherds" (left) and "Adora-tion of the Magi" (right) by Ricci; the vault frescoes are also his. The right wall has the monument of Bishop Mattia Grifoni (d. 1507), and the left that of the London-born Cardinal Thomas Weld (1773–1837), titular (1830–1837).

(5) The wooden crucifix on the altar is from the fourteenth century and escaped injury during the 1519 fire. The vault has *Perin del Vaga*'s "Creation of Eve" (1525); the other two panels have the evangelists. Mark and John (left) are by Perin del Vaga, while Matthew and Luke (right) are by *Daniele da Volterra*. On the left wall is the neoclassical tomb of Cardinal Ercole Consalvi (1757–1824), secretary of state under Pius VII (1800–1823); the statue depicts Religion and the tomb (1831) is by *Rinaldo Rinaldi*. Under the altar's table is a third-century stone, discovered in 1909 when work was being done on the premises. The stone's sides are deco-rated with military symbols and the front has a panel of polychrome marble (*opus sectile*) from the twelfth century.

(6) This chapel is dedicated to S. Pellegrino Laziosi (1265–1345), a Servite. The altar has *Aureliano Milani*'s "St. Pellegrino Cured by the Redeemer" (1725). The walls also have Milani's "Miracle of Our Lady of the Fire" (left) and "St. Pellegrino Heals a Blind Man" (right). *Pietro Bracci*'s monument (1726) to Cardinal Fabrizio Paolucci (d. 1726) is on the right wall.

(7) Sacristy. On the wall is a "Crucifixion" attributed to *Anthony Van Dyck* and the ceiling has a fresco of "St. Marcellus in Glory" by an unidentified seventeenth-century artist.

(8) The frescoes in the apse have scenes of the Virgin's life by Ricci. Prophets flank the three upper windows, while Servite saints flank the two lower windows. The inside arch has the evangelists with the Eternal

S. Marcello al Corso (G. Vasi, 1756)

Father, while the sides have the Doctors of the Western Church (Ambrose, Gregory, Jerome, Augustine). David (left) and Isaiah (right) are on the arch's front. The mediocre painting of "Pope St. Marcellus in Glory" (1867) is by *Silverio Capparoni*. The relics of St. Marcellus were brought to the church in the eighth century, from the cemetery of St. Priscilla, and are in the urn beneath the altar. The choir stalls date from 1612.

(9) *Pier Leone Ghezzi*'s painting (1725) on the altar shows "St. Philip Benizi, Assisted by St. Alessio Falconieri, Gives the Book of Rules to St. Guiliana Falconieri." The side walls have "St. Philip Benizi's Miracle of the Bread" (left) and "St. Philip Benizi's Funeral" (right), both by *Bernardino Gagliardi*.

(10) This is the chapel of the Frangipani, a famous Roman family. The altarpiece (1559) is the striking "Conversion of St. Paul," by *Federico Zuccari*; the side walls have *Taddeo Zuccari*'s "Blinding of Elymas" (left) and "St. Paul Cures a Paralytic" (right). The tombs with busts of the Frangipani occupy the lower portions of both walls. Antonino and his sons Mario and Curzio are on the left wall, with busts by an anonymous sixteenth-century artist; the tombs and expressive busts of Muzio and his sons Lelio and Roberto on the right are by *Alessandro Algardi*.

(11) The altarpiece is *Paolo Naldini*'s "Our Lady of Sorrows." The walls have *Domenico Corvi*'s "Finding of Moses" (left) and "Abraham's Sacrifice of Isaac" (right), both prior to 1763. *Antonio Bicchierari*'s "Presentation in the Temple" (ca. 1730) is in the vault.

(12) The painting (1728) of St. Mary Magdalene is by *Giacomo Triga*. The vault frescoes are "Annunciation" (left) and "Nativity" (right). The paintings on the side walls, by *Giuseppe Tommasi*, are of Blessed Francesco Patrizi (left) and Blessed Gioacchino Piccolomini (right).

(13) The chapel is dedicated to the Seven Holy Founders of the Servite order, represented in *Agostino Masucci*'s painting (1727). Naldini's frescoes of "Deposition from the Cross" (left) and "Way to Calvary" (right) decorate the side walls.

(14) This chapel is dedicated to St. Anthony Mary Pucci (1819–1892), a Servite, canonized in 1962. On the left wall is the tomb of Cardinal Alexis Lépicier (1863–1936), a renowned theologian; he was elected superior general of the Servites in 1913 and created cardinal in 1927.

(15) This double Renaissance tomb is attributed to *Iacopo Sansovino*. The figure on top shows Cardinal Giovanni Michiel (d. 1503) and that below his nephew, Bishop Antonio Orso (d. 1511). The books beneath the bishop's figure recall his bequeathing 730 valuable codices to the convent of S. Marcello.

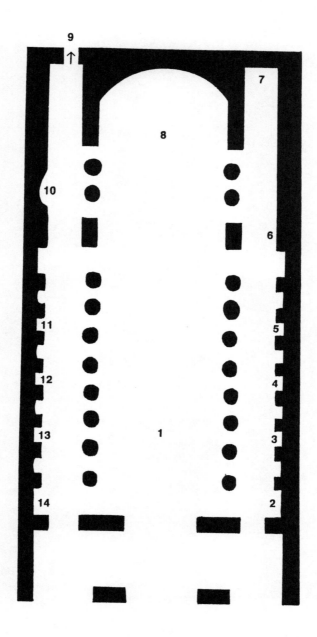

S. Marco

29 S. Marco**
Piazza di S. Marco

History. The church is said to have been founded by Pope St. Mark (336), and some would like to think on the site of the house in which St. Mark the Evangelist stayed when he was in Rome. The church was rebuilt in the fifth century after a disastrous fire; Hadrian I (772–795) restored it in 792 and Gregory IV (827–844) embellished (833) it and commissioned the apse mosaic. The building underwent further transformation (1455–1471) when the Venetian Cardinal Pietro Barbo, later Paul II (1464–1471), incorporated it into the Palazzo Venezia. Final major restoration (1740–1750) was done by *Filippo Barigioni*, who gave the church its baroque interior at the request of Cardinal Angelo Quirini (d. 1755), titular (1728–1755). Excavations (1948–1951) beneath the church have uncovered the outer walls of the fourth-century church, together with fragments of wall paintings and floor mosaics.

Exterior. The facade is formed by a charming Renaissance portico on the lower level, with three arcades divided by semicolumns, and a loggia above divided by pilasters. The portico is attributed to *Leon Battista Alberti*. The Romanesque campanile is from the twelfth century.

The portico's walls have architectural fragments and portions of early Christian tombstones imbedded in them. The ten small columns in the left wall were once (1145) part of the tabernacle over the main altar. On the right wall's lower right is the funerary stone of Vannozza Catanei (1442–1518), the mistress of Rodrigo Borgia (1431–1503) prior to his becoming Alexander VI (1492–1503), and the mother of Cesare and Lucrezia Borgia. Vannozza was buried in S. Maria del Popolo; it is not known how her tombstone came to be here at S. Marco.

Three doorways give entrance into the church; the central one is by far the most elegant. The fluted pilasters support an architrave decorated with festoons and fruit, with Paul II's coat of arms in the center. Above is a relief (1464) of a seated St. Mark the Evangelist attributed to *Isaia da Pisa*. Two medieval lions flank the entrance. The decoration of the other two portals is due to Cardinal Marco Barbo (1420–1491), who succeeded (1467) his uncle, as titular. Thus the inscription over the left door reads: "Mark Cardinal of St. Mark."

Interior. (1) The church is basilican in style, with a nave and two aisles separated by pilasters, against which are twenty columns with a

veneer of Sicilian jasper. The form of the church is that given it by Paul
II, but the baroque decorations are from the eighteenth century. In the
rear of the church, on the right, is the upper portion of a medieval well
(ninth-tenth century), with an interesting inscription (eleventh century)
inviting the thirsty to drink of the well, but cursing the one who should
charge for the water drawn from it. Until recently this had been in the
portico.

The gilded coffered ceiling, with Paul II's coat of arms, dates from
1474. The only other Roman church that has a ceiling dating from this
early period is S. Maria Maggiore. The upper portion of the nave is decorated with frescoes done by various artists in the seventeenth century, and
reliefs done by different sculptors in the eighteenth-century. The four frescoes, on the left from the rear, depict scenes from the life of Pope St. Mark;
the fresco nearest the altar is "St. Lawrence Giustiniani Takes Possession
of the Diocese of Venice," by *Domenico Corvi*. St. Lawrence Giustiniani
(1381-1456) was the first patriarch of Venice. The frescoes on the right
wall illustrate scenes from the lives of the third-century Roman martyrs
Sts. Abdon and Sennen, whose relics are in the crypt beneath the main
altar. The fresco nearest the altar is "Clement XIII Approves the Decree
of Beatification of Gregory Barbarigo," also by Corvi. Barbarigo
(1625-1697), a Venetian and cardinal of Padua, was beatified in 1761. The
twelve stucco reliefs (1740-1750) between the frescoes represent incidents
in the lives of the apostles.

(2) "Resurrection" by *Palma il Giovane* is on the altar.

(3) *Luigi Gentile*'s "Virgin with the Child and Sts. John the Baptist
and Anthony of Padua" is the altarpiece. To the left is the tomb of Canon
Luigi Oreste Borgia (d. 1916). Since this was the church of the Venetians
in Rome, many of them chose to be buried here.

(4) The altar has *Carlo Maratta*'s "Adoration of the Magi." To the
left is the tomb of the Venetian, Cardinal Cristoforo Vidman (d. 1660),
by *Cosimo Fancelli*. The urn is alabaster. Fancelli also did the cardinal's
portrait.

(5) *Bernardino Gagliardi*'s "Pietà" is over the altar. To the left is the
tomb of Francesco Erizzo (d. 1700), son of the Venetian ambassador in
Rome. The tomb is by *Francesco Maratta*. The lunette over the door on
the left is "Rout of the Midianites" by *Jacques Courtois*, famous for his
battle scenes.

(6) The monument to the right, as one ascends the stairs at the end
of the right nave, is to the sixteen-year-old Leonardo Pesaro (d. 1796),
son of Pietro Pesaro, last Venetian ambassador to Rome. The tomb is by
Antonio Canova.

(7) The chapel was designed by *Pietro da Cortona*. The painting of

"Pope St. Mark" on the altar is attributed to *Melozzo di Forlì*. The seventeenth-century canvases on the walls, by *Guillaume Courtois*, represent "Aaron Gathers Manna" (left) and "Aaron's Sacrifice" (right). The stucco work in the cupola is by Fancelli and *Ercole Ferrata*. The pavement (1478) here (and in the presbytery) is in the cosmatesque style. In front of the chapel is the stone marking the place of burial of Cardinal Marco Barbo (d. 1491).

(8) The **apse mosaic** was executed (833–844) during Gregory IV's pontificate. The figures are Byzantine in style, rigid and unlike the earlier mosaics in Ss. Cosma e Damiano, and the later mosaics in S. Maria in Trastevere. An oversized Christ, austere in visage and clad in royal purple, stands on a footstool that bears the Greek letters Alpha and Omega. His right hand is held in benediction, after the Greek manner, and in his left he holds a book with the words: "I am the light, I am the life, I am the resurrection." Above his head is the hand of the Father holding a crown and below him the phoenix, the symbol of the resurrection. On Christ's right are St. Felicissimus and St. Mark the Evangelist with his right hand on Gregory IV's shoulder. The square nimbus framing Gregory's head indicates that he was alive when the mosaic was done. He holds a model of the church. The figures on Christ's left are Pope St. Mark, St. Agapitus, and St. Agnes. Sts. Felicissimus and Agapitus were deacons martyred in 258 with Pope St. Sixtus II (257–258).

Below is the Lamb of God standing in the center on a mound from which flow four rivers and toward which the twelve lambs, symbols of the apostles (and faithful) approach. Beneath this is a Latin inscription in which Gregory dedicates the church to St. Mark the Evangelist and asks his intercession that God grant the pope life in heaven.

The outside of the triumphal arch, also in mosaic, has a bust of Christ, much less severe, and symbols of the four evangelists floating amid clouds. Lower down, Sts. Paul (left) and Peter (right) point toward Christ.

The middle fresco in the presbytery is *Giovanni Francesco Romanelli*'s "St. Mark in Glory." That on the right is "Capture of St. Mark" with "Martyrdom of St. Mark" on the left, both by Guillaume Courtois. Above the center seat in the choir is a gilded bronze medallion bearing the portrait of Paul II, placed here by Cardinal Quirini in 1735.

Beneath the altar in an ancient porphyry urn is the body of Pope St. Mark, and in the crypt below, the tomb of the third-century Roman martyrs Abdon and Sennen. Cardinal Marco Barbo had these relics placed here in 1474. Portions of the floor here are also cosmatesque.

(9) The **sacristy** has a remarkable fifteen-century ciborium, which had been in the presbytery but was transferred here at the time of the eighteenth-century renovations. The Eternal Father at the top is by *Mino*

da Fiesole, as is "Melchizedek Offers Bread and Wine to Abraham" on the right. The two angels at the top are by *Giovanni Dalmata,* as is "Isaac Grants Primogeniture to Jacob" on the left. There is also a thirteenth-century crucifix fresco, said to be of the school of *Pietro Cavallini,* and *Melozzo di Forlì*'s "St. Mark Writes His Gospel."

(10) The altar has *Pier Francesco Mola*'s "Immaculate Conception." To the left is the Renaissance tomb (1476) of Paolo Capranica (d. 1428), who had been secretary to Martin V (1417–1431) and archbishop of Benevento. The fresco in the lunette above the tomb and the doorway is "Victory of Joshua" by Jacques Courtois. Then left of the door is the tomb of Cardinal Pietro Basadonna (d. 1684) by *Filippo Carcani;* the statues are Faith (left) and Fortitude (right).

(11) "St. Michael Overcomes Lucifer" is also by Mola. The tomb to the left is of the Venetian, Cardinal Luigi Prioli (d. 1720); the statues are of Justice (left) and Charity (right).

(12) The painting of "St. Dominic Restores Life to a Child" is attributed to *Baccio Ciarpi.* The frescoes on the sides are of St. Nicholas of Bari (left) by *Ciro Ferri* and of St. Francis of Assisi (right) by *Lazzaro Baldi.*

(13) The chapel was constructed in 1764 to honor the recently beatified (1761) Gregory Barbarigo. The relief by *Antonio D'Este,* a student of Canova, shows the blessed giving alms. Barbarigo was canonized in 1960. To the left is the tomb of the Venetian, Cardinal Marcantonio Bragadino (d. 1658), by *Lazzaro Morelli.*

(14) The frescoes in the baptistery are attributed to Maratta. That of the Virgin in the oval is beyond recognition; Innocence is on the left and Prudence on the right.

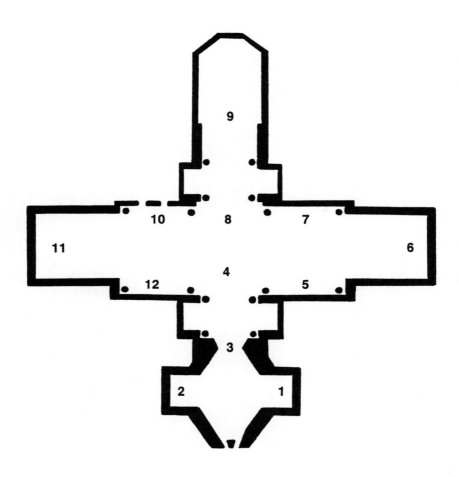

S. Maria degli Angeli

30 S. Maria degli Angeli**
Piazza della Repubblica

History. The building in which the church of St. Mary of the Angels is located was formerly the Baths of Diocletian (emperor 284–305), built between 298 and 305. Of the public baths in Rome at the time, these were the largest. Pope Pius IV (1559–1565), having been persuaded by the Sicilian priest Antonio Del Duca, who is said to have had a vision of a very bright light rising from these ruins, commissioned (1561) the eighty-six-year-old *Michelangelo* to convert the central hall (*tepidarium*) and adjoining ruins into a church. Work began in 1563, but, when Michelangelo died the following year, the project was continued by his student, *Giacomo Del Duca*, nephew of the priest mentioned above. The church (completed in 1566) was entrusted to the Carthusians, who were also given the monastery built in the baths. After additional chapels had been built in the church during the first half of the eighteenth century, the monks asked (1749) *Luigi Vanvitelli* to bring some unity and harmony to the building's interior. This he did, but he changed the orientation of the church, transforming Michelangelo's nave into the present transept. Vanvitelli likewise placed the entrance where it is today. The Carthusians remained here until 1873; the monastery subsequently became the home of a museum.

Exterior. The church does not have a proper facade. Vanvitelli's facade was demolished in 1912, and what we see is the original brick wall of a niche of the *calidarium*, with two doorways. The church's full name is "St. Mary of the Angels and Martyrs."

Interior. The church is in the shape of a Greek cross, with a transept disproportionately longer than the nave. To advance into the nave one first passes through a vestibule.

(1) The circular vestibule has two altars and several funerary monuments. The monument immediately to the right of the entrance is to *Carlo Maratta* (1625–1713), who was, in his day, the most successful painter in Rome. The artist's bust (1704–1708) is by his brother *Francesco*. The Latin inscription at the top says: "I believe I will see the good things of the Lord in the land of the living."

The altar to the left has "Christ on the Cross," thought to be the work of a certain *Giacomo Rocca*. Immediately to the altar's left is the tomb of the sculptor *Pietro Tenerani* (1789–1869); the bust is a self-portrait. Left of the chapel is the tomb of Cardinal Francesco Alciati (d. 1580), a famous jurist; his epitaph translates: "He lived in virtue, he lives in memory, he will live in glory."

(2) The altar has as an altarpiece *Hendrick van der Broeck*'s "The Risen Christ Appears to Mary Magdalene" (ca. 1579), one of the artist's more important paintings. The tomb on the left, near the entrance, is that of the Neapolitan painter and poet *Salvator Rosa* (1615–1673). The monument was erected by his son, Augusto, who, in the epitaph, describes his father as "Second to no painter of his time, and equal to the princes of poets of all time." The artist's bust is by *Bernardo Fioriti*. On the chapel's right is the tomb of Cardinal Pietro Paolo Parisi (d. 1545), with the epitaph: "The body turns to earth, fame is flitting, the spirit reaches the heavens."

(3) **St. Bruno** (d. 1101) was the founder of the Carthusians, and his statue (1766–1767) by *Jean-Antoine Houdon* was done during the sculptor's stay in Rome. This statue helped establish Houdon's reputation. Near the niche is an attractive angel (holy water font) from the first part of the eighteenth century by *Giovanni Battista Rossi*. The matching angel is a modern imitation.

The chapel to the right has a painting of St. Bruno by an anonymous seventeenth-century artist. The chapel opposite is dedicated to St. Peter; the altarpiece is *Girolamo Muziano*'s "Christ Gives the Keys to St. Peter." The walls have "St. Peter Being Freed from Prison" (left) and "Sts. Peter and Paul" (right), both by *M. Carloni*. On the arch above, facing the transept, is *Francesco Trevisani*'s large oval painting "Expulsion of Adam and Eve."

(4) It is on entering the **transept** that we experience the vastness of the building (298 feet long, 88 feet wide, and 92 feet high), and appreciate the grandeur that once was classical Rome. When Michelangelo converted this central hall into a church, he followed the lines of the original building. The transept is filled with light and the colors of red (pilasters [cottanello marble at the ends of the transepts, others are painted to simulate it]) and white (capitals and magnificent cornices) predominate. The eight massive monolithic columns of red granite (45 feet high and 5 feet 3 inches in diameter) supporting the vault are from the original building, while the other columns (four near the vestibule area and four in the area leading to the presbytery) are painted brick and were added by Vanvitelli to create a unified building. Michelangelo raised the level of the floor about six feet and, thus, portions of the bases of the eight original columns are below the level of the pavement, which is from the time of Gregory XIII (1572–1585).

In the pavement, beginning in the right corner of the right transept, is the *Linea Clementina*, a meridian line which Clement XI (1700–1721) had asked the astronomers Francesco Bianchini and Giacomo Maraldi to install (1702). The line is a brass strip imbedded in the pavement, and when the sun's rays enter through a small opening in the coat of arms above the right edge of the arch in the right transept (note how the cornice has been cut to permit the sun's rays to enter), they mark noon. Along the side of the brass strip are marble inlays depicting the signs of the zodiac. From the time of its installation to 1846, clocks in Rome were regulated by this meridian; since that time a cannon shot from the Janiculum Hill announces noon.

(5) The transept walls have eight large paintings, placed here by Vanvitelli. Most of these came (1727 and later) from St. Peter's, after they had been replaced by mosaic copies. The two paintings on the right wall are "Fall of Simon Magus" (left), by *Pierre-Charles Tremollière*, and "Crucifixion of Peter" (right), by *Niccolò Ricciolini*. Above, on either side of the windows, are paintings by Trevisani, used as cartoons for mosaics in the baptistery area in St. Peter's.

(6) The altar with its trompe l'oeil architectural effects is dedicated to Blessed Nicholas Albergati (1375–1443), Carthusian cardinal. After Nicholas was beatified in 1744, the Carthusians had *Clemente Orlandi* erect (1746) an altar to his honor; it is an exact copy of the altar in the left transept. *Ercole Graziani*'s painting on the altar depicts a miracle (1435) in which Blessed Nicholas changes white bread into dark bread (and vice-versa) in the presence of Duke Philip of Burgundy. Popes Martin V (1417–1431) and Eugene IV (1431–1447) had several times sent the cardinal as their special legate to European rulers. The side walls have paintings by Trevisani relating to baptism; on the left is 'Baptism of Water" and on the right "Baptism of Desire." These were models for the mosaics in the cupola near the baptistery in St. Peter's. The vault has Doctors of the Church.

On the walls beneath the paintings are tombs of two Italian heroes. On the left is the tomb of Grand Admiral Paolo Thaon di Revel (1859–1948), commander-in-chief of the Allied forces in the Adriatic (1917–1918), and on the right that of Vittorio Emanuele Orlando (1860–1952), outstanding jurist and minister of state. Both tombs are by *Pietro Canonica*.

(7) The paintings on the wall are Muziano's "Preaching of St. Jerome" (left) and next to it "A Miracle of St. Peter," by *Francesco Mancini*. Below is the tomb of Armando Diaz (1861–1928), marshall of Italy and commander-in-chief during World War I. The tomb is by *Antonio Muñoz*.

(8) The altar on the right has the altarpiece "Virgin and Child with Sts. Raymond and Hyacinth" (1610), by *Giovanni Baglione*. The side walls have "Sts. Cecilia and Valerian Receive Crowns from an Angel" (left) and

"St. Francis Receives the Stigmata" (right), likewise by Baglione. The chapel on the left has "Incarnation of Jesus" on the altar, with "Pope at Prayer" (left) and "Souls of Purgatory" (right) on the sides. The artists are unknown.

(9) Vanvitelli extended the apse to compensate for the shortness of the nave. The presbytery has more large paintings, originally from St. Peter's. From left to right: "Punishment of Ananias and Saphira," painted (1601–1606) on slate by *Cristoforo Roncalli;* "Baptism of Jesus" (1696–1698) by Maratta, one of his most famous works; "Martyrdom of St. Sebastian" (1629), a fresco by *Domenichino;* "Presentation of Mary in the Temple" (1639–1642), by *Giovanni Francesco Romanelli.* The vault frescoes are by *Daniel Seiter.*

The main altar dates from about 1762. The painting on the apse wall is of "St. Mary of the Angels" by an anonymous Venetian artist. It was commissioned in 1543 by Antonio Del Duca, the Sicilian priest who promoted the church's construction. He died in 1564 and was buried in the presbytery; his remains are now in the right wall, beneath the paintings. A marble tablet marks the place.

In the curve of the apse, on the left, is the tomb of Pius IV (d. 1565), who ordered the church's construction; his remains were brought here in 1583. On the right is the tomb of his nephew, Cardinal Giovanni Antonio Serbelloni (d. 1591); the nephew's tomb is a copy of that of his uncle.

(10) The paintings on the right wall of the left transept: on the left is *Placido Costanzi's* "St. Peter Raises Tabitha" and on the right "Immaculate Conception with Saints" (ca. 1735), by *Pietro Bianchi.*

(11) The altar in the left transept with its trompe l'oeil effects is said to have been designed by Maratta in 1698 and is dedicated to St. Bruno. The altar has *Giovanni Odazzi's* graceful fresco (ca. 1700) of "Virgin with Sts. Bruno and Peter." The statues (1874–1875) of Meditation (left) and Prayer (right) are by *Francesco Fabi-Altini* and are copies of his statues at the entrance to Campo Verano cemetery. The paintings on the side walls are by Trevisani and depict "Baptism of Blood"; these too were models for mosaics in the cupola near the baptistery in St. Peter's. The vault frescoes (ca. 1700) are by *Andrea Procaccini* and depict the evangelists.

(12) The paintings on the wall are "Fall of Simon Magus" (1760–1761), by *Pompeo Batoni* and "Mass of St. Basil" (1749), by *Pierre Subleyras.*

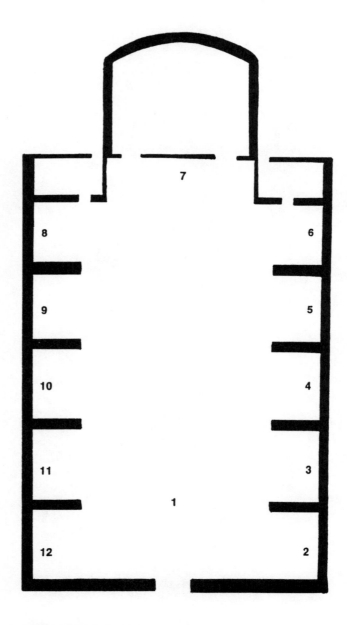

S. Maria della Concezione

31 S. Maria della Concezione*
Via Vittorio Veneto

History. The church is dedicated to Our Lady of the Immaculate Conception, but is more commonly known as *I Cappuccini*, the church of the Capuchin friars, a branch of the Franciscan order. The church's founder was Cardinal Antonio Barberini (1569–1646), a Capuchin since 1592. He built (1626–1630) the church as well as a convent next to it, but the convent had to yield (1886) to the new Via Veneto. On 4 October 1626, the cardinal's elder brother, Pope Urban VIII (1621–1644), laid the first stone and dedicated the church. The architects were *Antonio Casoni* and the Capuchin friar *Michele da Bergamo*.

Exterior. Two flights of stairs lead up to the church. The extraordinarily simple brick facade is of two orders; the lower has six pilasters forming five bays, with the doorway in the middle and small windows in the end bays. A cherub's head is in the tympanum over the door. The upper order has a window and the facade is surmounted by a triangular pediment. The coat of arms is that of the Capuchin order. On the first landing on the right is the entrance to the cemetery, discussed below.

Interior. (1) The church's interior is restrained baroque, with ornamentation at a minimum. It has a wide nave with five interconnecting chapels on the sides. The vault has *Liborio Coccetti's* fresco (1796) of the "Assumption."

(2) *Guido Reni's* St. Michael (1635) is the altarpiece. During Victorian times this painting was so popular that every English visitor to Rome felt that he or she could not leave the city without seeing it. On the left is *Gerrit van Honthorst's* Caravaggesque "Mocking of Christ," transferred here from the old convent.

(3) The altar has *Mario Balassi's* "Transfiguration." On the left is a "Nativity" attributed to *Giovanni Lanfranco*. Since this is a Capuchin church, many of the walls of the side altars have paintings of Capuchin saints; on the right is Blessed Bernard of Corleone (1605–1667) by Fra *Luigi da Crema*.

(4) The altar's "St. Francis in Ecstasy" (1635), by *Domenichino*, was the artist's personal gift to the church. Another "St. Francis in Ecstasy" is on the left wall, a fresco, also by Domenichino, originally in the cloister of the old convent. On the right is "St. Crispin of Viterbo Converses with Theologians," by Fra Luigi da Crema. St. Crispin (1668–1750) lived and died in the convent; he was canonized in 1982.

(5) *Baccio Ciarpi*'s "Christ in the Garden of Gethsemane" (1631–1632) is over the altar, and Fra *Herzog*'s painting of Christ giving a crown of thorns to St. Veronica Giuliani (1660–1727) is on the right wall. The painting dates from 1839, the year of the saint's canonization.

(6) The altar's painting (1640) is *Andrea Sacchi*'s "St. Anthony Raises a Dead Man to Life." The left wall has an eighteenth-century depiction, by an unidentified artist, of a Capuchin monk (perhaps St. Seraphim of Montegranaro [1540–1604]) in heaven, and on the right, also by an unknown artist, is St. Fidelis of Sigmaringen (1578–1622). The sculptor *Camillo Rusconi* (1658–1728) is buried in front of the altar. The door in the left wall leads to a private chapel, built for Urban VIII and later restored by Queen Margaret of Savoy (1851–1925), who used to attend Mass here. Further on are the reconstructed cells of Sts. Felix of Cantalice (see #11) and Crispin of Viterbo.

(7) The main altar is the only altar in the church that is totally of marble. It was the gift of Urban VIII; the pope celebrated the first Mass here on 8 September 1630. The Barberini coat of arms, with its three bees, is at the base of the columns. The polychrome marble used here came from old St. Peter's. The nineteenth-century painting of the "Immaculate Conception" over the altar is by *Gioacchino Bombelli*; the altar originally had one by Lanfranco, but it suffered damage in a fire (1813) during the French occupation of Rome. This is a reasonable copy of the original. The choir, reserved for the friars, is behind the main altar; paintings hang on the walls.

In the pavement, directly in front of the presbytery, is a tombstone that bears neither name nor date, but merely "Hic iacet pulvis, cinis et nihil," ("Here lie dust, ashes and nothing"). This is the tomb of the church's founder, Cardinal Barberini. On the pilaster to the left of the main altar is the tomb of Prince Alexander Sobieski, son of John III, king of Poland, liberator of Vienna. The prince died in Rome in 1714; the monument is by Rusconi.

(8) Sacchi's painting of "St. Bonaventure Venerates the Virgin and Child" (1645) is the altarpiece. The painting on the left by Fra *Raffaele da Roma* represents St. Joseph of Leonessa (1556–1612), and that on the right, by *Sebastiano Conca*, has Christ giving Communion to St. Lawrence of Brindisi (1559–1619).

(9) The altar has a nineteenth-century painting of "Our Lady of Hope" by an unidentified artist.

(10) "Deposition from the Cross" (1635), by *Andrea Camassei*, is the altarpiece. The left wall has "St. Francis Receives the Stigmata," attributed to *Girolamo Muziano*. On the right is the tomb of Cardinal Gabriele Ferretti (1795–1860).

(11) The chapel is dedicated to St. Felix of Cantalice (1515–1587), a Capuchin brother, who lived and died in the monastery. He was the first Capuchin to be canonized (1712). The saint's body is beneath the altar in an ancient Roman sarcophagus. The painting (1635) on the altar, showing the saint receiving the Christ Child from the Virgin, is by *Alessandro Turchi*. The other paintings represent two of the saint's miracles; on the left he restores sight to a child, and on the right he heals a paralytic. The painting on the left is by Fra Luigi da Crema, and that on the right by Fra *Simplicio da Verona*.

(12) The altar has one of *Pietro da Cortona*'s great paintings (1631), "Ananias Restores St. Paul's Sight." On the right is a wooden crucifix.

Cemetery. When the Capuchins moved from their convent near the Quirinal to their new home, they brought the bones of some four thousand of their brethren with them. It is impossible to give a precise date when these rooms were arranged as they now appear, but it is thought that it was toward the end of the eighteenth century. The first explicit reference to such a cemetery is in July 1818, when a certain Captain Spencer, together with some English gentlemen, received permission from the pope to visit it.

The cemetery is located directly beneath the chapels on the right side of the church. Off a long corridor there are six alcoves or rooms. Five have bones arranged in a variety of patterns on walls and ceiling; there are also skeletons clad in Capuchin robes. The second alcove is a chapel in whose lunette is Our Lady of Mercy together with Sts. Felix of Cantalice, Francis of Assisi, and Anthony of Padua, all helping the souls in purgatory. Two of the chapels have soil from the Holy Land.

When the monks arranged these rooms they did not do it as a macabre tourist attraction, but wanted the visitor to recall the transitory nature of human life and to reflect on death, a reality that we all must experience. The sign in the final alcove tells it as it is: "You are what we once were; you will be what we now are."

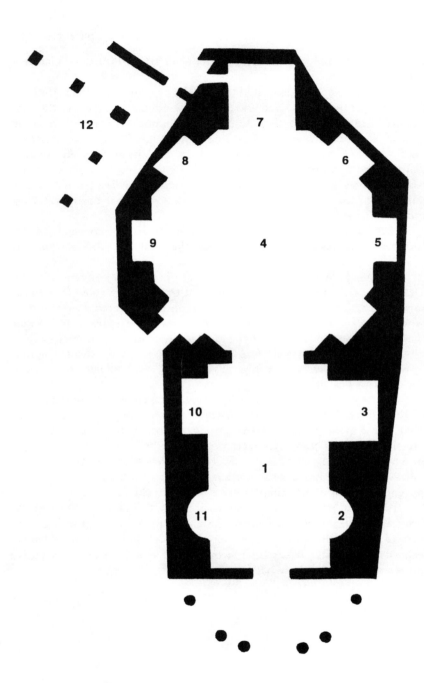

S. Maria della Pace

32 S. Maria della Pace***

Via della Pace

History. The church dates from the time of Sixtus IV (1471–1484) and is usually attributed to the architect *Baccio Pontelli*. It was built (1480–1483) on the site of a twelfth-century church, which was first dedicated to S. Andrea de Aquaricariis or "St. Andrew of the Water-vendors," and later (1192) renamed S. Maria de Aquaricariis. The octagonal cupola was constructed in 1524 by *Iacopo Ungarino*, after designs by *Antonio da Sangallo the Younger*. *Carlo Maderno* added (1611–1614) the presbytery area and Alexander VII (1655–1667) restored the church and gave it a new facade.

Exterior. The slightly convex baroque facade, the creation (1656) of *Pietro da Cortona*, is preceded by a semicircular pronaos, with six Doric columns. This replaces Pontelli's rectangular portico. The inscription is from Psalm 72:3 and translates: "The mountains shall yield peace for the people, and the hills justice." The vertical lines of the columns of the pronaos are repeated in the columns and pilasters of the facade's upper order. A large window is in the center and the entire facade is surmounted by a double pediment: segmental within triangular. The coat of arms of Alexander VII is now beyond recognition. The facade is flanked by two concave wings; the left has a medallion of Alexander VII, and the right of Sixtus IV. The doorway leading into the church dates from the time of Sixtus IV; his coat of arms is over the door, and the inscription translates: "This temple [is] dedicated to the Virgin of Peace by Pope Sixtus IV." In the tympanum above is the coat of arms of Alexander VII. If closed, enter at number 5, Vicolo del Arco della Pace, on the church's left.

Interior. (1) The church has a rectangular nave with four side altars and an octagonal area (serving as a transept) with four additional altars, and a presbytery. The pavement (1656) is from the time of Alexander VII's restorations; his heraldic charges (mountains and star) are used as decorative devices.

(2) The altar's expressive bronze relief, "Angels Support the Dead Savior" (1656), is by *Cosimo Fancelli*, who also did the statue of St. Catherine of Siena (right). That of St. Bernardine of Siena (left) is by *Ercole Ferrata*. The putti on the sides, holding instruments of the passion, are likewise by Ferrata (left) and Fancelli (right). On the outside arch, above the altar,

211

but below the cornice, is *Raphael's* **fresco** (1514) of four sibyls (left to right: Cumaean, Persian, Phrygian, and Tiburtine), who are shown writing down revelations given them by angels. The coat of arms on the cornice is that of Agostino Chigi (ca. 1465–1520), the wealthy Sienese banker, the chapel's founder. The lunette next to the window above has four prophets: Habakkuk and Jonah (left), David and Daniel (right). Their names appear beneath; the figures (1514–1515) are by Raphael's disciple *Timoteo Viti*.

(3) The chapel, designed by Antonio da Sangallo the Younger, has an overly ornate but excellently worked Renaissance front, the agreed masterpiece of *Simone Mosca*. The statues of Sts. Peter (left) and Paul (right), and the relief of the prophets and angels above are by *Vincenzo De Rossi*. Above is a fresco by *Filippo Lauri* depicting Adam and Eve. The Cesi family coat of arms is on the arch. Next to the altar are the tombs, supported by sphinxes, of Angelo Cesi (left) and Franceschina Cardoli Cesi (right), parents of Cardinal Federico Cesi (1500–1565). The figures on the tombs are also by De Rossi. The altar has "Holy Family with St. Ann" (ca. 1660), by *Carlo Cesi*.

(4) This area is octagonally shaped and the walls have four large canvases with scenes from the life of the Virgin. Left to right: "Death of the Virgin," by *Giovanni Maria Morandi*; "Nativity of the Virgin," by *Raffaele Vanni*; a rather crowded "Presentation of Mary in the Temple" (ca. 1516), by *Baldassarre Peruzzi*, and a charming "Visitation" (ca. 1655), by *Carlo Maratta*. The cupola has stucco decorations with hexagonal designs. In the lantern is *Francesco Cozza's* "Eternal Father."

(5) The altar has a mediocre painting of "Savior appears to St. Margaret Mary."

(6) Orazio Gentileschi's "Baptism of Christ" is the altarpiece; he likewise did the three frescoes in the vault with scenes from the Baptist's life. The attractive paintings on the sides are by *Bernardino Mei*; on the left is "Arrest of John the Baptist" and on the right "John the Baptist before Herod."

(7) The presbytery and main altar were designed by Maderno. The fifteenth-century image of Our Lady of Peace was originally under the portico of the earlier church. When struck by a ball during a game, or by an angry player, the image is said to have bled. Sixtus IV came to the church and promised to build a new one, if peace were restored to Italy. The papal war with Florence ended in 1480 and the Turks left Otranto in 1482; hence Sixtus' new church was named S. Maria della Pace and the image was placed on its main altar. Columns of verde antico marble flank the image and support a pediment on which Justice (left) and Peace (right) recline; these statues (1614) are by *Stefano Maderno*. The vault's "Assumption" (1612–1614) and the lunette over the altar, "Allegory of

Justice and Peace," are by *Francesco Albani.* The left wall has *Passignano's* "Annunciation"; his "Nativity of Mary" is on the right. Both are from 1611–1612. The pilaster on the left has St. Catherine of Siena (bottom) and St. Cecilia (top); the right pilaster has St. Agnes (top) and St. Clare (bottom). These four panels are by *Lavinia Fontana.* Albani also did the David and Isaiah on the outside arch.

(8) A fifteenth-century crucifix is over the Renaissance altar (1490); it was given the church by Innocent VIII (1484–1492). The altar is attributed to *Pasquale da Caravaggio;* Innocent's coat of arms is at its base. The frescoes in the vault, "Descent from Cross" (left) and "Burial of Christ" (right) are by an unidentified artist. The paintings on the altar's sides represent the two Marys who came to the tomb to anoint the dead Savior; the one on the left is surely Mary Magdalene.

(9) The altar has *Sermoneta's* "Nativity"; his are also the frescoes of Adam and Eve in the vault. The St. Sebastian on the altar's right is by an unidentified artist, as is the unidentifiable saint on the left.

(10) *Marcello Venusti's* painting of "Virgin with Sts. Ubaldo and Jerome" is over the altar. Next to the window, scenes with Adam and Eve, similar to those over the opposite chapel; here Adam and Eve are expelled from paradise (left) and shown with their children Cain and Abel (right).

(11) The altarpiece is Peruzzi's "Virgin with Sts. Brigid and Catherine of Alexandria" and includes the kneeling Cardinal Ferdinando Ponzetti (d. 1527), the chapel's donor. Peruzzi likewise did (1516–1517) the New and Old Testament scenes in the half-dome. The large Old Testament figures above the altar are also his. Outside the arch are monuments (1505 and 1509) of members of the Ponzetti family. The one on the right is in memory of the children Beatrice and Lavinia, six and eight years old, who died on the same day in 1505 as a result of the plague.

(12) The two-story cloister is thought to be *Donato Bramante's* earliest work in Rome. It was commissioned by the Neapolitan Cardinal Oliviero Carafa (1430–1511), and appears today as it was when completed. The lower level has arcades formed by pilasters with Ionic capitals, while the upper has columns (rising from the center of the arches below) alternating with pilasters. An inscription on the cloister's four sides tells us that the convent was built in honor of the Virgin of Peace, that canons of the Lateran lived there, that it was erected by Cardinal Carafa, and that it was completed in 1504. Under the portico, on the wall opposite the street entrance, is the Renaissance tomb of Bishop Giovanni Andrea Bocciacci of Modena (d. 1495). The tomb (1497) is by followers of *Luigi Capponi.*

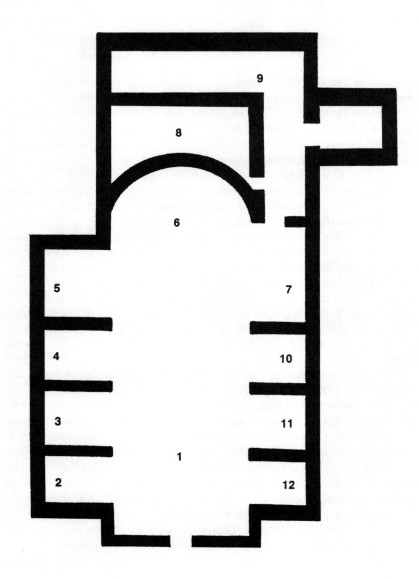

S. Maria della Vittoria

33   S. Maria della Vittoria***

Via XX Settembre

History. The church of St. Mary of Victory was built (1608–1620) by *Carlo Maderno* during the pontificate of Paul V (1605–1621). The church was first dedicated to St. Paul, since it replaced a small chapel to that saint on the site. In 1622, when the church received a miraculous image of the Virgin, its name was changed.

On 8 November 1620, the Catholic army of Maximilian I, Duke of Bavaria, won an astonishing victory over the Protestant forces of Frederick V of Saxony in the Battle of White Mountain near Prague, during the Thirty Years' War. A short time before, the Carmelite priest Dominic of Jesus and Mary (1559–1630), who was with the army as chaplain, found an image of our Lady in the ruins of the castle of Strakonitz. When time came for battle, he placed the image about his neck and accompanied the soldiers to the field. The Catholic forces were outnumbered four to one, but after an hour of fighting they were victorious. When Maximilian sent word to Paul V announcing victory, he wrote: "I came, I saw, but it is God who is the victor." The image of our Lady was then brought to Rome and on 8 May 1622 Gregory XV (1621–1623) gave it to this recently built church and renamed it St. Mary of Victory.

Exterior. The facade (1624–1626) is by *Giovanni Battista Soria,* and is of two orders; the lower has a handsome portal with a niche on either side, while the upper has a large window over a segmental pediment. The coat of arms of Cardinal Scipione Borghese (1576–1633) is in the tympanum, and the cardinal's insignia (eagle and winged dragon) are on the side scrolls. The facade was the cardinal's gift to the Carmelites in exchange for the Greek statue of the *Sleeping Hermaphrodite,* discovered when the church's foundations were being dug. The statue is now in the Louvre in Paris.

Interior. (1) The church has a nave with three lateral altars on each side, a transept, an apse, and a dome. This is one of the more richly decorated baroque churches in the city. The decorations date from the early part of the eighteenth century; the pilasters were covered with marble in 1705–1714, and there is much gilded stucco work. The cornice is especially elegant. The vault in the nave has "Triumph of Mary over Heresy," a fresco (ca. 1663) by *Gian Domenico Cerrini.* The pendentives, as well

215

as the cupola with its "Assumption," are also by Cerrini. The rich decorations of the choir gallery over the main entrance are by one of *Gian Lorenzo Bernini's* students.

(2) "Martyrdom of St. Andrew" on the altar is by an anonymous artist.

(3) The altarpiece of "Jesus Appears to St. John of the Cross" is by *Nicolas de Bar*, as are the two panels on the walls, depicting episodes in the saint's life. St. John of the Cross (1542–1591) was a Spanish mystic and one of the founders of the Discalced Carmelite reform.

(4) *Guercino's* "Most Holy Trinity" is over the altar; on the right is the tomb of Cardinal Berlinghiero Gessi (d. 1639), one of Galileo's judges. The cardinal's portrait above the tomb is by *Guido Reni*.

(5) The Cornaro Chapel is in the left transept. Bernini designed and executed it (1647–1652) at the request of Cardinal Federico Cornaro [Cornèr] (1579–1653), who wanted it as a funerary chapel. Bernini created an exceptionally beautiful altar with africano columns and behind them he placed his masterpiece, **"St. Teresa in Ecstasy,"** as in a frame. His genius, which set him above the artists of his time, lies in his ability to portray in stone the supreme moment of emotion, and here, in particular, that of ecstatic rapture.

St. Teresa (1515–1582) was a Carmelite nun and mystic, and Bernini depicts an episode in her life (ca. 1559), which she describes in her autobiography. She wrote that an angel was near her holding a golden spear, whose tip was on fire. "He seemed to pierce my heart several times. . . . So intense was the pain that I uttered several moans; so great was the sweetness caused by the pain that one never wants to lose it. Nor will anyone be satisfied with anything less than God. It is not a bodily pain, but spiritual . . ." (*Life*, chap. 29). Though the statue is of marble, the viewer sees a saint who is weightless, passively accepting and enjoying the divine intrusion into her soul. The angel's smile is his happiness in being God's instrument in bringing so inestimable a grace to a chosen one.

On both side walls of the chapel are marble portraits of members of the Cornaro family; they appear to be discussing the miracle of which they are witnesses. Cardinal Federico is said to be second from the right on the right side, looking into the body of the church. The other figures, all deceased at the time that the chapel was erected, include the cardinal's father, Giovanni Cornèr (1551–1629), doge of Venice, and six members of the family who had been cardinals. These figures are by Bernini's students. Cardinal Federico is buried in the chapel.

(6) The miraculous tiny image of our Lady, brought from Bohemia, was placed on the main altar and remained here until the night of 29 June 1833, when the altar and apse were destroyed by fire. These were rebuilt

in 1880 through the munificence of Prince Alessandro Torlonia (1800–1886). A copy of the original image is now on the altar, set within a large, overwhelming sunburst arrangement. Since the apse fresco was also destroyed, *Luigi Serra* replaced (1885) it. It depicts the "Victorious Catholic Army Entering Prague"; Fr. Dominic, on a white horse, carries the holy image.

(7) The chapel in the right transept was designed to match the chapel opposite. The architectural structure is the same, but the altar has the marble group "St. Joseph's Dream," by *Domenico Guidi*. It is well done but lacks Bernini's extra virtuosity. On the left wall is a relief of "Nativity of Jesus" and on the right "Flight into Egypt" (1699), both by *Étienne Monnot*. Under the altar is St. Victora, martyred during the persecution of Diocletian (emperor 284–305). Her relics were brought here in the nineteenth century.

(8) In the choir: in the center is "St. Paul Raised to the Third Heaven," by the Dutch artist *Gerrit van Honthorst*.

(9) The sacristy has four large paintings, by an unidentified artist, depicting four phases of the Battle of White Mountain. There is a full portrait of Fr. Dominic, as well as *Sebastiano Conca*'s "Duke Maximilian Gives a Horse to Fr. Dominic." In Conca's painting, Fr. Dominic has the image of the Madonna about his neck; presumably, the scene is shortly before the battle. In the glass enclosed cases are several military standards, captured during various battles and given to the church by the victors.

(10) The marble group on the altar is "Our Lady Gives the Scapular to St. Simon Stock," by the nineteenth-century sculptor *Alfonso Balzico*.

(11) The altar has the painting of "Our Lady Offers the Child to St. Francis." On the side walls are frescoes: "St. Francis Receives the Stigmata" (left) and "St. Francis in Ecstasy" (right). These were *Domenichino*'s last Roman works.

(12) The painting (1926) of St. Thérèse of the Child Jesus (1873–1897) is by *G. Szoldatics*. St. Thérèse was canonized in 1925.

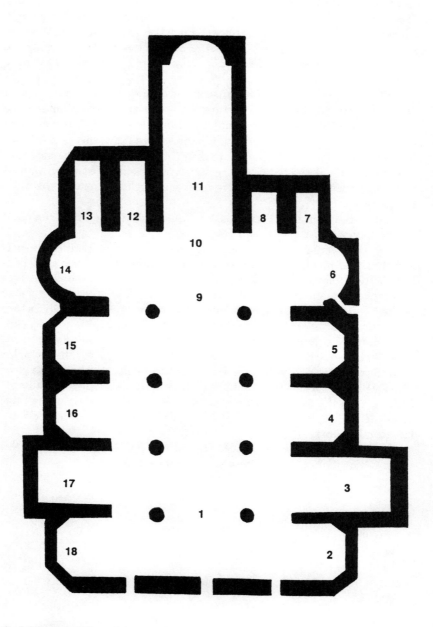

S. Maria del Popolo

34   S. Maria del Popolo***

Piazza del Popolo

History. In 1099 Pope Paschal II (1099–1118) built an oratory over the tombs of the Domitia, an ancient Roman family, at the foot of the Pincian Hill. Nero (emperor 54–68) had been buried here, after having committed suicide, and the Romans, during Paschal's time, believed that Nero's restless spirit haunted the area and that the crows inhabiting a huge oak tree nearby were his demon servants. To show the absurdity of this belief, Paschal himself cut down the tree, scattered Nero's ashes, and had an oratory erected; he dedicated it to the Virgin Mary. The oratory was rebuilt ca. 1230 by Gregory IX (1227–1241), and it was replaced by Sixtus IV (1471–1484). The present church, built between 1472 and 1477, has been attributed to *Baccio Pontelli*. When Martin Luther (1483–1546) visited Rome (1511) he stayed in the Augustinian monastery attached to the church; that monastery was destroyed during the Sack of Rome (1527). The church derives its name "del popolo" from the fact that it was a parish church, that is, for the people living in the vicinity.

Exterior. The travertine facade, recently cleaned, is remarkably simple; a good example of an early Renaissance facade. There are three doorways; the central door has a tympanum with an image of the Virgin, while the other two have large windows above them. Both side doors bear the name of Sixtus IV and 1477, the year when the facade was completed. The addition (1818–1821) on the church's right is by *Giuseppe Valadier*.

Interior. (1) The church is built in the form of a Latin cross, with nave and two aisles and lateral altars. Julius II (1503–1513) had *Donato Bramante* extend the apse, and Alexander VII (1655–1667) had *Gian Lorenzo Bernini* add (1655–1660) the baroque decorations to the interior. Bernini's hand is seen in the cornice above the arches, in the figures reclining on it, and in the transept where angels support the organ lofts. The pavement includes tombstones, both medieval and Renaissance; after centuries of wear many are beyond recognition.

(2) Della Rovere Chapel. The altar has a delightful fresco (1485–1489) by *Pinturicchio* depicting the nativity. The four lunettes have fading frescoes with scenes from the life of St. Jerome; in these Pinturicchio had the assistance of *Tiberio d'Assisi*. On the left is the Renaissance tomb that Cardinal Domenico Della Rovere (d. 1501) had erected for his brother,

Cardinal Cristoforo (d. 1478), and in which he too was buried. Both were nephews of Sixtus IV. The tomb may be the work of *Andrea Bregno;* the Virgin in the lunette is by *Mino da Fiesole.* On the opposite wall is the tomb of Cardinal Giovanni De Castro (d. 1506), perhaps by *Antonio da Sangallo the Younger;* it was originally located elsewhere in the church. The emblem of the Della Rovere family was the oak tree; this is conspicuously visible in the balustrade and in other places in the church.

(3) Cybo Chapel. This is among the more handsome chapels in the city; its architectural design, the form of a Greek cross, is due to *Carlo Fontana.* The chapel was built (1682–1687) with rich and variously colored marbles that produce a harmonious effect. The sixteen columns are of Sicilian jasper. The altarpiece (ca. 1686), "Immaculate Conception with Saints" (John the Evangelist, Gregory the Great, John Chrysostom, and Augustine), is by *Carlo Maratta.* On the sides are the twin tombs of the Cybo cardinals; that of Lorenzo (d. 1503) on the left, done in 1683, and of Alderano (d. 1700) on the right, done in 1684. The busts are by *Francesco Cavallini.* The dome has "Eternal Father in Glory," a fresco by *Luigi Garzi.* The paintings near the chapel's entrance depict the martyrdoms of St. Lawrence (left) and St. Catherine of Alexandria (right), by *Daniel Seiter.*

(4) The frescoes (1504–1507) in this Basso Della Rovere Chapel are by Pinturicchio's disciples. On the altar is "Virgin and Four Saints" with the Eternal Father above. The five lunettes in the vault have scenes from the life of the Virgin, and the left wall has a striking "Assumption." The pillars that frame the altar and windows are painted, and along the walls are four trompe l'oeil benches, whose backrests are in grisaille. The four scenes, left to right, represent: "Martyrdom of St. Peter," "St. Augustine in Dispute," "Martyrdom of St. Catherine," and "Martyrdom of St. Paul." On the right wall is the tomb of Giovanni Basso Della Rovere (d. 1483), brother-in-law of Sixtus IV, by a disciple of Bregno.

(5) The Renaissance altarpiece is a marble triptych (1489) of Sts. Catherine (center), Vincent the Deacon (left), and Anthony of Padua (right) by Bregno's disciples. The founder of this chapel was Cardinal Jorge da Costa (d. 1508) of Portugal; his tomb is on the left wall. On the right is the tomb of Marcantonio Albertoni (d. 1485) by *Iacopo d'Andrea.* The frescoes (1489) in the lunettes depict Doctors of the Church.

(6) The altar in the right transept was designed by Bernini and has *Giovanni Maria Morandi's* "Visitation" (1659). The painting stands in a marble frame held by two angels, the work of Bernini's students. On the right wall is the tomb of Cardinal Lodovico Podocataro of Cyprus (d. 1508); the lower portion has an interesting "Pietà."

(7) In this chapel, dedicated to St. Rita of Cascia, Juan, duke of

S. Maria del Popolo (G. Vasi, 1752)

Gandía, son of Alexander VI (1492–1503), was buried after he had been assassinated in Rome in June 1497. The duke's mother, Vannozza Catanei, was likewise buried here, but there is nothing to mark the spot. Above and between this and the next chapel is an organ loft supported by angels holding Alexander VII's coat of arms, which includes the Della Rovere oak tree. Bernini gave free reign to his baroque imagination—oak branches entwine about the organ pipes.

(8) The altarpiece depicts the Augustinian St. Thomas of Villanova (d. 1555), archbishop of Valencia. He was known for his charity toward the poor, and in this painting, by an unidentified artist, the saint is distributing alms.

(9) The dome is without a lantern, and has a fresco (1656–1658) of "Virgin in Glory" by *Raffaele Vanni*, in very poor condition. The pendentives are his and they depict four illustrious women of the Old Testament: Ruth, Judith, Esther, and Deborah.

(10) The main altar dates from 1627. The image of the Virgin, from the early thirteenth century, was brought here from the Lateran by Gregory IX, when he rebuilt the church ca. 1230. Above and below the image is the saying: "You are the honor of our people." The statues are of two Augustinian saints: Nicholas of Tolentino (1245–1305) on the left, and William of Maleval (d. 1157) on the right. The underarch has five gilded stucco panels depicting the church's legendary origins.

221

(11) The choir area behind the altar was extended (1505–1509) by Julius II, and contains masterworks. The two walls have almost identical tombs by *Andrea Sansovino;* on the left is the tomb of Cardinal Ascanio Sforza (d. 1505) and on the right that of Cardinal Girolamo Basso Della Rovere (d. 1507). It was Sansovino's genius that gave the tombs an architectural setting, a pattern that was followed in succeeding centuries. The cardinals rest in peaceful sleep, with heads supported by arm or hand.

The vault above has Pinturicchio's masterful **frescoes** (1508–1509): "Coronation of the Virgin" is in the center and is surrounded by four evangelists and four sibyls, with Doctors of the Church (Gregory, Ambrose, Augustine, Jerome) in the pendentives. The stained glass windows are likewise remarkable; they were commissioned by Julius II and done (1509) by *Guillaume de Marcillat.*

(12) *Caravaggio's* masterpieces are housed in this chapel. On the altar's left is **"Crucifixion of St. Peter"** and on the right **"Conversion of St. Paul."** Both were commissioned (1600) by Tiberio Cerasi (1544–1601) and were painted in 1601. The altarpiece is **"Assumption"** (1601), by *Annibale Carracci,* and is in superb color. Cerasi's monument is on the upper left wall, near the entrance to the chapel.

(13) The statue of St. Catherine of Alexandria on the altar is by *Giulio Mazzoni;* his Sts. Peter and Paul are on the sides as one enters the chapel. The walls have *Giacomo Triga's* "Annunciation," with the angel on the left and the Virgin on the right.

(14) *Bernardino Mei's* painting (1659) of the "Holy Family" is in the left transept, and the angels supporting it are by Bernini's students. On the left wall is the tomb of Cardinal Bernardino Lonati (d. 1497); not a successful piece.

(15) This chapel is dedicated to the crucifix. The frescoes (1635–1640) are the work of the Flemish artist, *Pieter van Lint;* the panels in the vault have angels with instruments of the passion, and prophets are in the lunettes. The large fresco on the left is "St. Helen Finds the True Cross," and on the right "Heraclius Returns the Cross to Jerusalem."

(16) This is the Mellini Chapel, with many funerary monuments. On the left is the very fine tomb of Cardinal Garzia Mellini (d. 1629), with a half-figure of the deceased by *Alessandro Algardi,* who also did the realistic busts of Urban (left) and Mario (right) Mellini on the altar's sides. On the lower portion of the right wall is the tomb with reclining figure of Cardinal Giovanni Battista Mellini (d. 1478); that of his brother Pietro (d. 1483) is nearer the altar below the tomb of Mario. The tomb of Cardinal Savio Mellini (d. 1701) is on the upper right wall. The painting of "Virgin with Sts. Augustine and Nicholas of Tolentino" is the work of *Agostino Masucci;* the frescoes in the vault are scenes from the life of St. Nicholas,

and the lunettes have the four cardinal virtues, by *Giovanni da San Giovanni*.

(17) The Chigi Chapel, the richest in the church, is named after its founder, Agostino Chigi (1465–1520), the renowned Sienese banker; it is octagonal in shape and was built (1513–1516) in accord with *Raphael's* designs. Raphael prepared the cartoons for the mosaics in the dome, which were then executed (1516) by another. These depict God as creator of the heavens, surrounded by the symbols of the planets, each of which is guided by an angel. The eight frescoes (ca. 1550) between the windows depict the Creation and Fall of Adam and Eve and are by *Francesco Salviati*, as are the Seasons in the pendentives. On the altar is "Nativity of the Virgin," by *Sebastiano del Piombo*, his last painting; the artist lived near here and is supposed to have been buried in this church. The altar frontal, "Christ and the Woman of Samaria," is by *Lorenzetto*.

To the left of the altar is a statue of the young Jonah (1520) and diagonally across the prophet Elijah (1530), both by Lorenzetto. The other two statues, Daniel (1655–1657) and Habakkuk (1655–1661) are by Bernini. According to Daniel 14:33-39, Habakkuk was about to take a basket of food to reapers in a field, but an angel appeared and commanded him to take it, instead, to the famished Daniel in the lions' den in Babylon. Bernini dramatizes Habakkuk's protest by having the prophet point in the direction to where he wants to go. The angel, on the other hand, takes him by the hair and points to where they are going, namely to Daniel (in the other niche). When the food arrives, Daniel gives thanks to God for having heard his prayer.

The pyramidal tombs of Agostino Chigi (d. 1520) and his brother Sigismondo (d. 1526) are on the chapel's sides. The portraits on the tombs are by Bernini. The figure of death in the pavement, with the Chigi coat of arms and the inscription "Death [is the way] to heaven," was added by Bernini.

Left of the Chigi Chapel is a curious and dreadfully over-done monument, erected in 1771, in memory of Princess Maria Flaminia Odescalchi, who died at age twenty, giving birth to her third child.

(18) The baptistery has "Baptism of Christ" by *Pasquale Posi*. On the altar's sides and placed within niches are two small fifteenth-century marble altars with friezes and saints, attributed to Bregno. On the left wall is the tomb of Cardinal Antoniotto Pallavinci (d. 1507) by a follower of Bregno, and on the right that of Cardinal Francesco Castiglione (d. 1568). Standing on the floor in the center is the sarcophagus of Bishop Gerolamo Foscari (d. 1463), attributed to *Lorenzo di Pietro*, commonly known as "il Vecchietta."

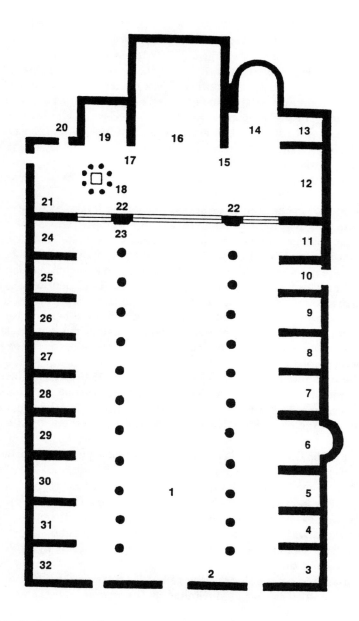

S. Maria in Aracoeli

35 S. Maria in Aracoeli***

Piazza d'Ara Coeli

History. The church is on the highest point of the Capitoline, one of Rome's seven hills, and may go as far back as the sixth century. The first monks to be associated with it were Greek, then the Benedictines in the ninth century; the Franciscans have been here since 1250, when it was given them by Innocent IV (1243–1254). The church was first called "S. Maria in Capitolio," and only about the thirteenth century did it become known as S. Maria in Aracoeli. It was the common belief during the Middle Ages that Augustus (emperor 27 B.C.–A.D. 14), on a visit to the Tiburtine Sibyl at the Temple of Juno Moneta, heard the prophecy: "Haec est ara primogeniti Dei," ("This is the altar of the first-born of God"). The emperor, the story continues, then erected an altar on the site to this deity. A church was subsequently built over the imperial altar and many years later it became known as *Ara coeli,* "altar of heaven." The legend is sometimes further embellished by adding that the Virgin and Child had also appeared to Augustus. When the Franciscans took over the church, they redid it in its present Romanesque form.

Exterior. If one does not feel sufficiently energetic to climb the 124 steps leading up to the church, there is a side entrance. The staircase was constructed (1348) by the Roman people in gratitude to God for the city's safety during the plague of 1346. The Roman tribune Cola di Rienzo (1313–1354) was the first to ascend it.

The church's thirteenth-century brick facade is unfinished. There are three doorways; the center one has an arch supported by corbels with carved hands. The side doorways have lunettes with sixteenth-century bas-reliefs: St. John (left) and St. Matthew (right). Small rose windows are above the side doors and a larger window above the main door. The upper portion of the facade once had a mosaic; remnants on the right side are visible from Piazza del Campidoglio. The inscription on the left of the main door commemorates the architect of the stairs, a certain Lorenzo Simeone Andreozzi. In front of the main doorway is the tombstone of the humanist Flavio Biondo (1392–1463).

The side entrance to the church, with a less taxing ascent, is up the ramp to the right of the stairs; pass the building on the left (Museo Capitolino) and then take a left up the stairs, then another left. This brings one to a hidden entrance built (1564) in the church's old Romanesque bell tower. The lunette above the door has a striking thirteenth-century mosaic of the Virgin and Child with angels, attributed to the Cosmati.

Interior. (1) The church is in the basilican style, with a wide central nave and two aisles separated by twenty-two varying columns taken from older Roman buildings. The third column from the rear, on the left, has, toward its top, *A Cubiculo Augustorum*, "from the room of the Augusti"; perhaps it did come from one of the imperial palaces. Above the columns are oval portraits of Franciscan saints; twelve female saints on the left and twelve male saints on the right. Above, on both sides of the nave, is a series of eighteenth-century frescoes of the life of the Virgin.

The coffered ceiling (1572–1585) commemorates the Christian victory (7 October 1571) over the Turks at Lepanto. The city of Rome provided the funds and hence its coat of arms (SPQR) is twice found on it. In the center is the Virgin; near the entrance is the coat of arms of Pius V (1566–1572), during whose pontificate it was begun, and near the altar that of Gregory XIII (1572–1585), during whose pontificate it was completed. The ceiling also has a variety of naval symbols. It was in this church that the papal admiral Marcantonio Colonna (1535–1584) held his triumph. The dedication inscription above the triumphal arch bears the date 1575.

Two altars stand in the nave; the one on the left has a fifteenth-century Sienese-school fresco of "Our Lady Refuge of Sinners," and the one opposite is dedicated to St. James Della Marca (1394–1476). The cosmatesque pavement is from the thirteenth century; marble slabs and tombstones are separated by strips of marble mosaics. At the foot of the fifth column on the left from the rear is the tombstone of a Franciscan friar, bearing the inscription: "Here lies the builder Aldo, who supervised the building of this church. May his soul rest in peace. Pray for him."

High on the rear wall is a large inscription (1634) honoring Urban VIII (1623–1644); *Gian Lorenzo Bernini* ingeniously made the window a part of Urban's coat of arms.

(2) Left of the main door is the handsome Renaissance tomb of Cardinal Louis d'Albret (d. 1465) by *Andrea Bregno*. A well-executed St. Michael is on the tomb's left, with St. Francis on the right. Above are St. Peter (left) and St. Paul (right). The tomb still has traces of gold. Imbedded in the pilaster on the left is *Donatello's* tombstone of Giovanni Crivelli (d. 1432), archdeacon of Aquileia. The stone was originally in the pavement in the left aisle, but was moved here in 1881. The inscription is almost totally worn away; left of the face, and still legible, are the words *opus Donatelli florentini*, "work of Donatello of Florence."

(3) Chapel of St. Bernardine of Siena. The chapel, dedicated to St. Bernardine (1380–1444), is one of the church's gems, and the frescoes (1485)

S. Maria in Aracoeli (G. B. Falda, 1665)

are among *Pinturicchio*'s masterpieces. During his lifetime, the saint reconciled the Bufalini and Baglione families, and in memory of the event, Niccolò Bufalini commissioned the artist to decorate his chapel with scenes from the saint's life. The back wall has "St. Bernardine in Glory"; the saint stands in the center with St. Louis of Toulouse (1274–1297) on the viewer's left, and St. Anthony of Padua (1195–1231) on the right. The Savior is in a mandorla above, surrounded by angels.

The left wall has "Burial of St. Bernardine." The saint died in Aquila on 20 May 1444, and was canonized in 1450. The gentleman on the far left, holding a candle, is N. Bufalini. The lunette above has "Young Bernardine at Prayer." The right wall has three frescoes: "St. Bernardine Receives the Habit," portraits of five unknown individuals, seemingly trying to look into the chapel, and "St. Francis Receives the Stigmata." The evangelists in the vault are probably by one of Pinturicchio's students. N. Bufalini (d. 1506) and other members of his family are buried here.

(4) The altar has *Marco da Siena*'s "Pietà"; on the left wall is *Cristoforo Roncalli*'s "Deposition from the Cross," and on the right his "Burial of Christ." Outside the chapel, to the left, a statue of Gregory XIII by *Pier Paolo Olivieri*, moved here from the Roman Senate in 1876.

(5) *Giovanni De Vecchi*'s St. Jerome is the altarpiece; the same artist did the frescoes with scenes from that saint's life in the vault. The left lunette depicts St. Jerome (ca. 340–420), while the one on the right has St. Bonaventure (1221–1274). The figures on the left wall are of Blessed

227

Alexander of Hales (ca. 1185–1245) and St. Anthony of Padua; those on the right Blessed Duns Scotus (ca. 1265–ca. 1308) and Blessed John of Parma (1209–1289). These four were eminent Franciscan theologians.

(6) The crucifix on the altar was carved (ca. 1690) by the Franciscan friar Vincenzo da Bassiano. The right wall has *Sermoneta's* "Transfiguration."

(7) The chapel is dedicated to St. Matthew. *Girolamo Muziano's* "St. Matthew and the Virgin" is over the altar; his "Martyrdom of St. Matthew" is on the left and "Miracle of St. Matthew" on the right. The floor is of inlaid marble, marking the places of burial of members of the Mattei family, donors of the chapel.

(8) On the altar is *Michel Maille's* statue of the Franciscan St. Peter of Alcántara (1499–1562) in ecstasy. He also did the angels holding portraits of Sts. Stephen (left) and Ranier (right). The sculptures are from 1682.

(9) S. Diego of Alcalá (ca. 1400–1463) was likewise a Franciscan and a painting of him by De Vecchi is on the altar. The paintings on the walls are by *Vespasiano Strada:* "St. Diego Changes Bread into Flowers" (left) and "St. Diego Cures a Possessed Person" (right).

(10) This is the vestibule for the side entrance. The sixteenth-century tomb on the left wall is that of Bishop Pietro Manzi of Cesena (d. 1504), and is by *Andrea Sansovino.* The tomb opposite is of the young Florentine Cecchino Bracci (d. 1544) who died in Rome at age sixteen; the tomb was designed by *Michelangelo* and executed by *Pietro Urbino;* the bust of the youth may be by *Raffaello da Montelupo.*

(11) The chapel is dedicated to another Franciscan, St. Paschal Baylon (1540–1592). The altarpiece is by *Vincenzo Vittoria;* the paintings on the walls are by *Daniel Seiter* and depict two of St. Paschal's miracles.

(12) St. Francis of Assisi (1182–1226) was the founder of the Friars Minor (Franciscans), and here are several paintings (1729) of him by *Francesco Trevisani.* "St. Francis in Ecstasy" is over the altar; on the left wall is "St. Francis Receives Papal Approval for his Order" and on the right "Innocent III's Dream."

Also on the left wall is the thirteenth-century **tomb of Luca Savelli** (d. 1266), Roman senator, nephew of Pope Honorius III (1216–1227), and father of Honorius IV (1285–1287). The tomb is attributed to *Arnolfo di Cambio* and Roman mosaicists. The lower portion is a third-century Roman sarcophagus with genii holding festoons of fruit. Resting on the sarcophagus is a casket, decorated with mosaics and bearing the Savelli coat of arms. In the pilaster to the tomb's left, a stone indicating where the bones of St. Francis' companion Brother Juniper (d. 1258) are preserved.

On the opposite wall is the thirteenth-century tomb of Luca's wife, Giovanna Aldobrandeschi, mother of Honorius IV. When Honorius died he was buried in old St. Peter's, but with the building of the new basilica, Paul III (1534–1549) had Honorius' remains placed (1545) with those of his mother and an effigy of the pope placed on top. The Aldobrandeschi coat of arms is in the center.

(13) This small chapel is dedicated to St. Rose of Viterbo (ca. 1233–ca. 1252) and has paintings depicting episodes from her life by *Pasqualino De Rossi.* High on the left wall is the thirteenth-century mosaic "Virgin and Child with Saints"; on the left St. Francis presents the donor to the Virgin, and on the right is St. John the Baptist.

(14) The chapel was originally dedicated to St. Francis Solano (1549–1610), but now a statue of the Virgin (Neapolitan school [1722]) is on the altar. The large lunette on the left wall, "Death of St. Francis Solano," is by *Antonio Gherardi.* The "Immaculate Conception" and the four tondi in the vault are by *Giuseppe Ghezzi.*

(15) The painting of St. Charles Borromeo is by an unidentified seventeenth-century artist.

(16) The main altar, as we see it today, is from 1723. The image of the Virgin is perhaps from the tenth century. The two statues flanking the altar are of Sts. Bernardine of Siena (left) and John Capistrano (right). The choir area dates from the time of Pius IV (1559–1565), who, unfortunately, had the original apse with *Pietro Cavallini*'s fresco demolished. The present frescoes are by *Nicolò Trometta;* in the center is "Virgin with Child and Angels," and on the sides "Augustus with the Sibyl" and "Nativity of Christ."

On the choir's left wall is the Renaissance tomb of Giovanni Battista Savelli (d. 1498), by the school of Andrea Bregno. His epitaph reads: "Twice elected to the cardinalate during changing and malevolent times." Paul II (1464–1471) first made him a cardinal, but the pope died before announcing it in a public consistory; Sixtus IV (1471–1484) then made him one in 1480. Also in the choir floor is a simple marker indicating the burial place of Sigismondo Conti (1432–1512), secretary of Julius II (1503–1513). It was Conti who commissioned *Raphael* to paint (1512) "Madonna of Foligno." That painting was here on the main altar until 1565, when an heir of his had it removed to Foligno. It is now in the Vatican. *Giulio Romano*'s "Holy Family" (presently in the sacristy) was then on the main altar until 1723, when the present Madonna was transferred here.

The outside arch has a sibyl in its left spandrel and Emperor Augustus in the other; in the center is a variation on the sibyl's prophetic words, "Haec est ara coeli" ("This is the altar of God").

(17) A seventeenth-century "Betrothal of Mary and Joseph" by an anonymous artist.

(18) The chapel of St. Helen (ca. 255–330), mother of Constantine (emperor 306–337), dates from the seventeenth century; it was severely damaged during the Napoleonic occupation of Rome (1798), and was reconstructed in the nineteenth century. Eight columns of giallo antico support a cupola, under which is a porphyry urn containing relics of St. Helen. The saint's statue is from 1972. Beneath the urn and lower down (visible from the side nearest the main altar), is the altar (*ara coeli*) that legend claims Emperor Augustus had constructed on this site.

(19) The altar has *Giacomo Semenza*'s "St. Gregory with the Virgin and St. Francis." Under the altar is the preserved body of Blessed John of Triora (1760–1816), Franciscan missionary martyred in China.

(20) This is the nineteenth-century Chapel of the Santo Bambino. The statue is of olive wood and is said to have been carved by a Franciscan monk in Jerusalem, toward the end of the fifteenth century, using wood from the garden of Gethsemane. The letters next to the statue come from various parts of the world, asking for blessings.

(21) The **Gothic tomb** of Cardinal Matteo d'Acquasparta (d. 1302) is by *Giovanni di Cosma*. The deceased became minister-general of the Franciscans in 1287 and the following year a cardinal. Dante refers to him in his *Paradiso* (canto 12, verse 124). The fresco of "Madonna with Child and Two Saints" is attributed to Cavallini; St. Matthew is on the left, and on the right St. Francis presents the cardinal to the Virgin. To the left is the statue of Leo X (1513–1521) by *Domenico Aimo*. The statue (ca. 1514) was moved here from the Roman Senate in 1876.

(22) The church originally had one twelfth-century pulpit by *Lorenzo di Cosma* and his son *Giacomo*; it had been dismantled and later made into two. The reconstruction is somewhat unfortunate; nevertheless, the artistic beauty of the Cosmati can still be appreciated in the individual parts. The pulpit on the right (as one faces the main altar) bears the signature "Lorenzo, with his son Giacomo, was the master of this work." This is found at very top of the vertical panel that faces the main altar. Over the steps leading to the other pulpit is the tombstone of Queen Catherine of Bosnia (d. 1478).

(23) The painting of St. John of Capistrano is by an unidentified artist.

(24) The altar painting of Our Lady of Loreto is by *Marzio Ganassini*. The walls have "Birth of the Virgin" (left) and "Death of the Virgin" (right) by *Marzio di Colantonio*, who also did the vault. On the lower right wall, outside the chapel, the tomb of Felice Freddi (d. 1529), who discovered (1506) the famous Laocoon group, now in the Vatican museum.

(25) The altar has "St. Margaret of Cortona in Ecstasy" (1827), by *G. Sales*. The walls have *Marco Benefial*'s finest works (1729): "Death

of St. Margaret of Cortona" (left) and "Margaret Finds the Body of Her Lover and Is Converted" (right).

(26) The St. Michael on the altar is by an anonymous seventeenth-century artist.

(27) The altar has a copy of Muziano's "Ascension."

(28) The painting of St. Paul on the altar is by Muziano; those on the walls of "St. Paul Preaching" (left) and "Martyrdom of St. Paul" (right) are by Roncalli, who also did the vault. In the left wall is the simple but elegant tomb of Filippo della Valle (d. 1494); since the deceased was a humanist the sculptor, perhaps *Michele Marini*, has books supporting the body.

(29) The altarpiece depicts the Poor Clare Blessed Catherine (Serafina) Sforza (1434–1478) in ecstasy; it is by Trevisani.

(30) The superb fresco (ca. 1449) of St. Anthony of Padua over the altar is by *Benozzo Gozzoli*. With St. Anthony are two donors. The left wall has "St. Anthony Heals an Injured Leg," and in the lunette above "St. Anthony Preaches to Fish"; the right has "Miracle of the Ass Adoring the Blessed Sacrament" and above "St. Anthony with the Child Jesus." These are by a student of Muziano. Trometta's "Paradise" is in the vault. On the right is the Renaissance tomb of Antonio Albertoni (d. 1509). Outside the chapel, to the left, is a statue of Paul III, moved here (1876) from the Roman Senate.

(31) This chapel is only open during Christmas and Epiphany seasons; it was made into a permanent *presepio* in 1833. During these seasons the Santo Bambino is placed in the chapel, and children are accustomed to come and recite poetry in front of it.

(32) The altar has Ganassini's "Immaculate Conception." The walls and vault were painted by Trometta; the paintings refer to Mary's immaculate conception as typified in the Old Testament and the Book of Revelation.

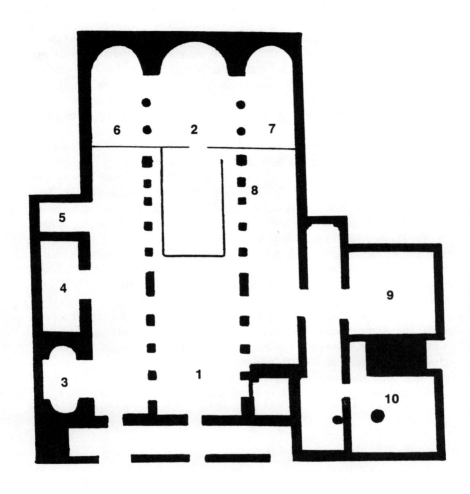

S. Maria in Cosmedin (in Schola Graeca)

36 S. Maria in Cosmedin (in Schola Graeca)***
Piazza della Bocca di Verità

History. In ancient Roman times this area was the *Forum Boarium*, the city's grain market. During the fourth century A.D., a *Statio annonae*, or market inspector's office, was set up in the loggia of the temple (constructed in the third century B.C.) dedicated to Ceres, goddess of agriculture. In the sixth century A.D. the *statio* was converted into a deaconry (*diakonia*), or food distribution center for the poor, with an oratory within. When the adjacent temple threatened to collapse in the eighth century, Hadrian I (772–795) had it demolished, and transformed the oratory into a church with three naves. He then entrusted the church to the Greek community (*schola Graeca*), which had settled in Rome after fleeing persecution in the East. The Greeks dedicated the church to the Virgin and added *in Cosmedin*, after a district in Constantinople. Since the church suffered during the Norman invasion (1084), Cardinal John of Gaeta, titular (1088–1118), began restoring it, and continued after he had been elected Pope Gelasius II (1118–1119). The rebuilding was completed under his successor, Callistus II (1119–1124). By the seventeenth century the church was in great disrepair; Cardinal Annibale Albani (1682–1751), titular (1716–1722), had *Giuseppe Sardi* give (1718) the church a baroque facade, and succeeding titulars had baroque decorations introduced within the church. It was Cardinal Gaetano De Ruggiero (1816–1896), titular (1889–1896), who sponsored the last major restoration (1892–1899) under *Giovanni Battista Giovenale*, who returned the church to its twelfth-century appearance.

Exterior. The church is preceded by a twelfth-century portico of seven arches and a porch (*prothyron*) with two granite and two marble columns. The tall, seven-story Romanesque campanile, from the time of Gelasius, is among Rome's best. The decoration (eleventh century) around the main door is by *Giovanni da Venezia*. The ninth-century inscriptions on the sides of the door record donations. To the door's right, the tomb of the papal chamberlain Alfano (d. 1150), who supervised the church's restorations under Callistus II. The lunette over the tomb and the one left of the doorway once had frescoes of the Annunciation and Nativity. On the far left wall is the large stone disk known as *Bocca della Verità*. It was, most probably, a manhole or cistern cover and has the face of Oceanus or a river god sculpted on it. A medieval legend has it that the disk will bite the hand of the one who tells falsehoods and dares to place his hand in its mouth. The disk was placed here in 1632; prior to this it was, for centuries, on an outside wall of the church. The piazza gets its name from the disk.

Interior. (1) The church is austere and basically the same as what the twelfth-century Christians saw when they entered it. It has a central nave with two side aisles separated by two piers with three sets of three columns on each side. The columns, taken from older Roman buildings, are of different materials and sizes and have a variety of capitals and bases. The upper portion of the triumphal arch and of the nave around the windows have remnants of medieval frescoes. The nave's left wall has two uncovered patches revealing earlier masonry; the patch nearer the altar shows brick-work from the sixth (left) and eighth century (right), and the other reveals sixth (right) and eleventh-century (left) work. The flat ceiling is modern (1965–1966).

The pavement is pre-cosmatesque *opus sectile*, from the time of Callistus' rebuilding. The marble fluted columns on the sides of the central door were part of the loggia of the *Statio annonae*. Four more such columns are in the left aisle, all in their original positions. Next to the columns on this rear wall are small niches with purplish-black marble stones; these are Roman weights, once used in the market and discovered here during the late-nineteenth-century restoration. The tablet on the bell tower's base recalls that Cardinal Francesco Roberti (1889–1977), titular (1958–1967), sponsored further restorations between 1960 and 1964.

The *schola cantorum*, with its panels and pulpits, stands in the center of the nave and is from the twelfth century. It had been dismantled during the sixteenth and was reconstructed in the nineteenth. The floor within is exceptionally beautiful. The *pergola* that separates the presbytery from the body of the church and *schola cantorum* was also dismantled in the sixteenth century and later reconstructed. The attractive paschal candle near the pulpit is from the eighteenth century; the small lion clasping its base, however, is from the thirteenth.

(2) The graceful Gothic baldachin over the altar is by *Deodato*, a member of the Cosmati family, and rests on four red granite columns. It is signed and dated 1294. The upper portion has mosaic decorations. The urn beneath is of porphyry and contains the relics of Roman martyrs (Cirilla, Coronatus, and Hilary). Next to the apse wall is the episcopal chair, which dates from the twelfth century; its backrest is a marble disk with a cosmatesque design; its armrests are lions.

The fresco in this apse and those in the other two are nineteenth-century efforts to imitate twelfth-century work. The half-dome has an en-

S. Maria in Cosmedin (G. Vasi, 1753)

throned Virgin and Child in the center, with Sts. Augustine and Felix on the viewer's left, and Sts. Denis and Nicholas on the right. The four scenes on the apse wall are "Annunciation" and "Nativity" (left), with "Epiphany" and "Presentation" (right).

(3) The baroque baptistery was constructed (1727) by Cardinal Alessandro Albani (1692–1779), titular (1722–1741). The font's basin is of finely worked marble, from the imperial Roman period. Outside the baptistery, in the corner to the left and on the wall to the right, are four columns from the loggia of the *Statio annonae*.

(4) The chapel was restored (1860) on the occasion of the beatification (1859) of St. John Baptist De Rossi (1698–1764); he was canonized in 1881. The saint had been a canon of this basilica and had lived in the adjoining building. The painting on the altar by *Giovanni Battista Brughi* depicts the saint among the poor.

(5) The chapel of the crucifix was added at the end of the nineteenth century.

(6) The fresco in the half-dome has the Virgin and Child in a mandorla; they sit on the Holy House as the angels transport it to Loreto. Below, on the window's left is "Nativity of Mary" and on the right "Death of Mary." The altar is recent and was designed to match the one in the right aisle. The pavement is a modern cosmatesque imitation.

(7) The half-dome has the Lamb of God in the center surrounded by an acanthus leaf design. The frescoes on the sides of the window have

235

scenes from the life of John the Baptist; on the left is "John the Baptist Preaching" and on the right "Beheading of John the Baptist." Beneath the window is a medallion of the Baptist. The altar's base is from a Roman column, with a modern marble top. The pavement here is also a modern cosmatesque imitation.

(8) On the left is one of the stairways leading down to the crypt, dug into the foundation of the Temple of Ceres, during the renovations of Hadrian I (eighth century). It is a miniature basilica, with three naves separated by six columns with an apse and altar. The columns are imbedded in the pavement. The crypt was reopened in 1717.

(9) This is known as the "winter choir." The altar has *Theotokos*, "Mother of God," and the inscription on the bottom translates: "To the ever Virgin Mother of God." The image is from the thirteenth century; it was repainted during the Renaissance and later retouched. From 1618 to 1900 it was over the episcopal chair in the middle apse; it was then transferred here. The four statues in the corners represent virtues. The vault has "Assumption" (1900).

(10) On the way to the sacristy, to the right of the doorway, is one of the original Roman columns of the *Statio annonae*, and another is in the center of the sacristy itself. The most interesting item here is the **mosaic fragment** on the wall opposite the entrance. About 706 John VII (705–707) built an oratory in old St. Peter's and had it decorated with mosaics. At the time of the building of the new St. Peter's, Paul V (1605–1621) had the oratory demolished, but portions of the mosaic were preserved and given to various individuals and churches. This fragment was kept in the Vatican sacristy; under Urban VIII (1623–1644) it was brought (2 September 1636) to this church and placed over the main entrance. It was later transferred (1767) to the sacristy. The mosaic depicts the Virgin and Child, with St. Joseph at her shoulder and an angel on the right. Since a hand offers a gift to the Child, it is presumed that the mosaic also included the Magi.

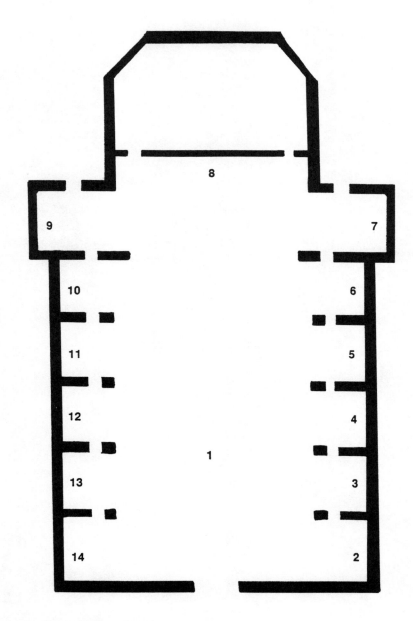

S. Maria in Traspontina

37 S. Maria in Traspontina
Via della Conciliazione

History. The first church of this name was built by Hadrian I (772–795), near Castel Sant' Angelo. It was dedicated to the Virgin Mary and was called *in Traspontina,* perhaps because of its location "on the other side of the bridge." On the occasion of imperial coronations in St. Peter's basilica, it was there that the imperial cortege gathered and vested prior to processing to the ceremonies. In 1484 Innocent VIII (1484–1492) gave the church to the Carmelites. The church was demolished in 1564, the better to fortify Castel Sant' Angelo, and a new one was built on the present site. The new church was begun in 1566 under *Sallustio Peruzzi,* and after his death (1573) it was continued (beginning in 1581) by *Ottaviano Mascherino* and completed (1635–1637) by *Francesco Peperelli,* who added the transept and choir area. The Calced Carmelites continue to serve the church.

Exterior. The facade, made of travertine, taken, for the most part, from the Colosseum, was designed by Peruzzi and constructed by Mascherino. It has two orders: the lower has three portals and two niches, one at either side, while the upper has a large central window and two blind ones. Over the main entrance is a niche with an eighteenth-century Madonna. The cupola is without a drum, so as not to obstruct, in time of crisis, the artillery at Castel Sant' Angelo. The Romans had not forgotten the Sack of Rome (1527).

Interior. (1) The church is in the form of a Latin cross, having a single nave with five interconnecting chapels on each side and one at each end of the transept. The pavement dates from 1873, and the pilasters were faced with yellow marble in 1895. The painting (1894) on the nave's vault is "Our Lady Gives the Scapular to St. Simon Stock" by *Cesare Caroselli.*
(2) The chapel is dedicated to St. Barbara and was sponsored by the artillery unit at Castel Sant' Angelo. The painting (1597) of the saint, patron of artillerymen (she holds lightning in her left hand), is by *Cavalier d'Arpino.* The frescoes in the vault and on the side walls depict scenes from the saint's life and martyrdom; these are by *Cesare Rossetti.* On the right is a monument to O. Malatesta degli Abbati (1730). Decorative motifs on the pilasters, pavement, and balustrade include firearms, in keeping with the chapel's sponsor.

(3) The altarpiece (1686) by *Daniel Seiter* represents St. Canute (1043–1086), king of Denmark and martyr. The vault, with "St. Canute in Glory," and the lunettes, with angels, are by *Alessandro Francesi*. The circular disk in front of the altar indicates the former burial place for Danish Catholics in Rome.

(4) The chapel area is taken up with a statue (1922) of Our Lady of Mount Carmel, patron of the Carmelite order. The walls have medallions (1895) of St. Ann (left) and of St. Joachim (right) by Caroselli.

(5) The altar has a crucifix (from the old church) with a painted (1590) Virgin and John on the sides by *Cesare Conti*. The walls and vault have scenes (1649) of the passion by *Bernardino Gagliardi*: the left wall has "Christ in the Garden" and above "Christ Scourged"; on the right "Way to Calvary" and above "Christ Mocked."

(6) The painting over the altar depicts the Carmelite, St. Albert of Trapani (d. 1307). It is by *Antonio Circignani*, who likewise did the frescoes on the walls illustrating episodes in his life, that is, a miracle (left) and his death (right).

(7) The altarpiece (1639) in the right transept is "St. Mary Magdalene de' Pazzi," attributed to *Gian Domenico Cerrini*.

(8) The main altar was designed by *Carlo Fontana* and built in 1674. In design it is different from the usual Roman altar, and this is, perhaps, what makes it interesting. Eight slender columns of red marble support a large crown (of the same marble) that serves as a baldachin over an image of the Virgin, set on a pedestal. This image is especially venerated by the Carmelites. There is a tradition that at the beginning of the thirteenth century, when the Carmelites left the Holy Land, they carried this image with them all through Europe. Nearest the altar are statues of the prophets Elijah (left) and Elisha (right), the other two are of the Carmelite saints Angelo of Sicily (left) and Albert of Trapani (right).

The cupola was decorated (1893) by *F. Cangini*; the artist who did the pendentives with Elijah and Elisha (facing the nave) and St. Andrew Corsini and Blessed Peter Thomas (facing the main altar) remains unidentified.

(9) The left transept has a painting of St. Andrew Corsini by *Giovanni Paolo Melchiorri*. St. Andrew Corsini (1302–1373) had been bishop of Fiesole, and during the battle of Anghiari (1440), he miraculously appeared and helped the Florentines achieve a victory. The fresco (1697) in the vault above, by *Biagio Puccini*, depicts the saint's appearance during the battle.

(10) *Giovanni Battista Ricci*'s "St. Angelo of Sicily Preaching" is over the altar. The walls and vault have events from the life of St. Angelo (1185–1225), also by Ricci.

(11) The altarpiece (1698) is *Antonio Gherardi*'s dramatic "St. Teresa

in Ecstasy." The paintings in the ovals on the sides are: "St. Teresa in Conversation with the Savior and Virgin" (left) and "St. Teresa in Glory" (right).

(12) The altar's painting is Ricci's "Sts. Peter and Paul Bound to Columns." At either side of the altar is a portion of a column to which, a pious but unfounded tradition claims, Peter and Paul were bound, when they were scourged before martyrdom. The left wall has a fresco of "St. Peter's Crucifixion" and above "Christ Gives the Keys to St. Peter"; on the right wall "St. Paul's Martyrdom" and above "St. Paul's Conversion." These are likewise by Ricci.

(13) "Prophet Elijah with St. Anthony the Abbot and Blessed Franco Lippi of Siena" (1639) is by *Giacinto Calandrucci*. The walls also have his "Elijah and the Sunamite" (left) and "Elijah beneath the Juniper Tree" (right). Elijah has traditionally been considered the founder of the Carmelite order.

(14) The terra-cotta "Pietà" on the altar dates from the thirteenth century and comes from the old church. The angels on the sides are of wood, school of *Ercole Ferrata*. The vault and walls have anonymous eighteenth-century frescoes: "Baptism of Christ" on the left wall; "Holy Spirit" in the vault; "Sts. Andrew and Charles Borromeo" on the right.

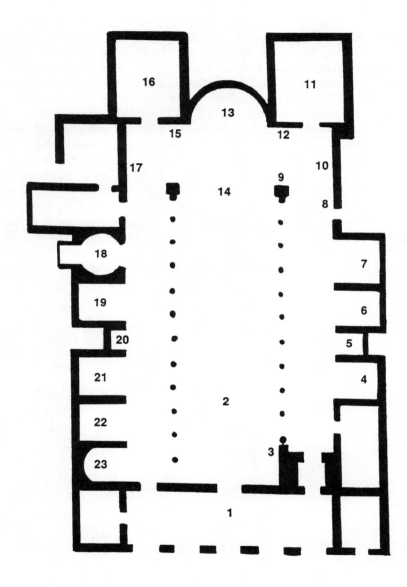

S. Maria in Trastevere

38 S. Maria in Trastevere***

Piazza di S. Maria in Trastevere

History. The church goes back to the days of Pope Callistus I (217–222), who is said to have built an oratory on the site of or near a *Taberna meritoria,* a hospice for veteran and invalid soldiers. That particular place was chosen because in the year 716 after the founding of Rome (38 B.C.) a jet of oil (*fons olei*) is said to have appeared and flowed for an entire day. Later, in the Christian era, this phenomenon was interpreted as a divine sign foretelling the birth of Christ, the Anointed One, through whom grace would flow to the world. Callistus' oratory here may have been the first place of public Christian worship in Rome. Julius I (337–352) replaced (ca. 340) the oratory with a church, which underwent subsequent restorations until Innocent II (1130–1143) constructed (1140–1148) an entirely new edifice, using material (columns, capitals, etc.) from the third-century Baths of Caracalla. The last major restoration was done (1866–1874) by *Virginio Vespignani* at the request of Pius IX (1846–1878).

Exterior. The portico, with four grey granite columns and five arches, was added in 1702 by *Carlo Fontana.* Above the portico is a balustrade with eighteenth-century statues (Sts. Callistus, Cornelius, Julius, Calepodius—their relics are beneath the main altar). The lower portion of the facade has three windows with still visible nineteenth-century frescoes by *Silverio Capparoni* of palm trees and grazing lambs. Above the windows is a twelfth-thirteenth-century mosaic with the Virgin and Child; five female figures are on either side, each holds a burning lamp, except the two on the Virgin's left. These two are also dressed differently and do not have crowns on their heads. No satisfactory explanation has been offered to explain the mosaic, and it is clearly not a depiction of the "wise and foolish virgins," since there are eight with burning lamps. Nor would one expect the foolish virgins to have halos. The two small figures at the Virgin's feet are not identifiable, though some think they are Innocent II, founder of the church, and Eugenius III (1145–1153), during whose pontificate the church was completed.

The fresco of Christ, angels, and evangelists in the tympanum, also by Capparoni, is almost totally obliterated. The campanile is from the twelfth century, and near its top there is a small aedicule with a mosaic Virgin and Child.

244 S. Maria in Trastevere

(1) Portico. Two fifteenth-century frescoes of the "Annunciation" are beneath the portico—one on the left wall and the other left of the main portal. The nondescript fresco of the "Nativity," to the right, is from the nineteenth century. The walls have many inscriptions, architectural fragments, and tombstones; two sarcophagi stand against the left wall. Especially beautiful are the cornices with acanthus leaves from imperial Roman times used to frame the three portals. Over the main door is a roundel with Greek letters, an abbreviation meaning "To the Mother of God."

Interior. (2) The church is basilican in style, with a main nave and two aisles, separated by twenty-one granite columns, taken from Caracalla's baths. The columns have nonmatching capitals (Ionic and Corinthian) and a variety of bases. The coffered ceiling has an intricate geometrical pattern of stars and crosses, designed (1617) by *Domenichino*. His "Assumption" is in the center. The ceiling was the gift of Cardinal Pietro Aldobrandini (1572–1621), as the inscription near the entrance indicates. His coat of arms is likewise in the ceiling.

The arch at the end of the nave rests on two granite columns with Corinthian capitals; their decorated cornices are fragments from an earlier Roman building. The fresco (1870) on the arch is by *Luigi Cochetti*. The Virgin and Child are in the center, with angels on either side; Moses is on the left and Noah on the right. The nave's walls have a series of saints between the windows; all are from the nineteenth-century. The pavement in cosmatesque style was reset in 1870, after the floor had been lowered so that the bases of the columns could be visible.

(3) This fifteenth-century marble tabernacle with gilt highlighting is by *Mino del Reame*; his signature (*opus Mini*) is visible near the bottom. In the right aisle near the entrance, high on the right wall, is an attractive fifteenth-century fresco of the Virgin and Child.

(4) The painting over the altar is "St. Frances of Rome Receives Communion." St. Frances of Rome (1384–1440) is closely connected with this church; she was a native of Trastevere, her spiritual director was pastor here, and she experienced several revelations here. On the left wall is a monument to Cardinal Giovanni Battista Bussi (d. 1726), and on the right one to Cardinal Pietro Francesco Bussi (d. 1765).

(5) The rococo chapel was designed by *Filippo Raguzzini; Étienne Parrocel's* "Nativity" is on the altar.

(6) The wooden crucifix is from the fifteenth century.

(7) The altar has *Giuseppe Vasconio's* "Christ Gives the Keys to Peter."

(8) At the end of the right aisle, and before walking up to the right transept, there is a niche in the wall containing chains supposedly worn by martyrs and a stone, which, at one time, was thought to be the stone

S. Maria in Trastevere (G. Vasi, 1753)

that had been tied to St. Callistus, when he was martyred by being thrown into a well.

(9) The coffered wooden ceiling in the transept is from 1596, the gift of Cardinal Giulio Antonio Santori (1532–1602). A polychrome "Assumption" is in the center and at this end is the cardinal's coat of arms; at the other end is that of Pius IX, who had the ceiling restored (1872).

(10) The monument of Cardinal Francesco Armellini (1469–1527) is by *Michelangelo Senese*. The cardinal commissioned the tomb in 1524; his figure is on the left and that of his father, Benvenuto (d. 1524), on the right. Statues of Sts. Lawrence (left) and Francis of Assisi (right) are in the center, with that of the Eternal Father above. Both reliefs in the roundels are of the Virgin and Child. The cardinal died as a consequence of the Sack of Rome (1527) and was buried elsewhere. The organ is above, and at its sides are sixteenth-century frescoes of David (left) and Isaiah (right). The "Angel Musicians" are attributed to *Gaspare Celio*.

(11) Strada Cupa Chapel. The chapel (1625) was designed by Domenichino to house the image of the Virgin known as *Madonna della Strada Cupa*. The fresco, painted by *Perin del Vaga*, receives its name from the fact that it was originally on a wall on Cupa Street. Because it was considered miraculous, it was brought to the church in 1624. The present altar was the gift of Cardinal Henry Stuart (1725–1807), duke of York and titular (1759–1761); his coat of arms is over the chapel's entrance.

245

The left wall has *Carlo Maratta's* "Rest on the Flight to Egypt" and on the right "St. John the Baptist" attributed to *Annibale Carracci.*

(12) This is the tomb of the eminent Polish theologian Cardinal Stanislaus Hosius (1504–1579), papal legate at the Council of Trent. He was a staunch defender of the faith against the Reformers, hence the inscription: "I have written this to you about those who are seducing you. Whoever disagrees with the Roman Church in matters of faith is not a Catholic."

(13) The **mosaics in the apse** are truly stupendous and are from the time (1140) of Innocent II. The upper part of the triumphal arch has a cross with the Greek letters Alpha and Omega, together with seven candlesticks and the symbols of the four evangelists. The figure on the left is Isaiah, who holds a scroll which reads: "Behold a Virgin shall conceive and bear a son," and on the right is Jeremiah whose scroll has: "The Lord Christ is held captive by our sins." The captive Christ is symbolized by the bird in the cage.

In the top portion of the apse Christ is in the center with Mary on his right, both sitting on the same throne. Christ wears a blue tunic with gold wrap, while Mary, wearing the same colors, has a jeweled bodice. Christ's right hand is on Mary's right shoulder. The book in his left hand has "Come, my chosen one, I will give you my throne," taken from the liturgy for the feast of the Assumption. The book in Mary's hand has "His left hand is under my head, and his right arm embraces me" (Cant 2:6). On Christ's left are Sts. Peter, Cornelius, Julius I, and Calepodius. The last three are here because their relics are beneath the main altar. On Mary's right is Sts. Callistus and Lawrence, and Innocent II, who holds a model of the church in his hand. Reaching down from the heavens above is the hand of God over Christ's head.

The next level of the mosaic has the Lamb of God in the center with the twelve lambs (apostles) approaching from the mystical cities of Bethlehem and Jerusalem. Above this frieze is an inscription which states that Innocent restored the church and offers it to the Mother of God.

Below the lambs are six magnificent mosaics by *Pietro Cavallini,* done about 1290. The series, which depicts scenes from the Virgin's life, begins and ends on the triumphal arch. The first on the left is "Birth of Mary," then "Annunciation." There follows "Nativity of Christ"; below the reclining Virgin there is a small building with the name *Taberna meritoria* with oil flowing out, continuing the tradition that Christ's nativity was the fulfillment of that sign. Then comes "Adoration of the Magi," followed by "Presentation in the Temple," and lastly "Dormition of Mary." Jesus stands next to the Virgin, and in his hands he holds her soul.

Beneath these mosaics there is another by Cavallini, in the center; the Virgin and Child are in a roundel, with St. Paul (left) and St. Peter (right). St. Peter gently places his right hand on the kneeling Bertholdo Stefaneschi, who had commissioned the series from Cavallini. The frescoes (1600) on either side of this mosaic are by *Agostino Ciampelli* and have angels holding symbols connected with the Virgin Mary. In the center of the choir stalls is a twelfth-century marble episcopal chair, with two winged griffins as armrests.

(14) The main altar was restored (ca. 1865) by Vespignani; four porphyry columns support the baldachin. Beneath the altar are the relics of Sts. Callistus, Cornelius, Julius, and Calepodius, placed here by Gregory IV (827–844) in 828. On the balustrade on the right of the steps leading up to the altar, there is a bronze plate with the words *fons olei*, and in the pavement in front of it an inscription that says: "Here oil flowed when Christ was born of the Virgin." There is an especially beautiful thirteenth-century cosmatesque candlestick on the altar's right.

(15) Tomb of Roberto Altemps (1566–1586), duke of Wales, prefect of pontifical police in Avignon.

(16) The Altemps Chapel was built (ca. 1584–1585) by *Martino Longhi the Elder* for Cardinal Marcus Sittich d'Altemps (1533–1595), titular (1580–1595). The cardinal was the nephew of Pius IV (1559–1565), who made him a cardinal on 26 February 1561 and on 10 November of that year appointed him one of the five papal legates to the Council of Trent. Hence the two large wall frescoes (1588) deal with that council: on the left is "Council of Trent in Session" and on the right "Pius IV Promulgates the Bull 'Benedictus Deus' Approving the Acts of the Council." These are by *Pasquale Cati*, who also did the frescoes of the life of the Virgin in the vault, with "Assumption" in the center, and the four evangelists in the corners. The vault also has excellent stucco work. In 1593 an eighth-century icon of Our Lady of Clemency was placed on the altar; it has recently been restored. In a window-like niche above the altar is a painting of Pius IV and his nephew. Cardinal Altemps is buried in the chapel.

(17) What is now the altar dedicated to Sts. Philip and James was part of the tomb of Cardinal Philippe d'Alençon (1319–1397), son of Charles II of Valois and nephew of Philip the Fair. The tomb was moved here (1584) from another part of the church. The Gothic tabernacle formerly held the reclining image of the cardinal, now on the altar's left. The cardinal died on 15 August and, thus, the bas-relief below his image is the "Dormition of the Virgin," and the "Assumption" was above it, still in the upper part of the altar's tabernacle. The altar now has a painting of the "Martyrdom of Sts. Philip and James," attributed to *Palma il Giovane.*

On the altar's right is the tomb of Cardinal Pietro Stefaneschi (d. 1417) by *Paolo Romano.*

(18) The Avila Chapel was designed (ca. 1680) by *Antonio Gherardi*; he likewise painted (1686) the "St. Jerome" on the altar. The chapel is somehow more secular than sacred.

(19) *Francesco Gagliardi*'s "Sacred Heart of Jesus' is the altarpiece.

(20) Tomb of Innocent II (1130–1143). Innocent, who built the basilica, was of the Papareschi family and a native of Rome's Trastevere section. He was first buried in the Lateran, but after the fire of 1308, his ashes were brought here. During Pius IX's renovations, he received a new tomb (1869) of Carrara marble, designed by Vespignani. The lunette above depicts Innocent II receiving the submission (23 May 1138) of antipope Victor IV.

(21) "St. Francis of Assisi Receives the Stigmata," by *Ferrau Fenzone*, is over the altar. The same artist may have done the left lunette, the vault fresco of the Eternal Father, as well as the pendentives with Doctors of the Church.

(22) The altar has an icon of "Our Lady of Divine Love."

(23) The design of the baptistery is due to Raguzzini, similar to #5. The artists *Ciro Ferri* (1634–1689) and *Giovanni Lanfranco* (1582–1647) were buried in the church, but the places of burial are no longer known.

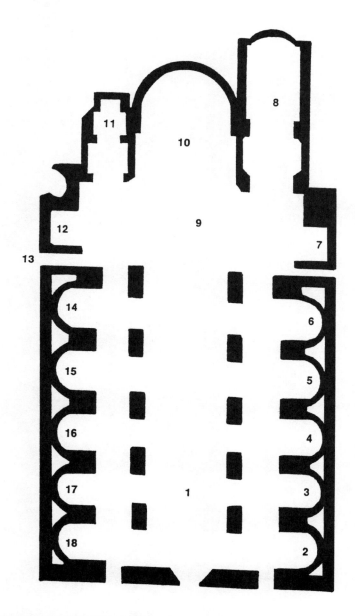

S. Maria in Vallicella (Chiesa Nuova)

39   S. Maria in Vallicella (Chiesa Nuova)**
Piazza della Chiesa Nuova

History. The church is closely connected with the life and work of St. Philip Neri (1515–1595). Philip was a Florentine who had come to Rome and worked among the city's poor. So well known did he become in the city, and so greatly did he help it, that he is today one of Rome's patron saints. In 1575 he and the priests who worked with him formed a congregation known as the Fathers of the Oratory, and so that this new congregation could have its own church in the city, Gregory XIII (1572–1585) gave (1575) Philip the twelfth-century church of S. Maria in Vallicella (which may also have been dedicated to St. Gregory the Great). It was called "in Vallicella" because of its location in a "little valley," now filled in. Since the church was not large enough for the purposes of the Oratorians, Philip decided to build another church on the site. The present church was begun in 1575 according to the plans of *Matteo da Città di Castello* and *Martino Longhi the Elder.* The saint came to live here in 1583 and spent his last years here; he died on 26 May 1595. The church was immediately dubbed by the Romans as *Chiesa Nuova,* or "New Church," and this is still its preferred name among the people.

Exterior. The facade was designed by *Faustolo Rughesi* and completed in 1605. The lower order has three doorways; the central one is framed by tall, double, Corinthian columns, surmounted by a segmental pediment, whose tympanum has a Virgin and Child. The inscription over the main door bears the dedication: "To the Virgin Mother of God and St. Gregory the Great." The inscription on the architrave recalls the facade's donor: "Angelo Cesi, Bishop of Todi, erected [this] in the year of Our Lord 1605." There are two statues in niches in the second order: St. Gregory the Great (left) and St. Jerome (right). The palazzo on the left of the church was built (1637–1650), after a design by *Francesco Borromini,* as a residence for the Oratorians, and to house their library, meeting rooms, etc.

Interior. (1) The church, richly decorated with gilded stucco, is in the form of a Latin cross, with five lateral chapels on each side. Tall fluted Corinthian pilasters rise to a trabeation with a painted frieze and elegant cornice that goes throughout the church. The vault has *Pietro da Cortona*'s "St. Philip Neri's Vision of Our Lady during the Church's Construction" (1664–1665). It is said that Philip had a vision in which our Lady averted tragedy by holding up a loose beam, which threatened the building's collapse. The day after the vision Philip notified the workmen and the loose beam was repaired. The stucco work in the vault (1662–1665), ornate but restrained, is by *Cosimo Fancelli* and *Ercole Ferrata*. Over the arches in the nave, as well as in the transept and presbytery, there is a total of fifteen paintings with scenes from the Old and New Testaments. These date from about 1700 and are by various artists: *Lazzaro Baldi* (two in presbytery), *Giuseppe Ghezzi* (two in transept and two in nave), *Daniel Seiter* (four in nave and one on rear wall), *Domenico Parodi* (two in nave), and *Giuseppe Passeri* (two in nave). The pavement in the nave was restored in 1736.

On the rear wall, above the main door, is a large inscription recording the munificence of the Cesi brothers: Cardinal Pier Donato (1521–1586) paid for the apse and its decoration and the adjacent Oratorian residence, while his brother Angelo (1530–1606), bishop of Todi, provided the funds for the facade and the chapel in the left transept.

(2) The altarpiece is *Scipione Pulzone*'s "Crucifixion." The frescoed panels in the half-dome above have scenes from Christ's passion: "Crowning with Thorns" (left), "Scourging" (center), "Agony in the Garden" (right). The columns on the altar are of Carrara marble, inlaid with black marble to imitate fluting.

(3) The "Deposition from the Cross" is a nineteenth-century copy of *Caravaggio*'s painting, located here until it was taken to Paris in 1797. On its return to Italy, it was placed in the Vatican Pinacoteca. The columns are of portasanta marble.

(4) *Girolamo Muziano*'s "Ascension" is over the altar, flanked by columns of giallo antico. The three panels in the half-dome portray Sts. Patermutius, Copre, and Alexander, martyrs (363) in Egypt under Julian "the Apostate" (emperor 361–363), and whose bodies were brought to this church. Patermutius, a desert ascetic, was condemned to be thrown into a furnace, while Copre, his disciple, was to have his tongue cut out and then burned. When Alexander, a soldier, saw that neither was injured, he too became a Christian. The three were then beheaded. Patermutius is in the center panel.

(5) The painting (1603) is "The Descent of the Holy Spirit," probably by the Flemish artist *Wenceslas Cobergher*. The altar columns are of alabaster. The three panels in the vault refer to the Spirit: the seven candlesticks (left) refer to the Spirit's seven gifts; "Christ's Baptism" (center) has the Spirit appearing in the form of a dove, and "Moses Receives the Law" (right) to indicate that it is the Spirit who imprints the divine law in our hearts.

S. Maria in Vallicella (G. Vasi, 1756)

(6) *Aurelio Lomi*'s "Assumption" is on the altar and scenes from the life of the Virgin are in the vault.

(7) The altar with verde antico columns in the right transept has the "Coronation of the Virgin" (1593), by *Cavalier d'Arpino*, admittedly an inferior work. The statues, by *Flaminio Vacca*, are of Sts. John the Baptist (left) and John the Evangelist (right).

(8) This is the Spada Chapel, designed by *Carlo Rainaldi*, with Sicilian jasper columns and pilasters. The altarpiece (1685) is *Carlo Maratta*'s "Enthroned Madonna with Sts. Charles Borromeo and Ignatius of Loyola"; the left wall has *Giovanni Bonatti*'s "St. Charles Cares for the Plague Victims in Milan" and the other has *Luigi Scaramuccia*'s "St. Charles Distributes Alms to the Poor." Above the chapel's entrance is an organ loft with wood carvings; angels hold St. Philip Neri's "burning heart" emblem. A similar loft is in the left transept.

(9) The **cupola fresco** (1647–1650) is by Pietro da Cortona and depicts "Trinity in Glory"; the Father and Son, encircled by angels holding symbols of the passion, are on the lower level with the Holy Spirit in the lantern. The figures are large and easily visible, making this one of the more beautiful cupola frescoes in Rome. When the lighting is proper, the blues in this fresco and that of the apse, give a celestial tint to the church. The same artist likewise did the prophets in the pendentives (1659–1660): Isaiah (front left), which is especially fine, Jeremiah, Ezekiel, and Daniel.

253

(10) The painting over the main altar is of the Virgin and Child surrounded by angels, the work (1607) of the young *Peter Paul Rubens* during his sojourn in Rome. The oval painting of the Virgin is removable and beneath it is an earlier fresco, originally on the wall of a nearby house. When a player threw a ball against the image, it is said to have bled. It was then brought (ca. 1535) to the church formerly on this site. The four columns flanking the painting are of giallo antico. The seventeenth-century crucifix above the altar, handsomely framed, is by the French sculptor *Guillaume Bertholet.*

The other two paintings (1607–1608) in the presbytery are likewise by Rubens. That on the left depicts St. Gregory the Great with Sts. Maurus and Papius. Maurus is on Gregory's right. The painting on the other side represents St. Domitilla with Sts. Nereus and Achilleus. Nereus (on Domitilla's right) and Achilleus were her servants. Gregory is represented because the church is also dedicated to him; the others (Roman martyrs) are here because their relics were brought to the church about 1590 and placed (1599) beneath the main altar.

The inscription beneath the painting on the left narrates the principal events in the church's construction and history. On the same wall, to the left, a black marble tablet indicates the burial place of Cardinal Pier Donato Cesi, one of the church's principal benefactors. The black memorial stone (1608) on the opposite wall recalls the renowned cardinals, Francesco Maria Tarugi (1525–1608) and the historian Cesare Baronio (1538–1607); both were members of the Oratory and are buried here.

The fresco (1655–1660) in the apse above the altar is Pietro da Cortona's "Assumption of the Virgin"; St. Philip Neri is portrayed in the lower left portion. The marble floor in the presbytery was the gift of the Oratorian cardinal Leandro Colloredo (1639–1709); he is buried in front of the altar and his coat of arms takes up most of the presbytery's floor. Other cardinals and bishops are buried outside the presbytery; their colorful coats of arms form an attractive pavement design.

(11) The Chapel of St. Philip Neri dates from 1602, when the saint's body was brought here, seven years after his death. The body was placed in its present crystal urn in 1922. This is the richest chapel in the church, with a variety of marbles, inlaid with mother of pearl. The cupola is supported by four columns of Sicilian alabaster. The altar has a mosaic copy of *Guido Reni's* painting of St. Philip Neri; the original is in St. Philip's rooms upstairs. The wall paintings depict miracles connected with the saint; these are by *Cristoforo Roncalli.*

(12) The altar in the left transept, which matches the one in the right transept, has as its altarpiece (1594) the "Presentation of Mary in the

Temple" by *Barocci.* The walls have St. Peter (left) and St. Paul (right), statues by *Valsoldo.*

(13) The sacristy was designed (1629) by *Paolo Marucelli;* at the end is an altar with *Alessandro Algardi's* impressive "St. Philip Neri and an Angel" (1640). The altar has columns of rosso brecciato marble. The fresco in the ceiling (1633–1634), "Angels with Instruments of the Passion," is by Pietro da Cortona; this was the first work he did for the Oratorians in the church. Over the entrance door is the bronze bust of Gregory XV (1621–1623), also by Algardi; it was Gregory who canonized St. Philip in 1622.

(14) The painting of the "Annunciation" is by *Passignano;* the altar's fluted columns are of pavonazzetto.

(15) Barocci's "Visitation" (1583) is on the altar. This is one of the artist's more expressive works and it was especially beloved by St. Philip. Here the altar's columns are of lumachella marble. The panels above had three saints by *Carlo Saraceni,* now ruined by humidity. The St. John the Baptist in the center is still recognizable.

(16) *Durante Alberti's* "Nativity" is flanked by columns of giallo antico. The vault's frescoes have three saints by *Cristoforo Roncalli;* except for the St. Agnes, the others are hardly identifiable.

(17) The "Adoration of the Magi," by *Cesare Nebbia,* is the altarpiece.

(18) The altar has *Cavalier d'Arpino's* "Presentation of Jesus in the Temple," one of his early works. The Carrara columns have inlaid black marble.

On the feast of St. Philip (26 May), the rooms of St. Philip may be visited. They are located upstairs at the end of a spiral staircase. St. Philip lived on the other side of the church, but those rooms were partially destroyed by fire. These are a reasonable reproduction. There is a chapel, an oratory, and a small cell, which is now used as a sacristy for the other two. The altar in the chapel has Reni's original painting (1615), which was first located in the saint's chapel in the church. The fresco in the ceiling is "St. Philip in Ecstasy" by Pietro da Cortona. There are several mementoes of St. Philip here: the confessional he used in S. Girolamo della Carità, his bed, blankets, etc. The oratory, next to the chapel, was St. Philip's and was moved here in its entirety.

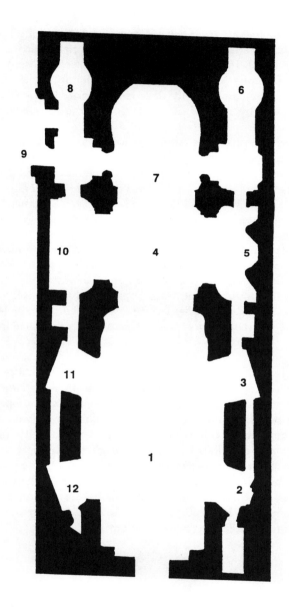

S. Maria Maddalena

40   S. Maria Maddalena*

Piazza della Maddalena

History. As early as 1403 a church dedicated to St. Mary Magdalene stood on this site, and next to it was a hospital. In 1586 the small run-down church was given to St. Camillus de Lellis (1550–1614), founder of the Order of the Servants of the Sick. In 1668 the Camillians, as they were commonly known, decided to build a new church, designed by *Carlo Fontana*. Construction halted in 1673 because of lack of funds, but then resumed in 1695 under *Giovanni Antonio De Rossi,* shortly before his death. It was finally completed in 1698 by *Giulio Carlo Quadri.*

Exterior. The concave facade was designed by *Giuseppe Sardi* and completed in 1735. Its style is rococo, with two orders; the lower has a single portal framed by two columns surmounted by a pediment. Over the door is the Latin inscription: "Hail, O Cross, only hope, increase grace in the pious," a quote from the sixth-century Latin hymn *Vexilla regis.* The left niche has St. Philip Neri and the right St. Camillus de Lellis; both statues are attributed to *Paolo Campana.* St. Philip Neri (1515–1595) was St. Camillus' spiritual director and had great influence on the saint and his congregation. The second order has a window in the center with a red cross, the symbol of the Camillians. In the left niche is St. Mary Magdalene and in the right St. Martha; these are attributed to *Joseph Canard.* The facade was cleaned in 1988.

Interior. (1) The church has the basic form of a Latin cross, with an elliptical nave, transept, dome, and apse. It is richly decorated (1751–1759) with polychrome marble in baroque-rococo style, a good example of a rare style in Rome. The statues in the nave are in niches directly above the confessionals, and illustrate qualities helpful to a fruitful sacramental confession of sin: on the left wall are (from rear to front) Humility, Secrecy, and Simplicity; on the right (from front to rear), Sorrow, Fidelity, and Shame. The first three are in marble; the other three in stucco.

Michelangelo Cerruti's frescoes (1732) in the vault depict episodes in the life of St. Mary Magdalene. The colorful "Resurrection of Lazarus" is in the center; near the windows are six other panels and two more are next to the window on the facade wall. Over the entrance is an uncommonly beautiful eighteenth-century organ loft of gilded carved wood with angels and allegorical figures in stucco; Charity (left) and Hope (right) sit on the balustrade, while Faith (left) and Religion (right) are on the upper level. The pavement in the church was restored in 1879.

(2) The painting (1720) on the altar is "St. Francis de Paola Raises a Dead Child," by *Biagio Puccini.*

(3) The sixteenth-century icon on the altar, known as "Our Lady, Health of the Sick," was given to the church in 1616 by a noble Roman lady. The altar has verde antico columns.

(4) The cupola was frescoed (1739) by *Étienne Parrocel* and depicts the "Most Holy Trinity in Glory" with Sts. Mary Magdalene, Camillus, Philip Neri, and others. The pendentives have Doctors of the Church, also by him.

(5) The chapel is dedicated to St. Camillus, founder (1584) of the Servants of the Sick who serve the church. The painting (1749) on the altar, "The Crucified Lord Comforts St. Camillus," is by *Placido Costanzi.* The altar has four fluted alabaster columns resting on giallo antico bases and supporting an ornate tympanum with angels. Beneath the altar is an urn containing the body of St. Camillus. The fresco in the vault is *Sebastiano Conca's* "St. Camillus in Glory." The left wall has "St. Philip Neri Sees Angels Wearing the Camillian Habit Helping the Sick," by *Giovanni Pannozza,* and the right "Sts. Camillus and Philip Neri," by *Gaspare Serenari.* Both these artists were Conca's students.

(6) On entering the passage to this chapel, on the right is a tall fifteenth-century wooden statue of St. Mary Magdalene by an unidentified artist. The sixteenth-century crucifix over the altar is the one that comforted and spoke (1582) to St. Camillus. Christ's words were: "Of what are you afraid, O weak one! Continue with your work, I will assist you; this work is mine and not yours."

(7) The painting (1698) over the main altar is "St. Mary Magdalene at Prayer," by *Michele Rocca.* The large bas-reliefs on the sides are by *Francesco Gesuelli:* "The Three Marys at the Sepulcher" (left) and "Mary Magdalene Meets the Risen Lord" (right). The fresco (1732) in the half-dome is *Aureliano Milani's* "Jesus Preaches to the Multitude"; Mary Magdalene is on the Lord's right. The underarch has Cerruti's interesting "Dinner in the House of the Pharisee"; Mary Magdalene is at the Savior's feet.

(8) The altar has *Agostino Gagliardi's* "Death of St. Joseph" (1868).

(9) The sacristy, one of the finest examples of the rococo style in Rome, dates from the eighteenth century. The architecture, wardrobes, and decoration form a harmonious unit. The vault fresco (1739), "Sts. Camillus and Philip Neri in Glory," is by *Girolamo Pesce.*

(10) *Baciccia's* brilliant "Christ, Virgin and St. Nicholas of Bari" (1698) is on the altar and illustrates a seventeenth-century legend about the saint. According to the legend, St. Nicholas, while attending the Council of

S. Maria Maddalena (G. Vasi, 1756)

Nicaea in 325 (which, in fact, he did not attend) had the symbols of his episcopal office taken from him after he had spoken out against the Arian heresy. Since Christ and the Virgin approved his manner of speaking, they return the symbols (book, pallium, crozier, and crown) to him. The altar is a handsome blend of cottanello columns with verde and giallo antico together with Sicilian jasper. The walls have paintings by *Bonaventura Lamberti* representing two of St. Nicholas' miracles.

(11) The chapel is dedicated to St. Lawrence Giustiniani (1381–1456); the painting, done (1704) by *Luca Giordano* a year before his death, depicts the saint adoring the Christ Child. The black marble columns are from the previous church.

(12) The altarpiece is Pesce's "Assumption of the Virgin."

St. Camillus lived in the adjoining monastery, and the room in which he died (14 July 1614) has been converted (1732) into a chapel (see sacristan). The walls have two paintings (1785) by *Matteo Toni*; on the right is "St. Camillus Receiving Holy Communion on His Deathbed," and on the left "Preparing St. Camillus' Body for Burial." The reliquary on the altar's left has the saint's heart.

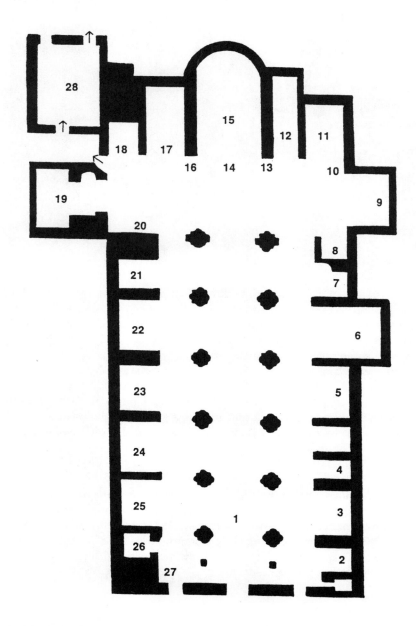

S. Maria sopra Minerva

41   S. Maria sopra Minerva***

Piazza della Minerva

History. The first church on this site was built by Pope Zacharias (741–752), on or near the ruins of a temple to Minerva that Pompey the Great (106–48 B.C.) had built (ca. 50 B.C.) in thanksgiving for his Asian victories. The church, thus, became known as "St. Mary on Minerva." In 1256 Alexander IV (1254–1261) gave the monastery next to the church to the Dominican Friars, and in 1275 they received the church. In 1280 the Dominicans, who still serve the church, began the present Gothic structure; the architects were probably Friars *Sisto* and *Ristoro*, who had earlier worked on the Dominican church of S. Maria Novella in Florence. The church was completed about 1370 and was dedicated to the Virgin of the Annunciation. It was the first Gothic church built in Rome. In the sixteenth century its Gothic interior was transformed into a Renaissance edifice with later baroque additions, but in the nineteenth century Fra *Girolamo Bianchedi* restored (1848–1855) it to its former Gothic state.

Exterior. The present facade is the from the seventeenth century, the gift of Cardinal Antonio Barberini (1569–1646). The three doorways are from the earlier facade (1453); the central doorway bears the inscription that it was restored in 1610 by Andrea Capranica Domenici. The side doorways have lunettes, whose frescoes are now almost totally obliterated. Above the main doorway's triangular pediment is the coat of arms of the Dominican Pope St. Pius V (1566–1572). The upper portion of the facade has three circular windows placed directly above the doorways. The several plaques on the facade to the right indicate the level the water reached during various floods in Rome from 1422 to 1870.

Interior. (1) The church is in the form of a Latin cross, with nave and aisles, transept, apse, and lateral altars. The non-descript decorations in the vault date from the nineteenth-century restoration; the medallions in the nave's upper portion portray Dominican saints. The inscription over the main door records that the restorations of 1848–1855 were done during the pontificate of Pius IX (1846–1878). Left of the main entrance is the Renaissance tomb of the Florentine lawyer Diotisalvi Neroni (ca. 1401–1482).

(2) The altar has *Baciccia*'s "St. Louis Bertrand in Ecstasy" (1671). St. Louis (1526–1581) was a sixteenth-century Dominican missionary in South America, and was canonized in 1671.

(3) *Lazzaro Baldi*'s painting (1671) of St. Rose of Lima (1586–1617) is on the altar. He likewise did the paintings on the side walls with scenes from the saint's life, as well as the attractive "St. Rose in Glory" in the vault. St. Rose was also canonized in 1671.

(4) "Martyrdom of St. Peter of Verona," by *Bonaventura Lamberti*, is the altarpiece (1688). St. Peter of Verona (d. 1252) is more commonly known as St. Peter Martyr. The wall paintings, "Nativity of Christ" (left) and "Resurrection" (right), with prophets and sibyls in the lunettes are by *Giovanni Battista Franco*. *Girolamo Muziano* did the vault frescoes.

(5) The chapel is dedicated to the Annunciation, and its patron was the Confraternity of the Annunciation, founded (1460) by the Spanish Cardinal Juan de Torquemada (1388–1468), to provide dowries for poor girls. The altar has *Antoniazzo Romano*'s charming painting (ca. 1500) of the "Annunciation," in which the Virgin gives purses (dowries) to three girls. Kneeling with the girls is Cardinal Torquemada. The cardinal is buried left of the altar. To the altar's right is the tomb of Cardinal Benedetto Giustiniani (d. 1621), also a confraternity benefactor. The paintings on the altar's sides, St. Dominic (left) and St. Hyacinth (right), are attributed to *Niccolò Stabbia*. The lunettes, with scenes from the life of the Virgin, are by *Cesare Nebbia*, perhaps his last works.

The niche in the left wall has a statue of Urban VII by *Ambrogio Buonvicino*. Urban, who was pope for only 12 days (15–27 September 1590), left his patrimony to the confraternity. His remains were brought here from the Vatican in 1606.

(6) Clement VIII (1592–1605) had the chapel decorated for the tombs of his parents. *Federico Barocci*'s "Institution of the Eucharist" (1594) is on the altar, with *Camillo Mariani*'s statues of Sts. Peter (left) and Paul (right) on the sides. Clement VIII's statue, in the niche on the left, is by *Ippolito Buzzi*; the pope, however, is buried in S. Maria Maggiore. St. Sebastian in the center (previously in the right niche) is now attributed to *Michelangelo*. The tomb of Clement's mother, Lesa Deti (d. 1557), is on the left, that of his father, Silvestro Aldobrandini (d. 1558), is on the right. These were designed by *Giacomo Della Porta* and *Girolamo Rainaldi*; the statues (1605) of the pope's parents are by *Nicolas Cordier*. The decorations in the lunettes and vault are by *Cherubino Alberti*.

(7) The altar has *Niccolò Magni*'s painting of Sts. Paul and Raymond of Penyafort. St. Raymond (ca. 1180–1275) was the third master-general of the Dominicans. The chapel has two Renaissance tombs: in the center of the left wall is the tomb of Benedetto Sopranzi (1447–1495), archbishop of Nicosia, and on the opposite wall that of Diego Diaz de Coca (ca. 1390–1477), bishop of Calahorra, by *Andrea Bregno*. Above the bishop's

S. Maria sopra Minerva (G. B. Falda, 1665)

figure is the fresco "Christ the Judge," perhaps by *Melozzo di Forlì*. Outside the chapel, on the left wall, is a fresco of Sts. Lucy and Agatha by *Sermoneta*.

(8) The chapel has a medieval Gothic entrance and within is a fifteenth-century carved crucifix. On the left wall is the tomb of Cardinal Clemente Micara (1879–1965), who was titular (1946–1965).

(9) Chapel of St. Thomas Aquinas. This magnificent chapel, built by Cardinal Oliviero Carafa (1430–1511), is dedicated to the Virgin of the Annunciation and to St. Thomas Aquinas (ca. 1225–1274), a Dominican and one of the Catholic Church's greatest theologians. The **frescoes** (1488–1492) are among *Filippino Lippi*'s best work. The altar has his "Annunciation" in which St. Thomas presents Cardinal Carafa to the Virgin. The wall behind the altar has the "Assumption," in which the Virgin is encircled by angels, while the apostles (on either side of the altar) gaze upward. The right wall has "St. Thomas' Teaching Triumphs over Error"; the saint holds a book and points to error that has been defeated. In the lunette above, the saint, praying before a crucifix, hears the Savior say: "Thomas, you have written well of me." The angels and sibyls in the vault are by *Lippi*'s pupil, *Raffaellino del Garbo*.

The niche in the left wall has the tomb of Paul IV (1555–1559); the columns flanking the tomb are verde antico, and the statue of the pontiff, in various marbles, is by *Giacomo* and *Tommaso Cassignola*.

(10) The **medieval Gothic tomb** of the Dominican Guillaume Durand, bishop of Mende (d. 1296), is by *Giovanni di Cosma.* The mosaic in the upper portion is of the Virgin and Child, between St. Privatus (left) and St. Dominic (right). St. Privatus, an early bishop of Mende, presents the kneeling Bishop Durand to the Virgin. Below the tomb and right of the small door is the well-executed bust of Onofrio Camaiani (d. 1574) of Arezzo.

(11) Clement X (1670–1676) had this chapel decorated in 1672. The altar has *Carlo Maratta's* painting (1675) of "Virgin with Saints"; the saints depicted are the five that Clement X had canonized in 1671, among them the two Dominicans, St. Louis Bertrand and St. Rose of Lima. Above the altar is Baciccia's "Trinity" (1671–1672). The left wall has the bust of Clement X's brother, Cardinal Giambattista Altieri (d. 1654), and the right his father, Lorenzo (d. 1638). Both busts (1672) are by *Cosimo Fancelli.*

Outside, on the wall above and between the two chapels, is one of the two organ lofts, given the church by Cardinal Scipione Borghese (1576–1633), cardinal protector of the Dominican order.

(12) In this chapel, dedicated to Our Lady of the Rosary, the body of St. Catherine of Siena (ca. 1347–1380), Dominican mystic, was venerated from 1430 to 1855, when it was transferred to the main altar. The sarcophagus that contained the body is in the left wall. The altar has "Virgin with Sts. Dominic and Catherine of Siena." *Giovanni De Vecchi's* frescoes on the walls depict scenes from St. Catherine's life; the panels in the vault represent the mysteries of the rosary and are by *Marcello Venusti,* except "Crowning with Thorns" (right side), which is by *Carlo Saraceni.* On the right wall is the splendid tomb of Cardinal Domenico Capranica (1400–1458), sculpted by Bregno.

(13) Statue of St. John the Baptist (1858) by *Giuseppe Obici.*

(14) Beneath the main altar are the relics of St. Catherine of Siena. The saint's figure (1430) is by *Isaia da Pisa.* In 1939 St. Catherine and St. Francis of Assisi (1182–1226) were proclaimed principal patrons of Italy, and hence the colors of Italy rest on her recumbent figure. In 1970 she was also proclaimed a Doctor of the Church. The paintings on the altar's sides are the cardinal virtues, by *Francesco Podesti.*

(15) The tombs of two Medici popes are in the choir area behind the altar. On the left is that of Leo X (1513–1521) and on the right Clement VII (1523–1534). The matching tombs are by *Antonio da Sangallo the Younger;* the statue of Leo (Giovanni de' Medici) is by *Raffaello da Montelupo* and that of Clement (Giulio de' Medici) is by *Nanni di Baccio Bigio.* The prophets (apostles?) in the side niches and the reliefs above (1536–1541) are by *Baccio Bandinelli.* In the floor, in front of the choir stalls on the

left, is the stone marking the burial place of the great Renaissance humanist Cardinal Pietro Bembo (1470-1547).

(16) Michelangelo's statue of "Christ the Risen Redeemer." It was begun in 1519 and sent unfinished to Rome in 1521; it was completed by one of his students. The bronze drape is of a later period.

(17) To the left, protected by an ornate grille, is the tomb of one of the great medieval artists, Fra *Angelico;* a better view is had from #18. Further down the vestibule are three baroque tombs: in the center of the left wall is the tomb of the Dominican Cardinal Michele Bonelli (d. 1598); above the door is the tomb of Cardinal Carlo Bonelli (d. 1676); in the center of the right wall is that of the Dominican Cardinal Domenico Pimentel (d. 1653).

(18) On the right is the **tomb of Beato Angelico** (1387-1455), known in the Dominican order as Fra Giovanni da Fiesole, who died in the adjacent monastery on 18 February 1455. The tombstone is perhaps by *Isaia da Pisa.* The altar has a fifteenth-century Virgin and Child, once thought to be by Angelico; after restoration (1966) it is said to have been only touched up by him. The paintings on the altar's sides are of St. Francis of Assisi (left) and St. Frances of Rome (right). Both are attributed to *Francesco Parone.*

The floor has three interesting fourteenth-century tombstones; the two on the left are of the Frangipane family and that on the right of the Capodiferro family, former patrons of this chapel. On the left wall is the tomb of Giovanni Arberini (ca. 1398-1473); the sarcophagus with a vigorous "Hercules Fights the Nemean Lion" is a Roman copy of a fifth-century B.C. Greek work.

(19) Chapel of St. Dominic. This chapel, decorated (1725) by the Dominican Pope Benedict XIII (1724-1730), is rich with black and white (colors of the Dominican Order) marble and is dedicated to St. Dominic (1170-1221), founder of the Order of Preachers. The painting on the altar, "Our Lady Displays an Image of St. Dominic," is by *Paolo de Matteis;* the painting of St. Dominic, however, is a modern copy of Angelico's painting of the saint. The vault frescoes are by *Cristoforo Roncalli.* The statues of four Dominican bishops (St. Albert the Great [ca. 1200-1280], St. Antoninus [1389-1459], Blessed Andrew Franchi [1335-1401], and Blessed Augustine Kazotic [ca. 1260-1323]) are by unidentified sculptors. Benedict XIII's tomb, designed by *Carlo Marchionni,* is on the right, as one enters. Marchionni also did the relief, "Benedict Presides at a Roman Council," on the sarcophagus. The statues of the pope and Purity (right) are by *Pietro Bracci;* that of Humility (left) is by *Bartolomeo Pincellotti.* Opposite the tomb is the alabaster group, "Virgin and Child with John the Baptist and John the Evangelist" (1670) by *Francesco Grassia.* The pedestal has an eighteenth-century sculpture of the "Nativity." The carved marble balustrade at the chapel's entrance is also worthy of inspection.

(20) The altarpiece is *Ottavio Lioni*'s "Virgin Appears to St. Hyacinth." To the left is the tomb (1506) of the great Renaissance sculptor *Andrea Bregno* (1418–1503).

(21) The chapel is dedicated to the Dominican Pope St. Pius V (1566–1572). *Andrea Proccacini*'s "Pius V Raises the Crucifix over the Conquered Turks" is on the altar; the Christian victory (7 October 1571) at Lepanto took place during Pius V's pontificate. Baldi's "Assumption" (left) and "Pius V at Prayer" (right) decorate the walls; beneath these are mementoes of the saint. The vault frescoes are by *Michelangelo Cerruti*.

(22) The altar has Venusti's St. James. The tomb on the left is of Carlotta and Livia Lante della Rovere (d. 1870), surmounted by a statue of the Savior. A relief of the two sisters with their father Giulio is at the bottom. The tomb on the right is of Maria Colonna (d. 1840) and Margaret of Savoy, with the angel of the resurrection above. Tombs and statues (1865) are by *Pietro Tenerani*.

(23) *Bernardo Castello*'s painting (1605) of "St. Vincent Ferrer Preaching at the Council of Constance" is on the altar. St. Vincent Ferrer (1350–1419) was known for his fiery sermons. The tomb on the left is of Cardinal Vincenzo Giustiniani (d. 1582), master general of the Dominicans, and on the right the tomb of Giuseppe Giustiniani (d. 1600).

(24) The small portrait of the Savior, done in the style of *Perugino*, was given to the church by Clement VIII. The statue (1603) of St. John the Baptist (left) is by Buonvicino, and that of St. Sebastian (right) is attributed to *Michele Marini*. The lunette above the altar with "Adoration of Shepherds" is by an anonymous artist of the late sixteenth or early seventeenth century. The walls have two beautiful Renaissance tombs: on the left that of the Venetian man of letters Benedetto Maffei (d. 1494) and on the right that of Bishop Agostino Maffei (d. 1490).

(25) The altar painting of St. John the Baptist, as well as the lunettes and dome frescoes, are by *Francesco Nappi*. The several monuments on the walls are to members of the Naro family; on the left is the tomb of Cardinal Gregorio Naro (d. 1634).

(26) The modern painting (1922) of "Sacred Heart with Sts. Catherine of Siena and Margaret Mary Alacoque" is by *Corrado Mezzana*. The frescoes of "Resurrection" in the lunette and of "Triumph of the Lamb" in the vault are also modern.

(27) Handsome Renaissance tomb of the young Florentine merchant, Francesco Tornabuoni (d. 1480), by *Mino da Fiesole*. Above is the tomb of Cardinal Giacomo Tebaldi (d. 1465), attributed to Bregno and *Giovanni Dalmata*.

(28) Sacristy and St. Catherine of Siena's room. The hall leading to the sacristy has on the left wall two reclining statues that were once part of the monument to Paul IV. Within the sacristy, the painting (1640) over the altar is "Crucifixion with Saints," by *Andrea Sacchi.* The vault's center has *Giuseppe Puglia's* "St. Dominic in Glory." Over the door is a fresco by *Giovanni Battista Speranza* recalling the celebration of two papal conclaves in this church: the first was in 1431 at which Eugenius IV (1431-1447) was elected, and the second in 1447 for the election of Nicholas V (1447-1455). Portraits of Dominican saints are on the walls; the walnut wardrobes are from the seventeenth century. The coat of arms with the bees is that of Cardinal Antonio Barberini (1569-1646), who had been a benefactor to the church.

Entrance to St. Catherine's room is to the altar's right. In 1630 Cardinal Barberini had the wall frescoes from the room where the saint died (29 April 1380) on Via S. Chiara number 14 moved here. The nine frescoes (1482) are by Antoniazzo Romano and pupils; a "Crucifixion with Saints" is the altarpiece. The oval painting of "St. Catherine of Siena" is a copy of a painting attributed to *Bronzino.*

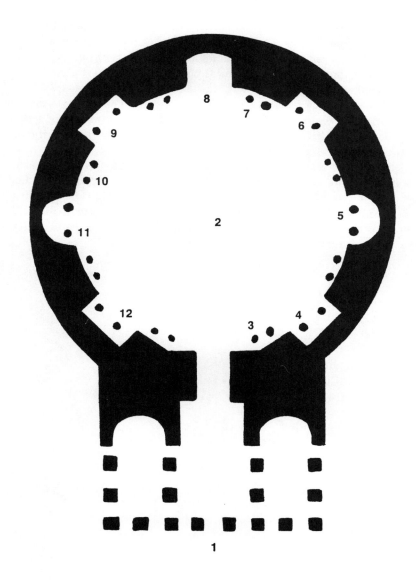

Pantheon (S. Maria ad Martyres)

42 Pantheon (S. Maria ad Martyres)***

Piazza della Rotonda

History. This is the best preserved building from ancient Roman times. It was built by Marcus Agrippa (63–12 B.C.), son-in-law of Augustus, in the year 27 B.C., during his third term as consul (as the Latin inscription on the architrave indicates). After fire damage in the year 80, the building was restored by Domitian (emperor 81–96), and after severe damage (lightning?) during the time of Trajan (emperor 98–117), it was totally rebuilt by Hadrian (emperor 117–138). Hadrian transformed Agrippa's building into the present structure; nevertheless, he placed Agrippa's name on the facade. Below this inscription there is another, smaller in size, which records that both Septimius Severus (emperor 193–211) and Caracalla (emperor 211–217) also did some restoring (probably on the inside). Inasmuch as this was a pagan temple, it was closed (391) by Theodosius the Great (emperor 379–395), and two centuries later Pope Boniface IV (608–615), having received the building from Phocas (emperor 602–610), converted (609) it into a church. Since Boniface had twenty-eight cartloads of martyrs' bones brought here from Rome's various cemeteries, he dedicated the church to S. Maria ad Martyres. In 663, when Constans II (emperor 641–668) came to Rome for a visit, he stripped the roof of its gilded bronze tiles and intended to take them to Constantinople, but the booty was captured by Saracens off Syracuse. In 735 Gregory III (731–741) gave the dome a lead covering, and other restorations followed in successive centuries. When bronze was needed for the baldachin in St. Peter's, Urban VIII (1623–1644) had the bronze trusses and girders removed from the portico and replaced with wood. This gave rise to the pun on the pope's family name: "Quod non fecerunt barbari, fecerunt Barberini" ("What the barbarians didn't do, the Barberini did").

Exterior. (1) The building is preceded by a pronaos of sixteen monolithic columns of red and grey granite with Corinthian capitals, and a triangular pediment, which once had a bronze relief. The front row has eight columns, with another eight in the rear forming three aisles. The columns are approximately 42 feet high and 15 feet in circumference; thirteen of the columns are original, while the three on the far left were replaced during the time of Urban VIII and Alexander VII (1655–1667), as the papal coats of arms in the capitals indicate. The medieval campanile was demolished ca. 1626 and two small towers were constructed (ca. 1634) at either end of the pronaos. The Romans did not take to them and called them "Berni-ni's ass's ears"; it is far from clear whether *Gian Lorenzo Bernini* was ac-tually responsible for them. They were removed in 1883. The walls of the building are of brick bearing consular dates from 115 to 124, and were originally faced with marble. The two niches in the portico once had colos-sal statues of Agrippa (left) and Augustus (right). The bronze doors were restored by Pius IV (1559–1565).

Interior. (2) The building is circular with a diameter equal to its height, about 142 feet. The spectacular coffered dome, whose weight is equally distributed on the supporting walls, has an *oculus* in the center (30 feet in diameter), the sole source of light in the building. In Roman times this was covered with a movable disk, a *clypeus.* The area above the cornice and below the base of the dome has a series of panels and blind windows; this marble decoration is from 1747, when *Pier Paolo Posi* replaced the original polychrome marble with the present marble. However, one sec-tion within this area (right of the main altar) still has the original (but restored) decoration. In the wall there are seven large niches, of which four are rectangular and three semicircular; each may have been conse-crated to one of the seven planetary gods, to whom the building was prob-ably first dedicated. The marble columns in front of these niches are of giallo antico. Between the niches are aedicules with segmental or triangu-lar pediments.The pavement was restored during the time of Pius IX (1846–1878).

(3) The aedicule has a late seventeenth-century painting of St. Nicholas of Bari, by an anonymous artist.

(4) The "Annunciation" fresco is attributed to *Melozzo da Forlì.* On the right is an attractive "St. Thomas with the Risen Lord" (1633), by *Pier Paolo Bonzi;* on the left is "St. Lawrence with St. Agnes" (ca. 1645), by *Clemente Maioli.* The two angels are done in Bernini's style. The aedicule on the left has a fifteenth-century fresco of "Coronation of the Virgin."

(5) Tomb of Vittorio Emanuele II (1820–1878), first king of Italy (1861–1878). The aedicule to the left has *Lorenzo Ottoni*'s statue of St. Ann and the Virgin.

(6) In the center is a fifteenth-century fresco of "Virgin with Sts. John the Baptist and Francis of Assisi." On the right wall is "Emperor Phocas Gives the Pantheon to Boniface IV (ca. 1750)," by an anonymous artist.

(7) The statue is of St. Anastasius, by *Bernardino Cametti*, and the aedicule on the other side of the main altar has a statue of St. Rasius, by *Francesco Moderati*. Both Anastasius and Rasius were Roman mar-tyrs. It was discovered in 1675 that of all the bones brought here by Boniface IV, none were identified except those of these two martyrs, which

Pantheon (S. Maria ad Martyres) (G. B. Falda, 1665)

were in a special casket. Clement X (1670–1676) had them encased in the main altar and, thus, these two saints have these central aedicules. Though nothing else is known about these martyrs, the sculptors have given them sacerdotal vestments.

(8) The altar dates from the early part of eighteenth century and has an image of the Virgin said to be from the seventh century. This image was the underpainting (discovered during restoration work in 1960) of a later Byzantine-style Virgin.

(9) The crucifix is from the fifteenth century. On the right wall is a monument (1824) by *Bertel Thorvaldsen*, containing the heart of Cardinal Ercole Consalvi (1757–1824), secretary of state to Pius VII (1800–1823). The cardinal is buried in S. Marcello, but the monument is here because this had been his titular church. On the left wall is "Pentecost" (1790), by *Pietro Labruzzi*, and a memorial to *Raphael* (1483–1520), whose tomb is to the left.

(10) Beneath the aedicule is Raphael's tomb. His remains are in an ancient marble sarcophagus, at the upper edge of which is the famous distich composed by the humanist and poet Cardinal Pietro Bembo (1470–1547). Alexander Pope translated it in the following manner: "Living, great nature feared he might outvie/Her works; and dying fears herself to die." Raphael died on 6 April 1520 and on the following day was buried here, according to his own request, near the tomb of his fiancée, Maria Bib-

biena. The marker indicating her place of burial is on the right of the aedicule, immediately below the empty niche. The statue in the aedicule is "Madonna del Sasso" (Madonna of the Rock) by *Lorenzetto*. In his last will Raphael asked Lorenzetto, his friend, to make a statue for his tomb. The Madonna is called "del Sasso" because her left foot rests on a rock. To the right of the aedicule, below the Maria Bibbiena marker, is a stone tablet indicating the place of burial of the great Bolognese artist *Annibale Carracci* (1560–1609).

The bust of Raphael (1833) in the niche, left of the aedicule, is by *Giuseppe Fabris;* below is Raphael's tombstone.

(11) Tomb of Umberto I (1844–1900), king of Italy (1878–1900), assassinated (29 July 1900) at Monza by an anarchist. Below is the tomb of Queen Margherita di Savoia (1851–1925), wife of Umberto I. The aedicule to the left has *Vincenzo Felici*'s statue of St. Agnes.

(12) The chapel (1543) is dedicated to "St. Joseph in the Holy Land"; soil from the Holy Land was used in building it. The "St. Joseph and Child Jesus" on the altar is by *Vincenzo De Rossi*. The reliefs (about 1720) on the side walls are "St. Joseph's Dream" (left) and "Flight into Egypt" (right), by *Carlo Monaldi*. The chapel was sponsored by the Confraternity of Virtuosi and on the feast of its patron (19 March) the confraternity met here and distributed dowries to poor girls. Some prominent artists are likewise buried here. Beneath *Francesco Cozza*'s fresco of the "Nativity," left of the altar, is the tombstone of the violin virtuoso and composer Arcangelo Corelli (1653–1713). On the right of the altar and below Cozza's "Adoration of the Magi" are the tombstones (left to right) of the following: architect *Bartolomeo Baronino* (1511–1554); Raphael's pupil *Perin del Vaga* (1500–1547); *Taddeo Zuccari* (1529–1566). Outside the chapel, left of the aedicule on the right, is the bust and tomb marker of the painter *Baldassarre Peruzzi* (1481–1536). Also buried in the Pantheon are the sculptor and architect *Flaminio Vacca* (1538–1605) and the painter *Giovanni da Udine* (1487–1564).

The aedicule to the left has *Andrea Cammasei*'s "Assumption" (1639).

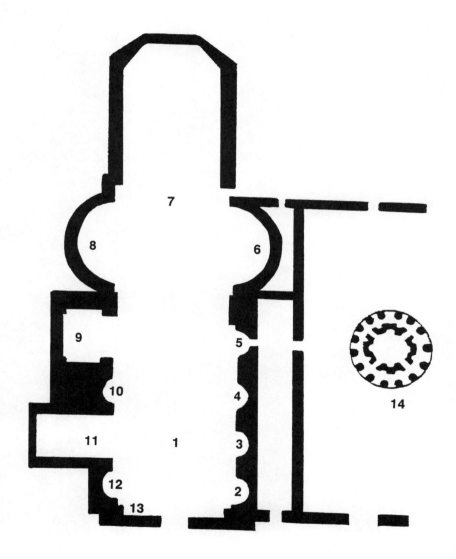

S. Pietro in Montorio

43   S. Pietro in Montorio***

Piazza di S. Pietro in Montorio

History. During the Middle Ages and the Renaissance it was piously believed that St. Peter the Apostle was martyred here on the Janiculum Hill. The church is thus dedicated to St. Peter and is known as "in Montorio" because the Janiculum, having yellow sand in its soil, was often referred to as *Mons aureus*. A church and monastery existed here before the ninth century. In 1472 Pope Sixtus IV (1471–1484) gave the church and monastery to Spanish Franciscans, who then had the church demolished, and with financial help from Ferdinand (1452–1516) and Isabella (1451–1504) of Spain, built (about 1481) the present church. The architects were probably *Baccio Pontelli* and *Meo Del Caprino*. During the French bombardment of Rome in June 1849, the church suffered severe damage and was subsequently restored in 1851. In 1870 the next door monastery was ceded to Spain; it is now the seat of the Spanish Academy of Fine Arts.

Exterior. The Renaissance facade is simple and is attributed to Del Caprino. It is of travertine and of two orders, with corner pilasters. The lower order has a single doorway; a rose window is in the upper and the facade is surmounted by a triangular pediment, in whose tympanum is the coat of arms of the kings of Spain. The construction of the piazza and of the double staircase leading up to the church is due (1605) to Philip III (1578–1621) of Spain; a stone tablet on the staircase bears his name. The inscription over the door reads: "Under the patronage of the Kings of Spain, during the reign of Alfonso XII, A.D. 1876."

Interior. (1) The church has a single nave with lateral chapels and a transept ending in two large chapels. The presbytery has a polygonal shape. The nave's vault is painted with monochromatic designs. The marble pavement is most probably from the time of the 1851 restorations.

(2) Painted directly on the wall is one of *Sebastiano del Piombo's* most powerful works, "Scourging of Christ" (ca. 1519), and based perhaps on a *Michelangelo* design. On the painting's left is his St. Peter and on the right St. Francis of Assisi. His are also the "Transfiguration" in the half-dome, and the prophets Isaiah (left) and Jeremiah (right) on the outside arch. It took the artist six years (1519–1525) to complete the chapel.

(3) The fresco of the "Madonna of the Letter" (ca. 1564), by *Niccolò Circignani*, was originally in a nearby wall shrine, but was brought within the church in 1714 by Clement XI (1700–1721). An inscription on the church's front stairs commemorates the transfer of the image to the church. The half-dome has an attractive "Coronation of the Virgin" by *Baldassarre Peruzzi*. His are also the cardinal virtues on the outside arch: (left to right) Fortitude, Prudence, Temperance, and Justice. The coat of arms in the center is that of the Spanish monarchs, also found elsewhere in the church. The charming relief on the altar's frontal is a replica of the fresco over the altar.

(4) The altarpiece is "Presentation of the Lord in the Temple," by an unidentified eighteenth-century artist. The frescoes on the sides are by *Michelangelo Cerruti;* on the left is his "Annunciation" and on the right "Immaculate Conception." On the outside arch are four sibyls; these are attributed to Peruzzi, since they match the figures on the outside arch of the previous chapel.

(5) A sixteenth-century fresco of the "Crucifixion" is in the half-dome.

(6) This chapel (1552) was designed by *Giorgio Vasari* at the request of Julius III (1550–1555) as a funerary chapel for his family. Vasari's "Ananias Restores St. Paul's Sight" (1551) is the altarpiece. The gentleman in black at the left edge of the painting may be a self-portrait. The frescoes in the half-dome, attributed to *Giulio Mazzoni,* represent scenes from St. Paul's life. On the altar's left is the tomb of Cardinal Antonio Del Monte (d. 1533), uncle of Julius III. Also buried here is Fabiano Del Monte. A statue of Religion is in the niche above the tomb. Justice is in the niche on the right. The statues (1550–1553) are by *Bartolomeo Ammannati,* who also did the putti in the balustrade.

On the left side of the outside arch are St. Augustine (bottom) and St. Gregory the Great (top). The four large figures above are the evangelists (in the center is Julius III's coat of arms) and on the right side St. Jerome. Below is the monument of Cardinal Fulvio Corneo (d. 1583). On the pilaster to the chapel's right is a monument to Julius III's nephew, Cardinal Roberto de' Nobili (d. 1559), who died when he was seventeen. His portrait is on the monument.

(7) The painting on the presbytery wall is *Vincenzo Camuccini's* copy of *Guido Reni's* "Crucifixion of St. Peter," now in the Vatican Pinacoteca. From 1523 to 1809, however, *Raphael's* "Transfiguration" was the altarpiece; it was commissioned by Cardinal Giulio de' Medici, who later became Clement VII (1523–1534). In 1809 the painting was taken to France by Napoleonic forces; when it was returned (1816), it was placed in the Vatican Pinacoteca.

The famous Beatrice Cenci (1577–1599) was buried under the altar's steps, but since the altar was moved forward during the last century, her remains now lie beneath the altar. The two marble angels flanking the altar are by *Giuseppe Setaccioli* and were originally sculpted for the Madonna of the Letter chapel. In the nave, in front of the presbytery, are the tombstones of three Irish patriots, who after the failure of the 1598 rising against Elizabeth I sought refuge in Rome: Hugh O'Neill, earl of Tyrone (d. 1616); his son Hugh, baron of Dungannon (d. 1609); and Roderick O'Donnell, earl of Tyrconnel (d. 1608).

(8) The chapel was designed by *Daniele da Volterra*, and his "Baptism of Christ," painted on slate, is on the altar. The Eternal Father in the center and two scenes from the Baptist's life, namely, his preaching (left) and martyrdom (right), are attributed to Mazzoni. The statues in the niches are St. Peter (left) and St. Paul (right), and are attributed to *Leonardo Sormani*. The tombs are of cardinals Giovanni Ricci (d. 1574) and Francesco Ricci (d. 1755). The prophets Isaiah and Jeremiah are on the outside arch, with the coat of arms of Cardinal Giovanni Ricci in the center. The balustrade copies the one directly opposite; the putti are said to be by Sormani.

(9) This chapel (1615–1620) is a gem; Mazzoni's stucco work is exceptional. The splendid "Burial of Christ" (1617) over the altar is by *Dirk van Baburen*, a follower of *Caravaggio*. The right wall has *David van Haen*'s moving "Way to Calvary"; its pendant on the left, "Christ with the Doctors in the Temple," is less successful and is by an anonymous artist of the Dutch school. The left lunette has "Christ in the Garden" and the opposite "Mocking of Christ." Over the outside arch are stucco figures of Fortitude (left) and Faith (right).

(10) The altarpiece is "St. Ann with the Virgin and Child" by a follower of *Antoniazzo Romano*. The fresco on the left is "Christ Meets His Mother on Way to Calvary" and that on the right "St. John the Baptist Points out Christ to Two Disciples." Both are by an anonymous seventeenth-century artist. The half-dome has the Eternal Father. On the outside arch are Solomon (left) and David (right), attributed to Peruzzi. The figure on the left holds a text from Song of Songs 4:7, "You are all-beautiful, my beloved, and there is no blemish in you," and the figure on the right holds a text from Psalm 45:5, "the holy dwelling of the Most High." Solomon is said to be the author of Songs and David the author of the Psalms but the identifications at the bottom appear to be mixed up.

(11) This handsome chapel was designed by *Gian Lorenzo Bernini*. The relief (1642–1646) over the altar, "St. Francis in Ecstasy," is by *Francesco Baratta*, a disciple of his. The fresco of "St. Francis in Paradise" in the vault, and the medallions with scenes of the saint's life, are by *Guidobaldo Abbatini*. The side walls have tombs with the Raimondi coat of arms at the top. The one on the left is of Girolamo Raimondi (d. 1628); two putti look into the open casket, one turns his head away and the other

extinguishes a torch. The relief on the urn is "Resurrection on the Day of Judgment." The tomb on the right is that of Francesco Raimondi (d. 1638). The relief on the urn has a triple scene: the joy of carnival (left), imposition of ashes on Ash Wednesday (center), and death and burial (right). The busts and reliefs are by *Andrea Bolgi.* Beneath is a simple but elegant frieze of birds amid rose branches.

(12) The sixteenth-century frescoes in this chapel are by *Giovanni De Vecchi.* The altar has "St. Francis Receives the Stigmata"; on the left is St. Nicholas of Bari and on right St. Catherine of Alexandria. Depicted in the half-dome is the funeral of Cardinal Clemente Dolera (d. 1568), benefactor of the church and of the Franciscan convent. In the center is the bier, on the left Mass is being celebrated for him, and on the right St. Pius V (1566–1572) kneels in prayer. Above, St. Francis intercedes for his soul. On the outside arch, also by De Vecchi, are two female figures; the angel on the left holds a scroll with "Sustain," and the other "Abstain."

(13) On the right of the doorway is the attractive monument (1510) by *Giovanni Antonio Dosio* of the Franciscan Giuliano Municipi da Volterra (d. 1508), archbishop of Ragusa. The lunette above the archbishop's recumbent figure has "Virgin and Two Saints"; the saint on the left appears to be a martyr, that on the right St. Bernardine of Siena. The epitaph reads: "To the good, both death and life are sweet."

(14) The Tempietto was constructed by *Donato Bramante* in 1502, commissioned by the Spanish monarchs, Ferdinand and Isabella. It stands on the spot which was then believed to be the site of St. Peter's martyrdom. The building is circular, and has three steps leading up to a peristyle of sixteen Doric columns. The lower portion of the building has three doorways and four windows. The granite columns support a trabeation with a balustrade; the cupola's drum has niches and windows and is surmounted by a lantern.

Inside, a sixteenth-century statue of a seated St. Peter is over a white marble altar, whose frontal has the coat of arms of the monarchs of Spain, and a center relief of an ark on water, symbol of the Church. Above the altar, but beneath the statue, is a frieze with three scenes from Peter's life: his condemnation, crucifixion, and being led to heaven. Statues of the evangelists are in the niches. The pavement is in the cosmatesque style.

Behind the tempietto are two sets of stairs leading down to a subterranean crypt. The walls have marble facing; the vault has stucco work (heavily ornate) with scenes from Peter's life. In front of the altar is the hole into which the cross of Peter, it had been believed, was placed at the time of his crucifixion. Peter was actually martyred in the circus of Nero, located just left of St. Peter's basilica. The inscription on the altar's front records the beneficence of Ferdinand and Isabella.

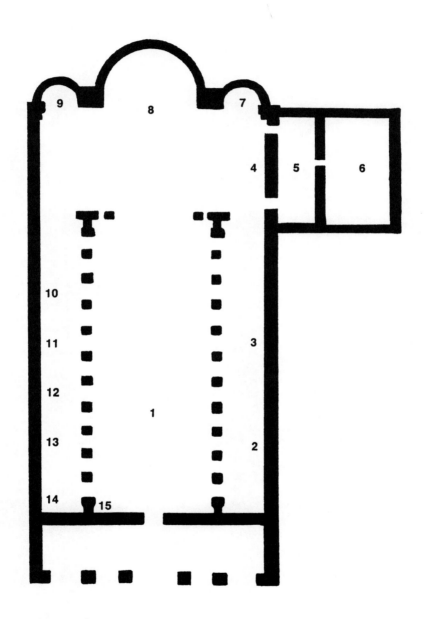

S. Pietro in Vincoli

44 S. Pietro in Vincoli***

Piazza di S. Pietro in Vincoli

History. The present building goes back to the first half of the fifth century, but was preceded by an earlier church dedicated to all the apostles, and built on Roman third-century B.C. ruins. About 438 Eudoxia, wife of Valentinian III (emperor 425–455 in the West), built the present basilica to house the chains with which St. Peter had been bound in Jerusalem and in Rome. The tradition behind the chains is that Eudoxia's mother, Eudocia, wife of Theodosius II (emperor 408–450 in the East), on a visit to Jerusalem, received from that Christian community the chains that held Peter in the Jerusalem prison. She kept one in Constantinople and sent the other to her daughter in Rome, asking that a basilica be built to house it. Eudoxia then gave the chain to Sixtus III (432–440) and, the tradition continues, when the pope placed it next to the chain that had bound Peter in Rome's Mamertime prison, both chains were miraculously joined together.

The basilica, about the same size as the earlier church, was consecrated by Sixtus III on 1 August 438–440, and dedicated to Sts. Peter and Paul. Since Eudoxia had built it, sources often refer to it as "Basilica Eudoxiana," but by the eleventh century it was more commonly known, as we know it today, as St. Peter in Chains. The basilica was restored by Hadrian I (772–795) and redone in the eleventh century after the Normans had sacked (1084) the city. Restorations were then done by Sixtus IV (1471–1484) and Cardinal Giuliano Della Rovere (1453–1513), titular (1471–1479) and later Julius II (1503–1513). The baroque additions inside date from the early eighteenth century under Clement XI (1700–1721). Pius IX (1846–1878) also made his contribution in constructing (1876–1877) the main altar and confession.

Exterior. The portico (1475), Cardinal Della Rovere's gift to the church, is most probably by *Meo Del Caprino;* it has five arches, separated by octagonal pilasters. The second story is an unfortunate later (1570–1578) addition; it completely conceals the church's facade. The large fifteenth-century doorway is also from the cardinal's period. In the corner, on the far right, is the entrance to the excavations done (1957–1959) beneath the pavement of the floor of the main nave; Roman ruins from third century B.C. to late third century A.D. were discovered, including the outline and foundations of the earlier church.

Interior. (1) The church has a main nave and two aisles, separated by twenty fluted white marble columns with Doric capitals. Since such columns were unknown in classical Rome, it is thought that they may have come from a Grecian temple. Two columns of red granite with Corinthian capitals support the triumphal arch between nave and transept.

The baroque coffered vault (1705–1706) is by *Francesco Fontana*. The inscription over the arch informs us that the vault was done during the pontificate of Clement XI, whose coat of arms is on the ceiling toward the front, and at the time when Cardinal Marcello Durazzo (d. 1710) was titular (1701–1710). The expense was borne by Prince Giovanni Battista Pamphili, whose coat of arms is near the entrance. In the center is the large fresco (1706) of "Miracle of the Chains," by *Giovanni Battista Parodi*; a count in the entourage of Otto I (emperor 936–973) is freed (969) from the devil's possession by touching the chains.

The marble pavement is from 1960; it was on the occasion of replacing the pavement that the above-mentioned excavations were made.

(2) The painting of St. Augustine on the altar is attributed to *Guercino*.

(3) The altarpiece is "Liberation of St. Peter from Prison," a copy by an unidentified artist of *Domenichino*'s painting in the ante-sacristy. To the right is the monument to Cardinal Lanfranco Margotti (d. 1611), titular (1610–1611), with the deceased's portrait by Domenichino, who also did the portrait on the monument to Cardinal Girolamo Agucchi (d. 1605), titular (1604–1605), on the left.

(4) This monument (1542–1545) to Julius II is a greatly reduced version of the one originally planned for St. Peter's basilica. In 1505 Pope Julius commissioned *Michelangelo* to prepare his tomb; it was to have four sides, be three stories high, have forty statues, and be conspicuously placed in the center of one of the tribunes of the new basilica, then under construction. Because of other tasks (e.g., Sistine ceiling), delays, Julius' death, and disinterest on the part of his successors, the grandiose tomb was five times scaled down. Finally, Paul III (1534–1549) ordered that the monument be completed and placed here. A frustrated Michelangelo left the monument's details to his students. The spectacular Moses, which the master sculpted ca. 1515, is the centerpiece. The sculptor depicts the prophet after he had come down from Mount Sinai and found the Hebrews yielding to idolatry—thus, his solemn pose and stern gaze. Michelangelo's other statues for the tomb were too large for the monument's new size; hence, they were never used and are now in Paris and Florence. Julius II is buried in St. Peter's but has no tomb. When he died, his body was placed in Sixtus IV's tomb, and when that was moved, the remains of both popes were then interred below the pavement in front of the tomb of Clement X.

S. Pietro in Vincoli (G. Vasi, 1753)

The statues (1542–1544) of Rachel (left) and Leah (right) were begun by Michelangelo but finished by his disciple *Raffaello da Montelupo*. The cramped recumbent figure of the pope above is by *Maso del Bosco* and the Virgin and Child by *Scherano da Settignano*. The sibyl (left) and prophet (right) are by Raffaello da Montelupo.

(5) Ante-sacristy. On the church wall is a large canvas, by an anonymous artist, showing the episcopal consecration of Giovanni Mastai Ferretti, later Pius IX, in this basilica on 3 June 1827. To its right, over the door, is *Pier Francesco Mola*'s St. Augustine, and Domenichino's "Liberation of St. Peter from Prison" (1604) is on the other wall.

(6) Sacristy. The vault has "Angel Leads St. Peter from Prison" in the center and four scenes from St. Peter's life. These are by *Paris Nogari*. On the altar, in the niche on the right, is an exceptionally fine fifteenth-century relief of Virgin and Child; the altar also has cosmatesque decorations.

(7) The altar in the right apse has *Guercino*'s St. Margaret (1617–1623).

(8) On the occasion of the fiftieth anniversary of his episcopal consecration, Pius IX had *Virginio Vespignani* redesign (1876–1877) the main altar and introduce a confession in front of it. The altar has four red granite columns with gilded bronze Corinthian capitals that support a handsome baldachin, similar to the one in S. Maria in Trastevere, which Vespignani had erected ten years previously. The elegant balustrade of polychrome marble is likewise his work.

The fresco in the half-dome, by *Iacopo Coppi*, is from 1577 (restored in 1706) and depicts the story of the Beirut crucifix, according to which an image of Christ was nailed to a cross in the eighth century and began to shed blood. His are also the three frescoes on the presbytery walls: "St. Peter Is Freed from Prison" (left), "Eudoxia Gives St. Peter's Chain to Pope Sixtus III" (center), and "Eudoxia Speaks with Pope Sixtus" (right).

St. Peter's chains are preserved in the confession beneath the baldachin. The reliquary containing the chains was designed (1856) by *Andrea Busiri Vici*. The gilded bronze doors (1477) were the gift of Sixtus IV and Cardinal Della Rovere and are attributed to *Caradosso*. The left door has Sixtus' coat of arms and a relief of "Peter's Condemnation"; that on the right has Cardinal Della Rovere's coat of arms and "Peter's Liberation."

Stairs lead down to a crypt in which a fourth-century Christian sarcophagus with seven compartments contains the remains of the seven Maccabee brothers (see 2 Macc 7). When the sarcophagus was discovered beneath the main altar on 2 September 1876 (at the time of building the confession), the first compartment had a lead plate indicating that these were the ashes of the seven Maccabees. It is very likely that the sarcophagus had been placed here at the time of the church's first dedication. The front has five scenes from the New Testament: (left to right) raising of Lazarus, multiplication of the loaves and fishes, Samaritan woman at the well, foretelling Peter's denial, and giving of the law. The fresco (1876–1877) above is by *Silverio Capparoni* and depicts the brothers' martyrdom.

(9) The altarpiece is "Immaculate Conception," by an unidentified artist.

(10) Baroque monument of Bishop Mariano Pietro Vecchiarelli (d. 1539), and in the pavement in front, the burial place of Cardinal Odoardo Vecchiarelli (d. 1667).

(11) This **mosaic icon** of a bearded St. Sebastian, clothed as a military officer in Byzantine style, is from 680. He holds a martyr's crown in his left hand. It was done after the city had invoked the saint's intercession during the plague that devastated Rome (June–September 680). The saint is represented as older and not the handsome youthful arrow-pierced saint of Renaissance artists. On the right are two marble tablets: the top one is a brief (1683) of an indulgence grant by Innocent XI (1676–1689), and below a fifteenth-century inscription in which St. Sebastian is called *Depulsor pestilitatis*, "one who repels plagues." The marble tablet on the left is an indulgence grant (1576) of Gregory XIII (1572–1585).

(12) Monument (1707) of Cardinal Cinzio Aldobrandini (d. 1610), titular (1605–1610).

(13) "Deposition from the Cross" by *Cristoforo Roncalli*.

(14) This relief (1465) of Cardinal Nicholas of Cusa with St. Peter

is by *Andrea Bregno*. The cardinal kneels on St. Peter's right; the angel who freed the saint from prison is on the other side. When Cardinal Nicholas (1401–1464) became titular (1448–1464) of the church, he had a new altar constructed on the left transept wall to hold the reliquary with the chains. When he died, he was buried in front of that altar, and this relief most probably formed part of it. The tombstone, to the relief's right, was his tombstone, once in the pavement in front of the altar. Both were moved here during renovations in the transept in the early part of the eighteenth century.

(15) Tomb of the brothers *Antonio* (1429–1498) and *Pietro* (1443–1496) *Pollaiolo*. Antonio is especially known for his bronze tombs of Sixtus IV (1471–1484) and Innocent VIII (1484–1492) in St. Peter's basilica, which the inscription on the monument also recalls. The tomb is attributed to *Luigi Capponi*. Above is a faded fresco (fifteenth century) depicting a procession praying for the end of the 1476 plague.

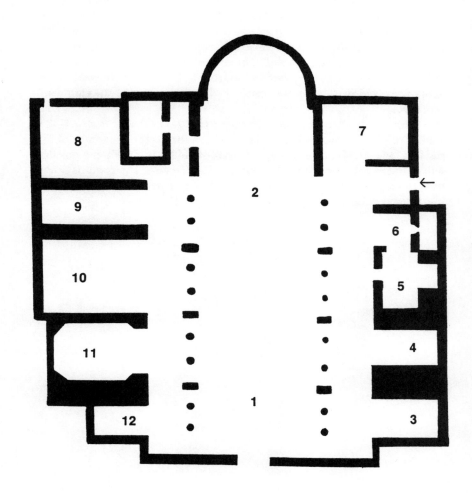

S. Prassede

45 S. Prassede***

Via di Santa Prassede

History. The church receives its name from the first-century Praxedes, who is said to have been a daughter of the Roman senator Pudens (mentioned in 2 Tim 4:21), and a sister of Pudenziana (see S. Pudenziana). Tradition uniformly depicts Praxedes and her sister as sheltering Christians in their home during the persecution of Nero (emperor 54–68), and of collecting the blood of the martyrs. After Praxedes' own martyrdom, she was buried next to her sister in what is now known as the Catacombs of St. Priscilla. The earliest historical reference to a church on this site, under the name of St. Praxedes, goes back to 489. The church was renovated by Pope Hadrian I (772–795), and then totally rebuilt and enlarged (822) by Paschal I (817–824) to house the relics of about twenty-three hundred martyrs that he had brought from the catacombs of S. Alessandro on Via Nomentana. The building underwent subsequent restorations, for example, at the time when St. Charles Borromeo (1538–1584) was titular (1564–1584), and later when Cardinal Ludovico Pico della Mirandola (d. 1743) was titular (1728–1731).

Exterior. The usual entrance to the church is from Via di Santa Prassede. The principal entrance, though it is rarely used, is on Via di San Martino ai Monti, where a Roman medieval porch (*prothyron*), with two granite columns (the now enclosed loggia was added in 1700), leads to a divided flight of stairs which, in turn, leads to a courtyard that opens on to the ninth-century simple brick facade with its single portal and three windows.

Interior. (1) The church has a main nave with two aisles separated by sixteen granite columns (others have been enclosed in piers to reinforce the building). The relatively unadorned coffered ceiling was redone (1721) by Cardinal Giuseppe Sacripante (d. 1727), and later restored (1864) by Pius IX (1846–1878).

The nave is frescoed (1594–1600) with angels and eight scenes from Christ's passion. The series, by various artists (for example, *Paris Nogari*, *Baldassarre Croce*, and *Giovanni Balducci*), begins with "Christ in the Garden" on the left wall near the triumphal arch and ends with "Christ on the Way to Calvary" on the opposite side. A fading "Annunciation," by *Stefano Pieri*, is on the rear wall. Apostles are on the pilasters.

The handsome pavement, with a variety of mosaic patterns, was reset in 1918. In the center, near the church's main door, is a large porphyry disk, encircled by the inscription: "Repository of the holy martyrs' relics in the house of St. Praxedes." It seems that a portion of the well, where the martyrs' blood had been preserved, was brought here from Pudens' home. Right of the main entrance, as one faces it, is an aedicule with a slab of marble on which, tradition claims, St. Praxedes slept. In front of it is a statue of the saint.

(2) The **mosaics** in the church are from about 822–824, the time of Paschal I. The mosaic on the triumphal arch represents the heavenly Jerusalem, elliptical in form and surrounded by gem-encrusted walls. An angel stands at each gate. In the center of the city is Christ, flanked by two angels; below him on the viewer's left are the Virgin, Sts. John the Baptist, Paul, and five apostles; on the viewer's right are Sts. Praxedes, Peter, and five apostles. On either side of the gates the just, carrying their crowns, approach to enter; on the right, Sts. Peter and Paul introduce the just to the angel, who, in turn, indicates that they may indeed enter. On both sides of the lower level there is a group of martyrs (men, women, and children) in white, carrying palms. This portion of the mosaic was damaged when Cardinal Borromeo constructed (1564) the aedicules, one on each side, in which relics were displayed for the faithful's veneration.

On the outside arch, the Lamb of God is in the center with seven candlesticks, angels, and the symbols of the evangelists. Below are the twenty-four elders of the Apocalypse, holding crowns in draped hands and offering them to the Lamb. The overhead vault simulates a star-studded sky.

The **apse mosaic** is similar to that in Ss. Cosma e Damiano, though a few centuries separate them. Christ, robed in gold, descends on clouds to greet Sts. Praxedes and Pudenziana, clothed in Byzantine style. On Christ's left St. Peter, with his arm around St. Pudenziana, presents her to the Savior; on the other side St. Paul, with arm around St. Praxedes, presents her. The other figures are Paschal I (the square nimbus signifies that he was still alive), who holds a model of the church, and St. Zeno. The hand reaching down from heaven, in the top center of the mosaic, is that of the Father, holding a crown over the Son's head. The palm trees are symbols of Paradise; the one on the left has a phoenix, symbol of the resurrection, on one of its branches. The Jordan flows beneath the group.

On the next level the Lamb of God is in the center standing on a mound from which flow the four rivers of Paradise; twelve lambs (apostles) approach from the cities of Jerusalem and Bethlehem. Beneath is an inscription which has Paschal's dedication to St. Praxedes. Both underarches have a colorful frieze of greenery with flowers and fruit, and with the name "Pascal" in the center.

A double staircase of rosso antico marble leads to the presbytery. The attractive baldachin (1730) with porphyry columns is by *Carlo Stefano Fontana*. Behind the altar in the apse is *Domenico Muratori*'s painting (1735), "St. Praxedes Gathers the Blood of the Martyrs." In the painting's upper right is a scene of Christians being martyred. The stone tablet on the left, in the apse, commemorates the restorations done by Cardinals Borromeo and Pico della Mirandola; that on the right describes the transfer of the martyrs' relics to this church at the time of Paschal I.

The crypt entrance is directly in front of the altar. In 1730 Cardinal Pico della Mirandola had four early Christian sarcophagi, with the relics of the martyrs, placed here; the sarcophagus on the lower right contains the relics of Sts. Praxedes and Pudenziana. The altar is a good example of the work of the Cosmati family. The now fading fresco over the altar is of the Virgin with Sts. Praxedes and Pudenziana.

(3) The church has been served by Benedictine monks of Vallombrosa since 1198, when they received it from Innocent III (1198–1216). The three paintings in this chapel depict two Vallombrosan saints and one blessed. *Filippo Luzi*'s painting over the altar represents the miracle of St. Bernard (d. 1133), cardinal bishop of Parma, stopping the flow of water in the Po River. The canvas (1716) on the left wall by *Angelo Soccorsi* shows St. Peter Aldobrandini (ca. 1000–1089) pass through fire unharmed, proving that the monks' accusation against the simoniacal bishop of Pavia was just. The ordeal is said to have taken place in 1063; in 1074 Gregory VII (1073–1085) made Peter cardinal bishop of Albano. The martyrdom of Blessed Tesauro Beccaria (d. 1258) is on the right wall. As abbot general of the Vallombrosan order, he was asked to reconcile the warring Guelphs and Ghibellines, but without success. The painting is by *Giovanni Domenico Piastrini.*

(4) The altarpiece is a modern (1954) painting of St. Pius X (1903–1914) by *Bartoli*; St. Pius was canonized in 1954, and his cause had been promoted by the monks of this monastery. On the left is "Adoration of the Magi" and on the right "Vision of Sts. Anne and Joachim," both by *Ciro Ferri*. The vault has "Eternal Father with Saints," by *Guillaume Courtois.* The lunette on the left depicts "Supporters of Henry V Attack Pope Gelasius II." Since Pope Gelasius (1118–1119) had excommunicated Emperor Henry V, the latter's supporters in Rome attacked (21 July 1118) the pope, while he was celebrating Mass in this church. The lunette on the right has "Countess Matilda Orders the Building of a Church over Pagan Ruins." Both lunettes are by Ferri.

(5) The Chapel of St. Zeno was built by Paschal I (817–824) as a mausoleum for his mother Theodora; it is named, however, after the early Roman martyr Zeno, whose relics Paschal had placed here. The chapel's entrance is flanked by two columns (one is black and white granite, the other black serpentine porphyry) supporting an ornate architrave, salvaged from a Roman monument, and surmounted by a third-century Roman funerary urn. A mosaic lunette with two rows of medallions frames the grated window above. The inner row has Virgin and Child in the center; the two male figures on the sides may be St. Zeno and his brother St. Valentine, a martyr whose relics were also brought here. Of the female figures perhaps the two uppermost are Sts. Praxedes and Pudenziana. The outside row has a blue background, in contrast to the gold of the inner row, and has Christ with the apostles. The two unidentifiable popes at the base of the lunette are of a later date. The figures at the top, outside the lunette, may be Moses and Elijah.

The chapel is in the form of a Greek cross. The mosaics cover the upper portion of the walls and vault; they are Byzantine in style and are the most important ninth-century mosaics in the city. Within the chapel one feels totally surrounded by gold, and since gold in Byzantine iconography symbolizes heaven, the chapel had been known as the "Garden of Paradise." The vault's center has a roundel with Christ; angels in white stand in the four corners and with extended arms hold the roundel.

The lunette on the wall with the altar has the Virgin (left) and St. John the Baptist (right); the underarch has a pattern of acanthus leaves with birds and animals.

The lunette on the left wall has Sts. Agnes and Pudenziana on the left, with St. Praxedes on the right; beneath the arch, on the same wall, is a small lunette with the Lamb of God on a mound, from which Paradise's four rivers flow and to which deer come to drink. Below are four feminine busts; the one on the far left is identified as *Theodora episcopa*, and has a square nimbus to indicate that she was still living when the mosaic was executed. Theodora is called *episcopa* because she was the mother of the bishop of Rome. The remaining three figures are St. Praxedes, with a crown, the Virgin Mary, and St. Pudenziana. The small mosaic on the wall to the right represents Christ's descent into hell and his liberation of the just.

The lunette over the entrance has a richly ornamented throne with a golden cross, symbolizing Christ, with Sts. Peter (left) and Paul (right). The lunette on the remaining wall has St. John on the left, with Sts. Andrew and James on the right. Beneath the arch is another lunette, with Christ and Sts. Zeno and Valentine. Over the altar is a niche with a thirteenth-century mosaic of the Virgin and Child with Sts. Praxedes (left) and Pudenziana (right).

The pavement in the chapel is an early example of *opus sectile* in polychrome marble. Beneath the porphyry disk Theodora and martyrs are buried.

In the small room to the right is a marble column which Cardinal Giovanni Colonna (d. 1245), titular (1212–1244) and papal legate to Constantinople, had brought with him on his return to Rome in 1223. Tradition claims that this is a part of the column to which our Lord was tied at the time of his scourging.

(6) Renaissance tomb of Cardinal Alain de Coetivy (1407–1474) by *Andrea Bregno*. Over the cardinal's effigy are busts of Sts. Peter and Paul; on the outside arch are St. Praxedes (left) and St. Pudenziana (right). The wall opposite the tomb has *Francesco Gai's* "Christ Being Scourged"; in the fresco the artist reproduces the column in the previous room.

(7) The wooden crucifix over the altar is from the sixteenth century. On the opposite wall is the tomb of Cardinal Pantaléon Ancher, nephew of Urban IV (1261–1264). The cardinal was titular of the church and is said to have been killed here on 1 November 1286, during a popular uprising. The tomb, a fine example of medieval sculpture, is by *Arnolfo di Cambio;* the vestments and drapery, with the rose and fleur-de-lis designs, are especially well done. Fragments and tomb slabs are attached to the walls.

(8) Over the altar in the sacristy is *Agostino Ciampelli's* "Christ Approves St. John Gualberto's Pardon of an Enemy" (1594). St. John Gualberto (ca. 995–1073) was the founder of the Vallombrosan Benedictine branch. The right wall has an expressive "Scourging of Christ" attributed to *Giulio Romano,* and *Giovanni De Vecchi's* "Christ Taken from the Cross." On the wall opposite the altar is Gai's "St. John Gualberto Dictates His Spiritual Testament," and on the left wall is Courtois's "St. John Gualberto of Vallombrosa."

(9) The Blessed Sacrament Chapel was redone in 1933. The niche over the altar has a mosaic of the founder, St. John Gualberto. The apse has "Virgin with Sts. John Gualberto and Humility," by *Giulio Bargellini.* St. Humility (ca. 1227–1310) was a Vallombrosan abbess. Bargellini's "St. John Gualberto Pardons his Kinsman's Murderer" is on the left wall; this episode in the saint's life occurred while he was still a knight. The other fresco, by the same artist, has "St. John Gualberto Defeats Simony and Nicolaitanism." This is an allegorical interpretation of the saint's conflict with the simoniacal archbishop of Florence and with those opposed to clerical celibacy.

Outside the chapel, on the left wall, is a superbly engraved tombstone. The inscription informs us that it was for John VI von Jenzentein, patriarch of Alexandria, who died in Rome on 17 June 1400. Beneath is a grey tablet, which says that the tombstone had been placed here in 1891, and now serves as but one example of the many wonderful tombstones that once paved the church floor.

(10) The fine frescoes in this Olgiati Chapel are by *Cavalier d'Arpino*, done between 1593 and 1595. The vault has his "Ascension" in the center, the triangular panels have the four Doctors of the Latin Church (Augustine, Ambrose, Jerome, and Gregory), while the others have angels, prophets, and sibyls. St. Andrew (left) and St. Bernard of Clairvaux (right) flank the altar. On the wall opposite the altar are: a fading "Assumption," "Last Supper," "Road to Emmaus," and "Mary Magdalene Meets the Risen Christ." *Federico Zuccari*'s "Christ Meets Veronica," a painting on slate, is over the altar. On the left wall is the table at which St. Charles Borromeo shared his meals with the poor. The three tombs on the side walls are of the Olgiati family.

(11) This is the chapel of St. Charles Borromeo. *Étienne Parrocel*'s "St. Charles in Prayer before a Crucifix" is over the altar; the walls have "St. Charles Meditating on Christ's Passion" (left) and "St. Charles in Ecstasy" (right), both by *Lodovico Stern*. The statues in the niches are of the four cardinal virtues. Near the altar, on the left, is the faldstool used by the saint. His coat of arms is in the center of the pavement. As titular of the church, St. Charles often resided in the adjoining monastery and frequently celebrated Mass in the church.

(12) The altar has *Giuseppe Severoni*'s "St. Peter Being Received in the House of Senator Pudens"; "St. John the Baptist" is on the left, with "Sts. Agnes and Emerenziana" on the right wall, also by Severoni.

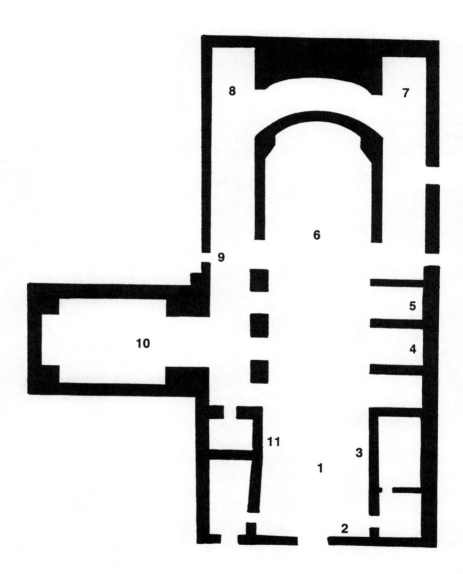

S. Pudenziana

46 S. Pudenziana***

Via Urbana

History. The church has an ancient tradition. This is supposedly the site of the house of Senator Pudens, who is said to have been St. Peter's host in Rome. Pudens is also said to have had two daughters, Pudenziana and Praxedes, and two sons, Timothy and Novatus. The family was among St. Peter's first converts. A Pudens is mentioned in 2 Timothy 4:21, but was he a senator? The early Christians may have, because of similarity of name, inadvertently turned two individuals into one. Tradition goes on to say that Pope Pius I (ca. 142–ca. 155) made the Pudens residence into a church, which was later incorporated into a public bath. During the time of Siricius (384–399) and Innocent I (401–417) a portion of that bath was transformed into a basilica. The church in early times was known in Latin as "Ecclesia Pudenziana," which means "Church of Pudens," but with the passage of time it came to be interpreted as "Church of Pudenziana." The basilica underwent various restorations, but perhaps the most unfortunate was that done in 1588 under *Francesco da Volterra*, at the request of Cardinal Enrico Caetani (1550–1599), titular (1585–1599).

Exterior. A double staircase (1870) leads down to the church, which is below street level. The facade was erected (1870) by *Antonio Manno*, commissioned by Cardinal Luciano Bonaparte (1828–1895), titular (1868–1879). The facade has two orders; a marble frieze separates them. The lower order has an especially elegant medieval portal with two spiral fluted columns supporting an eleventh-century sculpted architrave in which are five medallions: Pastor, Pudenziana, Praxedes, and Pudens, with the Lamb of God in the center. The inscription over the door reads: "Dedicated to St. Pudens and St. Pudenziana." The tympanum has a fading fresco of the Virgin and Child. The second order has two windows. The facade frescoes (1870) were done by *Pietro Gagliardi* and are now almost totally obliterated. St. Peter is in the center with Pudens on his right and Pudenziana on his left; on the far left is St. Pius I and on the far right St. Gregory the Great. The elaborate tympanum has the Savior with angels. The campanile is from the early part of the thirteenth century.

Interior. (1) The church has a main nave and two aisles, divided by ancient columns; the first three arches on the left and right are walled in, while the others have been reinforced by pilasters and sustaining arches.

The church, as we see it today, is the church after the 1588 renovation. The dome was also built in 1588, and the presbytery was altered at the same time. Early brick work is visible over the arches. The pavement was restored in 1963 by Cardinal Alberto Di Jorio (1884–1974), who was titular (1962–1974) and is buried at the end of the right aisle. His seal is in the center of the pavement.

(2) The back wall has a painting of "St. Peter Baptizes Pudens" and to its left, on the church's right wall, what appears to be its pendant, "Pudens Welcomes Sts. Peter and Paul." Both are by an anonymous sixteenth-century Tuscan artist.

(3) Tomb of Cardinal Włodzimierz Czacki (1834–1888) by *Pio Welonski*. The cardinal was titular (1883–1888); his effigy is in bronze.

(4) The altar has "Our Lady of Mercy." On the left is "Nativity of Mary" and "Nativity of Christ" is on the right; these are by *Lazzaro Baldi*.

(5) "The Virgin Appears to St. Bernard" is the altarpiece. The walls have "Christ Exchanges Hearts with St. Catherine of Siena" (left) and "St. Benedict in Ecstasy" (right); these are by *Michele Cippitello*.

(6) The **apse mosaic** dates from the end of the fourth century; it is Roman in style and antedates Byzantine influence in Roman mosaic production. This mosaic was, unfortunately, cut at the sides and at the bottom during the late sixteenth-century renovation. It depicts the heavenly Jerusalem; the upper portion has a jewelled cross (symbol of the victorious Christ) standing on a mound with the symbols of the evangelists floating amid colored clouds. The ox (Luke) is especially well done, the lion (Mark) much less so. The buildings in the background follow Roman architectural designs. The lower portion of the mosaic takes us within one of the buildings. Directly beneath the cross the Savior sits on a cushioned jewel-encrusted throne, with his apostles surrounding him. The Savior is in gold, wearing Roman dress, and holds a book in his left hand which reads: "The Lord, preserver of the Church of Pudenziana [*Ecclesia Pudenziana*]." St. Paul and four apostles are on his right, with St. Peter and another four on his left. Two apostles, one on each side, have been covered over or destroyed. Two female figures, holding crowns, stand behind Sts. Peter and Paul; these figures are sometimes said to be Sts. Pudenziana and Praxedes, but perhaps they are "the Church of the Circumcised" over Peter and "the Church of the Gentiles" over Paul.

The main altar is from the beginning of the nineteenth century; the painting (1803), "St. Pudenziana in Glory," is by *Bernardino Nocchi*. He likewise did the two figures flanking the altar, St. Timothy (left) and St. Novatus (right), Pudenziana's brothers.

The dome was constructed in 1588 and indifferently frescoed by *Cristoforo Roncalli*. Christ is in the center surrounded by angels; the figures near the base are Sts. Paul, Peter, and Pudens in the center, Sts. Pudenziana and Praxedes on the left, and Sts. Timothy and Novatus on the right.

(7) Sections of Roman floors, from the period when this was a public bath, are visible in the uneven floor. A statue of St. Paul is on the altar. On the right wall is a mosaic "Pietà" (1963), by *Sergio Ziveri*; this is the tomb of Cardinal Di Jorio (d. 1974).

(8) This richly decorated chapel is in honor of St. Peter. In the center over the altar is *Giovanni Battista Della Porta*'s marble group (1596), "Christ Gives the Keys to St. Peter." The marble inscription on the left wall informs us: "This house of St. Pudenziana was the first to give hospitality to St. Peter"; the inscription on the right refers to a piece of a wooden altar (now enclosed in the marble altar): "On this altar St. Peter . . . offered the Body and Blood of the Lord."

(9) Entrance to the Marian Oratory; the sacristan guides the visitor. In addition to fragments from excavations (1870, 1894 and 1928–1930) and a second-century mosaic pavement and wall, there are also eleventh-century frescoes, but in poor condition. Over the altar is "Virgin with Sts. Pudenziana and Praxedes"; on the left are "Paul Preaching" and "Baptism of Novatus and Timothy." Over the window is "Sts. Valerian, Tiburtius and Urban," and on the ceiling the "Lamb of God" with symbols of the evangelists. The frescoed "Crucifix" right of the altar is from the sixteenth century.

(10) This is the Caetani Chapel, erected by *Francesco da Volterra* at the request of Cardinal Enrico Caetani, but after the architect's death (1594) it was completed (1601) by *Carlo Maderno*. The chapel is especially ornate with polychrome marble and stucco, the work of G. B. Della Porta and *Valsoldo*. The vault has mosaic panels of the evangelists after designs by *Federico Zuccari*; the altar has a marble relief (ca. 1599) of the "Adoration of the Magi" by *Pier Paolo Olivieri*. The tomb of Cardinal Enrico (d. 1599) is on left, and that of Filippo Caetani (1565–1614), duke of Sermoneta, on the right. The tombs are attributed to Maderno. The niches have the four cardinal virtues.

Outside and on the right of the chapel's entrance is the tomb of Honorato Caetani (d. 1592), duke of Sermoneta. In the aisle is the well into which, tradition claims, Sts. Pudenziana and Praxedes placed the bodies of martyrs.

(11) A monument to Cardinal Luciano Bonaparte (d. 1895), titular. To the left is "Sts. Pudenziana and Praxedes Care for the Bodies of the Martyrs." St. Praxedes gathers the martyrs' blood, while St. Pudenziana places a severed head in the well. The painting is by an anonymous sixteenth-century Tuscan artist. On the rear wall of the facade is "St. Augustine Reflects on the Mystery of the Trinity," also by an unknown artist.

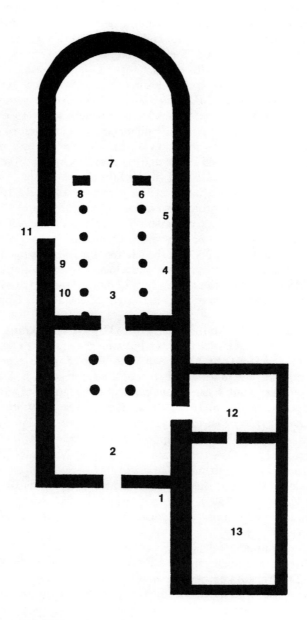

Ss. Quattro Coronati

47 Ss. Quattro Coronati**

Via dei Santi Quattro Coronati

History. The church is dedicated to "Four Crowned Saints," that is, four Roman soldiers who received the crown of martyrdom under Diocletian (emperor 284–305) for refusing to sacrifice to the pagan god Asclepius. Tradition has given them the names of Severus, Victorinus, Carpophorus, and Severinus. There was a church on this site by the end of the fifth century, and it may have been built in the time of Pope Melchiades (311–314). During the sixth century the church was regularly referred to as Ss. Quattro Coronati. Leo IV (847–855), who had been elected pope here, reconstructed the church, and brought the relics of these four saints to the church from the cemetery on Via Labicana, where they had been buried. About the same time he brought, from the same cemetery, the relics of the five sculptors (Claudius, Nicostratus, Castor, Sempronianus, and Simplicius), martyred in Pannonia (modern Hungary). These five were martyred because they refused to sculpt a statue of Asclepius. Because Leo's basilica had suffered severely when the Normans sacked (1084) Rome, Paschal II (1099–1118) rebuilt (1111) it, but on a smaller scale. In the sixteenth century Pius IV (1559–1565) gave (1560) the church and adjoining convent to Augustinian nuns, whose apostolate was caring for orphans. Augustinian nuns still inhabit the convent. In 1621–1623 Cardinal Giovanni Garzia Mellini (d. 1629), who was titular (1608–1627), had the apse decorated, as we see it today. The most recent extensive restorations were in 1912–1914 under *Antonio Muñoz*, who returned the body of the church to what it had been during the days of Paschal II.

Exterior. To advance to the church, one passes through a simple arched doorway, whose lunette fresco of the four martyrs has all but disappeared. Since the ninth-century tower is unlike other Romanesque bell towers in Rome—this one is truncated—its primary purpose may have been defense. A clock had been placed in the tower in 1625, but this century's restorations removed it. By passing beneath the tower, one enters the first courtyard, which was probably the *quadriporticus* of Leo IV's basilica.

(1) Under the portico on the right are two Tuscan school frescoes (1588) depicting the "Birth of the Virgin" (left) and "Presentation of Mary in the Temple" (right). The frescoes were damaged when the portico vault was lowered (1632). On the right is a doorway that leads to the Chapel

of St. Sylvester, which we shall visit after the basilica. The chapel was acquired by the stonecutters' and sculptors' guild in 1570 and, thus, the inscription in the architrave over the door bears that date. Above is a fresco of the Quattro Coronati. The doorway leading to the second courtyard is where Leo IV's basilica had its entrance.

(2) The second courtyard was once the rear portion of the central nave of the earlier basilica. Imbedded in the right wall are five columns that separated the church's nave from the right aisle. The underarch in the portico still has its ninth-century decoration. Above the entrance to the basilica is a fresco of the Quattro Coronati, with Augustinian nuns and orphan girls asking their intercession.

Interior. (3) The church is in basilican style, with a nave and two lateral aisles, separated by ancient grey granite columns of various thicknesses. The width of the present (Paschal II's) church is the width of Leo IV's nave, and the upper and lower portions of some of the columns that separated Leo's nave from the right aisle may still be seen in the present church's right wall. What was the right aisle in the ninth century is now the nuns' refectory. Remains of fourteenth-century frescoes still decorate the walls. Above the columns in the nave are women's galleries (*matronea*), each with three arches, supported by smaller columns.

The ceiling is of carved wood, dates from 1580, and has the coat of arms of Cardinal Henry of Portugal (1512–1580), who was titular (1547–1580), and king of Portugal (1578–1580). The pavement in the nave and in the transept area is cosmatesque from the twelfth century. The pavement in the side aisles is made up of slabs of marble taken from other buildings. The holy water stoups are carved out of bases of antique columns.

(4) The altarpiece is "Adoration of the Shepherds" by an unknown artist.

(5) Late baroque tomb of Luigi d'Aquino (1633–1679), auditor general of the Reverend Apostolic Chamber under five popes.

(6) A seventeenth-century fresco of the "Crucifixion."

(7) The apse, which extends the entire width of the church and not just the present nave, is too large for the present church; when Paschal rebuilt the church, he did not reduce Leo's apse. Cardinal Mellini had the Tuscan painter *Giovanni da San Giovanni* redecorate (1621–1623) the apse. The half-dome has his "Saints in the Glory of Paradise." The apse wall has three windows and six fluted pilasters dividing the area into seven bays. The panels on the wall are in two rows; the upper has four frescoes dedicated to the Quattro Coronati: (left to right) the four soldiers refuse to sacrifice to Asclepius; they are scourged to death; their bodies are left

unburied; Pope Melchiades and St. Sebastian bury the bodies on the Via Labicana.

The seven panels of the lower portion are dedicated to the five martyred sculptors of Pannonia: (left to right) Claudius converts Simplicius; Simplicius is baptized by Bishop Cyril of Antioch; the emperor orders the sculptors to make a statue of Asclepius; the five sculptors; they are scourged; the widow of the tribune Lampadius requests their death; Nicetas places the caskets with the live sculptors into the Sava River. The outside arch has the figures of Faith and Fortitude at the top; on the sides are frescoes of the individual Quattro Coronati. Behind the altar, in the center next to the wall, is an ornate seventeenth-century episcopal chair.

In the transept's left wall is the marble frontal from the twelfth-century altar. The central portion, which now has an image of the Virgin, was originally open so that the faithful could lower objects to touch the tombs of the martyrs. The left panel describes Leo IV's transfer of the relics to this church, and the right panel narrates Paschal II's search for them and their recognition.

The staircases at the ends of the transept go down to the ninth-century crypt, which Leo IV had constructed for the relics of the Quattro Coronati and the five Pannonian sculptors. In the twelfth century Paschal II verified that the relics were there, and in the seventeenth century Cardinal Mellini built the staircases to give access to the crypt. The relics of the martyrs are in four stone urns.

(8) A magnificently sculpted tabernacle with gilded decoration, from the time of Innocent VIII (1484–1492). It was originally in the presbytery but was moved here in the sixteenth century. It is attributed to *Andrea Bregno* and school, or to *Luigi Capponi*. It is surrounded on three sides by a seventeenth-century fresco of the Eternal Father with Sts. Peter and Paul.

(9) The altar has *Giovanni Baglione's* "Sts. Irene and Lucina Care for St. Sebastian" (ca. 1632). In the niche beneath the painting is a reliquary with St. Sebastian's skull. Cardinal Mellini discovered the reliquary when he had the crypt opened.

(10) "Annunciation," by Giovanni da San Giovanni. The grille below allowed the nuns in the convent to follow services in the church.

(11) A doorway in the left aisle leads to the cloister, which dates from the early years of the thirteenth century. The marble basin (twelfth century), now in the center since the beginning of this century, may have been originally in the *quadriporticus* or first courtyard. The walls have Roman fragments of inscriptions and of sarcophagi.

The entrance to St. Barbara's Chapel is from the cloister's left wing. The chapel is from the time of Leo IV; it has a cruciform vault in which remains of twelfth-century frescoes of the symbols of the evangelists may still be seen. The frescoes on the other walls depicted scenes from the life of St. Barbara; traces are still visible in a lunette and at the sides of the window. The chapel has three apses; one was converted into an entrance, and in the one facing that entrance a Virgin and Child is still visible. The doorway on the left was the entrance to the chapel from the ninth-century basilica's left nave.

(12) The entrance to St. Sylvester's Chapel is on the left, from the courtyard after one leaves the basilica. The room that serves as a vesti-bule to the chapel has on its walls the remains of a late thirteenth-century liturgical calendar. The calendar is in columns and names of various saints are easily read.

(13) To enter St. Sylvester's chapel, ring the bell and request the key from the nun in the porter's lodge. The chapel, rectangular in shape with a barrel vault, was built and decorated in 1246. The pavement is cos-matesque. On the rear wall, over the entrance, is a lunette of "Christ the Judge with the Virgin, St. John the Baptist and Apostles."

Beneath, the series of scenes taken from *Acts of Blessed Sylvester* (ca. 460) begins. This is a romantic and legendary account glorifying Pope Syl-vester I (314–335) and his dealings with Constantine (emperor 306–337). Beginning left to right: Constantine is afflicted with leprosy; the Apostles Peter and Paul appear to the emperor in a dream and suggest that he con-tact Pope Sylvester; Constantine sends three messengers to look for the pope; the messengers find the pope in a hermitage on Mount Soracte; Syl-vester returns to Rome and shows the emperor an image of Peter and Paul, whom Constantine identifies as those he had seen in his dream; Constan-tine is baptized and is cured; the emperor gives the pope the cap of au-thority and ceremonial umbrella; Constantine leads Sylvester, seated on a white horse, through the city; (on the opposite wall) the pope revives a dead bull; St. Helena, Constantine's mother, finds the true cross; (al-most totally lost) Sylvester frees the Roman people from the dragon. Below these scenes is a series of medallions with prophets.

When the sculptors' and stonecutters' guild acquired this chapel in 1570, they added the apse and had it frescoed by *Raffaellino da Reggio*. The altar has a "Crucifixion" and over the windows an "Annunciation." In the vault is the Savior with angels and evangelists. The pendentives have the Quattro Coronati. On the left wall is "Martyrdom of the Quat-tro Coronati," who are being scourged at the foot of a statue of Asclepius. The right wall has "Martyrdom of the Five Pannonian Sculptors," who are being placed in lead caskets before being cast alive into the Sava River. In the underarch are St. Sylvester (left) and Constantine (right).

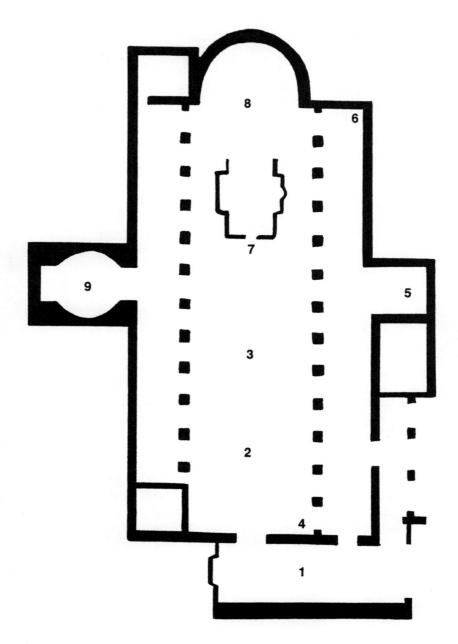

S. Sabina

48 S. Sabina***

Piazza di Pietro d'Illiria

History. The church was erected by the priest Peter of Illyria, during the time of Celestine I (422–432), and appears to have been constructed over the home of the Roman matron Sabina. Recent excavations beneath the nave have uncovered a third-century Roman house. Tradition connects Sabina with her servant Seraphia, a Christian, who converted her mistress to Christianity. During the ninth century the church was restored and Eugenius II (824–827) added a *schola cantorum* as well as a ciborium over the altar. In 1219 Honorius III (1216–1227) gave the church to St. Dominic (1170–1221), and the Dominicans continue to serve the church today. Major renovations were done (1587) by *Domenico Fontana* under Sixtus V (1585–1590); then during the early years (1919–1924, 1936–1938) of this century the church, under the supervision of *Antonio Muñoz*, was restored to its pristine appearance and beauty. When visitors enter the church today, they see, for the most part, what fifth-century Christians saw.

Exterior. The simple fifteenth-century portico with three arches, supported by two ancient columns, is attached to the side of the basilica. The doorway facing the viewer was introduced into the church wall at that time. The fresco over the door on the left depicts St. Dominic and two monks arriving at the monastery after having been led here, through the darkness, by an angel.

(1) The vestibule's vault is supported by four spiral fluted, pavonazzetto columns on one side and four granite columns on the other. The walls have fragments from earlier buildings as well as early Roman sarcophagi. The **large carved wooden doors** on the left are among the most important objects of Christian art. They are of cypress wood and date from the early fifth century. The eighteen panels, large and small, have scenes from the Old (five) and New (thirteen) Testaments. The "Crucifixion," at top left, may be the earliest representation of that scene in art. The large panel, lower level, second from the right, depicts "Crossing of the Red Sea." The reverse side of the door also has panels, but they have oriental and byzantine designs and are modern copies of those that once had been there. The statue in the niche on the left is of St. Rose of Lima (1586–1617), placed here at the time of her beatification (1668).

Through the small window in the wall, directly across from the carved doors, visitors of years gone by were able to see the orange tree that St. Dominic is said to have planted.

Interior. (2) The church is basilican in style, with a nave and two aisles, separated by fluted white Parian marble columns (total of twenty-four), joined together by arcades. This is said to be the earliest example in Rome, where the walls of the nave rest directly on the columns and not on an architrave. The columns are all matching, with Corinthian capitals; it is thought that they came from the same temple, perhaps that of Diana or Juno, once located here on the Aventine hill. The interior is spacious and bright, a magnificent example of an early Christian basilica. The fifth-century frieze above and between the arches is of colored marble; red porphyry and green serpentine are especially noticeable. Over the two arches, on both sides near the entrance, the design is painted. The windows in the upper nave have complex grating–like frames with selenite panels. In reopening these windows, most of which had been sealed in 1587, similar frames and panels were discovered. The wooden ceiling is recent (1936), but reproduces the type that a fifth-century basilica would have had. The pavement is mostly from the eighteenth and nineteenth centuries, and includes many tombstones and inscriptions. Some areas are ancient (e.g., in front of the entrance door).

On the rear wall, above the doors, is a fifth-century mosaic with an inscription in gold letters on a dark blue background. Written in metrical Latin, it informs the reader that Peter of Illyria, during the pontificate of Celestine, constructed the church. Celestine's name is in the first line, while Peter's is in the fourth. A female figure, dressed in purple, holding a book is on either end; the one on the left is identified as "Church from the Circumcision," and that on the right as "Church from the Gentiles." The former is the symbol of those members of the Church who came from a Jewish background, while the other symbolizes those who were non-Jewish. The mosaic was most probably done between 422 and 432, when Celestine was pope.

(3) The remarkable mosaic tombstone of Muñoz de Zamora, eighth master general of the Dominican order, who died in Rome in 1300. Some attribute it to *Iacopo Torriti*.

(4) The grille in the pavement indicates the entrance to the excavations beneath the nave, where the remains of a third-century Roman house were uncovered.

(5) Chapel of St. Hyacinth. St. Hyacinth (d. 1257) was a Pole who entered the Dominican order at S. Sabina, and received the religious habit from St. Dominic in 1220. The altar painting (1600), "St. Hyacinth be-

S. Sabina (G. Vasi, 1756)

fore the Virgin," is by *Lavinia Fontana*. The frescoes (1600) on walls and vault depict scenes from the saint's life, and are by *Federico Zuccari* and students. The left wall has "St. Hyacinth Receives the Habit from St. Dominic" and the right "Clement VIII Canonizes St. Hyacinth." St. Hyacinth was canonized in 1594, and the chapel was constructed in 1600 at the expense of the Dominican cardinal Girolamo Bernerio (d. 1611).

To the right of the chapel is the top portion of a column with a Corinthian capital. It is from an earlier building on the site, perhaps from the house of the matron Sabina.

(6) This is the tomb of Cardinal Valentino Auxias de Podio (d. 1483), archbishop of Monreale, Sicily, and titular (1477–1483). The elegant fifteenth-century tomb is by the school of *Andrea Bregno*. Above the recumbent figure are three reliefs; the center has Virgin and Child, with St. Catherine of Alexandria (left) and St. Catherine of Siena (right). The figures on the sides are the four cardinal virtues. The inscription on the tomb translates: "In order to live after death, he lived knowing that he was to die."

(7) A *schola cantorum* for singers was placed here by Eugenius II (824–827), but was dismantled during the 1587 renovations. During this century's restorations, portions of it were found imbedded in the floor, wall, and elsewhere. It was reconstructed; many pieces, however, are missing, and rather than replace them with modern substitutions, some panels

307

have designs etched in to continue the designs of the original. A pulpit is on either side for the reading of the Scriptures; these too are reconstructions.

(8) The fresco (1560) in the apse is by *Taddeo Zuccari* and students, done at the request of Cardinal Otto Truchsess (1514–1573), titular (1550–1561). It is said that it reproduces the theme of the mosaic that had once been here. Christ sits on a mound, teaching his apostles and disciples, who stand about him. The figures in the foreground are connected with this church; that is, their relics are preserved beneath the altar. The two female figures on the left are Sts. Sabina and Seraphia. On the right are two friars, one of whom is probably St. Dominic. There is some confusion, however, about the figures in the center. In the ninth century Eugenius II placed beneath the main altar the relics of the three martyrs Alexander, Eventius, and Theodulus. They were martyred ca. 119 on the Via Nomentana, several miles outside of Rome. In time, common belief identified the martyred Alexander with Pope Alexander I (ca. 109–ca. 116). Eventius is said to have been a priest, and Theodulus a deacon. In the fresco the artist has depicted a pope (Alexander I?) as well as two bishops (is one Eventius?), and a deacon (Theodulus?).

The lower part of the apse is faced with grey marble and porphyry stripes. A marble seat runs along the wall, as the early basilica had; the episcopal chair is a reconstruction from fragments found during the recent restorations.

The main altar also dates from the period of the restorations. Beneath the altar are the relics of Sts. Sabina, Seraphia, Alexander, Theodulus, and Eventius, placed here by Eugenius II, then discovered during Sixtus V's renovations.

(9) Chapel of St. Catherine of Siena. St. Catherine (1347–1380) was a Dominican tertiary and mystic; she was instrumental in having the pope leave Avignon and return (1377) to Rome. The chapel is in the baroque style and is attractive, though it does not exactly harmonize with the simplicity of the basilica. The chapel (1671) was designed by *Giovanni Battista Contini* for the family of the Sienese cardinal Scipione Pannocchieschi d'Elci (d. 1670), titular (1658–1670) of the basilica. The altarpiece is *Sassoferrato*'s "Madonna of the Rosary with Sts. Dominic and Catherine" (1643). The columns flanking the altar are of Sicilian jasper, as are some of the walls. The cupola has *Giovanni Odazzi*'s "St. Catherine in Glory"; the pendentives, also by Odazzi, represent four moments in the saint's life, namely, when she exchanges hearts with the Savior, receives Communion from him, chooses the crown of thorns, and receives the stigmata.

The Dominican convent next door has a fine thirteenth-century Romanesque cloister, with a modern well in the center. Within the convent the room in which St. Dominic lived, and that in which the Dominican pope St. Pius V (1566–1572) lived, are now chapels, and may be visited with the sacristan.

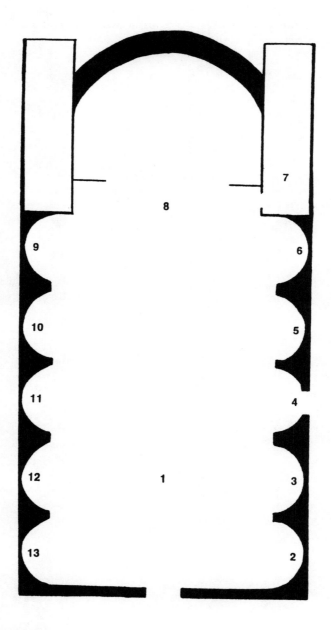

S. Spirito in Sassia

49 S. Spirito in Sassia*

Borgo S. Spirito

History. In 726 Ine, king of the West Saxons (688–726), abdicated his throne and with his wife, Queen Ethelburga, made a pilgrimage to Rome, where he died the year of his arrival. While in Rome the king established a hospice and a church, dedicated to the Virgin Mary, for the use of West Saxon pilgrims in the city. In time, that area, because of the presence of the Saxons, came to be known as *Saxia*. The church and much of the hospice were destroyed by fire during the time of Paschal I (817–824). They were rebuilt by Leo IV (847–855) and in 1198 Innocent III (1198–1216) converted the hospice into a hospital and entrusted its operation to the Hospitalers of the Holy Spirit and, thus, the church and the hospital, which is still in existence, bear the name of the Holy Spirit. The church suffered badly during the Sack of Rome (1527) and the present church was erected in its place. It was begun in 1536 by *Antonio da Sangallo the Younger*, during the pontificate of Paul III (1534–1549), and completed under Pius V (1566–1572).

Exterior. The late Renaissance facade is by *Ottaviano Mascherino* and was erected during the time of Sixtus V (1585–1590), whose coat of arms is over the window. The facade is of two orders; the lower has five bays formed by six pilasters with stylized Corinthian capitals. There is but a single tall doorway, simple and stately; niches are in the other bays. The second order repeats the lower except that there are three bays with a window and the papal coat of arms in the middle bay. The church is crowned with a triangular pediment in whose tympanum is a relief of the Holy Spirit. Semicircular stairs, having three levels, lead to the building. The pleasing campanile (1471) may be by *Baccio Pontelli*.

Interior. (1) The baroque church, fully decorated, has a single nave, lateral altars, and a deep apse. The rich ceiling, in gold, blue, and red, is from the time of Paul III (1534–1549); his coat of arms is nearest the main altar. The church was subsequently restored by Benedict XIV (1740–1758), whose coat of arms is near the entrance, and by Pius IX (1846–1878), whose heraldic coat is in the center.

On the rear wall, over the doorway, is *Antonino Calcagnadoro's* "Descent of the Holy Spirit." On either side of the door is an aedicule: the left has *Francesco Salviati's* "Visitation," and the right *Marco da Siena's* "Conversion of St. Paul."

(2) *Iacopo Zucchi*'s "Descent of the Holy Spirit" (1588) is on the altar and is framed by two columns of africano marble. The frescoes of St. John the Baptist (left), Joel (right), and those in the vault are also by Zucchi.

(3) The sixteenth-century "Assumption" over the altar is by *Livio Agresti*. On the left is "Nativity of Mary," by *Giovanni Battista Lombardelli*, and on the right "Circumcision," by *Paris Nogari*. The columns on the altar are copies of those that once stood around St. Peter's tomb in old St. Peter's and are now in the aedicules in the piers supporting St. Peter's dome.

(4) The loft holding the organ, with the coats of arms of Paul III and of the Hospital of the Holy Spirit, is from 1547; it is supported by two sets of double grey granite columns. The walls near this side entrance have sixteenth-century frescoes of "Last Supper" over the door and "Christ Washing the Feet of the Apostles" on the left.

(5) The nineteenth-century statue of the Sacred Heart of Jesus by *Raffaele Gagliardi* covers Agresti's "Trinity." Agresti's "Christ Heals the Paralytic" (left) and "Christ Heals a Blind Man" (right) are on the walls. Instead of the usual columns, the altar has caryatids supporting the pediment.

(6) *Giuseppe Valeriano*'s "Ascension" (1570) is the altarpiece. His is also the "Descent of the Spirit" in the vault. On the walls are Sts. Philip (left) and James (right). Instead of columns, the altar has heavy festoons of fruit as the flanking decorations.

(7) The sacristy has decorations by *Guidobaldi Abbatini*; they were done in the seventeenth century and depict the founding of the hospital and various events in its history. These are considered Abbatini's best work. He also did the stucco decorations. The altar has *Sermoneta*'s "Descent of the Spirit."

(8) The fresco (1583) in the apse, done in Florentine mannerist style, is Zucchi's masterpiece and represents the "Descent of the Holy Spirit." The artist has joined the apse's half-dome and the curved wall of the presbytery into one scene. In the half-dome the risen and ascended Lord sends the Holy Spirit upon the Virgin, apostles, and disciples gathered in a richly decorated Renaissance room below. Following the Florentine custom, the artist included portraits of some of his contemporaries, fellow artists, and literary figures in the fresco. The underarch has "Musical Angels" in the center with two scenes of "Descent of the Spirit" on the sides. The tondo in the center represents the Eternal Father.

The seventeenth-century altar is of various marbles and has two beautifully carved wooden angels holding up an attractive ciborium.

(9) A mediocre painting of John the Evangelist is on the altar, with an image of the Virgin known as "Madonna of King Ine." When King Ine founded the first church on this site, he is said to have given it an image of the Virgin, but over the centuries it has been lost. This is a modern substitution. The right wall has *Marcello Venusti's* fresco of "Martyrdom of St. John Evangelist." The other decorations are also from the sixteenth century.

(10) "Deposition from the Cross" on the altar is by Agresti. His are also the paintings on the walls, "Nativity" (left) and "Resurrection" (right). In the vault are his "Adam and Eve in Paradise" and "Expulsion from Paradise." Two statues take the place of columns on this altar.

(11) A sixteenth-century carved crucifix is the altarpiece, with sixteenth-century frescoes of scenes from the passion above. On the lower right is a monument to Blessed Agostina Pietrantoni (1864–1894), beatified in 1972. She was a Sister of Charity and a nurse in the adjoining hospital.

(12) *Cesare Nebbia's* "Coronation of Virgin" is on the altar; he also did the other frescoes, except the evangelists on the pilasters, which were done by *Andrea Lilio.*

(13) The statue (1880) of St. Aloysius Gonzaga is by *Ignazio Iacometti.* The frescoes are by Nebbia. The octagonal baptismal basin, with reliefs, is attributed to *Giacomo Della Porta.*

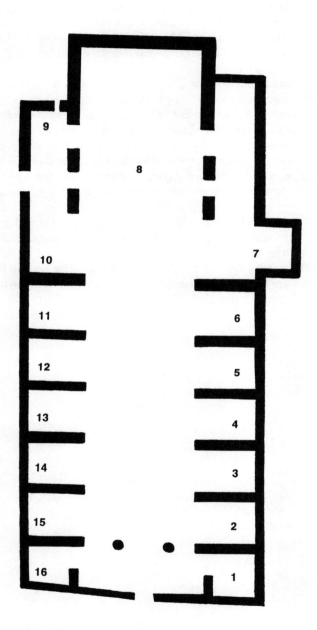

Trinità dei Monti

50 Trinità dei Monti**

Piazza della Trinità dei Monti

History. Charles VIII (king 1483–1498) of France, grateful to St. Francis of Paola (1416–1507) for assisting his dying father, Louis XI (king 1461–1483), and in admiration of the monk's holiness, had a small convent and church built (1494) for his monks (the Minims), here on Rome's Pincian Hill. The church was dedicated to the Most Holy Trinity. Though the first stone for the present church was laid in 1502, serious work did not begin until about ten years later. During the Sack of Rome (1527), the church and convent were still unfinished. The church was finally completed in 1584, the year the twin bell towers were constructed. The Italian monks, finding it difficult to coexist with the French (the property belongs to France), moved (1624) to S. Andrea delle Fratte nearby. The church then went through a period of decline and during the French occupation of Rome (1798–1799), it suffered such damage that it was totally abandoned. Not long after the accession of Louis XVIII (king 1815–1824), he had the architect *François-Charles Mazois*, associated with the French Academy next door, undertake its restoration (1816). In 1828 the church and convent were given to St. Madeleine-Sophie Barat (1779–1865), foundress of the Religious of the Sacred Heart, to be used as a school in Rome. The school is still in operation.

Exterior. The church overlooks the Piazza de Spagna. The facade is by *Carlo Maderno* and was finished by 1570. It has one order; pilasters divide it into three bays with a doorway, flanked by two columns and surmounted by a triangular pediment, in the center. Windows are in the other bays. The inscription tells the viewer that it was through the munificence of the kings of France and the alms of the faithful that the church was constructed. Above is an attic with a semi-circular window in the center and a clock on the left, placed here in 1613. The twin towers, with octagonal cupolas, built in 1584, are by *Antonio Ruspoli*, who followed a design by *Giacomo Della Porta*. A double flight of stairs, ordered by Sixtus V (1585–1590) and constructed (1587) by *Domenico Fontana*, lead to the entrance.

Interior. The church, Romanesque in style with few Gothic touches, has a single nave with lateral chapels. A iron grille allows the visitor to see the church only from the rear.

(1) The artwork (1573) here is by *Giovanni Battista Naldini*. Over the altar is "Baptism of Christ"; the left wall has "Herod's Banquet" and the lunette above "Beheading of John the Baptist." The vault has scenes from the Baptist's life. Prophets are on the altar's sides: Zechariah (left) and Isaiah (right).

(2) The altar has a nineteenth-century painting of St. Francis of Paola, done by one of the religious who lived in the adjoining convent. It is painted on boards supposedly used by the saint as a bed.

(3) The fresco of the "Assumption" is by *Daniele da Volterra*; in it he included a portrait of his teacher *Michelangelo*—the gentleman on the right in red, looking toward the viewer. "Slaughter of the Innocents" (left) and "Presentation of Mary in the Temple" (right) are by *Michele Alberti*. The frescoes in the vault, with scenes from the life of the Virgin, are by *Marco da Siena* and *Pellegrino Tibaldi*.

(4) *Louis Pallière*'s "Scourging of Christ" (1817) is the altarpiece. Pallière was a student at the French Academy at the time. The frescoes depicting scenes of the passion are by *Paris Nogari*. On the left is the tomb of Cardinal Rodolfo Pio di Carpi (d. 1564); on the right that of Countess Cecilia Orsini Franciotti (d. 1575) and her husband, Alberto Pio di Carpi (d. 1568). Both tombs are by *Leonardo Sormani*.

(5) Alberti's fresco of the "Nativity" is over the altar. The founder of the chapel was a certain Pierre Marcien; on the left he has himself kneeling at the feet of his patron, St. Peter; St. Paul is depicted on the right. The frescoes of "Circumcision" (left), "Adoration of the Magi" (right), and the four prophets (Daniel, Jeremiah, Isaiah, and David) are all attributed to the school of *Sodoma*.

(6) The frescoes in this chapel are of the school of *Perugino*. "Resurrection" is on the left wall, "Ascension" in the center, and "Pentecost" on the right. It was commonly believed that in the painting representing Christ's resurrection the artist included a likeness of Perugino (the gentleman in the center with upraised hand) and of *Raphael* (in the center with the red beret). It is also claimed that the painting of St. Francis of Paola on the left pilaster is a true likeness. St. Francis of Assisi is on the other pilaster. The altar is also worthy of close inspection.

(7) This right transept chapel is dedicated to St. Madeleine-Sophie Barat. The painting (1925) of the saint is by *Egisto Ferroni*. The frescoes in the vault are attributed to *Perin del Vaga*. On the left is *Domenico Corvi*'s "St. Michael," and on the right *Pierre Subleyras'* "Sorrowful Mother."

(8) The elegant main altar with its baroque top was designed by *Jean de Champagne*; the ciborium on the altar blends in well with the columns

Trinità dei Monti (G. B. Falda, 1669)

as its backdrop. The twisting side columns at the ends of the balustrade are from the thirteenth century.

(9) *Federico Zuccari's* "Coronation of the Virgin" is on the wall, and to its left is a copy of *Jean-Auguste Ingres'* "Giving the Keys to St. Peter," the original of which, now in the Louvre in Paris, was in one of the side chapels.

(10) The vault and lunettes have scenes from the life of the Virgin by Perin del Vaga. Because of the artist's death (1523), as a result of the plague, the chapel remained unfinished. *Taddeo Zuccari*, Federico's older brother, took over and did the "Death of Mary" on the left wall and began the "Assumption" over the altar. After his death (1566), Federico completed the chapel.

Outside the chapel there is a most interesting fresco by *A. Del Maino* of "St. Michael Appearing over Castel Sant' Angelo." It depicts Pope St. Gregory (590–604) in a penitential procession, seeking the end of the plague. The artist gave St. Gregory the face of Leo X (1513–1521) and shows what Castel Sant' Angelo looked like in the early years of the sixteenth century.

(11) The altar has a painting of the Sacred Heart of Jesus, by an unidentified artist. The left wall has *Alexander Maximilian Seitz's* "Prudent and Foolish Virgins" and the right his "Prodigal Son." Both are from 1838.

(12) *Giulio Romano's* "Risen Christ Appears to Mary Magdalene," much praised at the time, is the altarpiece. The monuments are of the Massimo family.

(13) The painting (1809) of St. Joseph is by *Jérôme Langlois,* done while studying at the French Academy. The Cardelli family monument (1872) on the left and that of the Marquis de Taurani (1866) on the right are by *Giuseppe Luchetti.*

(14) The altar has "Immacolata," by *Philipp Veit;* the walls have frescoes of "Annunciation" (left) and "Visitation" (right), by *Josef Thunner.* Both artists were members of Rome's Nazarene school of painting. On the right is the fine monument (1866) of Cardinal Louis de Rohan (1788–1833), titular (1831–1833), also by Luchetti.

(15) Daniele da Volterra's now faded and pale "Deposition from the Cross" is on the altar. When first executed it was as famous as Raphael's "Transfiguration" and hailed as one of the world's three great paintings. Time, however, has seen to its deterioration. Originally painted on wood, it was transferred (1811) to canvas. The side walls have frescoes of "Expulsion of Adam and Eve" (left) and "Adoration of the Magi" (right); both of these are by the Spaniard *Pablo de Céspedes.* His are also the evangelists and the scenes from the life of the Virgin in the vault. The Daniel (left) and David (right) on the arch's inside are from the nineteenth century and are by *Louis Dupré,* a student at the French Academy.

In front of the chapel, in the pavement, is a marker indicating where the great French landscape artist *Claude Lorrain* (1600–1682) was buried. Two other artists were likewise buried in the church: the painter *Paris Nogari* (1536–1601) and the sculptor *Nicolas Cordier* (1657–1612).

(16) *Wilhelm Achtermann's* group, "Deposition from the Cross" (1858), is the plaster model for sculptures the artist executed for the cathedral in Münster, Germany. The sculptures, however, were destroyed during World War II. The frescoes in the vault tell the story of Christ's passion and are by *Cesare Nebbia,* who also painted St. Francis (left) and St. Catherine (right) on the sides of the altar.

Bibliography

Armellini, M. *Le Chiese di Roma*. Rome, 1891.

Barberini, M. G. *I Santi Quattro Coronati a Roma*. Rome, 1989.

Basilica di San Giovanni in Laterano. Rome.

Basilica di San Marco al Campidoglio. Rome, 1982.

Beny, R., and P. Gunn. *Le Chiese di Roma*. Milan, 1982.

Berthier, J.-J. *L'Église de la Minerve à Rome*. Rome, 1910.

Boyle, L. *A Short Guide to St. Clement's Rome*. Rome, 1989.

Cecchelli, C. *San Clemente*. Rome [1930].

Cecchelli, C. *Santa Maria in Trastevere*. Rome, [1930].

Ceschi, C. *Le Chiese di Roma dagli Inizi del Neoclassico al 1961*. Rome, 1963.

Chandlery, P. J. *Pilgrim-Walks in Rome. A Guide to Its Holy Places*. London, 1903.

Chioccioni, P. *Illustrated Guide to the Basilica of Saints Cosmas and Damian*. Rome, 1973.

Colasanti, A. *Santa Maria in Aracoeli*. Rome, 1923.

Cruickshank, J. W. and A. M. *Christian Rome*. London, 1911.

D'Alatri, M., and G. Cattaneo di Ciaccia. *La Chiesa e il Cimitero della SS. Concezione*. Rome, 1988.

Dejonghe, M. *Roma, Santuario Mariano*. Rome, 1970.

Descrizione della Sacrosanta Basilica Vaticana. Rome, 1828.

Di Re, P. *Basilica di Santa Prassede*. Rome, 1986.

Drenkelfort, H. *The Basilica of the Holy Cross in Jerusalem*. Rome.

Faldi Guglielmi, C. *Basilica di San Lorenzo al Verano*. Rome.

Ferrua, A. *San Sebastiano fuori le Mura e la sua Catacomba*. Rome, 1968.

Frutaz, A. P. *Basilica di San Pietro in Vincoli, Roma*. Rome, 1981.

Galassi Paluzzi, C. *Chiese Romane*. 2 vols. Rome.

Galassi Paluzzi, C. *Les Cinq Basiliques Patriarchales de Rome*. Rome, 1970.

Galassi Paluzzi, C. *San Pietro in Vaticano*. 3 vols. Rome, 1963–1965.

Galassi Paluzzi, C. *La Basilica di S. Pietro*. Rome, 1975.

Gatti, I. L. *La Basilica dei Santi XII Apostoli*. Rome, 1988.

Giachi, G., and G. Matthiae. *San Andrea al Quirinale*. Rome, 1969.

Gigli, L. *Chiesa di San Marcello*. Rome, 1977.

Gradara, C. *Le Chiese minori di Roma*. Rome, 1922.

Grossi, I. P. *Basilica of Santa Maria sopra Minerva*. Rome, 1980.

Hare, A. J. C. *Walks in Rome*. London, 1925.

Jarawan, E. *Santa Maria in Cosmedin*. Rome, 1987.

John, R. T. *San Giorgio al Velabro*. Rome, 1980.

Krautheimer, R. *Rome: Profile of a City, 312-1308*. Princeton, 1980.

Lavagnino, E. *San Paolo sulla Via Ostiense*. Rome.

Lees-Milne, J. *Saint Peter's: The Story of Saint Peter's Basilica in Rome*. Boston, 1967.

Lloyd, J. B. *The Medieval Church and Canonry of S. Clemente in Rome*. Rome, 1989.

Luciani, R. *Saint Mary in Trastevere*. Rome, 1987.

Lugano, P. *Santa Maria Nova. (Santa Francesca Romana)*. Rome.

Lugli, G. *The Pantheon and Adjacent Monuments*. Rome, 1971.

Macadam, A. *Rome and Environs [Blue Guide]*. London, 1989.

Margarucci Italiani, B. M. *Il titolo di Pammachio. Santi Giovanni e Paolo*. Rome, 1985.

Martinetti, G. *Sant' Ignazio*. Rome, 1967.

Massimi, G. *La Chiesa di Santa Maria in Cosmedin (in Schola Graeca)*. Rome, 1989.

Masson, G. *The Companion Guide to Rome*. London, 1980.

Matthiae, G. *Santa Maria degli Angeli*. Rome, 1982.

Mortari, L. *Santa Maria Maddalena*. Rome, 1987.

Morton, H. V. *A Traveller in Rome*. New York, 1957.

Muñoz, A. *L'Église de Sainte Sabine à Rome*. Rome, 1924.

Nibby, A. *Roma nell'Anno MDCCCXXXVIII 1: Moderna*. Rome, 1839.

Ortolani, S. *Santa Croce in Gerusalemme*. Rome.

Parsi, P. *Chiese Romane*. Rome, 1950.

Pecchiai, P. *Il Gesù di Roma, descritto ed illustrato*. Rome, 1952.

Pericoli Ridolfini, C. *Chiesa del Gesù*. Rome, 1975.

Pericoli Ridolfini, C. *Saint Paul's Outside the Walls*. Rome, 1988.

Pericoli Ridolfini, C. *San Carlino alle 4 Fontane*. Rome.

Pericoli Ridolfini, C. *San Luigi dei Francesi*. Rome, 1983.

Pericoli Ridolfini, C. *Sant'Andrea della Valle*. Rome.

Pietrangeli, C., (ed.) *La Basilica Romana di Santa Maria Maggiore*. Rome, 1987.

Romanelli, E. *Santa Maria in Aracoeli, Roma*. Rome.

Ronci, A. *Sant'Agostino in Campo Marzio, Roma*. Rome.

Santa Maria in Vallicella. Chiesa Nuova, Roma. Rome, 1974.

Sharp, M. *A Traveller's Guide to the Churches of Rome*. London, 1967.

Strong, E. *La Chiesa Nuova. (Santa Maria in Vallicella)*. Rome, 1923.

Tencajoli, O. F. *Le Chiese Nazionali Italiane in Roma*. Rome, 1928.

Tesei, G. P. *Le Chiese di Roma*. Rome, 1986.

Toth, G. B. de, *L'Archibasilica di San Giovanni in Laterano*. Rome.

Thynne, R. *The Churches of Rome*. London, 1924.

Touring Club Italiano. *Roma e Dintorni*. Milan, 1962.

Vannicelli, P. L. *San Pietro in Montorio e il Tempietto del Bramante*. Rome, 1971.

Glossary

ACANTHUS — a plant, whose leaves are imitated in the capitals of the Corinthian and composite orders.

AEDICULE — a house-like niche.

AISLE — lateral divisions of a church flanking the nave.

AMBO — pulpit.

APSE — semicircular or polygonal area, usually at east end of a church, with a semi-dome as ceiling.

ARCADE — set of arches on piers or columns.

ARCHITRAVE — lowest part (beam) of an entablature, resting directly on columns; also a molding over (or around) a doorway.

ATRIUM — an unroofed court, often colonnaded, preceding a church.

ATTIC — low story or wall above the facade's cornice.

BALDACHIN — freestanding stone canopy over an altar or tomb, usually supported by four columns.

BALUSTRADE — an ornamental rail with a row of supporting balusters.

BAPTISTERY — area of a church (sometimes a separate building) containing the font for the baptismal rite.

BAROQUE — style of European architecture, painting and sculpture that flourished from the end of the sixteenth to the early eighteenth century; characterized by extreme ornamentation and dynamic movement.

BARREL VAULT — half-cylindrical vault.

BASILICA — rectangular church, having central nave, with two or four side aisles; central nave usually ends in vaulted apse.

BAS-RELIEF — sculpture in low relief in which the figures project slightly or less than one half their true proportions from the surrounding background, and no figure is undercut.

BAY — area or compartment between columns, pilasters, or piers.

BROKEN PEDIMENT — pediment in which the diagonal lines stop before meeting at the apex of the triangle.

321

CAMPANILE — bell tower.

CANTORIA — gallery for singers in a church; choir loft.

CAPITAL — topmost portion of a column or pilaster, e.g., Doric, Ionic, Corinthian, and composite.

CARTOON — a full-sized preliminary sketch to be copied in executing a fresco, mosaic, or tapestry.

CARYATID — sculptured female figure used as a column to support an entablature or pediment.

CIBORIUM — freestanding altar canopy; baldachin.

CLERESTORY — row of windows on the sides of the nave of a church, above the roof level of the aisles.

CLOISTER — covered way around a quadrangle in a monastery.

COFFER — ornamental sunken panels in a ceiling or dome.

COLONNADE — row of evenly spaced columns supporting arches or an entablature.

COLUMN — an upright shaft, usually cylindrical or slightly tapering.

COMPOSITE CAPITAL — ornamentation which is a union of Ionic and Corinthian styles.

CONFESSION — crypt-like shrine under the main altar where relics are preserved.

CORBEL — a block or bracket projecting from wall used to support a beam or vault, sometimes ornamented.

CORINTHIAN CAPITAL — decorated with carved acanthus leaves.

CORNICE — the projecting portion at the top of the entablature, usually an ornamental molding.

CROSSING — area where the transept and nave of a church intersect.

CUPOLA — dome.

DIPTYCH — formed by two painted panels, attached together to form a single altarpiece.

DORIC CAPITAL — the simplest of the classical orders; the capital has an ovolo (convex) molding beneath a square abacus (flat upper part of the column).

DRUM — circular wall (sometimes with windows) supporting a dome or cupola.

ENTABLATURE — the part supported by the columns including the architrave, frieze, and cornice.

FACADE — face or front of a building.

FINIAL — ornamentation placed on top of a gable, pediment, spire, etc.; in Gothic architecture usually in the form of a foliated fleur-de-lis.

FLUTE — shallow concave vertical groove in a column or pilaster.

FRESCO — wall painting on wet plaster.

FRIEZE — decorated band between architrave and cornice, or any ornamented band or strip on a wall.

GOTHIC — style of medieval architecture and medieval art in western Europe between the twelfth and sixteenth centuries; especially characterized by the use of pointed arches.

GREEK CROSS — cross in which the four arms are usually of the same length.

GRISAILLE — painting done in various tones of grey or neutral colors.

HIGH RELIEF — sculpture in which the figures project more than one half their true proportions from the surrounding background.

ICON — panel painting in Byzantine style of Christ, the Virgin, or a saint.

INTARSIA — mosaic of inlaid wood of different colors.

IONIC CAPITAL — capital with a volute or scroll-like ornamentation.

LANTERN — structure placed on top of a dome with windows or openings to allow light or ventilation.

LATIN CROSS — cross with one arm longer than the other three.

LOGGIA — gallery which is open on one or more sides; a balcony.

LUNETTE — semicircular area, over a window or enclosed by the arch of a vault; often decorated with a mosaic or a painting.

MANDORLA — almond-shaped design enclosing a figure of God the Father, Christ, the Virgin Mary, or, rarely, saints.

MANNERISM — style of European (principally Italian) art between the high Renaissance and baroque (1520–1600) periods; characterized by elongated and distorted forms in an attempt to represent beauty's ideal rather than natural images of it.

MOSAIC — design or picture made of small pieces of colored stone or glass set into cement or plaster.

NARTHEX — vestibule or entrance hall of a church between the porch and the nave.

NAVE — the main area of a church, from narthex to presbytery, and usually having aisles on the sides.

NEO-CLASSICISM — style of European art and architecture, from the late eighteenth to the early nineteenth century; characterized by a revival of antique forms and themes; a reaction against the baroque and rococo.

NIMBUS — halo of light surrounding the head of a saint or deity.

ORANT — standing figure in prayer, with hands spread and raised; common in early Christian art.

ORDER — a combination of base, column, and entablature.

PEDIMENT — a low-pitched gable, often triangular, usually over door and windows.

PENDENTIVE — any of the four triangular concave surfaces of vaulting, located in the corners of the structure supporting the dome.

PERGOLA — screen that separates the presbytery from the main body of the church.

PILASTER — rectangular shallow column attached to the face of a wall.

PLINTH — rectangular block at the base of a column.

POLYPTYCH — formed by several painted panels, attached together to form a single altarpiece.

PORTAL — door (way) or entrance.

PORTICO — entrance to a church, usually covered and colonnaded.

PRESBYTERY — area of the church reserved for the clergy, and where the altar is usually located; the sanctuary, the chancel.

PRONAOS — a projecting portico in front of a church.

PROTHYRON — the small porch of a medieval church.

PUTTO — chubby cherub.

QUADRIPORTICUS — four-sided colonnaded atrium.

RELIEF — sculptured figures that project from a background so that they are partly or almost entirely free of it.

RELIQUARY — receptacle for relics, especially of the saints.

RENAISSANCE — artistic movement which began in Italy in the fourteenth century and subsequently spread through Europe; the period between 1500 and 1520 is known as the high Renaissance, the years when Leonardo da Vinci, Michelangelo, and Raphael predominated the art scene.

ROCOCO — elaborately decorative style of art and architecture, begun in the eighteenth century which eventually supplanted the baroque; characterized by graceful ornamentation and lightheartedness.

ROMANESQUE — style of architecture in western and southern Europe from the ninth to the twelfth centuries characterized by massive masonry wall constructions, rounded arches, and groin vaults.

ROUNDEL — medallion; circular panel.

SCHOLA CANTORUM — in medieval churches the area reserved for the liturgical singers, usually in the center nave.

SEGMENTAL PEDIMENT — pediment in which instead of two diagonal lines converging, there is a single curve.

SEMICOLUMNS — not freestanding columns.

SHAFT — part of column between base and capital.

SOFFIT — the underside of an arch, usually decorated.

SPANDREL — triangular areas between the curve of an arch and the wall, or between two arches.

STUCCO — plaster reinforced with powdered marble and used for decoration and statues.

TONDO — a circular painting or carving.

TRABEATION — horizontal beams resting on columns, as opposed to arches.

TRANSEPT — projecting arms of a cross-shaped edifice, at right angles with the nave.

TRAVERTINE — porous rock from the district about Tivoli, Italy.

TRIPTYCH — three painted panels attached together to form a single altarpiece.

TYMPANUM — area enclosed within a pediment.

VAULT — curved ceiling or roof.

VOLUTE — scroll or spiral twisting form, especially used on Ionic capitals.

Artists

a = architect   m = mosaicist   p = painter   s = sculptor

Bl = Bologna   Fl = Florence   Np = Naples   Pa = Paris   Rm = Rome

Borromini, Francesco, a. (Bissone 1599–Rm 1667), 29, 30, 32, 69, 85, 111, 112, 165, 251

Bosio, Pietro, a., s. (Cremona late eighteenth century–Rm 1855), 55

Boulogne, Jean de, see Valentin

Bracci, Filippo, p. (Rome 1727–?), 96

Bracci, Pietro, a., s. (Rm 1700–Rm 1773), 14, 47, 90, 178, 190, 265

Bramante, Donato, a., p. (Fermignano 1444–Rm 1514), 1, 13, 213, 219, 278

Brandi, Giacinto, p. (Poli 1621–Rm 1691), 90, 92, 96, 148

Bravi, Giuseppe, p. (Recanati 1862–), 119

Bregno, Andrea, a., s. (Osteno 1418–Rm 1503), 83, 100, 107, 126, 220, 223, 226, 229, 262, 229, 262, 264, 266, 285, 291, 301, 307

Bricci, Plautilla, a., p. (Rm 1616–ca. 1700), 187

Bril, Paul, p. (Antwerp 1554–Rm 1626), 48, 117, 154

Broeck, Hendrick van der, p. (Mechlin ca. 1519–Rm 1597), 202

Bronzino [Allori, Allessandro], p. (Fl 1535–Fl 1607), 267

Brughi, Giovanni Battista, p. (nineteenth century), 235

Bruschi, Domenico, p. (Perugia 1840–Rm 1910), 108

Buonvicino, Ambrogio, s. (Milan ca. 1552–Rm 1622), 3, 4, 10, 34, 49, 50, 103, 262, 266

Busiri Vici, Andrea, a. (Rm 1818–Rm 1911), 181, 284

Buzzi, Ippolito, s. (Viggiù ca. 1562–Rm 1634), 50, 51, 262

Cades, Giuseppe, p. (Rm 1750–Rm 1799), 108

Caffà, Melchiorre, s. (Malta 1631/35–Rm 1667), 87, 91

Caffieri, Jean-Jacques, s. (Pa 1725–Pa 1792), 186

Calandrucci, Giacinto, p. (Palermo 1646–Palermo 1707), 241

Calcagnadoro, Antonino, p. (1874–1931), 311

Calcagno, Tiberio, a., s. (Fl 1532–Rm 1565), 51

Calderini, Guglielmo, a. (Perugia 1837–Rm 1916), 56

Camassei, Andrea, p. (Bevagna 1602–Rm 1649), 37, 208, 272

Cametti, Bernardino, s. (Rm ca. 1669–Rm 1736), 13, 156, 190, 270

Campana, Paolo, s., 257

Campi, Pietro, s. (Carrara, act. 1702–1735), 86

Camporese, Pietro, a. (Rm 1792–Rm 1873), 55

Camuccini, Vincenzo, p. (Rm 1771–Rm 1844), 59, 60, 276

Canard, Joseph, s., 257

Cangini, F., p. (nineteenth century), 240

Canini, Giovanni Angelo, p. (Rm 1609–Rm 1666), 52, 165

Canonica, Pietro, s. (Turin 1869–Rm 1959), 21, 203

Canova, Antonio, s. (Possagno 1757–Venice 1822), 15, 22, 26, 100, 105, 107, 155, 196, 198

Canuti, Domenico, p. (Bl 1626–Bl 1684), 147

Capalti, Alessandro, p. (Rm 1807–Rm 1868), 155

Capparoni, Silverio, p. (Rm 1831–Rm 1907), 100, 191, 243, 284

Capponi, Luigi, s. (Milan, act. Rm 1485–1496), 25, 126, 213, 285, 301

Caradosso [Foppa, Cristoforo], s. (Mondonico ca. 1452–1527), 284

Caravaggio [Merisi, Michelangelo] p. (Caravaggio 1571–Porto Ercole 1610), 92, 186, 187, 222, 252, 277

Carcani, Filippo, s. (act. Rm 1657–1685), 33, 52, 198
Cardi, Ludovico, "il Cigoli," p. (Cigoli di San Miniato 1559–Rm 1613), 50, 164
Carimini, Luca, a. (Rm 1830–Rm 1890), 107
Carlone, Giovanni Andrea, p. (Genoa 1639–Genoa 1697), 154
Carloni, M., p. (seventeenth century), 202
Caroselli, Angelo, p. (Rm 1585–Rm 1652), 14, 148, 239, 240
Caroselli, Cesare, p. (Genazzano 1847–Rm 1927), 100
Carracci, Annibale, p. (Bl 1560–Rm 1609), 76, 153, 222, 246, 272
Caslani, Giovanni, s. (Ticino sixteenth–seventeenth century), 4, 13, 20
Casoni, Antonio, a., s. (Ancona 1559–Rm 1634), 207
Cassignola, Giacomo, s. (act. 1567–1588), 263
Cassignola, Tommaso, s. (sixteenth century), 263
Castelli, Matteo, a. (Melide, seventeenth century), 103
Castello, Bernardo, p. (Genoa 1557–Genoa 1629), 266
Castiglione, G., s. (twentieth century), 25
Cati, Pascuale, p. (Iesi ca. 1550–Rm 1620), 247
Cavaceppi, Bartolomeo, s. (Rm ca. 1716–Rm 1799), 106
Cavalier d'Arpino [Cesari, Giuseppe], p. (Arpino 1568–Rm 1640), 8, 31, 34, 50,
    133, 140, 187, 239, 253, 255, 292
Cavallini, Francesco, s. (Carrara 1640–after 1703), 220
Cavallini, Pietro, m., p. (Rm ca. 1250–ca. 1330), 12, 59, 60, 120, 140, 160, 198,
    229, 230, 246
Ceccarini, Sebastiano, p. (Fano 1703–Fano 1783), 51
Celio, Gaspare, p. (Rm 1571–Rm 1640), 152, 245
Cerrini, Gian Domenico, p. (Perugia 1609–Rm 1681), 215, 216, 240
Cerruti, Michelangelo, p. (Rm 1663–Rm 1748), 257, 266, 276
Cesari, Bernardino, p. (?–Rm 1703), 34, 133
Cesi, Carlo, p. (Antrodoco 1626–Rieti 1686), 51, 212
Céspedes, Pablo de, p. (Cordoba 1538–Cordoba 1608), 318
Champagne, Jean de, a. (seventeenth century), 316
Chenevières, Jean de, a., s. (ca. 1490–Rm 1527), 185
Chiari, Giuseppe, p. (Rm 1654–Rm 1727), 21, 97, 108, 124, 176
Ciampelli, Agostino, p. (Fl 1565–Rm 1630), 34, 152, 153, 165, 247, 291
Ciarpi, Baccio, p. (Barga 1574–Rm 1654), 165, 198, 208
Cignani, Carlo, p. (Bl 1628–Forlì 1719), 102
Cioli, Aurelio, s. (Settignano ca. 1529–1599), 33
Cipitello, Michele, p., 296
Circignani, Antonio, "Pomarancio," p. (Pomarance ca. 1567–ca. 1630), 240
Circignani, Niccolò, "Pomarancio," p. (Pomarance 1530–after 1599), 72, 117, 157,
    165, 171, 275
Cisterna, Eugenio, p. (Genzano 1862–Genzano 1933), 83, 87
Cobergher, Wenceslas, p. (Antwerp 1561–1631), 252
Coccetti, Liborio, p. (Foligno 1739–Rm 1816), 207
Cochetti, Luigi, p. (Rm 1802–Rm 1884), 170, 244
Coghetti, Francesco, p. (Bergamo 1804–Rm 1875), 60
Conca, Sebastiano, p. (Gaeta 1680–Np 1764), 92, 116, 124, 126, 127, 208, 217, 258

Reni, Guido, p. (Calvenzano 1575–Bl 1642), 15, 19, 32, 37, 50, 117, 146, 182, 186, 207, 216, 254, 255, 276

Reti, Leonardo, s. (act. 1670–1709), 15, 152

Ricci, Giovanni Battista, p. (Novara 1537–Rm 1627), 24, 34, 43, 51, 91, 190, 240, 241

Ricci, Sebastiano, p. (Belluno 1659–Venice 1734), 108

Ricciolini, Niccolò, p. (Rm 1687–1772), 203

Rinaldi, Giovanni, s. (seventeenth century), 97

Rinaldi, Rinaldo, s. (Padua 1793–Rm 1873), 60, 61, 100, 190

Ristoro, Fra., a. (thirteenth century), 261

Rocca, Giacomo, p. (sixteenth century), 201

Rocca, Michele, p. (Parma 1670/75–Venice 1751), 258

Romanelli, Giovanni Francesco, p. (Viterbo 1610–Viterbo 1662), 21, 112, 157, 197, 204

Romano, Filippo, s. (seventeenth century), 31

Roncalli, Cristoforo, "il Pomarancio," p. (Pomarance ca. 1552–Rm 1626), 9, 19, 20, 34, 204, 227, 231, 254, 255, 265, 284, 296

Rondone, Francesco, s. (Rm ca. 1600–after 1670), 100

Rosa, Francesco, p. (Genoa ?–1687), 92

Rosa, Salvator, p. (Arenella 1615–Rm 1673), 164, 202

Rosa, Sigismondo, p. (eighteenth century), 182

Rossetti, Cesare, p. (seventeenth century), 239

Rossi, Giovanni Battista, s. (Rm, act. first half eighteenth century), 202

Rossi, Giovanni Francesco, s. (Fivizzano, Massa, act. 1640–1677), 86

Rubens, Peter Paul, p. (Siegen 1577–Antwerp 1640), 71, 133, 254

Rughesi, Faustolo, a. (Montepulciano, act. 1597–1605), 251

Rusconi, Camillo, s. (Milan 1658–Rm 1728), 13, 30, 178, 208

Ruspoli, Antonio, a. (Fl, sixteenth century), 315

Rusuti, Filippo, m., p. (Rm ?–1317/1321), 42

Sacchi, Andrea, p. (Nettuno 1599–Rm 1661), 20, 22, 34, 37, 208, 267

Sales, G., p. (nineteenth century), 230

Salimbeni, Ventura, p. (Siena 1567/1568–Siena 1613), 92, 152, 156

Salini, Tommaso, p. (Rm ca. 1575–Rm 1625), 90

Salviati, Francesco, p. (Fl 1510–Rm 1563), 190, 223, 311

Salvini, Salvio, p. (seventeenth century), 165

Sansovino, Andrea [Contucci, Andrea], a., s. (Monte San Sovino ca. 1460–ibid. 1529), 89, 222, 228

Sansovino, Iacopo [Tatti, Iacopo], a., s. (Fl 1486–Venice 1570), 70, 92, 163, 189, 192

Santi di Tito, p. (Sansepolcro 1536–Fl 1603), 164, 165

Saraceni, Carlo, p. (Venice 1580–Venice 1620), 133, 183, 255, 264

Sardi, Giuseppe, a. (S. Angelo in Vado ca. 1680–1753), 233, 257

Sarti, Antonio, a. (Budrio, Bl 1797–Rm 1880), 154

Sassoferrato (Salvi, G. B.), p. (Sassoferrato 1609–Rm 1685), 37, 308

Savonanzio, Emilio, p. (Bl 1580–ca. 1660), 66

Scaramuccia, Luigi, p. (Perugia 1616–Milano 1680), 253

Scherano da Settignano [Fancelli, Alessandro], s. (Settignano, sixteenth century), 283